SPORT ETHICS
Concepts and Cases in Sport and Recreation

SPORT ETHICS

Concepts and Cases in Sport and Recreation

SECOND EDITION

David Cruise Malloy, Ph.D.
University of Regina

Saul Ross, Ed.D.
University of Ottawa

and

Dwight H. Zakus, Ph.D.
Griffith University, Australia

THOMPSON EDUCATIONAL PUBLISHING, INC.

Requests for permission to make copies of any part of the work should be directed to the publisher: publisher@thompsonbooks.com.

Copies of this book may be ordered in the United States and Canada. For ordering information, please visit: **www.thompsonbooks.com**

National Library of Canada Cataloguing in Publication

Malloy, David Cruise, 1959-
    Sport ethics : concepts and cases in sport and recreation / David Cruise Malloy, Saul Ross and Dwight H. Zakus.

Includes bibliographical references and index.
ISBN 1-55077-129-9

    1. Sports--Moral and ethical aspects. I. Ross, Saul, 1934-
II. Zakus, Dwight Harry, 1951- III. Title.

GV706.3.M36 2003   175   C2002-905912-7

Copy editing: Elizabeth Phinney
Cover design: Elan Designs

We acknowledge the support of the Government of Canada through the Book Publishing Industry Development Program for our publishing activities.
Printed in Canada.
5 6 7   16 15 14

Table of Contents

Dedication

Each of us would like to dedicate this text to our very significant others.

I wish to dedicate this book to my wife Valerie, my children Connor, Gaelan, Bronwen, and Brigid, to my mother, Mary Whitlam Malloy, and fundamentally to my father, Group Captain Dennis Graland "Bud" Malloy, D.F.C., who was a gentleman of the highest caliber and the most honorable sportsman and competitor I have ever known.

David Cruise Malloy

This book is dedicated to very special and treasured people: daughter Karyn, son-in-law Brian, and their children, Quinton and Serena; daughter Dana and son-in-law John, and their son Colin; my mother, Goldie Ross, and to the memory of my late father, Al Ross; and to my wife, Pamela, for her constant encouragement and support.

Saul Ross

To Mum, constant, kind and loving; saint in disguise. To three women who have invariably made my life happy, sad, joyful, painful, and at times complete: Natasha, Margaret, and Ann. As the old adage goes, can't live with them but can't live without them. Finally, to my son Nicholas. We have lived at a distance but have not been distant. Our souls connect.

Dwight Harry Zakus

Acknowledgments

We express our gratitude to the many teachers who have enlightened us; those in the courses we have taken and those who, by putting their thoughts into writing, have helped us advance our thinking.

Some have had direct influence due to their presence and willingness to impart their wisdom. We single out the following: Dr. Leon Charette, Dr. Stewart A. Davidson, Arthur Kent Davis, Dr. Gerry Glassford, Dr. Rick Gruneau, Dr. Hal Hansen, Dr. Christopher Hodgkinson, Dr. Don Lang, Dr. Edward McCullough, Dr. Bob Morford, Dr. Christopher Olsen, Dr. Ruth Whitehead, Dr. Ruth Wright, Sören Kierkegaard, Aristotle, and JPG&R.

Preface

The realm of sport has always provided participants, administrators, and observers with a wide and often bizarre array of ethical issues. From the time of the ancient Greeks to the present we know that some of those involved in the world of sport have often missed the ideal ethical mark. For example, we may have looked on in shame, embarrassment, anger, or resignation at the behavior of the following:

- the bribery linked to the International Olympic Committee members;
- the drug abuse of Ben Johnson of Canada;
- the sexual abuse by Graham James of Canada;
- the physical assault linked to Tonya Harding of the U.S.A.;
- the hooliganism on the football pitches of the U.K.

Many may believe that human behavior in the supposed character-building environment of sport is far from where we wish it to be. While these incidents, and many others, have indeed occurred, they do provide a wonderful catalyst for an awakening or reawakening of our awareness of ethical conduct in sport. Can something be done? Can we make a difference?

In this text we endeavor to enhance this awakening in the reader by providing a variety of ethical "tools" and the means to implement these tools. The text is designed to empower students to think for themselves. It is written to enable students to explore and understand not only the ethics behind their own decision making and behavior but also the ethics and actions of others. While knowledge of one's own preferred ethical position does not lead necessarily to ethical conduct, it does provide the individual who is morally "armed" with a foundation to make more comprehensive and ethically informed decisions-ignorance is not bliss. By becoming ethical and critical thinkers each of us will become authentic human agents. In this text you will find:

- an introduction to ethical concepts and theories;
- two theoretical frameworks that will provide the grounding for comprehensive ethical decisions;
- a discussion of ethical principles to follow in the realm of sport and recreation;
- a variety of case studies that will enable you to put theory into practice.

The intent of the authors is to provide the reader with a firm grasp of ethical theory and method that will facilitate the application of theory to the case studies. We have intentionally refrained from including our perception of the "correct" decisions or processes with regard to the case studies. We believe it is up to the student, his or her colleagues, and the instructor to work through the cases, guided by the models provided, in order to render moral judgment.

Each of the three authors of this text have published their thoughts in scholarly journals on various aspects of ethics in the curricula of human movement, kinesiology, sport science, and various other academic programs. This text has provided an opportunity for synthesis of the ideas of Malloy, Ross, and Zakus on ethics and our profession. We hope it will be a useful tool to foster comprehensive ethical decision making, thus enabling the reader to make a difference in his or her personal and professional life.

> Man being condemned to be free carries the weight of the whole world on his shoulders; he is responsible for the world and for himself as a way of being (Sartre, 1998, p.52).

We hope that this book may help lighten the load a little.

The Second Edition

The first edition of *Sport Ethics: Concepts and Cases in Sport and Recreation* was well received. The combination of basic ethical theory with interesting and contemporary cases has been popular among professors and students in numerous universities in Canada, the United States, as well as in Australia and the United Kingdom. As a result, Thompson Educational Publishing Inc. has chosen to offer a Second Edition of this text. While we have made some significant modifications to the theoretical content in Chapters 1 to 7, the major changes have been in the form of additional cases involving events that have occurred since the First Edition's release in 2000 (e.g., the Salt Lake City Olympics and genetic modification of athletes).

As with any human endeavor sport changes constantly and throws up new and ethically challenging issues. Sound professional sport and leisure management demands that each of us keeps up to date with new knowledge, ideas, and techniques to deal with such issues and we have endeavored to do so in this Second Edition. We hope you enjoy the text and find these changes helpful in your scholarship and teaching.

1

New Approaches to Sport Education

T here is an adage that says the only two certain things in life are death and taxes. We would argue that there is at least one more thing that you can count on in your personal and professional life–you will be faced with ethical decisions. It may be the decision to commit a foul in order to save a goal, to take steroids to improve performance, to misrepresent an expense claim, or to report a friend who has sexually harassed a co-worker. Regardless of the particular nature or intensity of the choices that you must make, the extent to which you are able and willing to make an ethical decision may be a function of your understanding of what is good and bad, right and wrong, authentic and inauthentic behavior. The purpose of this text is to provide the student and the practitioner with frameworks for making comprehensive ethical decisions (i.e., good, right, and authentic).

Plato believed that no one knowingly acts unethically. He argued that all "unjust" behavior was the result of ignorance and therefore education must contain a *moral component.* He believed that each person had the capacity in his or her "soul" to be ethical and that education was the means to turn the soul from the darkness of ignorance to the light of knowledge and justice. While researchers have been active in enlightening the scientific and/or physical aspect of our field, historically the *moral component* has been left in darkness. This omission has been lamented by a number of scholars in recent years (e.g., Malloy, 1996; Macintosh & Whitson, 1990; Ross, 1994; Zakus & Malloy, 1995). A central theme among these scholars is their perception that the field has been dominated philosophically by positivism and technically by the human performance sciences at the expense of courses in philosophy and ethics in sport and recreation. Positivism is a philosophical view that places emphasis upon the verification of empirical or quantitative facts. If something cannot be measured, the positivist argues, it is not worthy of further consideration. This approach has been accepted as a "given" (and unquestioned) in both the social science and the human performance aspects of our field in both teaching and the funding and publication of research (Macintosh & Whitson, 1990; Ross,

1994). Social science has, in many respects, justified its existence by the adoption of positivism to quantify human conduct (cf., Hodgkinson, 1996; Saul, 1992). Saul (1995) goes so far as to say of social sciences generally that

> they labor still under the burden of being a false science. Their experiments do not provide any measurable progress in the manner of real science. In place of real evidence they are obliged to pile up overwhelming weights of documentation relating to human action—none of which is proof, little of it even illustration.... It is meant to create the impression of evidence by the force of weight (pp.68-69).

On the other hand, the field of human performance is by nature positivistic, as it is fundamentally natural science. The person as sentient being does not exist in this paradigm. Rather person as functioning athlete (a performing organism) is the general view taken. As a result of the implicit and explicit philosophical positivism in our field, which encompasses both the social and natural sciences, the non-quantifiable scholarly pursuits have been relegated, we believe unfortunately, to a secondary and/or insignificant position. When the sciences are given predominance, the perceived importance of the *moral component* is minimized. Certain consequences result from this hierarchical order. With regard to the field of medicine, Veatch (1977) made the following rather telling comment: "Physicians must no longer be educated as technical geniuses and moral imbeciles" (p.v). While this is somewhat of an overstatement of our position, it does indicate clearly our concern. Students are being taught to assess human performance in laboratories, to survey and statistically analyze human behavior, to develop and manage sport and recreation programming without consideration given to what Aristotle termed practical philosophy—ethics. The veracity of this speculation was confirmed in two studies that looked at the existence of ethics in Australian, Canadian, and American post-secondary curricula (Malloy, 1992; Malloy, Prapavessis & Zakus, 1994). The findings revealed that less than 25% of faculties and/or colleges in Australia, Canada, and the United States offered such courses. Typically the rationale for the omission of ethics and/or philosophy courses was that they were believed to have been part of other courses offered within the institution (e.g., current issues in leisure, sociology of sport and recreation, etc.). One can cynically make the assumption that ethics and/or philosophy was not deemed important to the students or faculty, as otherwise it would be on a similar footing in the curriculum with biomechanics, exercise physiology, or anatomy.

This dominance is undertaken at the expense of understanding human existence and essence in and through physical activity. We strive to teach our students to know the potential of the athlete's body to go higher, faster, and grow stronger, yet we seem to care little for the potential of the athlete as a sentient human, as a role model, as a member of the community. Ross (1994) states that

> it is only by studying the athlete from all purviews–reductionistic and holistic; biophysical, psychosocial and spiritual; as an ethical being concerned with right and wrong, good and bad, who is influenced by external stimuli and "internal" aspirations–that we will attain a comprehensive understanding of the athlete as an athlete and as a whole person. And, in so doing, this very process will lead us to a more profound understanding of ourselves as persons (p.115).

While Ross's comments focus upon the athlete, they can certainly be echoed for the practitioner (i.e., the administrator, coach, volunteer) as well. Those who are equipped with the cognitive ability to make ethical choices will have the option to act or not to act ethically–they will be able to choose. Those without these "tools" will not be able to choose or understand the appropriate path. This "state of the curriculum" is disconcerting because no one can avoid making ethical choices in their personal and professional lives. If students have not been exposed to ethical theories, concepts, principles, and decision-making models, they will be at a distinct disadvantage when faced with ethical dilemmas that are bound to arise throughout their lives and in their careers. Help in eliminating this disadvantage is forthcoming in this book.

Brief Overview of Content and Approach Used

Based on the material presented in the following chapters, it will become apparent that one of our goals is to blend ethical theory and applied ethics. Furthermore, through the study of the cases presented in the last two chapters, ample opportunity will exist for the readers to actually do applied ethics. To make that exercise meaningful and fruitful from an educational perspective, familiarity with some ethical theories is needed to serve as an intellectual foundation. Two models, one basic and the other more complex, are offered to help guide moral discourse. Taken together, these components serve as a framework within which moral reasoning is conducted. There is a logical flow to the order in which the material is introduced. Reference has already been made to the presence of an ethical component in all situations involving other players, coaches, administrators, and stakeholders. In Chapter 2, some of the political, social, cultural, and technological changes that have emerged recently are examined and some of the new conceptualizations that have appeared will be discussed. Attention is directed towards showing how these advances have not only highlighted certain ethical dilemmas but, at the same time, have created new, more difficult moral problems.

This is an introductory text. The instructor and student should be aware that the theories discussed in Chapters 3, 4, and 5 have been presented in their basic form, and of course, much more detail, discussion, and debate exists in the volumes of work published in ethics. Our intent is to provide the student with the basics and hope that this might "whet their appetite" for further reading and philosophical thinking.

The first steps in establishing a theoretical foundation are taken in Chapter 3. Basic concepts in ethics are introduced along with a number of definitions to help ensure a common understanding of the terms used. Three ethical theories are described very briefly in preparation for a more detailed discussion in the next chapter. An important feature is the emphasis placed on identifying and enunciating an ethical maxim that will serve as a yardstick against which behavior can be measured.

A basic, five-step model is presented to serve as a guide for moral discourse. This is a suggested procedure, one that need not be followed in a lock-step fashion, but which can be used to achieve a comprehensive discussion of the issue at hand. Utilization of this model facilitates the applied components of ethics since its goal is to help the user render moral judgment.

Chapter 4 contains a more detailed account of three ethical theories: consequentialism (teleology), non-consequentialism (deontology), and existentialism. As the explication evolves, the strengths and weaknesses, the advantages and disadvantages, as well as the limitations of each theory are discussed. Through this exploration the notions of good, right, and authentic become a little clearer.

Behavior is the overt manifestation of decisions made by the agent. To improve our understanding of appropriate behavior there is a need to examine various factors that influence the decision-making process. These factors are the focus of Chapter 5; their study provides deeper insight into what prompts people to act in certain ways. Reference to these moderators during moral discourse sheds additional light on the issues and may influence the final pronouncement.

A second, more sophisticated model to guide ethical decision-making is included here. This model takes into account aspects of individual moral development as well as psychological and social moderators. Its more comprehensive structure serves to remind those engaged in moral discourse or in making decisions to account for many more factors.

Emanating from Chapter 5, but geared towards facilitating the practical side, is a seven-step process to guide ethical decision making. Its applicability will be obvious to anyone faced with a true-life ethical dilemma; its usefulness will be seen when the cases presented in Chapter 9 are studied.

In Chapter 7, ethical principles that guide practice are identified. Each is principle expounded briefly to provide the specific context for the analysis of the cases. These principles include promise keeping, respect for persons, responsibility and/or duty, and balance. In addition, the notions of sportsmanship and fair play are discussed as well as different conceptions of sport.

A wide range of cases are presented in the last two chapters. One case is analyzed, guided by the models presented and considered within the context of the ethical principles noted in the preceding chapter. This analysis is meant as a demonstration of how to proceed. Now, armed with basic concepts in ethics, an understanding of three ethical theories, an appreciation for the use of an ethical maxim, and assisted by models that guide moral discourse, ample opportunities are available, in the form of actual cases, to engage in moral discourse, to do applied ethics.

Two well-known pedagogical principles—begin at the level of the learner and from there advance to more complex material, and learn by doing—have guided the approach used in this book. Based on the assumption that some readers have limited background in the study of ethics, basic concepts are introduced first. That step is followed by an exposition of three ethical theories that serve as a conceptual foundation for the applied aspect. Two models to guide moral discourse and ethical decision making are proffered to facilitate the blending of theory and practice.

Learning by doing is implemented in Chapters 8 and 9, where the case studies are presented. As each case is examined and analyzed, readers learn by doing. Since the cases cover a wide range of issues, many aspects of sport and recreation practice are explored as the readers practice their analytical skills during moral discourse. Wrestling with these cases will make the readers morally sensitive. Exploration of these moral dilemmas should provide future practitioners with some basis for addressing the difficult situations they will meet once they start practicing.

Advice on How to Use This Book

There is some reluctance on our part to offer pedagogical advice since each professor has her own favorite teaching methods as well as ideas on how best to proceed. That reluctance is tempered by the awareness that even the most experienced teachers can benefit from the suggestions offered by colleagues who have tried something different. Adopting new approaches is readily justified if the methods used facilitate learning.

A review of the table of contents and the elaboration presented in the preceding section would, at first glance, seem to indicate how to proceed: master the basic concepts, learn the theories, study the models, discuss the special principles that constitute the specific context of sport and recreation, and then institute small discussion groups to address the case studies. That certainly is one way to proceed but a caution might be in order: students may become restless if they are confined to the realm of theory for too long. Alternative approaches are available, procedures that will retain the blending of theory and practice and maintain the interest of students at a high level.

One possibility is to start the course with a case study. As the discussion evolves the instructor is in a position to question some of the comments made. These queries, formulated properly, will expose some of the lacunae due to the lack of knowledge of ethical theories. Lack of knowledge of ethical theory limits the scope and progress of the discussion. When such an intervention is successful, the need to study ethical theories becomes obvious to everyone.

As successful as that procedure may be it does not necessarily mean that all the theoretical material must be completed before any other cases are addressed. It is pedagogically possible, indeed feasible, to intersperse the study of theoretical material with small-group discussions, the applied component.

Another interesting approach can be attempted if there is sufficient time available. Very early in the course, before the theoretical aspects are studied, the discussion of a few cases can be recorded. After some aspects of theory have been addressed, the same cases can be revisited to determine if the discussion is now held on a higher level and if more penetrating comments are made that lead to new insights. Once again the theoretical and the practical can be blended in a different way.

As each case is studied the identification of an ethical maxim will serve as a yardstick against which behavior is measured. Promoting discussion of this challenging task can produce much educational benefit. At times difficulties may be encountered in enunciating a maxim and at other times consensus may not be reached regarding which specific maxim is directly applicable. When various suggestions are offered it indicates that the moral issue is defined or conceptualized in a different way by different members of the group. Much can be learned, from the perspective of ethics, from these debates.

Case studies, as a useful pedagogical procedure, are used in many academic settings. Each case provides a common base for discussion and, through participation in small groups, allows everyone to become actively involved. Through the give-and-take that ensues, new insights emerge as the discussion evolves. As positive as the benefits sound, there are some potential problems with small-group discussions: irrelevant material can be introduced, the group can become mired in dealing with minor points, and the discussion can become too narrowly focused or too broadly diffused. There may be times when all theoretical aspects are omitted as very "practical" solutions are sought. Although there are no assurances, it is anticipated that the judicious application of the models designed to guide moral discourse found in the text will serve to direct the discussion along the most fruitful path and keep the deliberation focused on the key issues.

References

Macintosh, D., & Whitson, D. (1990). *The game planners: Transforming Canada's sport system.* Montreal & Kingston: McGill-Queen's University Press.

Hodgkinson, C. (1996). *Administrative philosophy: Values and motivations in administrative life.* London: Pergamon Press.

Malloy, D.C. (1992). Ethics in Canadian university physical activity curricula. *CAHPER Journal,* 58, 2:27-31.

_____. (1996). A perspective on ethics in sport management curricula. *Avante,* 2, 1:79-83.

Malloy, D.C., Prapavessis, H., & Zakus, D.H. (1994). Ethics in human movement curricula: Do they exist? *Australian Council for Health Physical Education and Recreation Healthy Lifestyles Journal,* 41, 4:14-18.

Ross, S. (1994). Sport sciences and the whole person. *CAHPER Research Supplement,* 1, 1:109-116.

Sartre, J. (1998). *Existentialism and human emotions.* Toronto: Citadel Press.

Saul, J.R. (1992). *Voltaire's bastards: The dictatorship of reason in the West.* New York: Vintage Books.

_____. (1995). *The unconscious uncivilization.* Concord, Ont.: Anansi Press.

Veatch, R.M. (1977). *Case studies in medical ethics.* Cambridge: Harvard University Press.

Zakus, D.H., & Malloy, D.C. (1995). A critical evaluation of current pedagogical approaches in human movement studies: A suggested alternative. *Quest,* 48:501-517.

2

Recreation and Sport in the New Millennium

Imagine a conversation you might have with your grandparents over the nature of recreation and sport in their youth. "Ah, in my days we had to make our own fun, we found things to do, made our own equipment, played on any open space." Or, "Athletes were hard working, down-to-earth people—they worked hard and earned their money" and "They were part of the community." Grandparents would identify with athletes such as Mickey Mantle, Willie Mays, and Roger Maris in baseball; Gordie Howe, Rocket Richard, and Davey Keon in ice hockey; Jim Brown, Johnny Unitas, and Dick Butkus in gridiron football; Bob Cousy, Wilt Chamberlain, and Elgin Baylor in basketball; sport teams traveling by train; fewer major league teams and leagues; more regional and local competitions; shorter seasons and lower salaries; no national sport systems; and many opportunities to play in community recreation programs and sport. You would likely not know the athletes named or understand how sport was structured. Grandparents would lament that those were the "good old days."

Such a discussion with your parents presents another interesting scenario. They had a wide range of relatively inexpensive community leagues and sports systems that allowed them to compete; away games were within the region or state/province. Equipment and admission prices were within the range of most families. In all of the major sports, new teams, leagues, and competitions began that competed for athletes and fans. They would identify with the American Basketball Association, the American Football League, the World Hockey Association, and the American League in North American professional sports; Kerry Packer and World Series Cricket; the expansion of the Olympic Games and Avery Brundage's last days of protecting the amateur status of Olympians; air travel; the expansion of television; the Canada-Soviet Hockey series; and the Montreal and Munich Olympic Games. While all of these things were highly politicized, your parents too would lament the "good old days." They were or are living through the transition from a seemingly simpler time to the current, highly commercialized, globalized sport industry.

How will you discuss with your children and grandchildren the recreation and sport opportunities you enjoyed as a child and youth? What values and beliefs will form the moral and ethical framework of this discussion? Will your children or grandchildren understand or relate to this framework? A discussion of what "was/is" and what "will be" will vary with the historical times in which they are expressed and lived.

Here the student of sport is confronted with the classic questions of philosophy and life. How your grandparents, parents, and the generations before them and those to follow you understand the nature and structure of recreation and sport, how they understand athletes and how they compete, how they understand the cost, size, and volume of sports, sport competitions, and facilities will vary. Likewise, the identification of heroes and heroines and the myths that are established and recounted as cultural aspects of recreation and sport will vary. Questions around which values were central to past recreation and sport practices and organizations and how these value frameworks have changed are critically important. More centrally, how do they compare with those you currently hold or are currently operating? Clearly there will be several points of difference, changes in values, changes in ethics, and a wider debate.

Were things better in days gone by? Did athletes act differently and, by implication, better, in former times? Was their moral character better? Was their behavior ethically sound? More directly, what of the "sham-ateurs" (those who took payment for their performance while claiming amateur status)? Was government funding of programs and services better in previous times, and is this type of funding necessary for recreation and sport to operate currently? All of the above questions point to values, morals, and ethics. They also indicate dilemmas that confront managers and decision-makers. To wit, how do we reconcile what was or is and what might be in the future?

Each person must be cognizant of, and come to recognize, the moral and ethical frameworks that have been in operation. This demands contextualizing leisure and sport organizations and operations in historical terms. Likewise, each person must understand their own moral and ethical framework in order to manage in recreation and sport organizations. Obviously a temporal, generational shift in the nature and basis of the value, moral, and ethical frameworks that define this aspect of daily life changes. In fact, a debate arises constantly around these issues.

The basis of change. What, one must ask, is the nature of this debate in recreation and sport? Moreover, what are the forces that lead to change? Two things must be identified before going further into the details of elemental changes in recreation and sport. First, as a well-known political economist argued, economic factors initially are the basis and driving force of change. Changes in the way people materially survive leads to changes in the way they relate and interrelate, in the very way society becomes structured (e.g., in the actual social, political, and cultural structures). Over time the social, political, and cultural structures of society come to lead change in the way the economic processes operate and are structured. This process continues through time as the economy affects society and then society affects the economy and so on. Within these changes will be evolutions (and devolutions) in values, beliefs, ideologies, meanings, and norms. If these elements of culture change, so too will the moral frameworks and ethical behaviors that emanate from that culture. This is clearly marked in current times when globalization is evident, bringing more cultures, morals, and ethical codes into contact.

Most, if not all, readers of this book live in societies based on capitalist market economies, and the attendant social structures of such societies. Chesneaux (1976) argues that we can not understand any history without understanding the politics and power of this global economic force. So in order to understand sport and posit the changes in sport, we need to view the cultural changes within the context of economic changes. It is not possible to understand the former without some knowledge of the latter.

This indicates the second point. We argue that sport is the central focus for understanding the debate and for identifying and operating with an ethical framework. Sport provides a prototypic element of culture that exemplifies the debate. That is, within the changes in sport, we have a case study of the overall effect of change under capitalism. For it is the unrelenting changes brought on by the changes in capitalist operations that are harbingers of concomitant cultural changes. Change occurs at all levels of recreation and sport. Again, recreation and sport managers and specialists must have both a broad and specialized perspective in order to operate effectively and ethically. Finally, the focus on sport does not delegate recreation to secondary status. Clearly, much of what happens in recreational settings results from changes in sport.

The debate over tradition and current status of sport has a long discourse, one most often carried out in terms of the amateur versus professional dichotomy. Along with death and taxes, change is a certainty in life (all with underlying ethical aspects). Perhaps the debate is best described as one between nostalgia or tradition, and the rapid (distant or recent) changes found throughout the twentieth century. Challenges to beliefs, attitudes, cherished ideas, and ways of thinking and living have taken on major proportions. We argue that this debate embraces larger ideological elements as well. With the end of the century and a new millennium facing the world, the dissonance takes on greater proportions.

Sport traditionalists are left with the stuff of nostalgia. Their thoughts and discussions are informed by the past. Speak with your parents and grandparents to hear this nostalgia. Memorabilia, museum, movie and tourist industries, as specialized elements of the broader sport industry, all focus on and use sport nostalgia. They seek to make marketable the past that is glorified and promoted as a better time. Whether in products or services, people seek an idealized past to deal with the seemingly uncontrollable changes taking place in all parts of life. Sport marketeers use tradition as a way to sell their sport or sport product. We are inundated with images, words, slogans, myths, and a panoply of products that attempt to take us to that former place in sport. Undoubtedly sport is an element of culture that allows the tension between past, present, and future to be played out.

Purpose of chapter. We posit that recreation and sport managers or specialists need to understand the broader context and changes in these professional fields to be able to form and operate with a moral framework that enhances their ethical behavior. With an informed understanding and moral framework, you will be able to judge and act ethically and authentically in the face of other moral and ethical frameworks you will encounter. The following chapters are designed to provide the tools you will need to develop that ethical framework and models to assist your thinking and action.

This framework is complex, as is the real world of recreation and sport organizations. Both complexity and change make the work of practitioners that much more difficult and ethically variable. We encourage you, therefore, to know and understand the past in order to operate in the present and the future in a more ethical manner.

The purpose of this chapter is to examine several broad developments that have led to political, social, technological, and cultural changes in sport, and then recreation. More specific aspects of these changes are discussed in Chapter 5 as external moderators of the more complex ethical decision-making model. Once again, remember that all of this is only a temporal (historically specific) situation as change continues to alter the landscape in which you operate. The sport or recreation manager or specialist must understand the past to work in the present and the future. Without such ability the moral and ethical issues that ensue will surprise, challenge, and, perhaps, overwhelm the unaware.

New Sport Performers and Changing Global Markets: The Basis of Change in Sport

Markets are the basis of economic life. Producers and consumers come together to exchange goods and services of particular value to their best advantage. Some extra value leading to profits must be gleaned from this exchange for the economy to grow. Countries embracing this type of economy are capitalist in nature. As an economic system, capitalism has a long history. Over time, this economic system has changed in form but not substance in order to maintain itself. To understand this history would take a much longer analysis than is possible or necessary here. It is sufficient to state that capitalism has mutated in order to ensure the overall and continued economic growth of countries founded on capitalist principles.

Our focus here, again, will be on the sport industry. For sport, its industrial structure, and its many market elements, lead and even dictate how people dress, act, speak, and recreate. Central to this focus are the athletes, those whose performances are the core product that people pay to view, either live or on television, and who are central to spin-off aspects (community or national identity, endorsements, and an extensive array of products) of the sport market. Much of what is evident in recreation and at the developmental levels of sport can be traced back to the operation and organization of elite or professional sport.

The sport industry market is immense and varied. Moreover, this market has changed in the latter part of this century. At the basic level of the sport market we no longer have the debate over amateur and professional (except perhaps as residual elements and with athletes at recreational or developmental levels). While some ideological remnants endure of this debate, the issue of athletes receiving pay for their performance is moot. This change raises many new moral and ethical issues. The issues surround not only the producers (athletes) but also consumers (fans, spectators), goods manufacturers (e.g., sport equipment, stadium construction), the mass media, governments, and a host of sport governing organizations. In other words, sport is fully and centrally located in the broader market economy.

Athletes as laborers. To understand this movement, we must first understand how athletes are located in the market structures. In order to begin this discussion, it must be noted that athletes labeled professional have a longer history in this situation. There can be no argument that they have been centrally located in market economic relationships since the latter part of the nineteenth century. Here, therefore, we can observe industrial relations activity. Many sports struggled for collective bargaining rights. The formation of players' associations in many sports (soccer, baseball, U.S. football, rugby league and union, basketball, ice hockey, cricket, Australian rules football, among others) to collectively struggle against the unequal position enjoyed by owners and leagues has a long, if furtive, history. For example, baseball players attempted to unionize early in the twentieth century but were not successful until the mid-1960s. These struggles were never easy. In most of the major sports athletes made several attempts to form collective bargaining groups (players' associations, unions) and to apply collective bargaining negotiation techniques (strikes or threats to withdraw performance) (Staudohar, 1996).

Much of this struggle points to the nature of economic relationships under a capitalist economic structure. Sport merely reflects the broader issues and struggles where the direct producers seek to obtain a decent share of the wealth they create through their labor. It is not merely a teleological issue of more income (i.e., one of the good ends), but also a deontological one (i.e. one of the right means; to be discussed in detail in Chapters 3 and 4). Further, many critiques abound regarding the nature of work in this type of economy. Alienation and exploitation of workers, generally, and athletes, specifically, are seen as endemic under capitalism (Brohm, 1978; Ollman, 1984; Rigauer, 1981). In other words, direct producers find it difficult or are unable to find authenticity through their labor. In many cases, both teleological and deontological behaviors become morally and ethically suspect under such conditions. The overall efforts of most do not lead to experiences of completeness or satisfaction. This leads to questions regarding the nature of sport labor, its benefits to athletes' lives and health, and, on a broader scale, its benefits to society.

Where sport may differ is in its contradictory position in peoples' daily existence. While sport appears to centrally exist in the attention, discourse, and existence of many people, it is really peripheral. Would peoples' basic, daily life be adversely affected if sport or professional athletes no longer existed? While sport adherents would argue in the positive, in reality it would not matter (note: contrast this to the location of recreation activities, which points to an interesting contradiction).

Here an anachronistic situation exists. Is sport, as Brohm (1978) argues, the new opiate of the masses in late capitalism? Or, moreover, a hyper-reality par excellence as the postmodernists would argue? These sub-debates have raged on in the mass media and academic circles for some time. Clearly the economic strength of the sport industry points to a major saliency in peoples' lives and in economic activity. We need only look to the place of hockey in Canada, baseball, U.S. football, and basketball in the U.S.A., rugby in New Zealand, cricket in the West Indies, "Aussie Rules" football (and many other sports) in Australia, and the global phenomena of soccer in many countries to witness this contradiction.

When athletes, through their players' association, use traditional overt labor practices to support their claims, strikes affect the consumers. The last two decades of the twentieth century witnessed several work stoppages by professional sport unions; for example, baseball in 1981 and 1994-5, football in 1982 and 1987, ice hockey in 1994-5 (Staudohar, 1996), basketball in 1999, West Indian cricket in 1999, and several other threatened stoppages. On the surface the general population and many sport fans would have some difficulty aligning with a professional athlete suffering during such a work stoppage. When athletes struggle without a regular pay check (with many single checks being greater than that of most people's yearly income), the sympathy levels are low.

What is not recognized is that many athletes have short careers. True, many, but not most, do have considerable incomes. This depends on the sport and level of competition being discussed. A more important question here is—how much money is made in the overall operation of sport? Owners and their leagues are not philanthropists. They are in business to make money. Clearly much money is being made as most sport businesses pay approximately a quarter of their revenues to athletes. Perhaps the key issue is that people still view sport as being outside of the normal muck of labor relations and of everyday life. Is sport an opiate that consumers do not want muddied by the normal consequences of market relations?

Here then we can ask how the value frameworks have changed. Should professional (or more fundamentally all) athletes make as much as possible in the market? Are they being unreasonable when they unionize or strike? Do they not have the same labor rights as any other worker? How is this ethically contentious? We again confront an anomaly between the current market and industrial nature of sport with the broader canvas of life.

On the other hand, should sport franchise owners and manufacturers be able to use economic practices that seek the lowest possible labor costs, and which permit incredible profits? Should these people be able to control markets, especially those for athletic labor, beyond the sense of a "free" market? Clearly the values, beliefs, myths, attitudes, and practices take on a different hue under the changing operations of the capitalist marketplace.

Few sport managers will be involved with athletes at the elite or professional levels and with the attendant industrial relations activities. There will be situations, however, that demand negotiation skills. Sponsorships and other forms of sport marketing activities are more commonplace. This is an area where income or revenue maximization and hard bargaining might occur in your management role. You may be trying to obtain the best deal for or from an athlete or group of athletes. Further, as sport expands, so too do the number of athletes, in both state and professional development leagues, receiving payment for their performances. Here too is a location for clarifying your ethical stance on what is or is not appropriate recompense for performance.

Changing definitions of amateur and state involvement in sport. When we take this discussion to the formerly amateur situation we see major changes. The Cold War threw open the debate of what constitutes an amateur. The Western nations followed the mainly British model of class-based differentiation and exclusionary practice from traditions established in the late nineteenth century. The former socialist, Eastern bloc nations did not hold to these traditional class-based definitions and exclusions of amateurism. In fact, their entire sport structures were funded and operated with paid personnel, from athletes through to the upper levels of national sport organization administration. Even the prototypic amateur sport zealot Avery Brundage would not condemn the operation of sport in these countries (especially as the key United States athlete production system in college sport was not a purely amateur one). This Cold War rhetoric established much of the discourse of sport production and structure for the middle to late twentieth century.

In response, many of the British Commonwealth nations (especially Canada, Australia, and New Zealand), rather ironically, established Eastern bloc-like state sport systems. Canada, in fact, became identified as the East Germany of the West for its system. Initially this did not resolve the difficulty Western athletes had in obtaining incomes for their labor, but it did provide a large infrastructure of increasingly professionalized sport organizations. There were a number of concomitant processes in play at this time.

First, sport was seen as both an area in which states could increase economic activity (meet fiscal, economic, and social policy through social investment) and an area in which to build national identities. Second, this helped nations struggling to keep up with the sporting successes of the Eastern bloc nations. This was very much an ideological matter central to the Cold War debate of capitalism versus communism. Clearly more had to be provided if athletes were to be prepared properly and successfully. Third, sport became, as witnessed by the spread of professional sport, an attractive area for investment of capital (either directly, or indirectly through sponsorships and advertising). Here, clearly, are value differences (in the cultural sense) expressed through different norms of performance and organization. Not only were different national morals and ethics producing dilemmas in sport performance, but states were struggling with ideological differences that led to new ways of structuring and producing sport. In particular, teleological and deontological issues arose in the structuring and organizing of sport. These have yet to be resolved.

A sad irony of these developments is that athletes supported by the Western states were unable, initially, to obtain much income for their labor. Simply, their labor was not seen as typical of that of other workers in the economy. Much research (e.g., Beamish, 1993; Beamish & Burowy, 1987, 1988; Kidd & Eberts, 1982; Macintosh & Whitson, 1990) has argued that Canadian state athletes are employees within the normal definitions of law. Both MacAloon (1991) in the U.S. situation and Beamish and Burowy (1988) and Zakus (1988) in the Canadian situation point to the inequities resulting from this identification. In both countries the state sport system took up the bulk of the budget and left athletes to find their own financial resources. As with the professional context, some athletes were able to generate large trust funds, but these were the exceptions. Many athletes remained what Kidd identified as "sweat-suited philanthropists" (1988, p.298) and "underpaid state workers" (1982, p.300). Teleologically, many were in a better position, but not all. Deontologically, many were still seeking the right way to survive and produce in the confusion of Western state ideological contradictions and market drive conditions. Clearly the situation was inequitable and damaging to the overall life and success of many state athletes.

While some industrial action was threatened (e.g., Australian and Canadian state athletes threatening to strike before major games competitions), it did not occur. Changes made at the international level of sport governance permitted athletes to obtain more value (money) for their labor. In 1972 the International Olympic Committee (IOC) ruled that the definition of what constitutes a professional athlete was the purview of each international sport-governing body. Following this, athletes were able to establish trust funds to channel and contain any sponsorship revenues. The management of these funds was still under the aegis of the national sport-governing bodies, who were also able to access and use some of these funds for their own program operations. An improvement in the situation resulted but it was not an adequate one.

In 1980, with the ascendancy of Juan Antonio Samaranch to the presidency of the IOC, the whole matter of amateur athletes took a different hue. Seeking to have the best athletes available for the Olympic Games and in line with new IOC marketing and revenue-generating relationships, many "overtly" professional athletes were brought into Olympic competition. Professional tennis, basketball, figure skating, soccer, and ice hockey players become Olympians. Athletes in other sports sought and established lucrative marketing opportunities. One could say that issues of appropriate teleological and deontological agency became moot. Everything associated with amateurism and its outdated, class-based code was dead at the upper levels of sport. No more would the authenticity of so many athletes come into question or lead to personal crises of identity and ethical contradiction.

Again, many athletes were able to "cash in" on their name and image to generate huge sponsorships (see section on sport agents, "New marketing practices," p.28), but they were the exception and not the rule. In this open era, sport-governing bodies were also able to cash in by expanding sponsorship and marketing opportunities. In this melee, interesting situations eventuated as sport-governing bodies and athletes clashed over ownership and control of names and images. For example, in 1998 the clash between Rowing Australia and the 1996 Atlanta gold medallist mens' coxless four rowing team ensued over use of the label "oarsome foursome" for sponsorship purposes. A further example occurred in Barcelona during the 1992 Olympic Games. During the gold medal presentation to the U.S. basketball team, many athletes wore towels around their necks to cover the logo of company providing the U.S. team clothing. That is, the Reebok logo was covered so the Nike sponsored athletes were not photographed or televised with the wrong logo showing. There are many examples where different footwear and clothing sponsors lead to conflicts between athletes and their teams, sport-governing bodies, or Olympic association.

Overall, many young athletes continue to depend on family resources. While state financial support systems have assisted in talent development, they are still inadequate in the overall context. One could question the moral soundness of this situation. If democracy indicates that all have equal opportunity and access to resources to maximize their lives, that all sports are important as public goods, and that strong moral qualities are developed through sport, should the state not support equally all persons, all sports, and all organizations across the spectrum? Are there not conflicting values operating? Is this an example of George Orwell's famous anti-democratic dictum of "all are equal but some are more equal"?

In the overall context of elite sport production, both private and state sport systems have developed and provided a full range of human resource management policies, structures, and personnel (Chalip, 1995; Dabscheck, 1996, 1998; Slack, 1997). This process has a history longer than that of athletes receiving more value for their labor. Development of specialized sport organizations, the full professionalization of support and organizational staffs, and the ongoing development and expansion of these organizations is very much a feature of modern sport (and recreation) across the spectrum.

A number of studies have pointed to this development (e.g., Slack & Kikulis, 1989; Kikulis, Slack & Hinings, 1992; Macintosh & Whitson, 1990). The propensity of organizations to expand both in size and regulatory frameworks is clearly evident in all organizations throughout the world of sport. We can observe this expansion from local leisure providers through national sport bodies to the international sport organizations.

Perhaps the most deleterious effect of this has been the disproportion of funds spent on the organization of sport as opposed to the monies going to the direct producers, the athletes. MacAloon (1991), Beamish and Burowy (1987, 1988), and Zakus (1988) have shown that the amount spent for the operation of sport organizations and their attendant staffs is disproportionate to the financial support provided to athletes. These authors have raised this ethical dilemma, as it appears to reflect the amateur ideals as applied to athletes, but does not question the need for paid staff. Here the amateur board members (at local regional, national, and international levels) can still enjoy the lifestyle of the past, while not having the same responsibilities (since the paid staff takes these on). Board members receive extensive travel, expenses, and other perks while athletes are often left in "third-class" situations, fending for themselves. It is an inversion of the production pyramid. The monies and perks accrue to the administrative aspects of sport, while the actual producers receive less. One might ask how board members ethically justify this inversion and why it is that such conditions continue. Clearly many of the contentious issues arising during 1999 surrounding the unethical behavior of IOC members might not have arose if this were not the way sport is organized. Although athletes have benefitted from this expansion, it is not clear that the moral and ethical dimensions of this provision are acceptable. Whether a full professionalization of state athletes will occur, or be economically possible, is a question for the future.

Still the question of whether governments should support sport persons as government employees needs to be explored. Do we need professional state athletes, especially at the local or state levels? We can question how far the expansion of paid athletic labor can go. When we consider that children and youth (especially in youth-oriented sports such as gymnastics) and 15- to 18-year-olds (e.g., ice hockey) are paid for their performances, the logic, financing, and legal aspects become central—to say nothing of the obvious ethical implications that arise. Could you negotiate in these ethically laden circumstances? How would you do so? Upon what ethical rationale or framework? Certainly it is an issue that demands the attention of sport managers and specialists, as they are centrally located in these matters.

Expansion of the Sport Industry

Expansion of sport businesses. In the private sector of the sport industry we can observe that the sources of revenue for sport franchises have expanded considerably. First, sport franchises have banded together in industry-based associations (leagues) to (1) act in monopolistic (exclusive control of a commodity or service) and monopsonistic (exclusive control of the demand for a product by a single purchaser) ways and (2) to maximize merchandising, mass media, and sponsorship opportunities. These opportunities have resulted in considerable, new, extensive revenues. Second, sport franchises have sought community and regional market and media alignments to expand their own individual market opportunities. This is most recognized in team- or club-specific television programs and community relations. Finally, expansion of new teams and/or clubs, super leagues (such as those proposed in ice hockey and soccer), and global competitions (many sports going to World Cup formats) continue to provide new market and revenue sources. Overall, many sport franchises, throughout the spectrum of sport competition, have exploded in value.

No longer is it sport entrepreneurs who seek franchises. Major entertainment and non-sport corporations purchase sport franchises as part of their general expansion. The value or tax possibilities of sport franchises make them attractive economic, as well as status, investments (Beamish, 1988; Scully, 1995). Many of these corporations seek to vertically and horizontally integrate their holdings. Canadian hockey franchises in Vancouver and Montreal that were previously part of wider media and liquor corporations exemplify this process early in their history (Beamish, 1991). A more recent example is that of Rupert Murdoch, principle in News Corporation, who expanded his media empire through specialized sport broadcasting (e.g., Fox Sports, BskyB, Cablevision, among many others) and the purchase of professional sport teams (e.g., Los Angeles Dodgers, partial ownership of the New York Knicks and Rangers, and a failed offer to purchase the Manchester United soccer club), among other strategies. The morality and possible monopolistic control of sport arise here.

In late 1999, for example, two rugby league clubs in Australia were ruled out of the national, professional competition. The league has determined that it will only remain viable, financially and as a spectator sport attracting live and television audiences, if it reduces the number of teams (note: this situation has occurred in the English rugby league as well). The two teams were foundational clubs in the original league. In 1996, a "rugby league war" was fought between clubs in the existing league and a new "super" league financed by Rupert Murdoch and his media empire. The "war" was an expensive, divisive battle that led to the need to reduce the number of teams and the overall decline of the sport. As this situation was fundamentally over the control of sport television content (for Murdoch's cable sport stations), it points to the future of control and funding of sport. Whether sport can continue in a resource-dependent state on the mass media and maintain its integrity and viability is a large question. Rational decision making in the media and economic area will likely not follow or respond to the moral arguments for individual elements of the sport, both human and organization. This same sort of moral debate can be applied to franchise relocation such as that witnessed in the NFL (Baltimore, Los Angeles, Houston, Cleveland) and the NHL (Winnipeg, Quebec City, and possibly Edmonton and Calgary in the future). The morality of markets and money resources do not follow nostalgia and fandom subjectivity.

A final comment on this matter relates to the number of sport franchises that have floated share offers on various stock markets to obtain capital. This indicates that individual and organizational (especially pension funds) investors are targeted. Support for a club or team is now possible for the average fan and punter. The idea of publicly listed sport franchises will expand. As sport continues to grow economically, individual and corporate investors throughout the world will see it as a viable and desirable target for their portfolios. Ultimately, the question of difference between the world of sport and the wider world of corporate enterprise issues will disappear. Can the same moral frameworks be applied to these competing realities? Can corporate codes of conduct be applied directly to sport operations? Can sport managers respond to shareholders in the same manner as they would to fans and club boards? Can organizational effectiveness criteria be applied in both of these, albeit converging, realities?

"The Superstadium Game": Public provision for private profit? While state investment in sport systems is one way that fiscal and economic policy is met, there are two other dimensions to this matter. Often identified as public provision for private capital accumulation, public expenditure on sport infrastructure and on major competitions is widely noted. The central feature of the Canadian Summer and Winter Games policy was the provision of sport facilities for host cities. Extensions of this policy to major international sport festivals have similar purposes. Most often the facilities provided in the latter case are clearly for professional sport franchises. That is, they are publicly provided to attract private investment, and ultimately generate more economic activity and more state revenues.

The central concern of much of this public expenditure is on the morality of spending funds on facilities and events that the middle and upper classes will participate in, versus the provision of basic public goods (health, education, transport, and infrastructure facilities) that would benefit all members of society. Here again, different teleological and deontological positions are evident. With so many different institutions involved in these matters, is it possible to identify a standard moral or ethical basis? Is there any possibility of a standard, ethically sound process to resolve these issues? As sport and leisure organizations and operations are tightly coupled with institutions throughout society, sport and leisure managers or specialists must be aware of this wide variety of institutional cultures and ethical frameworks.

Professional sport teams are therefore provided with a key element in their productive process, an entertainment and training venue. For example, the bidding process for the Colts National Football League franchise between Indianapolis, Phoenix, and Baltimore (the then-current location) provides evidence of the incentives cities make available; these include new stadia, training facilities, guaranteed revenues, and other economic plums (see p.239 in Schimmel, Ingham & Howell, 1993, for the list). Other examples could be cited for each of the major professional sports. However, this situation occurs at various levels of the sport system. This is a feature long recognized by the mass media and sport studies academics. More often it is identified as the "superstadium game." Professional sport franchise owners use threats of moving the franchise elsewhere to obtain a newer, state-of-the-art facility and the best possible revenue-sharing deal (as well as the best possible rental and tax arrangement).

Although there are positive examples of stadia management following the public provision of the facility, most often local and state governments are left with development, operating, maintenance, policing, and debt-reduction costs. Public-debt financing is met from government revenues in various ways (public enterprise revenue, general obligation bonds, revenue bonds, and new directed taxes [e.g., hotel, restaurant, entertainment taxes]). The most common argument given to justify this public investment in large facilities is that increased tax revenue will be generated. This increased tax revenue, politicians argue, will come from direct taxes on items such as tickets, merchandise, and food and beverage sales at sport and other entertainment events in these facilities. As well, they argue that increased tax revenue will result from increased consumer activity in areas adjacent to the facility (such as hotel and motel room rentals, restaurant and bar sales, shopping, and other tourism consumption). In fact, these increased taxes fail to meet the huge capital investments made by these governments.

More often, tax increases are used to meet and then retire the debt created to build facilities for major competitions or directly for professional sport franchises. The same can be said of the operating costs to local, state, and federal governments for general infrastructure upgrades, extra public transportation, and policing during these events. Overall, this feature of public provision has often had debilitating effects on the host community and the benefits are limited to those who are economically well off (see Whitson & Macintosh, 1996). Again, the morality of allocation of public funds is central. In this situation the costs can accrue to generations of citizens, so the question of whether present generations of decision-makers can leave considerable debt for future citizens receives broad debate. Such decisions seem questionable teleologically.

Referred to in the above example of the Colts is the bidding process that city (and state) governments enter. In order to obtain the *raison d'etre* for expensive facilities, for franchises, and for international recognition, cities seek to obtain major games competitions and events and to bid (or steal) away sport franchises. Private enterprise uses a variety of techniques to favorably attract merger, acquisition, or take-over targets. The private sector also uses these techniques with governments to obtain concessions (tax and other), joint venture opportunities, and other favorable investment situations. Public and sport governments also apply these same tactics. Public governments have for decades structured their operation and organization to align with these normal business practices. Marketing, trade and development, and investment venture departments are examples of new government operations.

Perhaps the mostly widely publicized version of the dilemma surrounds bids for major games. In the late 1990s the bidding process for Olympic and Winter Olympic Games became a major ethical and financial issue. In the bids for all major games, not only the Olympic ones, considerable public money is invested along with some private funding. The host city, state, country, and peak sport body (i.e., the international sport body that is signature to the contract, such as the IOC or the Commonwealth Games Association) must sign contracts to ensure the financing of these games and also that monies are provided for sport-governing bodies and, more importantly, the global peak sport body. The bidding process itself is very complex and expensive (see Thoma & Chalip, 1996, on this topic). Each bidding city can expect to spend tens of millions of dollars in the final bid process and over a billion dollars on the actual preparation and hosting of the games (depending on the games under consideration). Games bids are serious and costly activities. Because of this, many socially conscious groups point to the social and economic folly of their locale hosting a games. Toronto witnessed such a group around their 1996 Olympic Games bid with the "Bread not Circuses Coalition" (see Kidd, 1992; Lenskyj, 1996).

Games bidding also came under incredible moral and ethical scrutiny during 1999 when the Board of Ethics of the Salt Lake City Organizing Committee (SLOC) for the 2002 Olympic Winter Games released its report (1999). The state of Utah and the city of Salt Lake City formed and funded its bid committee organization in 1966. This committee operated first to obtain the United States Olympic Committee's (USOC) right to bid for the Olympic Winter Games (OWG) and then unsuccessfully bid for the 1998 Games. In 1995, this committee finally won the right to host the 2002 OWG and transmogrified into the SLOC. In 1993, a code of ethics had been established for the bid committee. The Board of Ethics for SLOC was formed in December 1998. The five-person board, in a short time frame, reviewed large numbers of written records and carried out numerous interviews. In February, 1999, it released its report to the Board of Trustees for the SLOC.

The report contained damning evidence that IOC members had acted unethically in their demands for gifts and other special privileges. The evidence was damaging to the IOC and the entire bidding process. It implicated many individuals on the SLOC and its predecessor committee. A chain reaction was set off that led to the investigation of other bid processes, the establishment of an IOC code of ethics, a review of the entire IOC bidding process, the formation of an IOC Ethics Committee, and considerable embarrassment to the Olympic Movement.

For the first time in its history, the IOC expelled six members and strongly warned another nine members. The U.S. government also formed a senate investigation committee to review the allegations contained in this report. This was the strongest initiative by a national government to challenge the government and operation of the IOC (although nothing of substance has evolved from this challenge). The argument that ensued was whether the culture of the IOC would change as a result of this report and the limited crisis management completed by the IOC. Clearly, the IOC came off as a teleological, deontological, and existential nightmare.

New marketing practices. When sport governing bodies take on these same practices and structures what is witnessed is some ideological dissonance wherein sport is seen as separate from and above the mundane practices of the wider world. While traditionally professional sports moved into these operations in the 1960s, state and amateur sport governments were slower to adopt such elements and practices. The whole matter was given considerable impetus with the rise of sport agents and sport specialist marketing corporations.

Sport agents moved beyond merely representing and marketing athletes in the 1970s (see Steinberg, 1991). These entrepreneurs moved into event management and sponsorship in a major way. Much of this was vertical integration of existing business arrangements, but some of this change was new venture. Perhaps the most notable example of this is Mark McCormack's International Management Group (IMG).

IMG started as an sport agency for individual athletes. Now it is a large, vertically and horizontally integrated, global entertainment corporation. In 1997 it had revenue of over $1 billion U.S., employed over 2,000 people in 29 countries, and operated in several areas beyond celebrity client management. These other activities include: creating, developing, and operating major events in both sport and performing arts (including managing sponsorship and broadcast rights for events and providing promotion, marketing, and implementation services for events); managing events on behalf of other clients; ownership and management of events; and the operation of Trans-World International (a television production and media management subsidiary).

IMG is a prototypic example of mega-agencies that have been cloned by other entrepreneurs. What these businesses made evident was the incredible sponsorship possibilities for athletes and themselves. They also provided evidence of the vast amounts of money available in sport.

Sporting goods manufacturers were well aware of these possibilities some time earlier. It was the alliance between Horst Dassler and the

IOC in the late 1970s and early 1980s that set the pace for international and then national and local sport-governing bodies to market themselves (again, see Aris, 1990, chapter 12, for a fuller description of this situation). Dassler, through a subsidiary, International Sport and Leisure (ISL), became the IOC's marketing agent. While this history is more involved, what it set off was a quadrennial marketing plan (The Olympic Program–TOP) that has generated billions of dollars for the IOC. It also set an example for international, national, and state sport governments. As those in marketing often proclaim, "Marketing is everything." This has certainly been the case in sport since the early 1980s.

Sport organizations of every description have adopted business processes, structures, and cultures. It is not possible to separate sport-governing bodies from the regular routines of normal business practice. A business model and culture has been adopted and will continue to influence sport operations across the spectrum of the industry. Sport managers across the system will in some way be involved in this aspect of sport business–whether it is with a developing athlete's parents or an astute agent aligning with a young athlete with considerable potential. This necessitates challenges to existing moral and ethical frameworks. Different teleological, deontological, and existential questions and practices are presented, demanding new thought and action by leisure and sport specialists during these periods of change and transition.

The dark side of athletic production. Perhaps the most controversial issue of modern sport is that of drug use by athletes. What most people do not know is that this issue has a long history. Several academic studies (e.g., Hoberman, 1992; Todd, 1987) have clearly shown that sport has been a laboratory arena for human research. For example, Hoberman (1992) has made clear that pharmaceutical experiments have been carried out on athletes since the latter part of the nineteenth century and the drug scandals of today are nothing more than athletes being the "experimental subjects whose sufferings are a natural part of the drama of sport" (p.13). The depth and breadth of these experiments continues to be exposed as previously confidential Eastern-bloc state files are explored, and as athletes under these regimes sue coaches and administrators for the harm caused by this experimentation.

Clearly the ethical issues are paramount. Humans have legislatively protected animals from such testing, yet systematic doping as evidenced from the files of many states shows that humans have a long way to go towards ethical authenticity. How humans can take part in such practices raises a plethora of ethical issues. On the other hand, many athletes are complicit and condone such practices. Should sport and leisure managers or specialists view doping practices as an individual matter and leave the issue alone? Are humans not free, volitional, and rational agents with the right to act in ways they see as morally and ethically sound? Is it the position and role of organizations and governments to legislate against individual practices? There is no simple response to this matter.

It is not simply the matter of the communist side of the Cold War rhetoric that is problematic here. Canada exposed its colonial mentality by spending a good deal of time and money on the Dubin Inquiry following the Ben Johnson scandal in the 1988 Seoul Olympic Games. Numerous other countries and incidents point to fact that the matter of drugs in sport is widespread and virtually unstoppable. Further, evidence in the Dubin Inquiry indicated that teleological premises operated. These premises subordinated and denied any deontological morality. Clearly, many athletes felt some degree of authenticity in their behavior due to the actual or perceived prevalence of doping in sport. The whole matter continues to perplex sport administrators and governing boards throughout the sport system.

The question that goes begging is why drugs are used at all. Goldman (1987), citing a former East German sports physician, noted that "70 to 80 percent is talent. Twenty to 25 percent is training and maybe 5 percent is attributable to other influences, including drugs. True, if you can improve by 1 or 2 percent, you can go from sixth to first place." Others have suggested that if a whole team takes drugs, it will have about a 10 percent advantage over teams that don't take chemical aids (p.35). These experts further argue that a "placebo effect" occurs and possibly results whether or not drugs are taken. This further adds to the debate of whether drugs do or do not have the ability to improve performance. The argument that abounds is that sport as it is currently practiced and structured has inverted the foundational characteristic of fair play.

Sport is a viable career, one offering great possibility for attaining status and wealth. Yet can we simply put the drug issue and other malpractices down to economic possibilities? We must decide if we can support Goldman's (1987) notion that, "as someone has pointed out, when economic theory addresses capitalism, it says nothing about morality. In competitive markets, morality is sometimes compatible with competition, but usually must be legislated" (p.90). Does sport need to be legislated even further? Can the drug issue be legislated? Should sport organizations bother trying to deal with the drug issue? Will further legislation accomplish anything?

As with any other feature of a competitive system, athletes must seek to be the best. They must achieve great performance in order to maximize their status and subsequent income. This might be put into the adage of "to the victor go the spoils." While this may hold considerable saliency, we still must ask whether maximized performance results in maximized income. Clearly some sports exemplify the possibilities of this formula. Many sports do not hold the same possibilities. For example, Greco-Roman wrestlers, weight lifters, lawn bowlers, and luge athletes and sport organizations will not attract the same attention and sponsorship revenues as athletes in organizations for athletics, swimming, or any of the fully professional sports.

So the "cat and mouse" reality of sound drug testing and policing continues to defy medical logic and the sport system. The results of a summit on drugs in sport, held in Lausanne, Switzerland, in May 1999, made this clear. The IOC's proposal for a unified penalty framework was not supported by all recognized Olympic sports, leading to a watered-down policy. Further, the IOC's attempt to structure an international drug agency was attacked by the European Ministers of Sport. Clearly, the issue requires more discussion, more testing procedures, and more conclusive supporting action by sport-governing bodies if this issue is to be properly dealt with. So drugs continue as a feature of elite sport production in spite of their life threatening effects. This issue will not go away. It has been and continues to be a morally and ethically dilemmatic feature of sport. There is no good, right, or authentic substance to the issue, nor does it seem that codes can be formulated to deal with such practices.

Here, perhaps, is the greatest challenge to the recreation and sport manager or specialist. Public and private recreation facilities with strength-training equipment and programs may encounter drug issues. This dilemma may go beyond the use of performance-enhancing substances to include drug trafficking and other health-related matters (e.g., overdosing, used needles). Managers of these facilities must be able to identify the problem and even counsel those affected (see Peters, 1998). The issue demands that sport managers understand doping legislation and know testing procedures and protocols. An ethical position on the drug issue and how to handle the issue must be worked out, for it is bound to confront every sport manager at some point in his or her career.

Sport manufacturing and expansion of marketing practices. In capitalist economies, the need for new and different products to capture or retain markets is imperative. Research, development, and production in the sporting goods industry represents fully the two aspects of the basic economic dialectic—that of production and consumption. Each aspect reveals dilemmas, both technological and ethical in nature.

Production. In order to maximize profits from the production process, sporting goods manufacturers must seek the most attractive, in their terms, labor markets; that is, labor markets that are free of rights and benefits achieved by most labor collectives in the advanced economies. Countries that do not have, or have low levels of, wage legislation, workplace safety, unionization, and worker recognition, rights, and protection are those most often sought by manufacturers. Unfortunately these tend to be in "Third World" countries where inexpensive, mostly female, labor is available. These countries are those that seek to maintain favorable labor markets to attract and keep overseas corporate investments.

The "Nike Transnational Advocacy Network" and a number of other U.S. groups and mass media have exposed such labor practices in several countries throughout the world. The Nike Corporation is the most prescient of sporting goods manufacturers (among many other manufacturers across the spectrum) involved in this practice. Certainly it is not the only corporation to seek such labor markets. The practices are deplorable, yet are part of the history of capitalism. There is no teleological or deontological justification for such unethical behavior, regardless of whether it is indicative of the historical and future operation of such industries. Clearly, the ethical conduct and codes for such practices do not indicate an issue here. It is perhaps the attempts that such organizations publicly make towards morally justifying their behavior that rouses protest groups to action. While not condoning such practices, it must be recognized that they have existed in various forms for a very long period. Many businesses operate in this way. Minimizing labor costs, whether factory worker or athletic labor, is very central to profit maximization. Seeking the most attractive exchange of values in the marketplace also ensures profit maximization.

In this case it is highly recognized sport personalities that assist in attracting consumers to particular products. The incredible amounts paid in sponsorships are costs deducted in the accounting cycle before profits are declared. This should indicate the incredible amount of revenue generated in this segment of the overall economy. In the end it is the athlete name and image recognition that permits sporting goods industries to generate sales to the wider recreation and development-level markets and obtain revenues that lead to the huge endorsement contracts and huge profits. The immensity of the sporting goods industry must not be underestimated, nor the moral and ethical issues that manufacturers and athletes must face.

Some personalities have tried to rectify the issue of "sweat-shop" production by removing their endorsements or putting a spin on the situation, but this has been limited. As a sport manager, would you order products from companies that use such practices? Does your sport organization have any ethical guidelines on whom they will purchase from and from whom they will seek sponsorship? Would you recommend such guidelines, and what would they look like? Finally, how would you handle a situation in which one or more of your athletes were sponsored by a company that is morally and ethically suspect? The questions proliferate in this matter. Here one must question the teleological and deontological premises in operation to determine what might be done.

Consumption. On the consumption side, sporting goods manufacturers must constantly provide products that will attract sales. Often this requires ongoing product development, especially in terms of new technologies. While the sporting goods industry has a history of product development, it has been in the post-Cold War era that this development has taken on new and intriguing proportions. Military technology (e.g., space-age alloys, flak resistance materials, satellite technology) is now finding its way into the sporting goods industry, from the implements used to the materials worn in play or performance.

Such development is most evident in the equipment segment of the market. Footwear is the most ubiquitous of this trend. However, tennis racquet, golf club and ball, and bicycle manufacturers provide the most recognizable example of this development. The debate between traditionalists and new age sport enthusiasts rages here. For example, many argue that the golf club and ball technology is outstripping the challenge of golf courses, making golf a driver, wedge, putter game.

While this is an interesting debate, below the elite levels of performance, the human element is still a limiting factor. Existential limitations will override deontological practices. We must, however, question how far technology can develop before elite sport performance becomes a struggle between non-human technologies rather than the human technologies (performance in all of its aspects). Are cyborgs possible? How much of the human will be left in the "brave new world" of technologically advanced sport? How will this situation lead to authenticity?

It must be noted here that technology is advancing commensurably in the clothing industry and has a long history of development in the footwear industry. With endorsements from elite athletes, the consumption of these goods is large. This aspect of the sport industry continues to grow and to generate huge revenues and profits.

For recreation and sport managers, these ongoing developments present many dilemmas. One example would be in trying to keep up with the need for the latest and "best" equipment to service clients. How would a recreation center manager rectify client demand for the latest weight-training machinery with capital and operating budget costs and with staff-training requirements for the new equipment? In fact, recreation managers might find this to be a generally difficult aspect of their work—how to obtain, maintain, or upgrade equipment and facilities as newer, high-tech materials and designs are developed. Likewise, for managers, and parents, of developmental sport teams, the costs for general provision of equipment to athletes increases as new, safer equipment and facilities come into the market. Each of these dilemmas challenges the manager or specialist to identify goals, values, and the right ways to deliver on them. While these are not taxing moral or ethical matters, they present the type of daily issue with which professionals in the field must wrestle.

Here is where marketing, regulation, and finance cross paths, and perhaps swords. Marketing presents the latest recreation and sport products and an opportunity in an attractive way to generate wants and needs in consumers. Marketers have a particular intent, and this may conflict with consumer ability to consume. While this may seem somewhat trivial, the manager or specialist must be aware of promotional practices that might lead to ethically suspect behavior (e.g., kickbacks, free products or perks—compare this to pharmaceutical company relationships with medical practitioners). Sport-governing bodies must identify what type and level of quality equipment, travel, and facilities are required by participants. How far can they dictate what the basic requirements are for their sports? Then there are the costs of attracting and maintaining clients in recreation and sport activities. What will the market bear? With drop-out rates in some sports (e.g., ice hockey), this issue arises in all of its complexity. Clearly some sports are pricing themselves out of contention for new participants. Several points are salient for the future recreation or sport managers (specialists) in this. These will become even more evident in Chapters 4 and 5.

The legal expansion of "punting." A further development has been in the sub-industry aspect of gambling, or punting, as it is known in some countries. Sport has a long association with gambling. Perhaps the most prominent and sensationalized example of this occurred in the

1919 White Sox baseball scandal. By its very nature sport attracts such activity. While this is not problematic on the surface of the matter, when betting leads to corrupt practices, then the purity of sport and the uncertainty of its outcome is jeopardized.

Clearly racing in its various forms is traditionally, if not foundationally, linked to gambling. Boxing has a long, if not happy, association with gambling. There are not many sports that are not in some manner affected by this activity. In current times gambling has gone from a dark, sinister, unofficial, and covert activity to a fully institutionalized one. Governments have legalized gambling of all types and have created new sub-industries in sport. This is a key source of government revenue (and a way to control a vice industry). The early version of this activity was with racing but a wide variety of methods to "take a gamble" are now embraced.

While state legitimation, control, and rationalization of this aspect of the sport industry has alleviated many of the negative elements of the activity, it has not reduced potential corruption. Point shaving in college basketball, thrown games in soccer, and cricket players being charged in court for bribery are but a few examples of such negative activities. Such activities bring into question the very nature of sport and the belief that equals are competing for victory. With the advent of digital technology, the whole sport industry will witness an expansion of gambling opportunities. More immediate, diverse forms of betting will be possible (e.g., which athlete will draw which lane in an athletic race, what type of pitch will the baseball pitchers use next, by how many laps of a race will a particular swimmer break the current record time).

Bringing this matter back to the practical level, how would you as a manager handle a "friendly" wager between athletes about to compete, or even between athletes from your team or organization? Consider parents in this. If they offer rewards for goals, assists, tackles made, touchdowns, and so on, would you consider this a form of wagering? Are the athletes acting in teleologically sound ways? How are the parents affecting the deontological possibilities of their children's behavior? Ultimately, what is the link between authentic behavior and such practices? And more importantly, how would you deal with such practices? While much of the focus has been on high-level athletes betting on or manipulating the contest they are competing in, it is not beyond the realm of possibility that you will encounter the wagering (betting, punting) issue in your experience.

Recreation: Public Good or Economic Rationalization?

While the elite level of sport claims much attention, many changes have occurred at the level of public provision of leisure, recreation, and developmental levels of sport. In most of the Western, capitalist, liberal-democratic nations, there has been a change in the provision of opportunities, programs, facilities, and funding of government programs. Since the 1980s there has been a move towards economic rationalism. This political philosophy espouses the idea that the market should be allowed to operate freely (which in fact does not happen) and that many of the programs, facilities, and other necessary resources previously funded by various levels of the state should be either reduced or eliminated, privatized, or become self-funding entities.

Underlying philosophical rationales. Recreation and sport are viewed as necessary cultural activities in building a healthy, happy, and prosperous nation. In other words, these are fundamental methods of developing fully functional citizens. This indicates a social and socializing function of recreation and sport. Within this context, and within the claim made here that sport (elite and professional sport) drives the structure and function of recreational- and developmental-level sport, can we support this claim? Clearly if recreational- and developmental-level play and sport are aimed at product, performance, or competition outcomes, then we are on an incorrect path. This is, however, a philosophical argument that still has a basis in the underlying economic philosophy.

Clearly there is a larger, societal purpose for recreation and sport in the moral and ethical construction of citizens. One must ask here, do they continue to provide this function? Are they worthy of state funding and guidance? Should they be globally provided? How should they be funded? Again, morally and ethically charged questions proliferate.

In this political context many of the "welfare state" programs have devolved. Much public recreation and sport began in uncertain economic times and under a rational recreation control philosophy. In other words, the state provided activities, programs, equipment, human resources (e.g., program leaders, leisure managers, among others), and other funds towards ensuring that those from the lower income levels and the jobless (for example) had the opportunity for positive and socially appropriate recreation and sport activity. The agenda of these states was both to exercise social control and to ensure that all citizens had access to such activities and programs. The goal of existentially sound and, therefore, authentically behaving citizens was central. The debate over whether this was ever possible (or at least potential) continues. Can such state-based opportunities and provisions make individuals sound moral and ethical agents?

Much of this provision was at the local level of the state, although funding might come from all levels of the state. It must be noted that this provision also had a Keynesian economic basis. As with education, the state would benefit from a healthier, more productive citizenry that would in turn work, be taxed, and make a return on this public investment, an investment that would help overall economic advancement. The sport manager or specialist must understand this basis–the values that inform the ideology of public good.

Historically these state-provided opportunities allowed for the expansion and democratization of leisure and recreation, and also the "grass-roots" level of sport development. Where youth were previously left to their own devices and open public spaces to play sports, the "welfare state" provisions allowed more youth to participate and develop. Local clubs and leagues playing in public-supported facilities permitted this expansion. Equipment was either provided or rented, generally at an attainable cost to the provider (e.g., community, church, club, or parent). The volunteer structure of coaches, trainers, managers, and other such human resources were solicited, trained, and developed in state-supported programs and systems.

A philosophy of continual improvement and advancement of society has promulgated many of the non-economic changes. As recreational- and developmental-level sport become part of rationalized, professionalized state systems, this philosophy places greater stress on those systems. The demands on leaders, managers, coaches, administrators, and so on, in these systems magnify and require that the individuals filling these roles and functions have the knowledge and skills to perform adequately and completely. This often is beyond the ability, time, and energy levels of the individuals involved, especially those volunteering. Many volunteers are altruistic and find a sense of authenticity through participation in recreation or sport programs. The demands on these people must be regulated to ensure that quality people are attracted and that they are able to behave in morally sound ways.

Changes in economic policy. At the economic level, the change to an economic rationalist position meant that those using public facilities would have to provide more of the funding for those programs and places. A "user pays" philosophy shifted considerably the access to previously available recreation and sport opportunities. Added to this are the effects of inflation, increasing demands for profitability, public accountability (implementation of quality management programs), and professionalization of the human resources. Everything costs more currently. Increasingly, the economically disadvantaged are unable or inadequately able to access recreation and sport programs, equipment, and other necessary resources. This is in stark contrast to much public policy that supports large, expensive sport facilities subsidizing private sector investment and operation.

Two things are central here. While markets are argued to be efficient in economic terms, they result in unequal distributions of financial and other resources and of opportunity. Those seeking to provide recreation and sport in either public, privatized, or fully private situations are not doing so at a democratic or complete level. When state organizations seek to operate according to the market, they too become affected by market vagaries. Those fully privatized and the fully privately operated organizations are focused on returns on investment and funds to expand their operations. One can ask how well and how far quality management provisions, such as those demanded under British compulsory competitive tendering (CCT) processes, will ensure that privately operated, state-built recreation facilities will carry through this mandate (Robinson, 1998). Here the dilemma of profitability, a necessary aspect in a market economy, and provision meet. Once more we can observe that multifaceted institutions are involved in this process. As noted above, different moral and ethical frameworks are encountered. In these frameworks are divergent goals, values, and norms. It may be difficult to operate in such contexts due to the different notions of good, right, and measures of effectiveness.

In market-based societies, growth of the economy must occur for the continued health of the wider society. The moral argument here, then, is whether and to what degree wider market forces are used to dictate or govern the breadth and depth of public provision of facilities and programs. On the other hand, how universal and to what level of accountability can this provision be made? While these questions arise in many areas of provision in such societies (e.g., education, health care, pensions, welfare), they continue to be central to the incipient recreation or sport manager or specialist. In the end, the question comes back to one of public good versus market operation. Is there some third way for this dialectical situation can be attained? In many cases it is a juggling act for the professional. Individuals must identify their moral framework in order to "find their way."

Perhaps this situation has the greatest poignancy when we focus on marketing issues. How can you, as a manager of a public facility, rectify provision with cost efficiency and effectiveness? Or would it matter? Do you simply focus on the bottom line and objectives? If you were operating a privatized facility with quality management encumbrances, what type of market schemes would you implement? Clearly the matter of public good and profit collide here, demanding a clear ethical stance.

Summary. Within this move towards economic rationalism is a wide range of moral and ethical debates. Should not every society ensure that each citizen has access to recreation and sport? If these things are important to building solid, happy, healthy citizens, shouldn't all members of society be party to them so that each individual and society itself benefits? Can we expect every member of society to afford such experiences under current economic and social conditions? Can we rely on the market alone to ensure provision? Ultimately, what can be done to ensure that universal provision obtains?

The Need for Education in Ethics

Sport managers and specialists enter an ever-changing field. Further, as we have noted above, most do not come to the field with an ethical education (Malloy, 1992, 1996; Malloy, Prapavessis & Zakus, 1994). The need, therefore, for practitioners to inform themselves of the history of the sport industry and ongoing political, social, technological, and cultural developments is imperative. As the adage goes, "Those who forget or neglect the past are doomed to repeat it."

The nature of sport performance and production continues to change dramatically. At the basic level, the economic possibilities of sport have changed to the point where capital continues to seek investment in sport industries. From this athletes are able to realize value for their labor, although this is often achieved through more traditional, adversarial means. If we look at the amounts of money being bantered about in terms of salaries, infrastructure, and programs, it is evident that the sport industry is viable (i.e., one in which capital investments grow) and large. Further, state governments continue to invest public funds in order to attract, support, and extend private capital investment (i.e., provide attractive situations for capital accumulation), thereby assisting in the overall growth of capital. These investments by governments also assist in the growth of "public goods," which add to their overall legitimation function in society (i.e., their role in making a particular society a good place to live and one of which to be proud).

Sport consumption continues to rise overall. This is evident in the raw numbers of spectators at sport events, expanding markets for consumer goods, and the revenues and profits realized from these activities. Along with this continued consumerism is the need to identify, prepare, and market in ever-new ways. As sport changes, so do the markets for sport. New, adjunct industries arise within the broader sport industry.

In all of this one thing is certain: ethical dilemmas emerge. Attempting to deal with each situation as it arises, on a case-by-case basis, will prove to be difficult and frustrating, since there is no foundation upon which to base a decision. To confound matters, it is unlikely that there will be "textbook cases" that are amenable to standard solutions. Deciding moral questions, in all realms of the sport industry—practice, technology, research—requires a moral framework. That framework is usually called an ethical theory.

Ethical dilemmas cannot be avoided. It would be advantageous to have developed a reasoned moral stance before proceeding with any decision or action. Arriving at that position requires knowledge of some ethical theories and the development of critical and analytical skills based on a rational thought process. In all realms of human activity, more knowledge is better than less.

This also applies in management practice in the various fields of recreation and sport. It is incumbent upon the incipient manager to have wider knowledge of the political, social, technological, and cultural areas in order to develop a sound moral position. The succeeding chapters of this book are devoted to strengthening the ethical component of the development of sport and recreation specialists.

References

Aris, S. (1990). *Sportbiz: Inside the sports business.* London: Hutchinson.

Beamish, R. (1982). Sport and the logic of capitalism. In H. Cantelon & R. Gruneau (Eds.), *Sport, culture and the modern state,* pp.143-189. Toronto: University of Toronto Press.

_____. (1988). The political economy of professional sport. In J. Harvey & H. Cantelon (Eds.), *Not just a game: Essays in Canadian sport sociology,* pp.141-157. Ottawa: University of Ottawa Press.

_____. (1991). The impact of corporate ownership on labor-management relations in hockey. In P. Stadohar & J. Mangan (Eds.), *The business of professional sports,* pp.202-221. Urbana and Chicago: University of Illinois Press.

_____. (1993). Labor relations in sport: Central issues in their emergence and structure in high-performance sport. In A.G. Ingham & J.W. Loy (Eds.), *Sport in social development: Traditions, Transitions, and Transformations,* pp.187-210. Champaigne: Human Kinetics.

Beamish, R., & Burowy, J. (1987). High performance athletes in Canada: From status to contract. In T. Slack & C.R. Hinings (Eds.), *The organization and administration of sport,* pp.1-35. London, Ont.: Sport Dynamics Publishers.

_____. (1988). *Q. What do you do for a living? A. I'm an athlete.* Kingston, Ont.: The Sports Research Group.

Brohm, J.M. (1978). *Sport: A prison of measured time.* London: Inks Links.

Chalip, L. (1995). Policy analysis in sport management. *Journal of Sport Management,* 9, 1: 1-13.

Chesneaux, J. (1976). *Pasts and Futures or What is History For?* London: Thames and Hudson.

Dabscheck, B. (1996). Playing the team game: Unions in Australian professional team sports. *Journal of Industrial Relations,* 38, 4:600-628.

_____. (1998). Trying times: Collective bargaining in Australian Rugby Union. *Sporting Traditions,* 15, 1:25-49.

Goldman, R. (1987). *Death in the Locker Room: Steroids, Cocaine and Sports.* Tucson, AZ: The Body Press.

Hoberman, J. (1992). *Mortal Engines: The Science of Performance and the Dehumanization of Sport.* New York: Free Press.

Kidd, B. (1982). Sport, dependency and the Canadian state. In H. Cantelon & R. Gruneau (Eds.), *Sport, Culture and the Modern State,* pp.282-303. Toronto: University of Toronto Press.

_____. (1988). The elite athlete. In J. Harvey & H. Cantelon (Eds.), *Not Just a Game: Essays in Canadian Sport Sociology,* pp.287-307. Ottawa: University of Ottawa Press.

Kidd, B., & Eberts, M. (1982). *Athletes' Rights in Canada.* Toronto: Ministry of Tourism and Recreation.

Kikulis, L., Slack, T., & Hinings, C.R. (1992). Institutionally specific design archetypes: A framework for understanding change in national sport organizations. *International Review for the Sociology of Sport,* 27:343-370.

Lenskyj, H. (1996). When winners are losers: Toronto and Sydney bids for the summer Olympics. *Journal of Sport and Social Issues,* 24:392-410.

MacAloon, J.J. (1991). Are Olympic athletes professionals? Cultural categories and social control in U.S. sport. In P.D. Staudohar & J.A. Mangan (Eds.), *The business of professional sports,* pp.264-297. Urbana and Chicago: University of Illinois Press.

Macintosh, D., & Whitson, D. (1990). *The game planners: Transforming Canada's sport system.* Montreal and Kingston: McGill-Queen's University Press.

Malloy, D.C. (1992). Ethics in Canadian university physical education curricula. *CAHPER Journal,* 58, 2:27-31.

_____. (1996). A perspective on ethics in sport management curricula. *Avante,* 2, 1:79-83.

Malloy, D.C., Prapavessis, H., & Zakus, D.H. (1994). Teaching applied ethics in adult educational contexts: Instructional modules for the human movement student and practitioner. *The ACHPER Healthy Lifestyles Journal,* 41:14-17.

Ollman, B. (1984). *Alienation: Marx's conception of man in capitalist society* (2nd Ed.). Cambridge: Cambridge University Press.

Peters, R. (1997). Muscle-bound. *Australian Leisure Management,* December-January: 28-29.

Report to the Board of Trustees. (1999). Board of Ethics, Salt Lake City Organizing Committee for the Olympic Winter Games of 2002. Salt Lake City: SLOC (from web page <www.slc2002.org>).

Rigauer, B. (1981). Sport and Work (A. Guttmann, Trans.). New York: Columbia University Press.

Robinson, L. (1998). Quality management in public leisure services. In M. Collins & I. Cooper (Eds.), *Leisure management: Issues and applications,* pp.211-223. Wallingford, UK: CAB International.

Schimmel, K., Ingham, A.G., & Howell, J.W. (1993). Professional team sport and the American city: Urban politics and franchise relocation. In A.G. Ingham & J.W. Loy (Eds.), *Sport in social development: Traditions, transitions, and transformations,* pp.210-265. Champaign: Human Kinetics.

Scully, G. (1995). *The market structure of sports.* Chicago and London: The University of Chicago Press.

Slack, T. (1997). *Understanding sport organizations: The application of organization theory.* Champaign, Ill.: Human Kinetics.

Slack, T,. & Kikulis, L. (1989). The sociological study of sport organizations: Some observations on the situation in Canada. *International Review for the Sociology of Sport*, 24, 3:179-200.

Staudohar, P.D. (1996). *Playing for Dollars: Labor Relations and the Sports Business*. Ithaca and London: Cornell University Press.

Steinberg, L. (1991). The role of sports agents. In P.D. Staudohar & J.A. Mangan (Eds.), *The Business of Professional Sports*, pp.247-263. Urbana and Chicago: University of Illinois Press.

Thoma, J. & Chalip, L. (1996). *Sport governance in the global community*. Morgantown, WV, USA: Fitness Information Technology.

Todd, T. (1987). Anabolic steroids: The gremlins of sport. *Journal of Sport History*, 14:87-107.

Zakus, D.H. (1988). *A Preliminary Examination of the Dialectical Change in "Modern" Sport and the Intervention of the Canadian State in Sport Between 1968 and 1988*. Unpublished doctoral dissertation, University of Alberta.

3

Introduction to Ethics

"That's cheating!"

"That's wrong!"

"That's bad!"

"That's improper behavior!"

"That's a violation of policy!"

"That may not be an actual violation, but it certainly goes against the spirit of the rules."

"No, it's not!"

"No, it's perfectly alright!"

"No, it isn't!"

"No, it's not!"

"No, it isn't!"

"If it's not a violation of the rules, then it is perfectly acceptable."

Comments such as these all reflect a concern for ethics and ethical behavior. Each comment is an expression of a moral judgment about some behavior exhibited. Each comment uttered is the result of an evaluation or assessment made of the behavior in relation to an explicit or implicit standard. These comments are usually uttered based on observations of the behavior exhibited. The assessments originate from the observer's own set of beliefs about what is right or wrong, what is good or bad, or what is permissible or unacceptable.

A critical question emerges from the preceding comments: From where does the standard come that the person uses to assess behavior and then render judgment? The beginning of an answer to the possible bases for ethical standards will be presented later in this chapter and a more elaborate treatment is reserved for the fourth chapter, "Sources of Ethical Decision-Making."

From this brief digression we return to an examination of the ways we make moral judgments. Frequently there is no critical examination nor probing of the set of beliefs, the actual basis for rendering moral judgment, used by the person making such comments. In part this is due to the paucity of attention paid to the study of ethics, generally, and to sport ethics, particularly, at all levels of schooling. While each individual has a personal sense of morality, without the serious, disciplined study of ethics it is not surprising to discover that most people are unaware of the bases for moral judgment. This text aims to considerably reduce this lack of knowledge through the information provided below.

In ordinary, everyday circumstances, human behavior is not pre-ana-
lyzed for us. There are, however, some instances when this does occur.
For example, there are times when teachers, parents, administrators,
religious officials, writers of articles for newspapers and magazines, or
authors of books discuss certain events. Then, through their analyses,
they point out the good and the bad, the right and the wrong. These
instances are few compared to the many times when we have to analyze
the situation by ourselves. Consequently, there is an obvious need to
comprehend the realm of ethics and to learn how to conduct moral reasoning.

Divergent Assessment of Behavior

A list of contradictory statements appears at the start of this chapter.
These comments result from observations of blatant acts. If both
observers (in each set of statements) saw the same action, yet came to
hold different opinions, there is a need to (1) explore how two observers could possibly hold such divergent views, and (2) devise a method
that should enable them, and us, to decide which is a justified view. We
shortly will undertake these tasks. To help us deal with these challenges
we need to turn our attention first to some preliminary matters: (1) the
definition and elaboration of terms such as ethics, morals, values, and
norms, and (2) briefly deal with some historical aspects of ethics (additional information on this topic is presented in Chapter 4). These discussions will provide the basis for the development of the first model
for rendering moral judgments. A second, more elaborate, and complex
model will be presented in the third chapter, "Factors Influencing Decision Making."

Axiological Framework

In one sense it seems almost redundant to provide definitions for
such common terms as ethics, morals, values, and norms since these
words are often used in everyday speech. Ironically, it is because of the
widespread use (and misuse at times) of these words that they have
taken on many meanings, thus indicating a need for the provision of
definitions to standardize our understanding. Definitions are provided,
along with pertinent elaborations, to clarify current usage and to provide additional insights into the axiological framework. Understandings
derived from the definitions will facilitate the reading of the text.

Ethics is a sub-discipline of philosophy. Ethics, as the word is com-
monly used, is concerned with issues of right and wrong in human conduct. It is concerned with what is good and what is bad; what is

authentic and is not authentic. Ethics is also concerned with the notions of duty, obligation, and moral responsibility. As such, ethics are manifested in behavior and assessed through the application of ethical inquiry and critical moral reasoning.

An understanding of what is, and what ought to be, is basic to assessing behavior in terms of right/wrong, good/bad, or authentic/inauthentic. To assess behavior, what is ethical, as a basis for rendering moral judgment, we need to know what is right, what is good, and what is authentic. Although the three terms, right, good, and authentic, refer to ethical standards, there are differences among them. Generally, we employ the terms right and wrong in situations where rules and laws are applicable; we use the terms good and bad when we focus our attention on the consequences of the act; and we apply the terms authentic and inauthentic to situations where the person examines his or her own behavior critically. The section entitled "Three Ethical Bases" below contains additional information regarding these differences.

Ethics, as the study of morals, refers to that specific branch of philosophy that critically examines, clarifies, and reframes the basic concepts and presuppositions of ethical theories and of morality generally. The contemporary organization of this branch of philosophy is comprised, roughly, into two categories, metaethics and applied ethics.

Metaethics is more theoretical in nature as it trains its sights on the logic, coherence, and presuppositions found in each ethical theory. In contrast, as the term suggests, *applied ethics* is much more concerned with examining behavior in terms of right and wrong, good or bad, authentic and inauthentic.

Both metaethics and applied ethics interrelate at the level of theory and practice. We must ground ethical theory in actual human existence, for if that were not so, it would be difficult to imagine its applicability. And, as we base moral judgment on some standard or ethical maxim, we must invoke some ethical theory. Ethical theory unavoidably forms the basis of moral judgment.

Morals, generally, is the term more often used when referring to actions, behavior, and the principles that guide them. Technically speaking, morality is a central concept of ethics but it is not the whole of ethics. Morality often refers to certain principles that seem to make absolute and universal claims (e.g., thou shalt not kill).

In contemporary times, moral is the term applied to an individual's actions. Through moral categories we can judge if that particular behavior was right or wrong, good or bad, virtuous or evil.

Figure 3.1: Axiological Framework:
The Interrelationship between Values, Norms, and Ethics

VALUES	NORMS	ETHICS
Individual beliefs which motivate and guide behavior.	Group or societal standards or generally held criteria for acceptable conduct.	Objective basis upon which judgments are rendered regarding right or wrong, good or bad, authentic or inauthentic behavior.

Ethics and Morals

Two features of these terms, as currently used, merit highlighting.

1. Interchangeability. Most often ethical and moral are interchangeable terms. An ethical issue is a moral issue; a moral issue is an ethical issue.

2 This feature refers to the fact that we use both terms, ethical and moral, in two distinctly different ways. In one way both terms cover the full gamut of appraisals. The spectrum ranges from absolute good or right, to absolute bad or wrong, with various shades of grey between. When these terms are used in this manner, it is the aim of the speaker or writer to direct our attention to a particular feature, the ethical or moral, of the behavior in question. This invites us to focus on the rightness or wrongness of the action. Within this context ethics and morals can refer to good and proper behavior and to bad and improper behavior. We say that someone who constantly violates the rules has the ethics or morality of an "alley cat." Yet, if a player calls an infraction on himself or herself, which the referee did not notice, we call that behavior ethical or moral.

The terms ethical and moral are often used in another way. When used to describe behavior, motivation, or a person, it will be a positive comment meaning right or good, in keeping with common usage. The context within which the word is placed will reveal its usage.

Values are those deeply held views that serve to motivate and guide our behavior. A value is an enduring belief that a particular way of behaving and living is personally and socially preferable to other ways of behaving and living. Values are enduring qualities that set out the path of life we follow. Values can be positive or negative, depending on the person's perspective. While the word value, like ethics and morals, covers the gamut of behavior from good to bad, when used as a descriptor it generally has a positive connotation.

Norms, a contraction of the term normative, refers to standards or a generally held set of criteria. We can use these criteria as a maxim or measuring rod to assess behavior. Norms, used in conjunction with judgments (about actions, about how people should behave, about values, and about which goals are worth pursuing), provide this framework (Figure 3.1). Juxtaposing values, norms, and ethics in this manner serves to clarify the relationship between these three concepts. Any action observed in the physical education, sport, or recreation environment can be analyzed to (1) identify the values held by that person or group, and (2) compare that act to the norm(s) for that particular situation. Various theories of ethics can then be employed as objective criteria upon which moral judgments will be rendered.

Three Ethical Bases

Throughout history, serious thinkers have explored and proposed a wide range of sources as the base for ethics. These bases are often called ethical theories. Some approaches have persisted over time as generally accepted bases for ethics. Three are of particular interest (Figure 3.2). A brief introductory comment is presented here to serve as the basis for a more extensive discussion in the next chapter.

Deontology is a rule-based approach, focusing on obligation and duty, similar to the orientation found in the Bible. Since attention is directed to the act itself, this approach is non-consequentialist.

Teleology is an approach that focuses on the consequences of the action, one that conceives of ethics as concerned with measuring the amount of goodness, or badness, arising from behavior. Attention is directed towards assessing the consequences of a particular action rather than examining the act itself.

In contemporary times, under the influence of post-World War II European thought, generally called *existentialism,* attention was directed squarely on the individual. Concepts such as authenticity, which refers

Figure 3.2: Focus of Ethical Theory

DEONTOLOGY	TELEOLOGY	EXISTENTIALISM
Behavior based upon what is **Right**.	Behavior based upon what is **Good**.	Behavior based upon what is **Authentic**.

to how true the person is to himself or herself, integrity, and genuineness are factors that must be considered in judging each individual act at that particular time within the context of the unique circumstances prevailing.

Each of the three bases or approaches listed above identifies a source from which we derive ethical maxims. Problems can, and usually will, arise during moral discourse if there is no explicit agreement reached regarding which ethical maxim will serve as the measuring rod. Using different ethical bases can lead to divergent judgments.

An example will serve to illustrate the case. A hockey player on Team A is about to skate free on a breakaway with the likelihood of scoring a goal. A defender on Team B deliberately trips the opposing player to prevent the goal and the television announcer, in reporting the play, adds that it was a good foul. Phrased in this manner, the announcer is praising a violation of the rules. If a rule-based orientation is the source of the ethical maxim, then clearly the defender deliberately violated a rule and, therefore, it is judged as wrong or bad. However, if one takes a consequentialist approach, one can argue that the defender, by tripping the opponent, ensured a win for Team B. This, thereby, produces more good/happiness for the defending team than bad/sadness for the opposing team. Since the good/happiness for one team outweighs the bad/sadness of the other team, the deliberate rule violation was, in reality, a good foul. From an existential perspective, the player committing the foul would need to examine his or her conscience to decide whether a deliberate violation of the rules is an instance of authentic behavior.

Ethical Bases and Values Clarification

Three different and distinct sources have been briefly sketched; ethical maxims can be derived from each of these three sources. As illustrated in the case just described, the behavior under scrutiny can be assessed from all three ethical bases and, on occasion, somewhat surprisingly, contrary ethical judgments can be rendered. This creates a new problem that needs addressing. Which of the three moral judgments do we accept and which do we reject?

Confronting this problem requires, among other things, the clarification of your own values. Do you regard adhering to higher principles and obeying the rules as more important or valuable than evaluating the goodness (or badness) resulting from an action? Or do you subscribe to the view that the end justifies the means, particularly in situations where the end creates more goodness than badness? If this is your belief, are you prepared to break rules in cases where, on balance, you predict more goodness than badness will result from your actions? How important is it for you to be authentic, to behave in a way that is consistent with what you truly believe in?

When faced with a choice, which do you value more highly: Obeying the rules under any circumstances? Or making certain that the result of your actions produces more goodness than badness, no matter the behavior used to attain that goal? Or is it maintaining authenticity, that is, being true to yourself at all times without regard for adherence to the rules and possible outcomes regarding goodness and badness? As you rank these options in order of your personal preference you are engaging in a values clarification exercise through which you will (1) learn more about yourself, and (2) obtain some insights into which ethical base (theory), deontology (rules, non-consequentialism), teleology (outcome, consequentialism), or existentialism (authenticity), is more likely to influence your thinking and moral reasoning.

Moral Discourse and Moral Reasoning

Many philosophers draw a sharp distinction between ethics, which they regard as the study of behavior from a moral perspective, and moralizing, which is a normative activity often conducted by parents, teachers, coaches, and religious officials. Our approach differs from the traditional philosophical undertaking that has as its goal greater intellectual understanding of ethical issues and dilemmas without crossing the threshold into moralizing. We start with the assumption that whatever happens to us has an impact on our thinking and that, in turn, influences how we behave. In real life, events cannot be isolated, nor compartmentalized. More profound ethical knowledge should lead to improved moral behavior.

Why Be Ethical?

There is an ethical dimension embedded in all of our behavior. This observation applies equally to individuals and to organizations, as people comprise these groups and make decisions that lead to action. Ethics permeates all of our behavior, encompassing our interactions with other human beings, with animals, and with the environment. Viewed in this light, we suggest that ethical considerations are more than vague theoretical abstractions, since they apply to every move we make. Usually the moral component remains unnoticed because we generally treat each other ethically. When behavior departs from the norm, we quickly become aware of the ethical aspect.

Since there is an ethical dimension to all of our behavior, it behooves us to consider carefully how we ought to behave. Why should administrators, leaders, teachers, coaches, players, students, participants, and professionals in all fields behave morally?

We can use three lines of argumentation to answer the question just posed. First, we will start with a basic premise about human interaction. Then we will take a negative tack by exploring what would actually happen if people refused to follow rules. Finally, we will posit that an ethical mode of conduct, rather than one that is unethical, is preferred since it is conducive to what Aristotle would describe as the "good life."

Human Interaction

Parents, teachers, employers, and psychologists are keenly aware that how we treat people influences how they will treat us. This treatment usually sets the tone for the manner in which others will behave, particularly the way they will reciprocate. In dealing with others, if we choose to bend the rules, disregard agreements made, and surreptitiously attempt to gain an unfair advantage, it should not be a surprise if we receive the same behavior in return. If we persist in our immoral actions, most people will refuse to associate with us. Recall the situation in your childhood on the playground when you and your friends played without adult supervision. You warned the cheater to play by the rules. If the cheating persisted, you expelled the miscreant from the game. A firm commitment to abide by the rules was exacted as the price of readmission.

Refusal to Obey the Rules

A game is about to start and all the players are in position, ready to play. A tacit agreement exists among the players that they will abide by the rules. As well, there is a tacit assumption that the players know the rules of the game, for without knowledge of the rules it is impossible to play that particular game. Imagine what would happen if, upon being questioned by the referee, some, or all, of the players maintain that they will not abide by the rules. If that were the case, the game could not begin since the actual playing of the game is dependent upon everyone obeying the rules. If the referee ignores the replies and attempts to start the game anyway, the result would be chaos instead of a contest.

At the administrative level, refusal to abide by the rules and to live up to agreements would produce chaos as well. This consequence would result within organizations whose members do not treat each other ethically, and it applies equally to interorganizational relations. Organizations can only continue to function if the people involved obey the rules and treat each other ethically. Adherence to rules and ethical treatment of others promotes cooperation among members as they work to attain the goals of the organization. This type of behavior is a prerequisite for the advancement of all organizations.

Interorganizational relations also depend upon adherence to the rules and ethical treatment. For example, organizations who are members of a league tacitly agree to abide by the rules. This understanding must prevail to ensure that no team gains an unfair advantage. Rules governing conduct are found in the league constitution; included are sanctions imposed for violations. If, perchance, one organization (team) persistently violates the rules, it runs the risk of expulsion. No league or recreational activity can exist unless the members treat each other ethically. Richard Taylor (1970), the well-known contemporary philosopher, has written about the role of rules in regulating human conduct. He points out, cogently, the importance of abiding by the rules to avoid open conflict. He enlarges the concept of rules to encompass "practices or ways of behaving that are more or less regular, and that can, therefore, be expected" (p.110). Breaking rules is, in one sense, an abrogation of an agreement, a practice that violates the notion of regular behavior. Breaking rules leads to conflict; abiding by the rules promotes cooperation and harmony.

Goodness Is Preferable to Evil

Behaving ethically advances and enhances the notion of fairness. Unethical behavior, in contrast, promotes unfairness that, in turn, provokes feelings of anger, resentment, and, often, the desire for revenge. Fairness produces a better life for all members of society. Behaving ethically shows social responsibility, a notion understood as a concern for the welfare of family, friend, and neighbor. Another contemporary philosopher, Rodger Beehler (1978), believes that the basis of morality is the fact that human beings care for each other. Morality is a manifestation of that caring. It then follows, logically, that immoral behavior disregards the feelings of others. Given the option of residing among people who care for us, by acting morally, or living in a place where people show they do not care for us by behaving unethically, there is no hesitation in making a choice.

As children, we were taught by our parents to behave ethically. There is a host of valid reasons for inculcating those values in us. Evil actions engender evil and promote chaos; good actions engender goodness, promote cooperation, and enhance life. Wherever inculcation of this credo occurs, any deviation from that pathway would be an instance of inauthentic behavior.

Rendering Moral Judgment

Differences of opinion over moral issues have probably existed since the beginning of time, since our forebears began interacting with each other. A review of contemporary writings reveals disagreement and controversy between philosophers, professional practitioners, theologians, and throughout the public. We cannot expect to find unanimity in ethics and in moral judgments except on rare occasions. When we find agreement, it occurs mostly when the exhibited behavior is at either one of the extreme ends of the moral spectrum. Behavior that contains minimal ethical content is rarely subject to scrutiny or cause for dispute. Since we readily reach agreement in such cases without serious discussion we learn very little. Similarly, blatant, flagrant, obvious immoral acts provoke little, if any, moral disagreement. In such cases discussion tends to focus on the motivation that prompted the act or on the sanctions likely to be applied.

Between these two extremes are countless acts that invite moral judgment. Ethical dilemmas emerge daily in every facet of professional practice, incidents and events that demand our scrutiny. When we begin discussing those incidents and behavior we are engaged in doing ethics. Doing ethics involves judging human beings in terms of ends or goals attained and the means used to achieve them. Included in this approach is an examination of the relationship between the means and the ends. Doing ethics involves using data and it also requires techniques of describing, assessing, judging, and making decisions.

Examining data critically to render moral judgment is part of a process called *moral reasoning*. Moral reasoning is a systematic approach that enables us to probe deeply in order to see things with greater clarity. It frees us from dogmatic, preconceived, and prejudiced thinking. Freedom from these intellectual restrictions creates cognitive independence. Issues and statements are analyzed critically using rational thought in place of emotional appeal. An integral part of moral reasoning is the requirement to provide reasons to support the position taken or the rendered moral judgment.

Providing reasons places the discussion above the level of mere opinion. If the discussion remains at the level of mere opinion, we make little, if any, advancement or progress. All opinions are of equal value. We are each entitled to our opinion. Stating, and restating, opinion gains us very little, although this is often the case in moral discussion. When we offer reasons in support of the view expressed, the impasse is often broken. Once we offer reasons, we can evaluate them in terms of their pertinence, cogency, and force. By comparing the total strength of the reasons provided in support of one view to the total force of a contrary view, we can determine which is the more logical and/or stronger case.

Through critical examination of the reasons given, faulty logic, inconsistent thinking or inapplicable rationales can be detected. Disciplined, impartial, logical thinking is required to criticize the reasons given and to ferret out discrepancies. This analytical process, difficult and arduous at times, leads to greater moral insights, thus placing the dialogue well beyond the realm of mere opinion. When moral reasoning is used, the discussion is placed on a different level, one well above what is found in a "bull session." Based on rational thought and sound reasoning, the moral judgments rendered through this process are apt to better withstand criticism.

Moral reasoning is not conducted as an exercise in abstract thought. As applied ethics, moral reasoning aims to identify and delineate right conduct and correct behavior. As cases in Chapters 8 and 9 are explored and analyzed, we become aware of the moral options available to us as well as the wide range of ethical dilemmas that are encountered as real-life issues. Caution must be used before declaring an action absolutely right or absolutely wrong, absolutely good or absolutely bad. There are shades of grey when judging human conduct.

Moral reasoning is a skill that needs to be acquired. Like all other skills, practice, often guided by a more knowledgeable person, is required in order to improve one's ability. Ample opportunity to practice moral reasoning skills is provided in Chapters 8 and 9, where a wide array of case studies are found. As you tackle each one you will be engaged in moral discourse.

Agent Accountability

A person is accountable for his or her actions. Technically, we identify that person as an agent. To understand what it means to be accountable requires an understanding of what it means to be an agent. An agent has free will and the power to act. Having free will and the power to act allows the agent to choose, from among options, which action to do. By choosing to act in a certain way, an agent accepts responsibility for that action and its consequences. An agent is accountable for actions done intentionally; here we link accountability to intention, which is an integral part of action. ~~Involuntary actions and accidental actions are~~ ~~generally placed in another moral category~~. Both motivation and intention are not always obvious. Difficulties may be encountered in determining the status of motivation and intention in the act.

Five Steps for Rendering Ethical Judgment–Model I

Step One: Obtain and clarify all the pertinent facts of the case or incident.

To ensure that everyone involved in the discussion is operating from the same base, it is important that all the facts be presented. Everyone needs to know exactly what occurred. We must consider the incident, not only in its proper chronological order, but also in terms of who was present and their roles, responsibilities, and understandings (both tacit and explicit) that prevailed then. This step is similar to evidence being presented at a trial in court. In order for the judge and jury to arrive at a just verdict, all the facts of the case need to be presented. The same line of thinking applies to moral reasoning.

Step Two: Identify and enunciate the ethical maxim(s) to be used.

Omission of this step will likely add confusion as the use of different implicit maxims will create a situation where people talk past each other. The identification and enunciation of an ethical maxim serves to direct the discussion along one path of moral reasoning. Here we can focus the debate as everyone involved understands the yardstick being used as the measuring rod.

An ethical maxim is a general moral principle, rule, law, or moral doctrine one adopts or formulates to serve as a yardstick against which behavior is to be measured. It can be understood as a moral rule of thumb and, as such, it can also serve to guide behavior.

As explained earlier, the three ethical theories, deontology, teleology, and existentialism, are sources from which ethical maxims can be derived. From a deontological (non-consequential) perspective we can ask the following questions: Are there any specific rules which apply? Are there any "unwritten" but generally accepted procedures which are pertinent? Do any of the policies of the institution cover the issue at hand? Are there broader social standards that can be invoked? Do any of the particular laws of the jurisdiction apply? If there is a rule governing that behavior then that rule serves as an ethical maxim. If no rule is applicable the next step may be to consult the institution's policies, and procedures. Generally speaking, it is easier to arrive at consensus where explicit rules or clear statements are available. A consensus is more difficult to obtain in the realm of "unwritten" rules and social standards since these areas are amenable to a wider array of interpretation. Laws, clearly, can serve as ethical maxims. Laws, rules, policies, and procedures can also be terribly wrong (more on this in the next chapter).

A teleological (consequential) approach focuses on the end results produced. Did that particular action generate more good than bad? Ethical maxims, formulated within this context, will be phrased in a way that allows for the comparison of benefits (goods) and drawbacks (bad) resulting from the action (e.g., ergogenic aids in sport). Attempting such calculations is a difficult challenge since goodness and badness are not readily amenable to quantification. Estimates can be made of the impact the action is likely to have on everyone involved in that particular event. This step assists us in calculating the sum total of good and sum total of bad resulting from the incident.

Consideration given to the greatest good for the greatest number serves as a general guide in public policy but that notion is more difficult to apply to individuals. Despite this caveat we can often determine if an event had minimal or major impact. In calculating the sum of goodness and the sum of badness, consideration needs to be given both to quantity and quality; some events have more profound impact than others (this will be discussed further in Chapter 5).

From an existential perspective, the focus is trained on the person as agent with freedom of choice and responsibility, that is, authenticity. Authenticity is a characteristic based upon the concept of congruence—congruence within the person (affective and cognitive domains) and congruence between the person, the person's actions, and the world. A person is authentic to the degree to which the person's being in the world is fundamentally in accord with the basis of that person's own nature and own conception of the world. An authentic person thinks, feels, and acts in a consistent, congruent manner.

Authenticity is a personal matter. Only the person can know the authenticity of his or her own being. To be genuine, honest, congruent, or "real" means to be authentic to oneself. The person is the only one who can know what is going on inside his or her self.

The search for an ethical maxim cannot be conducted in isolation, separate and apart from the incident under scrutiny. Step Two cannot be the exclusive focus of attention; some consideration needs to be given to Step One at the same time.

More than one ethical maxim can be found to serve as the moral yardstick against which we can measure behavior. Invoking more than one ethical maxim promotes a wider-ranging moral discourse. A more comprehensive examination of the behavior/act/incident/event is preferable to a narrower review, since the former produces greater insights and therefore more, rather than less, ethical knowledge.

Step Three: Time.

Chronologically we can look to (1) the time before the incident, (2) the time of the incident, and (3) the consequences that resulted because of the incident. In the quest for a comprehensive description of what occurred, it is usually advantageous to know what prompted the action under examination. That knowledge often helps us to understand the act itself. Knowing precisely, and in detail, what happened when the incident occurred adds to the foundation upon which we conduct moral reasoning. Assessing the consequences helps us to determine the gravity or severity of the situation. As the moral reasoning exercise evolves, knowledge of what happened before the incident, what indeed happened, and the consequences resulting will be considered. All this information helps to satisfy the requirements of Step One in the Model.

In the first period, the time before the action, two factors may be present that demand consideration: motivation and intention. What motivated the action? At times good motives produce bad results and, conversely, evil motives produce good results. Knowledge of the motivation involved, which is not readily or easily attained, is usually a factor considered in moral reasoning. From the individual's own perspective authenticity is a moral characteristic that applies at all times (i.e., prior to, during, and following the act). Intention, the other factor, can often be discerned from the act itself–but that is not always the case. In the absence of a statement from the agent, there is no alternative other than assessment of the act to impute intention (Figure 3.3).

This schema can also serve as a very general checklist of factors to consider in an attempt to arrive at a complete description of what occurred.

Figure 3.3: Time and the Act

PRIOR TO THE ACT	DURING THE ACT	FOLLOWING THE ACT
Individual motivation and intention.	Established rules. Unwritten rules or norms.	Consequences.

Step Four: Identify and discuss extenuating or special circumstances.

At times special or extenuating circumstances exist that shed light on what occurred. For example, in an 800-meter race the runner in second place stumbles, due to a pothole in the track, just as she is about to pass the leader. This jolt is of sufficient force to cause the leader to lose her balance. Thrown off-balance, the leading runner pauses to right herself and in so doing drops back into second place. Somehow that collision helps the stumbling runner regain her balance and launches her into the lead that she maintains for the rest of the race. The second place finisher lodges a protest as she felt she deserved the gold medal. A pothole in the track, easily discovered only after the incident, represents a special circumstance that needs to be considered when rendering moral judgment.

Another scenario will add to the explanation. Team Alpha arrives at the visitors' dressing room to discover the theft of their soccer sweaters. League rules are strict and firm, requiring teams to dress in uniforms bearing the color and design registered. Without proper dress the team cannot play. In addition, another rule says that games must start on time. The opposing team receives one goal for each five-minute delay. With full knowledge that a rule violation will occur, the manager of team Alpha requests permission to use the home team's practice jerseys. She further asks for a 20-minute delay in the start of the game and that no penalty be applied. Here is a special circumstance that merits consideration in moral reasoning.

In Step Four, the facts of the case or incident are further amplified. Circumstances are best identified as extenuating or special after a full basic description of the case has been provided.

Step Five: Render judgment.

This, in one sense, is the culmination of moral reasoning. We should render judgment only after all the facts of the case have been considered and we reach agreement on the ethical maxim(s) applicable.

Once we know as many facts as possible, and consider the special or extenuating circumstances, is it possible to reach a consensus among those involved in that particular moral reasoning exercise. Not always is it possible to decide absolutely in terms of black or white, right or wrong, good or bad. Ethics also comes in shades of grey, that is, qualified judgments that find some right or good and some wrong or bad in a particular act. Reasons given for the judgments rendered serve as warrants to support the decision reached.

**Figure 3.4: Model I—A Five-Step Approach for
Rendering Ethical Judgment**

1. Obtain and clarify all the pertinent facts of the case or incident.

2. Identify and enunciate the ethical maxim(s). This is the standard against which the behavior/action/incident/event is measured.

3. Time.

4. Identify and discuss any extenuating circumstances.

5. Render judgment.

Summary

Professional practitioners and laypersons utter ethical pronouncements on certain acts that occur within the realm of that specific specialty and in all aspects of life. Too often these judgments are based on inadequate knowledge of moral reasoning and a lack of awareness of the various bases from where ethical maxims can be derived to serve as yardsticks against which behavior is measured. Despite the need for professionals in all fields to be aware of the ethical dimension of their practice, very little attention is paid to this topic in the curriculum that comprises their respective professional education.

In this chapter, basic terms were introduced and defined. A preliminary explanation was provided for each of the three ethical sources (teleology, deontology, and existentialism) from where ethical maxims can be derived. A Five-Step Model was elaborated that can serve as both a framework and a guide for the conduct of moral reasoning. The next chapter, which is more theoretical in its orientation, provides additional details about the three bases for moral reasoning.

References

Beehler, R. (1978). *Moral Life*. Oxford: Basil Blackwell.

Taylor, R. (1970). *Good and Evil: A New Direction*. New York: MacMillan.

4

Sources of Ethical Decision Making

Brief Historical Overview

Moral issues have existed since the beginning of civilization. In Western society, our traditions derive from two sources, the Bible and the ancient Greek philosophers. From the Bible we obtain both a historical account and a major ethical resource in the Ten Commandments. These Commandments contain a summation, in one sentence, of an important moral guide: Do unto others as you would have them do unto you. Clear rules of conduct are set out in the Ten Commandments. These rules detail both actions prohibited (e.g., thou shalt not kill, steal, covet property or person) and encouraged behavior (e.g., honor thy father and mother). Based on the rules set out in the Ten Commandments, we identify additional laws to cover all aspects of human life.

The premise, "do unto others," as a moral guide, dictates that we treat everyone with consideration and fairness. Here the assumption is that you, as the agent about to act, also wants consideration and fairness. The Bible, believed to be the revealed word of God, provides a base for ethics in theology. In this tradition the focus is on the ideals of righteousness before God and the love of God and one's neighbor as the source of morality.

In sharp contrast to the biblical tradition is the thought of the ancient Greek philosophers. They looked at human beings in a very different way as they sought a source for ethics. The early Greeks were among the first to consider the realm of ideal human conduct as a function of intellectual reason and secular thought. Socrates, Plato, and Pythagoras argued for the supremacy of the intellect over the perceived constraints of society. Socrates's dictum, "The unexamined life is not worth living," is testimony to the intellectual introspection and evaluation that we must apply to live full lives–to actualize ourselves as complete human beings. Plato equated knowledge with virtue based on the assumption that the more knowledge a person acquired the more virtuous would be that person's behavior. Aristotle was interested in examining the rationality of the emotions in his quest to find the basis for moral character. Aristotle also taught us about the importance of questioning the motives or intention underlying behavior as a key factor to be considered when rendering moral judgment. The "good life," with happiness (i.e., a life virtuously lived) as the desired end, is basic to this tradition of ethics.

The Bible, supported by theological interpretations of Plato, formed the base of ethics early in the Middle Ages. Here we see a return to the sacred basis of thought and action. What was good and right was what the Church's interpretation deemed it to be. The individual was a representative of the Church's doctrine, not an independent agent of moral critique. Existence on earth was about doing God's work as defined by Church doctrine. As the Middle Ages passed into the Renaissance and Reformation ethics again gradually became more secular. Ethical views independent of the Church emerged as the state became the central body of moral interpretation and regulation.

Reason was not to be the only guide for individuals. Empiricism and science also became a determining framework for what was ethical conduct. Here rational, formal, empirical thought was the order. Contemporary ethical thought combines and refines much of what the philosophers of the past two thousand years have explored. There has been, however, one school of thought that has rejected, not only the perceived dogma of the Church, but also the perceived convictions of science itself. Existentialism loosely defines this approach. It can be seen as a revolt against philosophy. In many respects existentialism returns us to the original position of Socrates, in which individuals are the primary source of defining their own existence.

Throughout history thinkers have explored and proposed a wide range of sources as the base for ethics. Some proposed sources include the pleasant life, self-interest, the love of God, respect for persons, duty, the greatest good for the greatest number, sympathy, social justice, using a scientific approach to assess behavior, and radical freedom (existentialism). Over the years brilliant minds have investigated these alternatives (and others, as well). While it is beyond the scope of this book to analyze each source, it is important to apprise the reader of the existence of alternative sources.

In the previous chapter we provided a brief overview of three ethical approaches—deontology (non-consequentialism), teleology (consequentialism), and existentialism. The purpose of this chapter is to further explain and elaborate upon these three diverse approaches in order for the reader to develop a basic grounding in ethical theory.

Consequentialism: What Is Good Behavior?

Background

Consequentialism is an approach that argues that one must consider the ends or results of behavior rather than the intent or means used in order to render moral judgment; hence, it is situational. Within the consequential ethical orientation there exists a number of perspectives that can be classified under the headings of subjective and objective consequentialism (Macdonald & Beck-Dudley, 1994). Subjective consequentialism includes the approaches that are based upon the subjective perception of what is the best end or result to be sought; objective consequentialism or virtue ethics argues that there are basic virtues that should be adhered to, regardless of personal perception, in order to seek the best end for the individual and society. Subjective consequentialism is concerned with what should be done in a particular situation; objective consequentialism is concerned with how one should live one's life to achieve the ultimate end–happiness. Each of these orientations will be addressed in the following sections.

Subjective Consequentialism

Generally, this classification includes the ethical theories of hedonism and utilitarianism. While both are similar in the belief that the end to be sought is the greatest pleasure or good and least pain or evil, they differ in focus. This end is determined by a *test of coherence*, that is, what agrees with individual or group beliefs and desires. *Hedonism* argues that the individual should determine what is good and ethical for himself or herself by choosing whatever results in the best ratio of personal pleasure over pain. Though some hedonists argue that some pleasures are better than others (e.g., Epicurus [341-270 BC] believed that pleasures of the mind were of a higher order than pleasures of the body unlike the Cyrenaics who favored the satisfaction of desire), it remains a subjective evaluation. For example, an individual who chooses a career in kinesiology because it gives him or her financial reward, a personally exciting career, and/or intrinsic pleasure to work with the public to improve their health can be said to be acting hedonistically.

The utilitarian focus as advocated by Jeremy Bentham (1748-1832) and J.S. Mill (1806-1873) is much more broad than that of the hedonist, as it seeks the greatest pleasure and least pain for the greatest number. Determining what is the greatest pleasure continues to be a subjective calculation–a test of coherence with a belief of what is perceived to be best for the masses. Utilitarianism itself can be viewed in two distinct ways. *Act-utilitarianism* is the perspective that advocates any action that results in the greatest pleasure for the greatest number. From this view, rules, laws, policies, procedures, traditions, and individual justice can be overlooked if the results are best for the masses. For example, a researcher in biomechanics conducting potentially harmful weight-bearing experiments on pre-adolescent patients without informed consent, and who attempts to justify his or her action based upon the premise that it will assist more people (and win more gold medals for the nation) than it may potentially harm, would be using an act-utilitarian argument.

A second form of utilitarianism is termed *rule-utilitarianism*. Here, rules are the subject of the test—"the greatest good for the greatest number." Rules that are followed that result in the greatest good are ones that should be maintained in all circumstances; those that do not should be discarded. In contrast to the rationale provided in the previous example by the act-utilitarian, the rule-utilitarian would seek to determine if "informed consent" was a rule that would result in the greatest good. If it was perceived to do so, then, regardless of the potential outcome, breaching this rule would be unacceptable for the rule-utilitarian.

Generally, the utilitarian perspective has been more widely accepted than has hedonism as it has the tendency to promote or at least maintain some form of social awareness and responsibility. Utilitarianism is in fact the basis of not only liberal-democratic political ideology (i.e., liberalism) and economic theory (e.g., Pareto optimality), but is also the forerunner of the modern separation of ethics from religious authority. See Box A on page 74 for examples of hedonism, act- and rule-utilitarianism.

The Subjective Consequential Method

The subjective consequential method has been described as the *hedonistic calculus*. It refers to a process developed by the utilitarians (i.e., Bentham) for assessing the perceived outcome of possible actions or decisions. The decision-maker is to determine the ratio of *utiles* or units of utility or pleasure for each alternative and then choose that which results in the best overall ratio of pleasure over pain. Ascertaining what would be pleasurable and painful for the masses is a function of what is perceived to cohere with the belief of the masses. For example, the utilitarian may argue that there are more units of pleasure derived by the greatest number of people by having a recreation program geared to sport for all regardless of economic status. In contrast, the hedonist may perceive, if he or she were wealthy, that a private and relatively expensive sport program would result in the greatest pleasure or, perhaps, the least pain for him or her.

The Advantages and Disadvantages of Subjective Consequentialism

The subjective consequentialist position has many positive aspects. First is its orientation towards the future. We do not base goodness on the past or upon tradition. Rather we base it upon what will result in the greatest future goodness. As a result, this perspective is dynamic and innovative and is capable of adapting to changing structures, innovation, and perceptions of goodness. In a world that is changing as rapidly as ours, and with a more rapid pace of change anticipated in the twenty-first century, an ethical approach that is fluid may be essential. What was good (and possible) for us in the 1960s may not prove to be sufficient to guide us ethically in the decades to come.

While flexibility and fluidity provide a dynamic ethics, subjective consequentialism may result in a weakened or unstable sense of ethical behavior. Many critics argue that the general malaise of our times is in part due to the situational nature of our ethical conduct. Where traditional ethical guidelines (or values) are no longer an explicit and stable part of our educational and societal paradigms, the resulting tendency has been an entrenchment of ruthless and self-serving behavior by individuals, organizations, communities, and nations. If ethics are dynamic, how can we establish foundations for conduct resulting in goodness? Specifically, how can we ensure that the direction of the ethical dynamic is one that fosters goodness as opposed to evil and chaos?

A second advantage of subjective consequentialism is its attempt to measure goodness (i.e., the hedonistic calculus). This process fosters a rational and secular method to determine ethical conduct. Presumably, where societal and theological doctrines are diminished, ethics can enter a more detached and scientific realm. However, can ethical issues be treated in the same manner as a sport administrator's financial statement or a health researcher's regression analysis? How does one assess and measure the relative merit or utility of one ethical dilemma over another?

Critics of the hedonistic calculus argue that it is difficult, indeed impossible, to quantify a concept such as *goodness*. How, for example, does one weigh the utility of programming focused upon mass participation versus elite sport? Furthermore, is it possible for the decision-maker to forecast accurately the consequence of his or her action? Can the decision-maker ever exhaust all possible alternatives without incurring decision paralysis? Finally, does one know, in fact, what is

Box A
Examples of Hedonism, Act-Utilitarianism, and Rule-Utilitarianism in Coaching

Hedonism. A coach saw the opportunity to make the jump from a national to an international level position if his wrestling team performed well at the next competition. In an attempt to ensure the team's success, and therefore his own, he encouraged, to the point of manipulation, one of his star competitors to participate in the forthcoming meet. This was done even though the athlete had suffered a concussion in the previous competition and had been given medical advice to cease all training for two weeks while neurological tests were performed. The athlete competed and, fortunately, there was no further injury.

Act-utilitarianism. To win was perceived by a coach to be the fundamental end of sport. She believed that seeking this ultimate goal would result in the maximization of happiness for all. This perspective was communicated forcefully and frequently to her players. Two outcomes occurred. First, her teams were generally very successful in terms of skill development and performance. Second, her play-

ers were relatively unaware of and unconcerned about the values attached to the concept of the "spirit of sport." That is, the perspective that sees sport as a means to develop character of the individual. (See the Spirit of Sport Foundation website at:
http://www.spiritofsport.ca/)

Rule-utilitarianism. A veteran volleyball coach involved at the intercollegiate level was very competitive and goal driven. Her teams had always been winners, and the upcoming season was going to be no exception to this continued success. The coach had a proven formula of incorporating tremendous offensive strategies and strict training regimes with uncompromising adherence to league regulations. She knew that by following this formula her teams would continue to be winners. This was not only good for the athletes but also good for the student body in general who had a great deal of pride in the university's athletic successes.

good? How well does the decision-maker's perception cohere with that of the greatest number? Does the decision-maker's subjective perception of coherence not destroy the supposed scientific basis of this method? Is it possible to determine a consensus at all regarding what is *good*?

Subjective consequentialism, in its utilitarian form, provides an explicit concern for the welfare of the masses. Its dictum "the greatest good for the greatest number" is testimony to the decision-maker's obligation to the populace as opposed to personal survival. However, can we warrant forsaking the minority's or the individual's rights to serve the majority's will? For example, should we place less emphasis on the participation in sport of individuals with Down's syndrome because they are less functional or productive members of society? Can we condone the actions of inner-city recreation administrators who close centers with low participation rates in favor of cost-benefit ratios and the general efficient operations of the municipal recreation system despite the real possibility that some individual underprivileged child may suffer as a result? Yet, fundamental to utilitarianism is faith in the collective will being just to the greatest number.

Can we be sure that this collective wisdom satisfies our perception or our intuitive belief in what is ethical conduct? Further, can we be so certain of the actual coherence of the wisdom of the collective? The populace can be notoriously wrong, superficial, uninformed, and inconsistent. To see that collective wisdom and common sense can be erroneous, one needs only to recall such historical examples as the letting of blood for various ills, the firm belief that "evil" was the cause of the Black Plague of the medieval era, and the jailing of Copernicus for suggesting that the earth orbited the sun.

Objective Consequentialism

Objective consequentialism or virtue ethics is usually associated with the traditional teleological perspective advocated by Aristotle (384-322 BC) in his treatise *Nichomachean Ethics*. Where subjective consequentialism relies on the *test of coherence*, that is, coheres with other perceptions or beliefs, objective consequentialism is based upon the *test of correspondence*. This view, it is argued, corresponds with what is believed to be objectively true of human nature and human potentiality. As a result, it is less a preference or emotional desire than a standard that any human as a human ought to follow because it corresponds with what it is to be a fulfilled human.

According to Aristotle, human behavior is end-driven (i.e., teleological). As the end of the health and fitness profession is the general health of the population, the ultimate end of all human endeavor is happiness or *eudaemonia*. Happiness in this sense is not the happiness one may feel when receiving a raise in pay or completing one's education or falling in love. Rather happiness is the end point of all of one's efforts to flourish as a human. In other words, one seeks happiness as the ultimate end of a life well lived. To flourish as a human, Aristotle believed that one must live virtuously (and have good luck). To live virtuously is to habitually base one's actions upon virtues such as courage, wisdom, temperance, and justice. Each virtue is a mean between deficiency and excess. For example, courage is the mean between cowardice and recklessness; generosity is the mean between stinginess and extravagance. Virtues are

particular or natural to humans and distinguish us from non-rational
animals—they make us uniquely human. Aristotle argues that

> neither by nature ... nor contrary to nature do the virtues arise in
> us; rather we are adapted to receive them, and are made perfect by
> habit.... [T]he virtues we get by first exercising them, as also hap-
> pens in the case of the arts as well. For the things we have to learn
> before we can do them, e.g., men become builders by building and
> lyre players by playing the lyre; so too we become just by doing
> just acts, temperate by doing temperate acts, brave by doing brave
> acts (1968, p.952).

We have the ability though to choose not to actualize and habitualize
these virtues; that is, to make decisions that are not in accordance with
virtue. Consequently, it is possible not to lead fulfilled or virtuous lives
and thus fail to achieve true happiness or *eudaemonia* (as opposed to
apparent happiness). However, if we are able to distinguish between
excess and deficit and choose the mean between these extremes, then,
presumably, virtuous behavior and happiness are within our grasp with
good habits and good luck.

While this approach may appear to be highly individualistic, it must
be noted that Aristotle believed that virtuous behavior (and, in particular, just behavior) ultimately led to a just and happy society. The virtuous individual was considered the essential building block for the good
society. This is in contrast with the utilitarian focus upon "the greatest
good for the greatest number" and its obfuscation of the individual.

Aristotle would argue that virtuous kinesiology professionals would
exhibit these virtues not only in their professional lives but also in their
private lives in order to achieve happiness or a fulfilled life as a human.
As happiness is the "activity of the soul in accordance with virtue," any
behavior, professional or personal, that is not virtuous essentially dam-
ages the soul and thus inhibits the individual from achieving
eudaemonia.

The Objective Consequential Method

Objective consequentialism is an ethical theory of choice and of
habit. The decision-maker has the capacity to choose behavior that is in
accordance with virtue as well as to reject, ignore, or remain ignorant of
virtue. Objective consequentialism is an experiential ethical theory.
Aristotle argues that the decision-maker must experience virtuous
behavior in order to be virtuous. One must act prudently to be prudent,
act generously to be generous, courageously to be courageous. Further,
in order to realize *eudaemonia,* virtuous behavior must become habitual.

One virtuous act does not make a virtuous person. Thus, the decision-maker must become well grounded in choosing the "golden mean" between extremes and have this become second nature in order to live virtuously.

The Advantages and Disadvantages of Objective Consequentialism

One clear advantage of this school of thought is that it focuses not upon a particular incident (i.e., I am faced with an ethical dilemma, what should I do now?) but upon an ethical life well lived. It encourages life-long ethical or virtuous conduct rather than a concern for ethics when occasion demands.

This method can lead, however, to some ambiguity regarding what is accepted as a virtue (e.g., varying perceptions based upon cultural differences), how this virtue is to be interpreted into one's particular context (e.g., as a teacher, coach or administrator), and how one might deal with circumstances that call for the resolution between conflicting virtues.

Non-Consequentialism: What Is Right Behavior?

Background

Non-consequentialism is an approach that considers the means, principles, or personal duties as the foundation for "right" ethical conduct. This perspective is in obvious contrast with consequentialism, as the ends of action or decision making become secondary to the formal adherence to rule-based behavior. The basis or grounding of non-consequentialism varies and includes *theology, social contract,* and *intuition* orientations.

Theology. Religious doctrine is the basis of a theological orientation. The Bible, the Koran, and the Bhagavad Gita provide us with three examples of publications that contain theologically based principles of ethical conduct. As followers of any one of these or other possible religious teachings, it is the sacred duty of the believer to abide by the words of God or the gods. Thus, one measures one's behavior against established religious doctrine or rule. For example, the Ten Commandments and the Old Testament give clear direction for the ethical conduct of the Christian and the Jew. The more orthodox a person's religious beliefs, it appears, the more sacrosanct is the literal interpretation of the doctrine, and, arguably, the less room for individual interpretation.

Social contract. A second orientation of this approach argues for a secular set of rules. One must obey these rules, not only to make life better as a member of a collective, but also to avoid the persecution of the populace. The social contract made, both implicitly and explicitly, by all members of society establishes the parameters of acceptable and preferred "right" conduct. This contract is manifested in macro-perspectives through the laws governing society-at-large, as well as in micro-perspectives through those policies and procedures that form the basis for right conduct in our institutional life.

Why is it necessary, for example, to formalize rules of conduct in the workplace or on the tennis court? Generally we do so to enhance the quality of life for each individual. Hobbes has suggested that life without society (and rules/laws) is "nasty, brutish, and short." Aristotle argues that we are social or political animals. Achieving the "good life" that we all seek is, therefore, impossible without being a part of the collective; we cannot realize or express virtuous behavior alone. Rousseau (1979) says that

> although in civil society man surrenders some of the advantages that belong to a state of nature [i.e., a state of complete individual freedom], he gains in return greater ones.... Man acquires with civil society, moral freedom, which alone makes man the master of himself; for to be governed by appetite alone is slavery, while obedience to a law one prescribes to oneself is freedom (p.65).

For example, in organized sport, we enter competition based upon a mutually accepted code of conduct (i.e., the rules). This code is not heaven-sent nor is it necessarily the result of intuitive guidance. Individuals (sometimes generations of individuals) interested in playing a game in a particular manner create and agree upon the code or rules of the game. We play 18 holes of golf rather than 12 because of a historical social contract among early Scottish enthusiasts. Clearly, social conventions and mores become central to this orientation.

Intuition. A third view argues in favor of an intuitive approach. Intuition, in this context, is not considered to be a hunch or a gut reaction. We can logically defend intuition as it refers to a reasoned process. Perhaps the most famous proponent of this view is Immanuel Kant. He suggested that a profound commonality among all humans is the capacity to reason. Through this generic capacity, we are capable of coming to terms with universal notions of right, duty, and self-evident ethical conduct. According to Kant (1968), in what he formally termed the categorical imperative, we find the criterion for establishing right behavior. This imperative states that one ought to "act only according to that maxim by which you can at the same time will that it should become a universal law" (p.45). We, therefore, perceive such an act as ethically valid for all and for all time. One cannot lie, cheat, or steal unless one could argue that everyone ought to lie, cheat, and steal.

A second imperative that is relevant to us is the "practical imperative." It states that one must "so act as to treat humanity, whether in thine own person or in that of any other, in every case as an end with all, never as a means only" (Kant, 1785/2001, p.186). This imperative clearly extols us not to treat others as a means to our own end but rather as an end or a project in and of themselves. The administrative and coaching implications of this imperative are enormous. How often is an athlete treated as an expendable commodity? How many coaches or managers invest their efforts to develop the individual as a whole rather than perceive them as "homo mechanicus"? Thus Kant identifies for us two primary duties that form the parameters of ethical conduct for his version of deontology.

The essential feature, then, of non-consequentialism is doing one's duty. This duty is placed upon us from religious sources, from societal contracts, or from our innate and self-evident capacity to reason. To place this perspective in context, the example in Box B describes the non-consequentialist behavior of a sport administrator.

Justice. Theories of justice are, broadly speaking, non-consequential or deontological in nature as they are fundamentally rule-based. However, these theories generally provide much more prescriptive guidance for the decision-maker than does Kant's categorical imperative. Perhaps the two best-known positions come to us from both ancient and contemporary sources.

The notion of justice has a long philosophical tradition dating back to the Socratic era. Aristotle paid considerable attention to it in his *Nichomachean Ethics* in which he stated that "justice ... is not a part of virtue but the whole of virtue; its opposite, injustice, is not part of vice but the whole of vice" (1971, p.157). Aristotle distinguishes between distributive and rectificatory or corrective justice. Distributive justice refers to the principle that states that equals ought to be treated equally and unequals ought to be treated unequally (i.e., justice is proportionate). Rectificatory justice refers to the principle that suggests that inequalities ought to be restored to form just proportions.

Rawls (1971) provides a contemporary perspective of justice. His theory is concerned primarily with the notion of social justice and the means to obtain maximization of rewards for the disadvantaged. His approach begins with the introduction of the ideal observer who, under a "veil of ignorance," must develop principles of justice in a society where one cannot know one's station in life (i.e., advantaged or disadvantaged, Catholic or Buddhist, male or female). Rawls proposes that each person will be bound to the principles formulated

in future circumstances the peculiarities of which cannot be known and which
might well be such that the principle is then to his disadvantage.... The principles will express the conditions in accordance with which each person is the
least unwilling to have his interests limited in the design of practices, given the
competing interests of the others, on the supposition that the interests of the
others will be limited likewise (pp.373-374).

The result of this deductive process, according to Rawls, is the formulation of two principles—the liberty principle and the difference principle. The liberty principle refers to the equal access for all persons to
such basic human liberties as freedom of speech and religion, and freedom to own property. The second principle provides the conditions
allowing the first principle to be overridden. That is, inequality can be
accepted when the advantages to the least fortunate are the result of the
transgression of the liberty principle. For example, a physician has the
power to write prescriptions for patients. This unique role of the physician is a safeguard against the layperson acquiring drugs at will (i.e., the
liberty principle) that may be harmful to individuals and the public if
abused. This manifestation of the difference principle (i.e., the power to
write prescriptions) is accepted by the general population as a necessary
condition to override its liberty and thus enhances its general welfare.

Rawls suggests that individuals acting in their own self-interest will
generally place emphasis upon the principle of liberty and then agree to
the allowable departures from it. In other words, the individual will
choose to err on the side of one's own advantage. Rawls' theory of justice has particular relevance for the administrative aspect of the our
profession. Policies, procedures, and organizational hierarchies exist by
definition in bureaucracies and will inevitably create many inequities.

The Non-Consequential Method

Unlike the hedonistic calculus of the utilitarians, the
non-consequentialists do not employ a cost-benefit analysis or an
explicit formula to determine ethical worth. Rather, the decision-maker
is to refer to his or her intuitive and rational sense of what would be
universally right. This perspective represents a cognitive logic by which
truth and rightness become self-evident for all rational people. Or, the
decision-maker may appeal to sets of rules, codes, and principles established by religious or secular sources (i.e., societal, cultural, or organizational) (Hodgkinson, 1996).

The Advantages and Disadvantages of Non-Consequentialism

The primary advantage of this approach is that it considers the manner and intent of our actions as opposed to simply allowing the ends to
justify the means. This is in contrast, as we discovered, with most forms

of consequentialism. Non-consequentialism does not allow for the (tele-ological) suspension of what we instinctively reason to be just in order to achieve the best end. As a result, it can be argued, there is an appeal to our intuitive sense of rightness.

In addition, the notion of duty is a central feature of this view. As religion and society play a key role in this theory, traditional precepts and obligations represent significant criteria against which behavior is judged. We look to what tradition tells us is right. The impact of this formalism is stability in cultural ethical expectations.

The elements that point to the strengths of non-consequentialism also expose its inherent weaknesses. As rules and principles are the frameworks for ethical judgment, the individual's personal responsibility for ethical conduct is deferred to externally driven criteria (e.g., religion or society is to praise or to blame). For example, Adolph Eichmann, the architect of the slaughter of Jews in World War II, attempted to argue his innocence by suggesting that he was merely following orders (organizational principles). The problem is that some principles are eventually deemed to be unjust. An example of this was Martin Luther King, who argued from his jail cell that it is every person's responsibility to abide by just laws, yet, at the same time, we must reject those that are unjust (i.e., segregation).

Further, the reality of societal change places enormous pressure upon the validity, and perhaps the reliability, of traditional notions of ethical conduct. We need only look to the Olympic Games to see the blatant transgression or transformation of the principle of "amateurism" to illustrate this point. What is acceptable now would have been unspeakable to the founders of the modern Olympics. Interestingly, the ancient Greeks would have been surprised at Coubertin's nineteenth-century idealism and his use of the term amateur, which was unknown to them.

Where consequentialism's dynamics provide for flexibility as society changes, non-consequentialism's static nature may hinder it from providing a contemporary basis from which to judge rightness and wrongness. As a result, traditional notions of ethics may become static, dead, irrelevant, and ignored.

Having briefly surveyed the ends and means approaches to ethical behavior, the reader may wonder which way to turn to determine what, in fact, is moral behavior. One possible answer can be found in the next approach, which is a radical departure from consequentialism and non-consequentialism. Existentialism has been termed a revolt against traditional philosophy and argues for a paradigmatically different approach to ethical conduct compared to the former two theories.

Box B

An Example of Non-Consequentialism in Sport Administration—Rightness

A sport administrator is provided with concrete evidence that two individuals on the national team have taken IOC-banned, performance- enhancing substances. Despite the reality that many athletes at this level are equally guilty of this misconduct, and that there seems to be some grey areas in regard to this issue in the culture of this particular sport, the administrator feels that the ethical root of this dilemma must be uncovered first before any action is taken.

As an individual whose ethical basis is non-consequentialism, this administrator assesses the situation from three levels. First, the policies and procedures for this sport are consulted to see if any rules exists that deal specifically with the use of performance-enhancing substances. Second, legal sources are consulted to determine whether in fact a law has been broken and the athletes ought to be reported and charged for this offence. Finally, the sport administrator attempts to reason through the categorical imperative to determine whether or not the athletes' behavior can be condoned or rejected from the basis of a universal principle of right conduct.

As a result, of the administrator's review of organizational policy, societal law, and universal principle, a course of action seems more apparent as the following information was uncovered:

1. The sport association does have a policy regarding the use of performance-enhancing substances. If guilty, athletes are to receive lifetime bans from participating in the sport sanctioned by the association.

2. At present there is not a law which deems the possession and/or use of the particular drug in question as illegal. No law has been broken.

3. The categorical imperative forms the basis for a universally valid principle of ethical conduct. To condone the behavior of these "accused" athletes would result in the explicit and implicit acceptance of drug use by all athletes of all ages at all levels. The sport administrator clearly sees that such a message is not acceptable. As a result, the existing organizational policy is upheld with vigor by the individual.

Existentialism: What Is Authentic Behavior?

Background

Existentialism is a disjointed school of thought. It consists of a disparate and eclectic set of ideas gathered from a dissimilar group of philosophical thinkers. While existentialists, as individual thinkers, differ dramatically, two common threads of thought are woven throughout their ideas regarding the nature of ethical conduct. The first is the belief in the freedom of individuals to create their own essence, that is, to create who they are. Sartre, a twentieth-century French existentialist, argued that "existence precedes essence." This implies that we exist as humans, and we then become whom we decide to be through our free will or choice. We are not predetermined. Who we are is not purely the result of either societal reinforcement (nurture) or our genetic predisposition (nature). Existentialists would suggest that, through our capacity to exercise free will, we are the sum of the decisions made through that capacity.

The second component of existentialism is contained in the concept of responsibility for one's actions. What has been labeled the "terrible freedom," the "agony of thinking" or the "torment of choice" posits the responsibility for correct behavior squarely on the shoulders of the individual. That one is responsible for all of one's actions and the impact of these actions upon all of humanity is cause for the alleged fear and despair that the existentialist experiences as one's essence is created. As a result, behavior, "good" or "right," "bad" or "wrong," cannot be diverted to an external locus of control. For example, an individual ought not to praise or blame co-workers, policy, clients, patients, or society for the success or failure of his or her acts. Further, this individual cannot argue that responsibility will be taken for personal acts only. All action must be considered as it may influence all individuals, all of society, or all of humanity.

Though this theory is highly personal, it is neither about selfishness nor is it hedonistic. Rather, existentialism is a philosophy that insists that the individual is self-determined and must constantly battle to overcome the "averaging" effect of modern society. It acknowledges respect for individualism, yet acknowledges the tremendous responsibility that one's individualism and its accompanying decisions have for others. For example, the great existentialist Sartre (1997) suggests that

> when we say that man chooses himself, we do not mean that every one of us must choose himself; but by that we also mean that in choosing for himself he chooses for all men.... What we choose is always the better and nothing can be better unless it is better for all.... Our responsibility is thus much greater than we had supposed, for it concerns mankind as a whole (p.586).

Box C
An Example of Existentialism in Sport—Authenticity

An athlete, Z, is by nature non-violent. He is participating in a rather violent sport in which fighting is perceived by many to be "part of the game." In one match, a brawl develops between Z's team and another. In fact, it turns out to be a bench-clearing brawl. Z, who is opposed to this sort of behavior under any circumstance, remains on the bench—alone. The coach orders Z to join the fray to defend the honor of the team. The coach threatens Z with fines as well as with "benching" him if his participation in the fight is not immediate. Z remains on the bench, contemplating the weight of the decision that he has made and the outcome for the players, the children in the stands, and all the fans watching the violence of this game. Z is determined not to sacrifice personal integrity for conformity to other people's standards.

Thus, it is blatantly a misinterpretation to suggest that existentialism is glorified hedonism. An example of existential thinking in a sport context is provided below (see Box C).

The Existential Method

The method for the existentialist consists of one criterion– authenticity. All action must be judged against the individual's genuineness. To be authentic or genuine implies being honest with oneself and with others. Shakespeare's dictum "To thyne own self be true" is an appropriate metaphor for the existential method. As we have mentioned, this is perhaps the most difficult approach as there is no method, no formula, no rule, no principle or maxim to help in choosing a course of action. The existentialist will never have more than his or her authenticity and therefore will always experience the "agony of choice." As a person comes to accept "nothingness" (i.e., the constant state of becoming who he or she is), it is then possible to deal more readily with the solitude and responsibility of individual decision-making behavior. While this method may appear to be a non-method, that is, in fact, the existentialist's lot.

The Advantages and Disadvantages of Existentialism

Existentialism is one of the most demanding theories of ethical conduct. This is because the full weight of individual action rests upon the decision-maker. All choices must be made from within the soul or the will of the individual, as opposed to following externally driven, rational, cost-benefit analyses (consequentialism) or principles (non-consequentialism). This is the central advantage of existentialism, as it leads to complete honesty with oneself and with all others who may be influenced by one's actions.

The foremost disadvantage of existentialism is that it does not provide a clear means to deciding one's essence or authenticity. The individual is left entirely alone in deciding which is the best choice. No God, process, or societal norm can make the choice for the individual. Some may believe that this theory is too depressing, since existentialism argues that there is no meaning to the universe, that God is dead, and that we are essentially alone and nothing. This, however, has its optimistic side as well. That we are nothing also implies that we are capable of becoming. Individuals are completely free and unfettered to create whom, in fact, they wish to be if there is no God and no predestination and if society does not hold all the answers.

We have now discussed the essence of three very different approaches to ethical thought. In the following section, a composite of these views is provided, based upon the premise that this step will give the reader a more comprehensive perspective of ethical action and decision making.

Synthesis: Good, Right, and Authentic Behavior

Thus far we have discussed three disparate approaches that identify the good, the right, and the authentic aspects of ethical behavior. Taken individually, we have observed that each presents a particular view of what constitutes ethical conduct. On the other hand, each individually provides an incomplete perspective. Consequentialism identifies the good and dynamic change while neglecting the right and the authentic. Non-consequentialism considers the right and the stable (i.e., the traditional notions of right) yet overlooks the good and the authentic. Finally, existentialist thought views authenticity as primary, while perhaps obfuscating the good and the right. If each presents an incomplete picture, can there be an acceptable synthesis to create good, right, and authentic behavior? Is there a holistic behavior that meets all the criteria?

We argue that it is possible and preferable that individuals, when confronted with an ethical dilemma, incorporate criteria from each of these theories to form a complete ethical decision. This synthesis may be analogous to the ancient Roman God of the Gates. This god possessed two faces, which enabled him to look inwards to protect the people within the city and outwards to protect them from invaders. Our

Box D
An Example of Good, Right, and Authentic Behavior

In many sports there exists a term called "the good penalty," which condones an infraction of the rules when it serves the purposes of a team or an individual. An example, which was cited in Chapter 3, would be to trip a hockey player as he or she is skating towards the goalie on a breakaway. How does this behavior meet our criteria?

1. Does this behavior result in the best end for the greatest number? Clearly, this infraction will help the team committing the violation—a goal may be prevented. However, if we search beyond the immediate context of the particular game or play, the implication of this behavior may not be best for the greatest number. Can we argue that viewing a deliberate rule infraction is "good" for the majority of individuals watching this kind of behavior as fans, as players, or as potential players? Can this behavior (cheating) be the basis of modeling of similar behavior in future by players or soon-to-be players?

2. Is the decision consistent with intuitive, organizational, socio-cultural, and universal norms? This criterion is "clear," as a rule and a principle were conspicuously broken. Cheating behavior in its broadest sense in not generally condoned—it is not a value of our sporting community. From a global perspective, cheating cannot be justified for athletes as the very fabric of "structured" sport would be undermined.

3. Is this free, honest, and authentic behavior? How does this particular decision impact on oneself? And on others who will feel the impact? How this criterion is met can only be answered by that particular individual. We might argue that persons who condone cheating and are capable of feeling no remorse while being true to themselves when they exhibit this kind of behavior are behaving in a way that is markedly dysfunctional. Therefore, regarding this particular dilemma, what is good, right, and authentic is not to condone cheating of any kind despite its immediate outcome.

synthesis has this Janus-head, with three faces instead of two. One face looks towards the future, the dynamic and the good. Another looks backwards to the past, the stable and the right. Finally, one faces inward, at the essence, the freedom, the responsibility, and the authenticity of the individual.

Complete ethical decisions may be formulated within the following framework:

1. Does the decision accomplish the best end for the greatest number?

2. Is the decision consistent with intuitive, organizational, socio-cultural, and universal norms?

3. Is this free, honest, and authentic behavior? How does this particular decision impact on oneself? And on others who will feel the impact?

A decision based upon these criteria, then, can presumably be considered ethically complete–good, right, and authentic. That is, such a decision will accomplish the goal (the good), it will do so based upon inclusive means (the right), and it will be reflective of the decision-maker's authentic intent.

We argue that the synthesis of good, right, and authentic decision making is comprehensive. A decision that is not based upon these criteria, we suggest, cannot be considered ethically complete and must be re-evaluated–another alternative must be found. The search for this synthesis requires a great deal of contemplation. Such inquiry and introspection are difficult. Though the world of education, sport, leisure, dance, and recreation are each characterized by its fast pace, when it comes to ethical behavior we may wish to accept the notion that the person who does not hesitate (and reflect) may be lost. An example that describes such a scenario where ethical synthesis is accomplished follows (see Box D).

Summary

In this chapter we have briefly surveyed the consequential, non-consequential, and existential schools of ethical thought. While each theory argues for different criteria to judge ideal conduct, each provides us with an incomplete perspective. In response to this fragmented picture we provided the reader with a model in which the synthesis of the good, the right, and the authentic nature of complete ethical decisions is contained. In the next chapter we explore the many factors that may influence, to a greater or lesser extent, the decision-making behavior of the individual.

References

Adler, M.J. (1989). *Aristotle for everybody.* New York: Bantam Books.

Albert, E.M., Denise, T.C., & Peterfreund, S.P. (1988). *Great traditions in ethics.* Belmont, Calif.: Wadsworth Publishing Company.

Aristotle. (1968). The basic works of Aristotle, R. Keon, Trans. New York: Random House.

Aristotle. (1971). *Aristotle on man in the universe,* L.R. Looimis, Ed. Roslyn, N.Y., Walter J. Black, Inc.

Barnes, J. (1989). *Aristotle.* Oxford: Oxford University press.

Fry, J.P. (2000). Coaching a kingdom of ends. *Journal of the Philosophy of Sport,* 27:51-62.

Gaarder, J. (1994). *Sophie's world: A novel about the history of philosophy,* P. Moller (Trans.). New York: Harper Collins Canada Ltd.

Hodgkinson, C. (1996). *Administrative philosophy*. Oxford: Pergamon.

Kant, I. (1785/2001). *Fundamental principles of the metaphysics of morals,* A.W. Wood, (Trans.). New York: The Modern Library.

Macdonald J.E. & Beck-Dudley, C.L. (1994). A deontology and teleology mutually exclusive? *Jouranl of Business Ethics,* 13:615-623.

MacIntyre, A. (1966). *A short history of ethics.* New York: Macmillian Publishing Company.

_____. (1984). *After virtue.* Notre Dame, Ind.: University of Notre Dame Press.

Nietzsche, F. (1992). *The basic writings of Nietzsche,* W. Kaufman, (Trans.). New York: Random House.

Rawls, J. (1971). *Theory of justice.* Cambridge, Mass.: Harvard University Press.

Russell, B. (1979*). History of Western philosophy.* London: Unwin Paperbacks.

Sartre, J.P. (1966). *Being and nothingness,* H.E. Barnes, Trans. New York: Pocket Books.

———. (1997). Existentialism. In *Introducing Philosophy: A text with integrated readings,* R.C Solomon, (Ed.), pp.586-589. Toronto, Ont.: Harcourt Brace College Publishers.

Sayegh, N.S. (1988). *Philosophy and philosophers from Thales to Tillich.* Ottawa: Academy Books.

Sherman, N. (1997). *Making a necessity of virtue: Aristotle and Kant on virtue.* Cambridge: Cambridge University Press.

Singer, P. (Ed.) (1993). *A companion to ethics.* Oxford: Basil Blackwell Ltd.

Solomon, R.C. (1997). *Introducing philosophy.* Fort Worth: Harcourt Brace College Publishers.

Stumpf, S.E. (1993). *Socrates to Sartre: A history of philosophy.* New York: McGraw-Hill, Inc.

5

Moderators Influencing
Ethical Decision Making

As you have probably gathered from the preceding chapters, ethics is a rather complicated yet fascinating field of practical living and academic study. By now you have discovered that to say that an act is ethical or unethical can be too simplistic a statement. Having read thus far, you are aware that detecting the ethical disposition of an act requires complex patterns of analysis and thought, along with rigor in the application of moral reasoning. In this chapter and the next, we present our second model of ethical decision making (Figure 5.1).

Model II–A Comprehensive Approach

This model provides the reader with a more comprehensive approach to resolving moral dilemmas because it identifies a variety of moderators or variables that may, to a greater or lesser extent, influence the manner in which one makes ethical decisions. A significant aspect of this model is that it can be used, not only to render judgment of past events (as is the case with our first model), but it can also enable the decision-maker to assess comprehensively future courses of ethical conduct. We believe that by adopting this model, not only in the cases presented in Chapter 9, but also in actual day-to-day dilemmas, you will enhance the rigor, reduce the ambiguity, and increase the effectiveness of your ethical reasoning.

The manner in which we make decisions, ethical or unethical, is most often the result of a multitude of moderators. These moderators are shown in Figure 5.1. If we are to understand why individuals behave in the way they do, it is necessary to investigate some antecedent features. These features may, based on the individual's level of moral reasoning or psychological development, influence behavior. We have chosen to categorize these variables into five sets of moderators. The first set concerns those moderators that are particular to the individual (IM). They include such variables as ethical and value grounding, level of moral development, and demographic moderators, such as age, education, and gender.

The nature of the ethical dilemma itself or the issue-specific modera-

Figure 5.1: Ethical Decision-Making Model—Comprehensive Approach

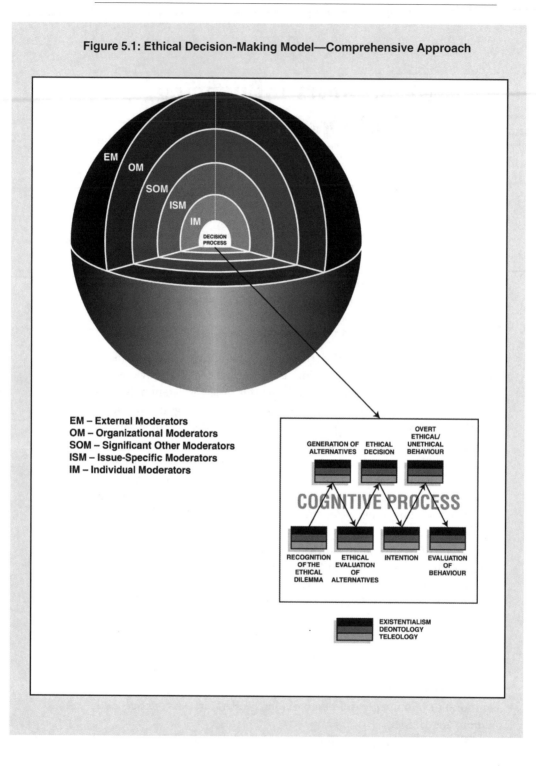

EM – External Moderators
OM – Organizational Moderators
SOM – Significant Other Moderators
ISM – Issue-Specific Moderators
IM – Individual Moderators

tors (ISM) is a second area that we consider to be a potential influence on ethical behavior. The third set contains moderators that involve the relationships that the decision-maker has with significant others (SOM). These relationships include those with family and friends, peers, group members, and individuals from other communities and organizations. The fourth set of moderators considers the organizational or team culture in which an individual is participating, working, or volunteering. The final category includes moderators that are external to the individual and organizational context. These moderators include political, social, economic, and technical variables that may influence the manner in which decisions are made, of an ethical or unethical nature. In the following paragraphs, each area will be explored in detail.

Individual Moderators of Ethical Decision Making

In this section we describe the effect that an individual's ethical orientation, level of moral development, and demographic profile may have upon decision-making behavior.

Ethical orientation. Ethical orientation forms the basis of the content of our behavior. Awareness of our ethical nature tells us to what extent we focus upon good, right, and authentic behavior and what is bad, wrong, and inauthentic. If our nature is to behave as a teleologist, the content of our behavior may be predisposed to seeking out the good ends in decision making. If, on the other hand, we tend to be more deontological in our behavior, the means become the dominant concern. For example, the teleologist's theme could be "to succeed at all cost," whereas the deontologist's theme could be "It is not to win or lose but how one plays the game."

In contrast to these dispositions is the existential view, which places all weight upon freedom, responsibility, and authenticity. The ends and the means pale in comparison to the importance of exercising freedom and one's own creative will. The existentialist theme is, as expressed so directly by Nietzsche, "Do something! Exist!"

Though we have identified, here and in earlier chapters, three extreme positions or archetypes, it is important to realize that few of us represent or exhibit pure forms of any one orientation. Research informs us that we are hybrids of all of these ethical positions and that our orientation is often contextually driven; it is an eclectic mix (e.g., Reidenbach & Robin, 1988, 1990).

Once identified, we must then decide if that ethical orientation is how we want to continue believing and behaving. Does my action follow my beliefs and values? Do I, for example, profess the existential

axiom of freedom yet seldom take responsibility for my action, or do I
spread the blame on those around me? Similarly, can we identify the
behavior of our co-workers and peers as focused upon the ends or the
means? Are we aware of their commitment to their own authenticity?
For example, can we conclude from our observation of an individual's
behavior that there is a propensity towards goal accomplishment, rule
following, or genuineness?

Ethical orientation influences how we behave. The schools of ethics
that we have covered provide us with tools with which we can describe
our own behavior and that of those around us. As a result, we have a
clearer idea of what we and those around do that is ethically good,
right, and authentic.

Values and value orientation. In Chapter 3 the term value was
described as being a belief or concept that motivates and guides behavior. We could say that a particular behavior is a function or manifestation of what one values. England, Dhigra, and Agarwal (1974) described
values in terms of their relative intensity. They described values as
being weak, adopted, intended, and operative. Weak values are superfi-
cially held by the individual and do not tend to motivate action (e.g., I
say I value X but in fact I do not). Adopted values are held situationally
by the individual and are perceived to be relatively important based
only upon the particular circumstance in which the individual finds
himself or herself (e.g., I value X when the situation calls for me to
value it–perhaps when I am being observed). Intended values are
important to the decision-maker. However, they tend not to be
employed in actual circumstances; instead they are conceptually held
(e.g., my intention is to value X but other things seem to get in the way
of my behavior reflecting X). Finally, operative values are seen to be
most influential in the actual behavior of an individual (e.g., I value X
and this is observable in my behavior). Operative values are indeed the
motivators and the origin for overt behavior.

From a different perspective, the administrative philosopher
Hodgkinson (1996) sees a hierarchical orientation of values as being
vital to understanding human behavior. He describes value orientations
or groundings as being based upon four levels. The lowest level indicates that a person values something for fundamentally selfish and/or
egocentric and hedonistic reasons–I behave the way I do because I like
it. The second level of valuing is utilitarian in orientation–I behave the
way I do because everyone else does it. The third level describes an orientation that is pragmatic or scientifically driven–I behave the way I do
because it is efficient and effective. The final level is deontological and

existential in nature. Valuing here is based upon one's individually driven principles–I behave the way I do because I have faith in my beliefs.

Hodgkinson's approach to value orientation may assist the decision-maker to better understand the basis of his or her own behavior as well as the behavior of others. If, for example, you wish to have a coach alter the style in which she motivates her players and if you are aware that a coach tends to make decision based upon pragmatism (i.e., what is fact, what is most efficient and effective in solving the "problem"), then any attempt to appeal to this person's sense of group pressure from players, volunteers, or the public (i.e., utilitarianism) may not be successful. Rather, this individual needs to see the facts in order to be convinced to use a different coaching style.

Cognitive moral development. From a different perspective, researchers in cognitive moral development have sought to explain moral behavior in terms of the level of the individual's cognitive complexity. Following Piaget's work studying the moral development of children, the research conducted by Laurence Kohlberg and his colleagues in the 1970s and 1980s as well as research that continues today employing Kohlberg's model and method, particularly in the area of applied ethics (e.g., business and administrative ethics), has examined the rationale for moral behavior among adolescents and adults. While Kohlberg's work has received substantial support, there are critics who have argued against his methodology and his theoretical assumptions. These criticisms were initially raised by Carol Gilligan (1982), who argued that the Kohlbergian model was biased against women. Her approach, which she termed the *Ethics of Care*, attempted to provide a feminine alternative to the so-called masculine model. In the following sections each of these perspectives will be discussed. [**N.B.** It should be noted that much of the debate between these two perspectives is based upon vying theoretical and empirical assumptions. We will not explore this debate and would recommend the following text as a good resource to explore the Kohlberg-Gilligan dialectic: Shogun, D. (1988), *Care and Moral Motivation,* Toronto, Ontario, OISE Press.]

Kohlberg's model. This model, developed from the responses of subjects to hypothetical moral dilemmas, is structured in three levels consisting of two stages per level. These levels are termed *pre-conventional, conventional,* and *post-conventional.* The *pre-conventional* level is characterized by reasoning focused upon the individual's own survival. It is a hedonistic orientation. At this level, pain is avoided and reward, as exchange, is sought. Behavior at this level is, therefore, not a

Figure 5.2: Kohlberg's (1969) Model of Moral Development

Level I—Pre-Conventional Morality

Stage 1	Punishment orientation	Obeys rules to avoid punishment.
Stage 2	Reward orientation	Conforms to obtain rewards, to have favors returned.

Level II—Conventional Morality

Stage 3	Good boy/nice girl orientation	Conforms to avoid disapproval of others.
Stage 4	Authority orientation	Blindly accepts social conventions and rules (i.e., law and order morality).

Level III—Post-Conventional Morality

Stage 5	Social contract orientation	Conforms to Hobbesian and Lockian contract theory. One's duty is to avoid violating contractual or natural rights.
Stage 6	Ethical principle orientation	Actions guided by self-chosen ethical principles.

function of lofty principles or concern for others. Rather, this level is egocentric and selfish. A pre-conventional employee is likely to strive to gain extrinsic rewards (e.g., money) or to avoid punishment (e.g., fear of physical, verbal, or monetary reprisals for poor performance).

The *conventional* level describes reasoning focused upon one's significant others and society-at-large. At this level, behavior is not self-centered; rather it is based upon the approval one seeks from those with whom one has close interpersonal relationships or from the greater community. Seeking the approval of the coach or co-workers or the public may drive the conventional individual to act in a particular manner. Individuals who reason from either the conventional or pre-conventional levels are externally driven. In other words, the rationale for their behavior is based upon sources external to themselves.

Individuals whose reasoning is complex and based upon their personal commitment to the profession specifically and to universal principles of justice generally would be considered by Kohlberg to be *post-conventional* in their cognitive moral development. These people reason not from selfishness, nor do they necessarily reason from the influence of the collective will of those around them. Rather, because of their own introspection, intelligence, moral advancement, and maturity, they have come to reason in complex and highly personal ways towards resolutions they hold as right, good, and authentic modes of behavior.

The proponents of this post-conventional approach argue that the way in which an individual can achieve more complex levels of moral reasoning is primarily through an environment that is progressively enriching. This environment, whether it is enriching educationally or experientially, provides opportunities for individuals to have their cognitive schema (i.e., the conceptual maps we have created to explain the world around us) challenged, critiqued, and broadened. Because of such challenges to our world view, we may rethink our positions and opt for a more complex explanation of reality. What we understand, in other words, does not simply align in dichotomies of black or white, right or wrong, good or bad, but is a result of many cognitive and affective "shades of grey."

The ethic of caring. Carol Gilligan (1982), a colleague of Kohlberg's at Harvard, believed that another cognitive approach was needed that would explain more accurately the manner in which females reason morally. Using open-ended interviews with female subjects, she found that the underlying rationale for the behavior of females was the notion of relationship and *caring* as opposed to justice. Her model consists of three levels and two transitional phases.

The first level is similar to Kohlberg's pre-conventional level as it is fundamentally self-centered and focused upon personal survival. Here, one cares only for oneself. This level is followed by the first transition in which the female begins to recognize that there are other individuals to whom she is responsible. In this stage, the female begins to break out of her egocentric perspective and starts to realize additional obligations and attachments to others. This transition is followed by the second level in which the female becomes altruistic in her concern for others at the expense of her own moral care. She is not only aware of her relations and responsibilities to others, she also believes that she must care for all of these individuals and becomes the *selfless mother* figure that Gilligan argues is a function of societal expectation as opposed to the truth (i.e., that altruism is not necessarily the same as goodness). This level leads to a second transition in which the woman recognizes that truth is not altruism and that she herself is in need of care and control.

The final stage of Gilligan's model describes the morality of non-violence or caring. Here the woman has rejected the traditional criterion of feminine morality (i.e., self-abnegation and self-sacrifice) in favor of one in which care becomes the universal obligation where "the worth of the self in relation to others, the claiming of the power to choose, and the acceptance of responsibility for choice" (p.507) now becomes the paramount issue. The woman now becomes

> the arbiter of an independent judgment that now subsumes both conventions and individual needs under the moral principle of nonviolence. Judgment remains psychological in its concern with the intention and consequence of action, but now it becomes universal in its condemnation of exploitation and hurt (p.492).

The work of Gilligan first revealed the unique feminine character of moral development (morality of caring). The implications of her research are significant particularly if the notion of moral development (i.e., Kohlberg's model) is conceptually inaccurate for the female population. Acknowledging the inherent differences in moral reasoning between genders may enhance the practitioner's ability to explain and understand ethical or unethical behavior.

The juxtaposition of the ethic of caring and the ethic of justice is important to our field, as athletes, students, and the public-at-large need to be considered as more than just bodies to be trained to be more efficient and effective. A holistic approach to body, mind, and emotion, and relationship therein is needed (see Malloy & Taylor, 1999; Ross, 1995).

The value of using an approach based upon cognitive moral development is two-fold. First, it provides a framework from which we may better understand the rationale for our own behavior and that of the individuals with whom we interact. Unlike ethics, which tells us the content or substance of behavior, cognitive developmental psychology explains why we make decisions the way we do. For example, do we abide by the law because of a pre-conventional fear of avoiding punishment or is it a post-conventional personal commitment to justice?

Demographic profile. Demography refers to the variety of background moderators, such as age, education, sex, race or ethnicity, cultural background, place of residence, among many other variables. Each of these variables may have a profound influence on the way in which individuals act and perceive ethical and unethical conduct. The research in this area is, however, rather mixed.

While there is some trend towards more enhanced ethical perception and behavior among older and more educated subjects, there is less consensus when gender and sexuality differences are measured.

Whether females and males reason differently about ethical issues and whether they employ different ethical criteria is far from conclusive.

From another perspective, cross-cultural research has demonstrated that significant differences exist in the way in which members of different cultures reason ethically. This is not to say, however, that any one ethnic culture portrays "superior" ethical reasoning or behavior. Suffice it to say that each of us brings a unique essence that may influence, to a greater or lesser extent, the manner in which ethical conduct is perceived and acted upon. It is up to us as unique individuals to recognize that our behavior forms and informs our own essence and to accept the consequences of, and responsibility for, all of our actions. Further, once one recognizes the positive and negative aspects of one's demographic profile, the decision to change or maintain one's ethical position can be made.

Issue-Specific Moderators—The Ethical Intensity of the Issue

The nature of the decision itself may have an impact upon the way in which we approach ethical dilemmas (e.g., Jones, 1991). Some issues simply may not be ethically contentious and require very little, if any, ethical consideration. On the other hand, some issues may be ethically loaded and the failure to recognize the moral intensity may result in dramatic outcomes for the individual and the organization. The moderators to be discussed in this section will help with the exploration of the ethical intensity of a dilemma. This will help us to decide the relative intellectual demands required of the decision-maker (the more ethically intense, the more ethically demanding).

Normative consensus. The decision-maker's awareness of the general perception of the group or community regarding a particular issue will help in deciding its relative ethical intensity. For example, if the perception of the community-at-large embraces a strong normative stand against the violent nature of hooliganism surrounding local English football matches, the relative ethical intensity is greater than another issue such as renaming the stadium after a local historical figure. The community's concern may (or should) heighten the level of the decision-maker's ethical reasoning regarding the particular issue.

As an individual or as a professional in a particular community, you must be aware of the normative intensity of issues around you. Far too often individual action, whether as an individual or as a professional, taken without seeking out the views and feelings of the broader community is dangerous and leads to attack or failure of the action. We must avoid making the assumption that we know or have insight into the broader normative stance of those around us or for whom we work. Here further investigation is necessary and fundamental to action. The community's concern may (or should) heighten the level of the decision-maker's ethical reasoning regarding the particular issue.

This is not to say that the norms of the community are necessarily right or good and must be followed. The caveat here is that the community's opinion will determine only the relative support or conflict that the decision-maker will have when he or she acts. The group has been known to be terribly wrong, as Socrates and Galileo experienced first hand!

Physical and psychological distance. The distance, physical or psychological, which separates the individual from the dilemma can have an effect upon the decision-maker's perception of ethical intensity. If an issue has occurred in a distant location, the decision-maker may not be compelled to act to the same degree as she or he would if the issue occurred locally. For example, the football hooliganism in England cited above may have little relevance to the fanatical baseball public of the United States or the ice hockey public of Canada.

Psychological distance refers to the extent to which the decision-maker is intimately involved with the issue or the circumstances surrounding it. When a coach is required to eliminate players trying out for a team, it is presumably more difficult to remain objective if the player is related to the coach.

Magnitude of the consequences. This moderator refers to the potential impact of the ethical issue upon the public or the individual. An issue that will result in very little negative or positive outcome is obviously less contentious and demanding than one that causes a great deal of harm or good. For example, the magnitude of consequence for a recreation director inadvertently securing incompetent individuals to cut grass in a park will have less negative impact upon the public than would the potential harm of hiring an recreation therapist who may prescribe unsafe activities for participants in a cardiac rehabilitation fitness program. The former will create some aesthetical discomfort, while the latter may result in fatalities.

Simply, a full analysis of the impact is part of any decision-making strategy. Included in this type of analysis is consideration of the positive and negative outcomes of different possible ways in which to proceed. Central to this process is a sound ethical basis from which to weigh the outcomes in both directions.

Probability of effect. This variable refers to the likelihood that a good or bad outcome of an action will actually occur. The greater the likelihood of an outcome taking place, the greater the moral intensity; the less likely, the less morally intensive. For example, the probability of violence occurring in a ball game between historical and violent rivals is greater than a similar match between teams that have no background of overly aggressive behavior. Organizers are well advised to take precautions of additional security in the former scenario, whereas in the latter, no extraordinary monitoring of players of public would appear to be required.

Concentration of effect. The extent to which good or harm is potentially distributed may influence a decision-maker's reasoning behavior. If the good or harm is distributed over a great number of individuals and everyone is affected minimally, it may be less contentious than if it affects one person severely.

For example, suppose pharmaceutical Company A introduces a vitamin supplement for athletes that is safe yet results in some minor intestinal discomfort for most users (i.e., it is effective but uncomfortable). Company B introduces a supplement that is more complex than Company A's vitamin, yet may result in some liver dysfunction for 3 percent of long-term users (i.e., extremely effective yet potentially dangerous for a minority of athletes). Therefore, the concentration of effect of Company A's product is less than that of Company B's product.

This variable has wide-ranging and diverse ramifications for all professional practices. Whether your field impacts upon public health, education, business, social policy, or the environment, there is constantly great potential to influence so many by what we do. As a result we cannot ignore or partition the fundamental role ethics plays in our decision-making behavior.

Immediacy. The time constraint placed upon the decision-maker may heighten or lessen the perceived intensity of an ethical dilemma. An issue that must be resolved immediately will undoubtedly hone the decision-maker's reasoning capacity to a greater degree than a resolution that can be delayed. For example, the decision to remove an abusive physical education teacher from the classroom is far more ethically pressing than the decision to develop a policy of teaching conduct. Both are necessary, but the former requires immediate attention, while the latter does not.

Strategic or tactical decision. The final moderator of ethical intensity describes the difference between strategic and tactical decisions. Strategic decisions deal with long-term and more global issues of an organization's functioning. The decisions that concern the organizational culture are typically strategic. Those decisions that focus upon the day-to-day operations of the team or organization are tactical. While both categories of decisions must be given attention, the implication of strategic decisions arguably transcends tactical ones and, therefore, must be given considerably more cognitive regard. For example, the decision to develop a mission statement for the organization (i.e., strategic) demands greater attention and is ethically more laden than a decision to change a team's uniform colors (i.e., tactical).

Significant Other Moderators of Ethical Decision Making

These moderators include interpersonal, interorganizational, and extra-organizational relationships that an individual has with other potentially influential persons. Interpersonal relationships are those special connections we have with family, friends, co-workers, and mentors. These persons may play a significant part in the development of our initial moral character.

These persons are the ones who perhaps initially taught us all the values we now unquestioningly hold. For many, behavior is based upon seeking approval from these significant others. As a result, the influence of these significant others upon our perceptions and behavior can be powerful.

A second grouping of relationships may also provide a strong incentive to behave ethically or unethically. Much research has been conducted into the impact of a co-worker's behavior and, more important, a supervisor's behavior, upon the individual. Supervisors are particularly relevant because they, as leaders, are perceived by many as role models and representatives of the culture of the organization. As a result, individuals may model their behavior after these persons, for better or worse. The leader's influence ought never to be underestimated.

The third group of individuals refers to those with whom we have established relationships from other organizations. For example, one may have relationships with individuals from different provinces, states, regions, districts, or countries. These relationships, though more distant than the former two categories, may nonetheless have a role to play in how we deal with ethical issues.

Organizational (Cultural) Moderators of Ethical Decision Making

Cultural moderators refer to the ideology, the explicit values, the observable behavior of members, and the physical structures of an organization. Together, these moderators combine to form what many call "the way we do things around here." Culture is a learned, shared, and meaningful way through which a group, team, or organization creates its own identity and way of existing and operating. Culture, in this usage, does not necessarily refer to ethnic culture. However, as discussed previously, ethnicity may play a role in the manner in which organizational members perceive and act ethically.

Edgar Schein (1990), in order to understand better the inner workings of organizations generally, developed a conceptual model based upon various dimensions of culture. In this model the organization is viewed in terms of three successive layers that extend outward from a foundational core. The inner core represents the implicit assumptions that the organization holds. These assumptions are a central feature of all organizational behavior yet are so ingrained in the individual member that they have become latent concepts from which problems have been successfully overcome. The first layer contains the values of the organization. These are explicit concepts that motivate organizational members to behave in certain ways. The second layer represents behaviors that can be observed. These behaviors are manifestations of the values found in the first layer. The final layer of the model is indicative of the physical artefacts that represent an organization's culture (i.e., the uniform of the military or the coat of arms of a university or clan).

Ideology. The ideology of an organization represents the philosophical basis for its culture. It consists of the implicit or unquestioned rationale for the existence of the organization. This may include the assumptions relating to the interaction with and relationship to the physical environment; the perceived nature and purpose of human activity; the nature of human relationships, both internal and external to the organization; and the perception of time, of reality, and of truth. These assumptions define the basic premises upon which the organization evolves and, ultimately, revolves. Ideologies also provide filters or screens through which conceptions and preconceptions are formed. As such, they form justifications, legitimations, and contested terrains for the organization.

Organizational values. Values are another essential feature of organizational culture. If ideology is the "blueprint" of organizational culture, we might consider values as the culture's conceptual "building blocks."

Earlier we defined a value as a concept that motivates behavior. This definition implies that a value is something abstract; that is, it is something that humans create, both for themselves and for their organizations. In addition, if a value is deemed desirable, that suggests that it is accepted by most. Thus when we speak of values, the desire of the group outweighs, usually, the desire of the individual. Finally, a value motivates us to do something.

A value strongly held will push us to behave in a particular manner. If, for example, an organizational value is competition in sport, members may be motivated to compete or, at the very least, to promote contests; or, if a cultural value is winning, members may promote elite-level sport over grassroots involvement. Thus you can surmise that organizational values have a significant role to play in understanding what and why we do what we do, or, in other words, what our organizational or team behavior might appear like.

We must also consider the extent to which a match exists between formal and informal organizational values. Formal values are those that are publicly and officially promoted by the team or the organization. Informal values are those that are not officially pronounced, yet are integral to the daily functioning of the organization, for better or for worse. For example, a municipal sport and recreation organization may, in its press documentation, declare its promotion as "Sport-For-All." This organization may unofficially discount the practical value of supporting all sub-groups of the population in favor of a more cost-effective strategy directed towards the preferences for certain programs among the mainstream population.

The extent to which there is a match between formal and informal value structures will determine the relative strength of the culture of the organization. Overall, if all individuals are operating from the same "blueprint," if they are using the same conceptual "building blocks," then the organization will, ideally, be more effective in accomplishing its goals. Should there not be a match, conflict may follow and the efficiency, effectiveness, and perhaps the humanistic aspect of the organization may suffer.

The physical structures of the organization provide us with another aspect or frame of culture. They are the objective artifacts that represent the culture of the organization. The things around us show where we place value. Does a school have a display case for its academic awards? Does it have a display case for its athletes' awards? Is the building, which houses organizational members, clean and safe? Are members provided with the equipment necessary to accomplish their task (e.g., computers, facsimile machines)? These items are often tangible indicators of the ideology and values of the organization being put into action.

As a final note on organizational culture, it has been argued that the fundamental role of leadership is the development and maintenance of organizational culture. This responsibility is perhaps a new dimension to be considered by many. It may be common sense to others. None-

theless, attending to the development of ethical culture and its maintenance through the "frames" of ideology, values, and structures can
result in effective, holistic, human, and humane organizational functioning.

External Moderators of Ethical Decision Making

External moderators consist of those variables that are outside the
confines of the organization. These moderators include economics, politics, technology, and society (domestic and international). These moderators may influence, to a greater or lesser extent, the actual
decision-making behavior of the individual. They have been placed at
the periphery of the model (Figure 5.1) to suggest less intense influence
than moderators more centrally situated.

Having stated this we refer the reader back to the introduction where
we pointed to two key ideas: first, the world, humans, and human activity are complex; and second, education, sport, recreation, and physical
education are not separate or isolated from the real world. Although
external modifiers are on the periphery of the model, we cannot rule
out or reduce the effects of their impact. Furthermore, the following
division of economy, politics, technology, and society is artificial. It is
done for ease of discussion. The reader must always bear in mind that
they are concomitantly parts of the complex whole of human social
existence.

Economy. The economy has perhaps an obvious influence upon the
way in which we make decisions. The extent to which an individual or
an organization is pressured economically to perform may result in
more, or less, tension to achieve ends at any cost. The power of corporate sponsorship could be the dominant factor in an individual's ethical
or unethical conduct.

Politics. Political pressure, as a form of power, whether domestic or
international, can have a significant effect upon ethical behavior. The
promise of increased economic activity by business, cities, provinces
and/or states, nations, and other political groups to achieve their ultimate ends has always been and will undoubtedly continue to be a political tool. This is evident in the funding of "mega-projects" of all sorts.
Obtaining tax-based revenues for these projects, while other more
socially necessary projects go wanting (e.g., stadia or arenas versus
schools or hospitals) continues (see Chapter 2 for a more elaborate discussion of economic factors).

A rationally ethical decision-maker acting in an ethically sound manner must be aware of and observe how other individuals and all organi-

zations act politically. We caution you not to restrict your examination to the behavior of elected officials, governments, and bureaucratic members. Politics operate at all levels of society and in all relationships.

Technology. The impact that new innovations may have upon human behavior can be significant. For example, the ability to enhance athletic performance, sanctioned or unsanctioned, overt or covert, has created a variety of new dilemmas that were unknown one or two decades ago. From this perspective it is critical that our ethical awareness, our ability to recognize ethically contentious issues, keeps pace with the rapid development of technology. In other words, while we celebrate the achievement of research, we must also temper the application and implication of new discoveries with respect for humanity and for the manner in which sport is developed, delivered, and played.

Society. We are social beings and need to interact with others to define our own "humaneness." How we go about relating to others involves a complex learning process, socialization, based on both our natural, genetic endowment and our cultural background. In all professions and in all occupations we go through a process of socialization. We learn our role within the culture of that social activity and structure. A constant challenge is presented to us through this process to determine the manner by which we develop our selves, our knowledge, and our action in acceptable and professionally relevant ways.

In terms of this moderator, we must constantly weigh the cultural elements that focus our thought and action. Furthermore, we must ask whether the values, ideologies, and structures surrounding these activities are meeting ethically sound goals for the individuals involved and for our societies.

Interaction Effect

The moderators we have thus far discussed in the model have been presented as layers surrounding a core of the decision-making process. To clarify the relations among these layers we present the following four propositions:

Proposition 1. The arrangement of the layers implies that those moderators closest to the core have potentially greater influence upon the process of ethical decision making than do those more distally from the core. Despite this logic, we suggest that occasionally the process may be influenced to a greater extent by distal layers or moderators than proximal ones. For example, though an organizational culture may pressure an individual to behave in a particular manner, the influence of this person's church may hold more relative power of persuasion. The point made here is that, although there exists some logic to a rather linear arrangement of moderators, this logic may not always hold and the decision-maker must be prepared for the unexpected.

Proposition 2. The extent to which any moderator influences the ethical process will be mediated by individual moderators. For example, those reasoning from a conventional realm will be influenced to a much greater extent than those functioning from a post-conventional level. The deontologist will be affected to a greater degree by organizational policy than will the existentialist or the teleologist.

Proposition 3. The actual decisions, particularly those generated from the core, can influence each moderator surrounding it. An individual's decision might affect in a profound way the behavior of significant others, the organization's culture, and perhaps even the societal or political structure generally.

Proposition 4. Moderators can influence each other reciprocally. For example, organizational culture can influence the behavior of significant others as well as a variety of external moderators and, in turn, may be influenced by them. Thus there is influence being generated towards the core, between layers of the model, and also from the core to external layers.

Summary

In this chapter we have presented the moderators of a comprehensive model of ethical decision making (Model II). Five layers of moderators were identified that may influence, to a greater or lesser extent, the decision-making process. Each layer represents a set of variables that should be considered in order for the individual to fully understand the complexity, breadth, and significance of decision-making behavior. While the significance of each layer will vary according to the nuances of any particular dilemma, Model II provides the reader with a framework from which comprehensive ethical decisions can be achieved.

In the next chapter a process of ethical decision making is introduced. This process, located at the core of Model II, operates as a framework for ethical action to be assessed and resolutions implemented.

References

Badaracco, J.L. (1995). *Business Ethics: Roles and Responsibilities.* Chicago: Irwin.

England, G.W., Dhingru, O.P., & Agarual, N.C. (1974). *The Manager and the Man: A Cross-Cultural Study of Personal Values.* Kent, OH: Kent State University Press.

6

The Process of Ethical
Decision Making

In the previous chapter, we discussed many variables or moderators that may, to a greater or lesser extent, influence the manner in which we make ethical or unethical decisions. In this chapter we will look at a process of ethical decision making that will provide the reader with a more comprehensive analysis and plan of ethics-in-action.

The use of any particular decision-making model will not always guarantee the best decision. The result depends on the decision-maker's ethical beliefs, cognitive abilities, intentions, and creativity. Having said this, we present the following as a framework for the analysis and development of a logical, consistent, and comprehensive ethical decision.

The process consists of seven stages (Figure 6.1). Within each stage, the reader is urged to consider the analysis from three separate ethical perspectives—teleology (good), deontology (right), and existentialism (authentic). By using this unique three-way ethical analysis, the reader assesses a particular dilemma in a more comprehensive way than by using only one theory or process or employing no conscious ethical stance at all (as is the typical manner in which most case studies are analyzed). The result is a better and conscious ethical decision that is good, right, and authentic.

The Seven Stages

1. Recognition of the ethical dilemma or cause. The first stage of the process is the actual acknowledgment that there is, in fact, a dilemma, and that it is ethically laden. If an individual perceives that an issue is in need of resolution, yet does not see its ethical nature, an attempt to solve the problem will go on without the insight of a conscious and comprehensive investigation of ethics. The problem is then solved with the decision-maker using an unconscious ethical bias. For example, as explained earlier, one may use, without examination, a teleological perspective to solve the dilemma. As a result, all the pitfalls of using this theory exclusively will befall the decision-maker (i.e., ends justifying means) and a relatively narrow resolution will be the outcome. Therefore, the initial stage in the process is an all-important one in order

Figure 6.1: A Process for Ethical Decision Making

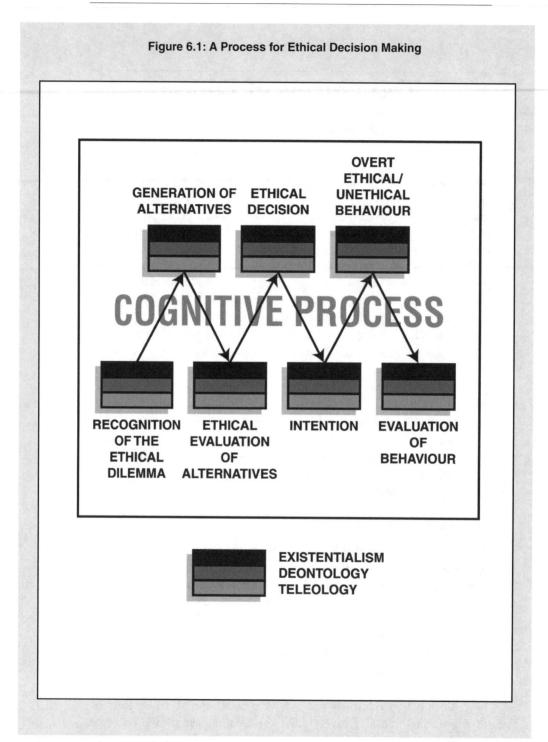

for the remaining six stages to contribute meaning to a good, right, and authentic ethical decision.

The *teleological recognition* will focus upon the degree to which the best ends are achieved for the group (utilitarianism) or the individual (hedonism). The decision-maker must assess the extent to which the dilemma presents barriers to the accomplishment of group or individual goals. The following questions may help the decision-maker in determining the teleological basis of the dilemma.

1. Does the dilemma prevent ends from being achieved for the individual?
2. Does the dilemma prevent ends from being achieved for the group?

These very simple questions provide the basis of teleological recognition.

The *deontological recognition* will focus upon the rules that have or have not been followed and the duty, implicit or explicit, which has or has not been assumed. The decision-maker may wish to ask the following questions to decide whether rules or duty are at issue.

1. a) Has a rule, a policy, a procedure, or a code of ethics been broken?

   b) Is it a bad rule, policy, procedure, or a code that ought to be broken?
2. a) Has a law been broken?

   b) Is it a bad law that ought to be changed?
3. What was the implicit and explicit duty of individuals in the case?
4. Was this sense of duty followed?

The issues these questions raise will provide the decision-maker with some needed information to determine the deontological aspect of dilemma recognition.

The *existential recognition* will focus upon the extent to which the dilemma has created a situation in which some aspect of the individual's authenticity is being restricted or denied. The decision-maker may wish to ask the following questions to determine whether authenticity is at issue.

1. Is there a restriction upon the individual's freedom to choose?
2. Is there a restriction upon the individual's freedom to take responsibility for action?

3. Is there an attempt in general to control an individual's or a group's behavior?

4. Is there an attempt to deny an individual's free will?

If any one of these questions can be answered positively then the dilemma has been recognized as having an existential feature. Eventually the decision-maker must address this feature through the choice of resolutions.

Through the perspectives of each ethical theory, the reader can discover a wide range of possible problems. Once each of these perspectives has been examined, the reader must then decide what, in fact, is the actual problem or cause. It may be that the problem is complex; a mosaic of sub-problems. However, the reader must detect which problem is the cause of the others. So often students analyzing cases make the error of identifying the first problem they discover and assume that it is, in fact, the issue to be addressed. Without careful consideration, students may choose a symptom of the primary cause rather than addressing the actual nub of the ethical dilemma. As a result, the analysis proceeds, the symptom is resolved, yet the primary issue remains unresolved. Therefore it is important that the reader is convinced that the problem identified is in fact the cause of all symptoms and not a symptom of a greater cause (cf., Malloy & Lang, 1993).

2. Generation of alternatives. The second stage of the process is the generation of alternative solutions based upon the tenets of each of the three ethical perspectives. The rationale, to reiterate, is to be ethically comprehensive at each stage of the process to provide good, right, and authentic solutions. The decision-maker must, therefore, develop plausible alternatives for the resolution of the dilemma from teleological, deontological, and existential positions.

The teleological position will be geared towards achieving group or individual ends. The deontological position will focus upon rules, policies, and duty. The existential position will contribute alternatives that involve free will and choice, responsibility and authenticity. The intent of this stage is not necessarily to be locked into a particular school of thought. It is quite probable and desirable that alternatives be composed of two or all three ethical positions, that is, alternatives that can resolve the dilemma in a good, right, and authentic manner. The reader may wish to generate alternatives from each position separately before attempting an amalgamation of two or more positions. Being locked into one ethical orientation may result in a constricted, rather than a comprehensive and rich, ethical analysis. This phase requires a great deal of effort and creativity from the reader, for it is from this stage that the eventual resolution to the dilemma arises. As Hodgkinson (1983) states, sometimes "he who does not hesitate [and reflect/examine] is lost" (p.104).

3. Evaluation of alternatives. The third stage of the process is the evaluation of alternatives. Each alternative is assessed, based upon the criteria of the three ethical theories. The decision-maker has to decide to what extent each alternative is good, right, and authentic. That is, does it accomplish the best end; does it follow or create a rule, a policy, a procedure, or a law? Does it allow the individual to be free to choose and to be responsible for all action? The alternative that best satisfies these criteria in the most comprehensive manner is presumably the ideal alternative to select.

4. Selection of the ideal solution. To restate, the ideal solution is the option that is the most comprehensively good, right, and authentic. The identification of the ideal or comprehensive alternative does not necessarily result in the use of the ideal solution. In any organizational setting, there will be many pressures and surprises that come up unexpectedly; the world of human interaction is often in a state of subtle or blatant chaos. These moderators, which upset the ideal or theoretical process, may influence the intent of the decision-maker to start the ideal solution.

5. Intention. One's intent, according to Aristotle and Kant, is perhaps the strongest determinant of ethical action. If your intention is to carry out an ideal resolution, then presumably and conceptually you will. Unless unforeseen circumstances that are beyond your control prevent you from doing so, the ideal decision will become the actual decision. If, however, your intention is not to carry out the ideal solution because of a variety of moderators (e.g., peer pressure, moral intensity, organizational climate, and culture or societal pressure), then the actual decision will differ from the ideal. For example, suppose that you have worked through the decision process and determine that the good, right, and authentic decision for a sport/leisure fundraising program is to prohibit funding from tobacco or alcohol sponsors. However, by doing so you will undoubtedly be the focus of the wrath of various powerful board members who demand a successful fundraising campaign whatever the ethics involved. Not only could you lose your job, but the organization will suffer, and some valuable traditional sources of revenue will be lost. As you have no immediate job opportunities at hand and your young family is dependent upon you, you choose not to carry out the ideal solution and opt instead for a weaker or watered-down resolution.

Figure 6.2: Summary of Case Study Analysis

THE MODERATORS

Individual: ethical orientation; level of moral development; demographic variables.

Issue-Specific: normative consensus; physical and psychological distance; magnitude of consequence; probability of effect; concentration of effect; immediacy, strategic/tactical orientation.

Significant Other: personal; interorganizational; extraorganizational.

Situational: organizational ideology; organizational culture and climate.

External: political; economic; technical; societal.

THE PROCESS

1. Identify the problem from each perspective.

2. Develop alternatives from each perspective.

3. Evaluate each alternative from each perspective.

4. Select the ideal solution.

5. Determine intention to act upon the ideal solution.

6. Actual decision.

7. Evaluation of the actual decision from each perspective.

6. The actual decision. The actual decision is, one would hope, the most comprehensively ethical decision. That is, it is good, right, and authentic. The actual decision is a function or product of the individual's discovery of the ideal decision, the moderating variables that will allow its implementation, and the individual intent to carry through with the ethical choice. The decision may or may not satisfy all criteria. However, this process has provided the decision-maker with the logic to consider a variety of perspectives that have ultimately resulted in a comprehensive and informed or conscious resolution.

7. Evaluation of the actual decision. As we have stated throughout this text, the decision-maker should seek to make good, right, and authentic decisions. At this point in the analysis, you must decide the extent to which the actual decision has met the comprehensive ethical criteria. Does it accomplish desired ends? Does it follow existing rules or have new ones been made? Does it allow for individual free will and the accompanying responsibility? If the actual decision does not meet each of the three criteria, can the decision-maker justify this less than comprehensive resolution? For example, perhaps a decision was made that was right and authentic, yet was not good. In other words, the decision followed the rules, was true to the decision-maker's heart, but did not accomplish the intended goals. Can such a decision be defended?

To conclude, we urge the reader to seek comprehensive ethical solutions that are good, right, and authentic. We also caution that such a comprehensive resolution may be difficult, if possible or desirable, to achieve. Figure 6.2 provides a summary of the moderators and process of this second model. While we believe that each of these stages of ethical analysis are extremely important, the reader is well advised to make use of those moderators which are pertinent to the dilemma or case study at hand. An example of the application of this second model is provided in Chapter 9.

References

Hodgkinson, C. (1983) *The Philosophy of Leadership.* Oxford: Basil Blackwell.

Malloy, D.C., & Lang, D.L. (1993). An Aristotelian approach to case study analysis. *Journal of Business Ethics,* 12:11-16.

7

Ethical Principles for Sport and Recreation

Two familiar and widely used terms, sportsmanship and fair play, have been employed as general ethical guides to influence the behavior of those who participate in sport. Often used interchangeably, they are meant to apply to athletes, coaches, managers, and trainers, indeed everyone associated with the sports contest. Both terms defy precise definition and are amenable to a variety of interpretations. These factors, combined with changes in social values, have prompted a number of authors (e.g., see the essays by R.M. Feezell, 1988; O. Leaman, 1988; and C.K. Lehman, 1988) to question their utility and applicability in present day sport. Since the sport contest is an arena for testing oneself physically, emotionally, intellectually, socially, and *ethically*, there continues to be a need to offer guidelines for moral conduct.

First, a disclaimer. There is no intent to discredit nor supplant the notions of sportsmanship and fair play. On the contrary, our aim is to strengthen these concepts since the presence of such behavior enhances the sports contest. Motivated by what exists in medicine (see Ross and Malloy, 1999, Chapter 7), we enunciate a set of ethical principles to guide behavior and practice in sport. Five ethical principles guide practice in medicine and also serve as standards against which behavior is judged. For sport, the ethical principles introduced later in this chapter are designed to promote moral behavior and can serve as benchmarks (ethical maxims) against which actions can be assessed. All behavior that is in accord with the proposed ethical principles can readily be subsumed under the headings of good sportsmanship and fair play.

Hardly a week passes without the media reporting another incident in sport that violates the basic concepts of sportsmanship and fair play. Both the popular and scholarly literature are replete with expressions of concern about what is happening to sport and the potentially negative impact such behavior is likely to have on children and youth. Many authors go so far as to call into question the future viability of sport. In recent years three books have been published that provide guidelines, which, if followed, would produce improved behavior in sport. Each one makes an important contribution but each has a limitation.

In *Right Actions in Sport: Ethics for Contestants*, Professor Fraleigh (1984) formulates a set of guidelines that apply to almost every conceivable situation in sport. He lists 30 guides, which frankly are too many to remember. More recently, two texts have appeared that offer their own guidelines. In *Sports Ethics: Application for Fair Play*, Lumpkin, Stoll and Beller (1994) focus on moral values as their guides. A somewhat different tack is taken by E.J. Shea (1996) in his book *Ethical Decisions in Sport: Interscholastic, Intercollegiate, Olympic and Professional.* The thrust here is the formulation of a method to aid judgment formation regarding the right decision or action in competitive sport. Without detracting from the validity and pertinence of the content, we find the treatment of the guidelines in both books too diffuse.

Prior to elaborating the four ethical principles we have selected—*promise keeping, respect for persons, responsibility/duty*, and *balance*—two tasks need to be addressed. First, a brief discussion of the two terms, sportsmanship and fair play, is presented to illuminate some of the foundational thinking and then to show why these terms are now problematic. Following that task, we turn our attention to delineating three different conceptions of sport. Once the three conceptions of sport have been outlined, the reader will be in a better position to see the applicability of the ethical principles to each conception of sport and, perhaps more important, where the greater challenges will lie in their future practice.

Sportsmanship. This is a vague concept that is difficult to define. Rooted in a set of lofty ideals that were more readily accepted 100-150 years ago, it requires athletes and coaches to behave in a way that demonstrates, by their actions, strict adherence to the rules as well as concern for their opponents. At least two components are involved, one concrete and the other more abstract. With regard to the former, abiding by all the explicit rules of the contest is an obvious requirement. It is in the latter category, the abstract realm of concern for one's opponent, that difficulties are encountered due to the wide variation of interpretations possible.

Sportsmanship involves an intense striving to win, that is, playing your very best against a worthy opponent but, at the same time, adhering strictly to both the letter and the spirit of the rules. When faced with the choice between using a shady ploy or questionable practice versus concern for the feelings of one's opponent, good sportsmanship would indicate shunning shady ploys and foregoing questionable practices. Such a decision is relatively easy to make when little is at stake. However, when great rewards are likely to ensue from winning, be it financial, fame, promotion to a higher league, or elevated status, the individual is really put to the test.

Many admirable qualities can be included under the heading of sportsmanship but that possibility seems to impoverish the term rather than enhance it. For example, Keating (1988) argues that

> sportsmanship is not merely an aggregate of moral qualities comprising a code of specialized behavior; it is also an attitude, a posture, a manner of interpreting what would otherwise be only a legal code. Yet the moral qualities believed to comprise the code have almost monopolized consideration and have proliferated to the point of depriving sportsmanship of any distinctiveness (p.244).

Any term that attempts to be so inclusive runs the risk of losing its cogency because it can be applied in too many diverse situations.

Another factor contributes to the difficulty of defining sportsmanship. Rosenberg (1993) explains that "sportsmanship is not a monolithic, unitary concept. It instead necessarily generates a plurality of relevant meanings and usages and a lack of consensus over a single interpretation" (p.16). A plurality of meanings and usages provides fertile ground for dispute and disagreement. Support for Rosenberg's contention that sportsmanship is multidimensional is found in an essay by P.J. Arnold (1984), who expounds the concept under three headings: as a form of social union, as a means in the promotion of pleasure, and as a form of altruism. Claiming a multidimensional character for sportsmanship enhances our understanding of the concept but, at the same time, creates additional grounds for dispute.

A comprehensive discussion of sportsmanship, one that is idealistic and rooted in the ethos of the nineteenth century English Public (i.e., in fact private and exclusive) Schools, is provided by Arnold (1984). At that time, character development was a clearly enunciated goal of the public schools (Rugby and Eton serve as examples). Although not explicitly defined, the educated young men (they were the ones who played sports in that era) readily understood what it meant to be a gentleman. Accepting that status, and the responsibilities imposed thereby, facilitated the understanding of sportsmanship as a concept and practice, one which included the virtues of fairness, honesty, magnanimity, courtesy, self-restraint, and a high sense of honor.

A much different ethos envelops sport in contemporary times. In place of the gentlemanly approach found in our English heritage, the current attitude can be derived from slogans enunciated by two icons of American sport. Leo Durocher, a fiery shortstop and long-time feisty baseball manager, maintained that "nice guys finish last." Clearly, if you want to finish first, you cannot do so by being a nice guy (gentleman).

More widely publicized is the slogan associated with Vince Lombardi: "Winning isn't everything, it's the only thing." If winning is the only thing, anything done to produce that result is justified. These slogans, and the values they represent, reject the foundation upon which the notion of sportsmanship rests.

The great emphasis placed on winning, on finishing first, seems to have eroded the notion of sportsmanship by creating a new set of values. This shift is described by Hoberman (1992), a perceptive observer of the contemporary sport scene:

> Traditionally, the rules of sportsmanship governed relations between athletes whose athletic abilities were less important than their honorable intentions, whose muscles counted less than their motives. The nineteenth-century "gentleman" did not approach athletic training with the single-mindedness of the contemporary lower-class "professional" who might even take drugs. This ethos of honorable self-restraint is by no means extinct, but it has lost ground to the modern fixation on performance and productivity that has come to supersede the ideal of fair play. In fact, the performance principle has virtually supplanted the ideal of "sportsmanlike" self-restraint in the prevailing ethos of elite sport (p.21).

A detailed account of sport's radical transformation in the twentieth century is provided by Professor Hoberman in his book *Mortal Engines* (1992). As his study progresses we are made aware of the evolution in how elite athletes are treated, changing from what was once a humanistic approach to a new conception of the athlete as a bodily machine. What was once confined to the elite level of sport can now be found at all levels.

Shortly after the Ben Johnson scandal (Seoul Olympics, 1988) the Canadian government appointed Judge Charles Dubin to head a commission of inquiry into the use of drugs and banned practices in sport. In his report he states that "as a society we have created a climate in sport in which the only good is perceived to be winning and the manner of doing so of no consequence" (Dubin, 1990, p.518). Comments by Dubin and Hoberman, along with many other concerned voices, attest to the need for increased efforts to remedy the ethical ills in contemporary sport. We agree with the sentiment expressed by Rosenberg (1993, p.22), that sportsmanship is a concept worth retaining. By presenting a set of ethical principles we aim to influence behavior positively so that future actions are in line with the noblest aspects of good sportsmanship.

Fair play. Similar to sportsmanship, fair play is an idealistic concept that is difficult to define. At the very least it means playing within the rules. Fair play rejects exploiting loopholes in the rules and abjures using shady or questionable ploys that produce an unfair advantage over one's opponent. Fair play involves a constraint on self-interest to ensure that every contestant has an equal opportunity. As such, consideration is given to one's opponent in the contest.

Fair play is derived from our English heritage. More than one hundred years ago the basic concepts of fair play were developed by "a generation of middle-class players who formulated the rules and codes of conduct of many games ... and did so on certain principles" (McIntosh, 1979, p.126). Given the ethos of the time, gentlemanly conduct was valued above winning and the relatively minor status ascribed to sport in that society meant the concept was readily acceptable. As time progressed and society changed, elevating sport to greater prominence and emphasizing victory, the notion of fair play was either relegated to a secondary position or altered radically. Where winning is the ultimate and dominant value, many practices that would have been condemned in the past, such as deliberately fouling, using intimidation and violence, and deceiving the referee, are now deemed fair (McIntosh, 1979, p.127).

Additional problems, at the theoretical level, beset the notion of fair play. As the term itself indicates, fair play is rooted in the concept of fairness. Determining what constitutes "fairness" involves a number of complex and subtle philosophic issues that are beyond the scope of this book. Suffice it to say that the philosophic literature on this topic is marked by a vigorous defense of a number of different, and at times conflicting, conceptions of fairness.

In keeping with the view expressed at the end of the discussion of sportsmanship, we are convinced fair play is a concept worth retaining. Its idealism needs to be promoted as a counterbalance to the negative practices engendered by the overemphasis placed on winning.

Three Conceptions of Sport–Models of Practice

A sports contest can be described in a number of ways: with reference to the level of skill exhibited; as an aesthetic experience; in terms of the excitement generated; as a successful or unsuccessful commercial venture; as a symbolic conflict substituting for war; as a venue for the display of bodily excellence (Weiss, 1969); as an arena for testing moral conduct (Ross, 1989, p.19); and, as a means of determining who won and who lost. Although all are valid descriptions—each one tells us something different about what transpired during the game—the range of possibilities has not been exhausted.

Another way to describe the sports contest is available, one which focuses on the significance attributed to process (how the game was

played) compared to end product (outcome) and the relative importance assigned to each. An account of the sports contest rendered
within these parameters facilitates the identification of values held by
the participants. At least two consequences ensue from the employment
of this line of thinking. First, this approach provides us with the elements used in detailing three conceptions of sport. Each conception is
also a model of practice. Second, an analysis of the sports contest within
this framework invokes the notions of sportsmanship and fair play since
these concepts are invariably involved when we examine how victory
was achieved. Such discussions fall within the realm of moral discourse.

By the manner in which they are structured, sports contests are
designed to produce a winner and a loser at the end of the game. Individuals and teams strive to achieve victory but, in so doing, a number of
ethical questions are raised but rarely addressed explicitly. What is the
proper competitive thrust in sport? This general question can be subdi-
vided into three more specific queries: How much emphasis should be
placed on winning? How scrupulously should contestants adhere to the
letter and the spirit of the rules? Does an emphasis on winning distort
the sport contest? Each of the three conceptions of sport presented
below provides a different answer to the questions just posed.

Conception I: Winning Is the Only Thing

"'Winning isn't everything, it's the only thing,' as a well-known rally-
ing cry in certain sport circles, leaves no doubt about the value
espoused and the forcefulness with which it is held" (Ross, 1987, p.269).
Acceptance of this viewpoint means that losing is equated with nothing
and hence has no value. Benefits only accrue from winning. If winning
is the only thing, then for the loser all potential benefits to be derived
from sports participation are dismissed out-of-hand since they fall outside of the category of the only thing. Health, social, and psychological
benefits, even financial benefits (think of the enormous salaries paid to
athletes and coaches of losing teams), no longer count where a literal
interpretation of the phrase, "winning is the only thing," transforms
everything else into nothing.

Fully subscribing to the view that winning is the only thing brings
inexorable pressure to bear since by losing the game one loses everything. Even without that pressure, due to the nature of the sports contest, there is something at stake when a game is played. As Hyland
(1990) points out, "it will always be tempting for a person immersed in
the intensity and passion of that competitive situation to push the rules
of the game, to cheat, to injure, and generally to `do anything to win'"

(p.35). That situation is exacerbated when the slogan, winning is the only thing, is adopted. Under this conception of sport, losing is equated with nothing. Since very few people are content to invest considerable time, effort, and energy into any activity that produces nothing as a benefit at the end, a strong rationale presents itself to justify doing anything to win.

This conception of sport focuses exclusively on the outcome, on victory. Since "winning is the only thing," anything done to ensure victory appears to be justified.

Conception II: How You Played the Game

Grantland Rice, the American sportswriter and author, composed a short poem that embodies a set of values that stands in sharp contrast to those espoused in Conception I:

When that One Great Scorer comes
To write against your name
He marks not that you won or lost
But how you played the game.

In place of a focus on outcome, attention is directed towards process, how the game was played. Abiding by the rules and concern for one's opponent are ranked at a higher level than achieving victory. Under this conception the notion "spirit of the rules" assumes a more central position since that orientation guides behavior along morally correct lines.

Within this conception of sport, victory is relegated to a secondary position, replaced by a greater concern for how well one behaves with regard to the letter and spirit of the rules. Process is more important than product (outcome).

Conception III: Mutual Quest for Excellence

Once the sports contest gets underway, and opponents strive for victory within the rules, they set challenges for each other. Throughout the ebb-and-flow of the game the situation is fluid, creating various scenarios that call for new responses. As these new challenges are met the contestants extend themselves, reaching beyond their previous levels to attain new heights. Viewed in this way, the sports contest can be seen "as the mutual quest for excellence in meeting challenge" (Simon, 1985, p.22). He adds that "excellence is to be attained through the response to challenges created by an opponent" (p.28).

Implicit in this conception is proper respect for oneself and for one's opponent. Proper respect for one's opponent means treating that person with dignity and integrity. Behaving towards others in this manner indicates that an opponent is treated as an end and not as a means. Treating a competitor as a means degrades that person's humanity and where such incidents occur excellence cannot be achieved no matter what the final score shows. In contrast, treating a competitor as an end is a morally defensible position, one that allows for the mutual quest for excellence (Malloy & Taylor, 1999). Additional commentary on the appropriate way to relate with others, teammates as well as opponents, will be found later in this chapter when the Second Principle, Respect for Persons, is elaborated.

Depicting the sports contest as a mutual quest for excellence encompasses a concern for both the process and the outcome. While the term *excellence* defies precise definition, there are some things that are incompatible with that notion (Kowal & Ross, 1999). Winning an athletic contest has been equated with excellence by James Keating (1978) who asks, "in short, can we, in any meaningful sense of the word, have excellence in a competitive engagement without victory?" (p.15). Excellence cannot be equated simply with victory; excellence cannot be applied to the winner of a contest where victory was achieved without playing well or where the opponent was so much weaker that the outcome was a foregone conclusion. From an ethical perspective, excellence cannot be achieved in victory if that end was attained by cheating or where rules were violated deliberately.

This conception of sport embraces both process and outcome.

Four Ethical Sport Principles

Based on the numerous, widely reported instances of inappropriate behavior by athletes, coaches, judges and even administrators (e.g., the recent IOC scandal), it would be difficult to refute the assertion that ethical behavior in sport has declined when compared to the standards exhibited in the past. Many observers place the blame for the deterioration on the overemphasis placed on winning, which now is identified as the dominant, or perhaps more accurately, the only, value. A number of practices, such as deliberately committing a foul, using intimidation to upset one's opponent, listing ineligible players on the roster, resorting to violence in order to gain an advantage, and explicitly or tacitly encouraging athletes to use banned substances, would have been condemned in the past. At present such behaviors appear to be excused if their use results in victory.

A speculative look forward envisages two possible diverse courses of action. One option is for administrators, educators, physical educators, and sports officials to wring their hands while uttering pious comments about the deterioration and claim they are helpless to change society's values. Predictable results will follow from the absence of action–further moral atrophy. An alternative is to renew our resolve to remedy the ethical ills in sport by striving to reverse the present trend. Simply staunching the decline is insufficient; a loftier target is required, one where moral atrophy is replaced by a constantly increasing number of ethically laudable actions performed by moral strivers (Malloy & Taylor, 1999; Malloy, 1996).

To assist in the achievement of this goal, four ethical principles are presented. A principle is a fundamental statement of truth, at times issuing from scientific facts and, at other times, emanating from philosophical concepts. Principles serve as universal guides. When a principle is adhered to, or followed, a specific effect is produced. With particular reference to the endeavor at hand, the four ethical sport principles are designed to serve as guides that, when applied, will help all decide which actions, intentions, and motives are morally acceptable and which are not.

The four ethical sport principles are both normative and prescriptive in nature since they indicate what is morally acceptable and also how people ought to act. Applied individually, or as an integrated entity, the principles selected will direct thinking along lines that will produce behavior in sport consistent with the loftiest ideals enshrined in the concepts of sportsmanship and fair play. Since there are only four principles, no difficulty will be encountered in remembering them. Furthermore, by concentrating our exposition of the principles in the forthcoming section, the discussion is located in one readily available place.

First Principle: Promise Keeping

Elaboration of the first principle starts with a consideration of the rules in sport.

The Function of Rules

Each sport is a creation of human imagination, the end product of innovative thinking. These activities, which have emerged over many years, differ in a number of ways: the terrain on which they are played, the equipment used, the standards used for determining competence, and the method of scoring used to decide who wins, to cite but a few. For example, baseball teams take turns at bat until there are three outs; water polo players advance the ball in the pool by swimming with it or passing it in order to get into position to score a goal; figure skaters have their routines assessed by a panel of judges; and golfers propel a small ball by stroking it with a club. As diverse as these activities are they all have one feature in common: each has a specific set of rules that govern play. All sports, individual and team, non-contact, contact and combative, are rule-governed contests. Indeed, the rules of each sport make it that sport and not any other.

Generally speaking, there are two types of rules that govern the sports contest, constitutive and proscriptive.

Constitutive rules. These rules guide play within the sport; they are the regulations that make a particular game what it is. These rules specify the dimensions of the playing surface, the duration of the contest, allowable equipment and material, what end is to be attained, and the permitted means used to achieve it. For example, the rules of basketball stipulate the dimensions of the court, the markings on it, the height of the basketball goal, the points awarded for goals scored (1 for a free throw, 2 for a regular goal from the field, and 3 for a goal scored from beyond a specified distance), and the number of players on a team. Included are the penalties to be imposed for infractions and rule violations (e.g., free throws, technical fouls, and ejection from the game).

Proscriptive rules. As the name indicates, these are rules that proscribe certain behaviors in each sport. For example, in basketball, advancing the ball by any means other than dribbling or passing is prohibited. In soccer, only the goalkeeper may play the ball with his or her hands and then only within a circumscribed area; any other player whose hand touches the ball in the field of play would be whistled for a violation. Contact team sports, such as football and hockey, have a number of proscriptive rules that serve to limit the degree of violence and reduce the incidents of injury. Blocking from the rear, chop blocking, and using the helmet as the first point of contact (spearing) are some of the actions proscribed in football. Cross-checking, charging, and high sticking are some of the actions proscribed in hockey.

Rules in sport, both constitutive and proscriptive, serve to provide equity for all participants; they are designed to create a situation that equalizes opportunity for success for all contestants. Rule books set down the conditions for winning, but these conditions can only be fulfilled properly if the rules are rigorously followed by all the competitors (Lehman, 1988, p.287). This matter will be revisited when the question of cheating and competing is discussed.

Two Presumptions

A player, entering the contest, is presumed to know the rules. This presumption must exist, for without knowledge of the rules that person would not know what is allowed and what is forbidden and hence could not play the game. It may not be necessary to know every rule of the game, for in some sports there are relatively minor rules that are rarely invoked, but for anyone to play the game a solid grasp of the main rules is a prerequisite.

A second presumption also prevails. By taking up a position on the field of play, an athlete signifies his or her tacit agreement to abide by the rules of that particular sport. Without this tacit agreement on the part of all contestants, the game cannot even start. Imagine, for a moment, if just prior to the beginning of the contest the referee asked the players if they intended to abide by the rules and received a "no" or "maybe" as a reply. Without this tacit agreement to abide by the rules the game cannot be played, at least not in the form intended by the rules.

Participants choose freely to enter the sports contest. Once that option has been exercised, that "choice obligates the athlete to uphold the accepted rules and to treat opponents in the same way that the athlete would treat himself" (Thomas, 1983, p.194). Freely entering the sports contest signifies an acceptance of the tacit agreement to abide by the rules.

Acceptance of the tacit agreement to abide by the rules imposes certain obligations on all participants: they "promise to fulfil a tacit social contract" (Fraleigh, 1984, p.137). Entry into the tacit agreement to abide by the rules occurs, technically, prior to the start of the contest, but is actually *a promise made to do so throughout the duration of the game.* This promise imposes certain responsibilities on the participants: Once I enter into this "social contract" I am required to live up to my end of the pact. Entry into this "social contract" imposes a duty on me to fulfil the promise I made; I am honor-bound to do so.

Playing fairly, abiding by the rules, fulfils the promise I made prior to the start of the contest. Behavior of this sort discharges the duty I undertook when the promise was made, and does so in an honest and honorable fashion. Living up to the promise made is a necessary condition for maintaining equal opportunity for all to succeed within the rules of that particular sport contest. I fulfil my promise to abide by the rules because it is the right and proper thing to do.

From all three ethical perspectives, deontological, teleological, and existential, promise keeping is the right, good, and proper thing to do. From a deontological perspective, fulfilling promises complies with a general social rule: promises made are expected to be kept. Teleologically, keeping one's promise has good consequences. Whatever the potential short-term gain available if a promise is broken it is surely outweighed by the long-term bad if the practice of promise breaking becomes prevalent. Existentially, since I gave my promise freely, I am bound to fulfil it; to do otherwise would be to act in an inauthentic way.

During the sports contest there are times when the rules are violated. Roughly speaking these violations can be divided into two categories: inadvertent or accidental and deliberate. What distinguishes between them is the intention of the contestant. In the first category, the infringement is unintended: in the heat of the game a basketball player dribbling the ball steps on the out-of-bounds line; a volleyball player mistakenly serves out-of-order; or a tennis player, rushing to return an opponent's drop shot, brushes against the net. In such cases the sanctions described in the rule books are imposed and the game continues. Since such acts are unintended, it is generally understood that the promise to abide by the rules still stands.

That is not the case when there is a deliberate violation of the rules. Such behavior is cheating and a different line of reasoning applies. As Professor Fraleigh (1984) points out, "cheating is [an] intentional violation which denies the implicit promise a sports participant makes in agreeing to contest, the promise to follow the rules"(p.73). Cheating in sport is promise breaking; it is also, at the very same time, an abrogation of a contractual relationship, one which was entered into freely prior to the start of the contest.

Intentional violations of the rules are instances of deceptive behavior. Deception is a deliberate attempt to mislead; it is fraudulent behavior. As noted earlier, prior to the start of the game all contestants enter into a tacit agreement to abide by the rules. Every deliberate rule violation denies that agreement and the commitment made, hence *it is actually a form of lying.* In a comprehensive examination of lying in public and private life, noted philosopher Sissela Bok (1978) finds no justification for such behavior. She concludes her investigation by stating, "Trust and integrity are precious resources, easily squandered, hard to regain. They can thrive only on a foundation of respect for veracity" (p.249). Lying is unacceptable behavior and, by logical extension, so is committing a deliberate rule violation. This assessment prevails within the three theories of ethics—deontology, teleology, and existentialism.

Deliberate rule violations destroy the vital frame of agreement that makes sport possible. A deliberate rule violation changes the nature of the event. Delattre (1988) states that "competing, winning and losing in athletics are intelligible only within the framework of rules which define a specific competitive sport; a person may cheat at a game or compete at it, but it is logically impossible for him to do both. To cheat is to cease to compete" (p.274). This important insight forcefully points out the deception involved, that is, promising to do one thing then surreptitiously doing something else. Victory can only be claimed, truthfully, by a contestant who has not cheated.

Even if the cheating remains undetected and the contestant who cheated claims victory, he knows how that was achieved. It is a hollow victory, signifying nothing, since the cheater competed under one set of rules while the opponent played under another set of rules. Under such circumstances the contest is not a test. Hence the cheater in claiming victory has proven nothing. A true sports contest can only exist where trust and integrity are found. For integrity to prevail, promises made must be kept.

Second Principle: Respect for Persons

An athlete is a person, a real, live, complex, existential human being. An athlete, as an entity separated from a person, is an abstraction, an imaginary being (Ross, 1994). When people play sports they are often called athletes to signify the nature of the activity they are engaged in, but that must not mislead us into thinking that when we speak about an athlete we are talking about something other than a person. Since there is a tendency on the part of some people to set sport apart from society it is important to remind ourselves constantly of this basic fact.

Human beings are by nature relational. No person can reach his or her potential as a human being (i.e., Aristotelian *eudaemonia*) by himself or herself; other people are needed to enable us to develop as persons. In sport, other people are needed—most games require the presence of another person, or many other people, as teammates, opponents, and officials. To speak of opponents in a sport context is to highlight the competitive nature of the activity, yet, at the very same time, it is a cooperative venture. Cooperation is manifested in the orderly fashion in which opponents line up prior to the start of the contest and in the proper manner in which they follow the protocol of that particular sport. Even when the sports contest is conceived of in purely competitive terms, the other, be it a single opponent or a team, is needed for the game to be played.

Sports are played by persons. A person is a highly complex, integrated being capable of responding to the environment in either of two contrasting modes: (1) with behavior originating in the psychobiological structures shared with lower forms of life, or (2) with behavior originating in the more elaborate and highly developed cognitive structures characteristic only of human beings, that is, self-consciousness and reflection. Human beings, whose behavior is governed chiefly by ideas, beliefs, attitudes, and meanings, are set above the other species in the world. Persons occupy a special place in the cosmos, one which commands full respect due to our humanity and humaneness.

Persons, as teammates in certain sports and as opponents in most games, are needed for the contest to be played. An opponent can be viewed in a number of ways: as an obstacle to be overcome, as a means to an end, as the enemy, as an end, or as a partner and colleague. Regarding an opponent as a partner and colleague facilitates the mutual quest for excellence for all participants. Unfortunately, all too often the opponent is regarded in negative terms, as an obstacle, as the means to an end, as the enemy. How the opponent is viewed will determine the nature of the relationship and will also, to a certain extent, determine how one's opponent will be treated.

Where winning is deemed to be the only thing, it should not surprise us to learn that one's opponent is regarded as an obstacle to be overcome. An overemphasis on winning leads to certain abuses, such as "a willingness to cheat, to hurt others, to treat members of the opposing team not as fellow human beings and athletes but as enemies—as objects to be defeated without respect or regard for their rights as human beings" (Hyland, 1990, p.3). Such behavior dehumanizes and denigrates opposing players. That process, in turn, seems to create a climate in which violent behavior comes to be regarded as an acceptable means to be used in the pursuit of victory.

This mode of competition leads to alienation, not only in competitors, but also in an increasing number of spectators who refuse to attend games or watch them on television. Hyland (1988) points out that there is another kind of competitive experience, one that is much different from that depicted in the preceding paragraph. Within this mode of competition, "our relation to our opponent can be that mode of positive encounter which deepens into a form of friendship" (Hyland, 1988, p.231). He notes that for many people participation in sports leads to the formation of friendships and sport is often used as an activity to enhance and solidify friendships. It is not uncommon to see a group of friends getting together to play sports.

Treating Other Persons

Sport, as a competitive activity, is a venue for human interaction. How people treat each other within the sports contest is one important factor in determining what is gained from the experience. Martin Buber, a noted twentieth-century existential philosopher, who has sometimes been called the philosopher of human relationships, addresses the issue of how people should treat each other in his famous book *I and Thou* (1954). He starts his book by offering a basic insight: "There is no I taken by itself, but only the I of the primary word I-thou and the I of the primary word I-it" (p.4). Two important lessons are derived from this cryptic comment. First, human beings are always in a relational mode, either I-thou or I-it; the I cannot stand alone, isolated. Second, two different ways of relating are possible, one on the level of I-thou and the other on the level of I-it. There is a basic difference between relating to a thing as an object which I observe, an "it," and to a person, a "thou," who addresses me and to whose address I respond in an appropriate manner.

An I-thou relationship is confined to human beings who acknowledge each other's value and treat each other with mutual respect and dignity. It is a relationship among equals where both behave in a manner that confirms the other as a person. An I-thou relationship is a genuine relationship where the persons involved relate to each other in a mutually affirming manner; each treats the other as an end in himself or herself, not as a means to an end. Each person's authenticity and humanity is affirmed and re-enforced.

In an I-it relationship the "it" is a thing and hence no mutuality is possible. An I-it relationship is characterized by the fact that it is not a genuine relationship because such a relationship is impossible *between* the I and the "it." An I-it relationship can involve an inanimate object or an animal and *it can also involve another human being.* An I-it relationship between two people is characterized by interaction in which the other is treated as an object, an obstacle to be overcome, a means rather than an end, as the enemy. When the "it" is a person, his or her humanity is debased and personhood is reduced to a status similar to other objects in the world.

Where an I-it relationship exists in sport, opponents are reduced to mere physical beings, in effect mere objects, a status that denies them their full personhood. Refusal to acknowledge and respect one's opponent as a person, thereby making an I-thou relationship impossible, places athletes, coaches, and administrators in the same category as racists and extreme chauvinists. In both these situations there is a refusal to grant full person-status, "thou" status, to other rational, adult human beings. A very subtle, but nonetheless powerful, message is conveyed: abuse, disrespect, and cheating are acceptable because one's opponent is an "it" rather than a "thou."

Countless sources exist that can teach us how to behave properly towards others. From the wide range available only two have been selected, one from the Bible and the other from the work of the influential philosopher Immanuel Kant.

"Do unto others as you would have them do unto you," the biblical Golden Rule, is an often-used directive to guide behavior. Following that advice entails taking the feelings of others into account since whatever is done must be mutually acceptable. As sound as that advice appears to be, it has one serious drawback. As formulated, the Golden Rule places the ethical standard within the person about to act. When that individual is a moral striver, one who is ethically aware and realizes the potential consequences of the impending action, whatever is done will, most likely, be acceptable to the other. However, when the person about to act is an individual with low moral scruples, or is somewhat naive ethically, the behavior may not be acceptable to the other. For example, if I believe cheating in sport is acceptable, that standard will guide what I do to others.

A different situation prevails when Kant's categorical imperative is applied. It states, "Act only according to that maxim by which you can at the same time will that it should become a universal law" (Kant, 1968, p.45). In place of locating the ethical standard within the person about to act, as in the Golden Rule, the categorical imperative functions as a universal principle. It is a principle of ideal moral conduct and also serves to guide moral judgment.

An additional component to Kant's categorical imperative bids us to respect each person as a free moral agent, as an end rather than a means. Since we do not want to be exploited by others we cannot exploit others by our behavior. An important feature of Kant's statement is pointed out by Osterhoudt (1973): "The rightful singularity of the categorical imperative as a moral principle entails it accounting for all conditions, all circumstances; that is, entails its necessity and universality" (p.285). It applies to all situations, within and outside of sport.

Kant's categorical imperative is applicable to sport and its principle of universalizability is a good criterion for justifying or negating various behaviors in sport. With regard to respect for persons, it serves as a guide to determine what acts are acceptable and which violate the notion of personhood. Under the heading of acceptable behavior, we list courtesy, mutual respect, and a regard for one's opponent as a facilitator (Fraleigh, 1984, p.89) in helping all contestants in their mutual quest for excellence. This list is not intended to be exhaustive; the items mentioned serve as examples.

On the negative side the list appears to be more extensive. Cheating is ruled out since no one wants to be a victim of deliberate deception. Harassment is unacceptable because it belittles the one badgered as a person. Intimidation, excessive use of force, and deliberate attempts to injure are prohibited because of the harm inflicted. This last comment raises a serious problem with regard to boxing. In boxing the goal is to inflict the greatest amount of injury on one's opponent. No matter how the activity is described, or what rationale is used to justify it, nothing can refute the reality that every punch thrown is a deliberate attempt to injure one's opponent. Under such circumstances there cannot be respect for persons. As noted above, this list is not intended to be exhaustive; the items mentioned here serve as examples.

An illuminating insight into one aspect of the sports contest is provided by Delattre (1988): "The testing of one's mettle in competitive athletics is a form of self-discovery, just as the preparation to compete is a form of self-creation" (p.273). In sports contests where respect for persons prevails, self-discovery and self-creation are facilitated. Under such circumstances the quality of the contest is elevated and the benefits derived by the participants are increased.

Third Principle: Responsibility and/or Duty

By taking up their positions on the field of play, sports contestants signal their agreement to abide by the rules of that particular sport. As explained earlier, that means the players tacitly enter into a social contract, one which provides them with a set of rights and, at the very same time, *imposes a range of obligations.* By virtue of being a contestant, be it in an individual or team sport, a "performance" is expected, indeed required, of each contestant. Such performances are assessed from at least three perspectives: skill execution, strategy employed, and the level of ethical behavior. Attention is paid to the manner in which each contestant fulfils his or her obligations.

Obligation, as a concept, is broad in scope. It usually encompasses two notions that are similar to it yet are somewhat different, responsibility and duty. I am responsible for fulfilling my obligations; indeed it is my duty to do so. These comments apply to all aspects of life, sport included. Since both concepts, responsibility and duty, are unavoidable in sport, further exposition is merited.

Responsibility. This concept generally refers to an overall thrust, or to an encompassing set of tasks for which one is accountable or answerable. Large segments of organizational and social life can be allocated as being the responsibility of certain people. As captain of my team I have certain responsibilities for my teammates and towards my coach. Responsibility is the concept used to explain the notion of agency that is invoked for the attribution of blame, which makes one liable for punishment or praise, which makes one liable for reward. Unless a person is judged personally responsible for some act or outcome, that individual would not normally be thought to *deserve* blame, punishment, praise, or reward.

People whose actions result from free will are held accountable for what they do. Sport, as a social institution is not, nor can it be, exempt from the notion of responsibility. Every participant is responsible for his or her behavior.

I, as an athlete, cannot renounce my responsibility to abide by the rules, nor can I delegate that responsibility to someone else such as the referee or umpire. It is I, and not the referee or umpire, who engages in the intentional actions needed to play the game and, as such, the concept of agency prevails. That allows for the attribution of moral approbation. Moral approbation is attributable to me because I am a person who is able to think, who can give reasons for my judgments, who can choose between alternatives, who can make decisions, and who can put into action the decisions made. In a word, as an athletic competitor I am an agent who acts and, as a consequence, is responsible for my intentional actions (Sartre, 1957).

Once I willingly enter into an agreement where other persons are involved, such as in a sports contest, then I cannot renounce nor delegate my responsibility without first obtaining their consent. If such consent were to be given in a sports contest, the game would be transformed into something else since it would no longer be governed by the original rules. But it is the original set of rules that makes that particular activity the game that it is. To hold a person responsible for something is to presuppose that he or she is a responsible agent. Entering the game, which signals the athlete's agreement to abide by the rules, validates the presumption.

Duty. This concept appears to be somewhat more concrete, referring to the things one is expected to do by virtue of having taken on a job or assumed some definite office. Once I become a parent I have a duty to care for and nurture my children. Duty is a more limited notion, one that is generally confined to specific actions and realms of behavior. As a coach my duty is to prepare my team for the season and for each game played. Duty is rooted in moral and legal obligations or in a sense of propriety. Duty ranks as one of the considerations, along with values and dedication to ethical behavior, which guide and constrain rational choice. Someone who neglects his duty rightfully deserves blame. Censure, if imposed, is usually commensurate with the degree of neglect, the importance of the task, and the magnitude of the consequences. Since duties are required, the actions taken when they are fulfilled rarely merit commendation. We reserve our praise for actions that are regarded as beyond the call of duty.

Applied to sport, I, as a player, have a duty to obey all the rules of the game. That duty emerges from the tacit agreement I entered into at the start of the game. Any time I violate the rules accidentally the sanctions found in the rule book are applied, but such behavior is not considered a remission of my duty because no intention was involved. A deliberate violation of the rules is another matter; in such cases I am definitely derelict in my duty. That kind of behavior destroys the original sense of trust that existed at the start of the game. Such violations are reprehensible acts that merit moral approbation no matter which theory of ethics is applied. Deontologically it is wrong because I unilaterally abrogated the tacit social contract I entered into freely. Teleologically it is bad since such actions create mistrust, a feeling that interferes with normal social interaction and impedes social progress. From an existential perspective such behavior is inauthentic since I reneged on a promise freely given.

Accepting responsibility and discharging one's duty applies to everyone involved in the sports contest. "Each [person] contributes some value to the sports contest by doing a certain kind of function.... Because that function is required, an athlete, coach, or athletic trainer each have certain duties" (Fraleigh, 1989, p.113). Although athletes, coaches, athletic trainers, and administrators operate in somewhat different realms, each one can either enhance or detract from the moral ground that pervades the sports contest. Whether I am an athlete, a coach, an athletic trainer, or a sport administrator, I cannot neglect my duty nor can I fail to fulfil my responsibilities. To do so breaks the tacit promise I made and shows disrespect for the other persons involved in the sports contest.

Fourth Principle: Balance

Balance. As understood in this context, balance refers to a state of equilibrium, a pleasing harmony among various elements and, at times, as a counterpoise designed to offset extreme influences. This conception is similar to, but more encompassing than, the notion of perspective. Balance, as a guide to ethical behavior in sport, means, first, that sport is only one component in life, along with family, school, work, social relationships, and other leisure-time pursuits. Attention and time devoted to each of the components mentioned leads one to a sense of the good life, in which fulfilment and self-actualization are attained in a variety of ways. Investing too much of oneself emotionally, socially, or financially in only one realm may bring great dividends at times, but in the vast majority of cases, it leads to disappointment and imbalance.

Within sport the issue of balance invariably emerges in relation to the emphasis, or overemphasis, placed on winning. Earlier in this chapter a number of questions were posed, querying what constitutes proper competitive thrust. How much emphasis should be placed on winning? Does an emphasis on winning create an imbalance in the ethos surrounding sport? Can the other values of sport be highlighted sufficiently so that a fair balance exists amongst them? Hyland (1990) argues that "putting equitable emphasis on other values in sport, for example, good health, the ethical lessons to be learned such as teamwork and sportsmanship, the friendships we gain, the fun we have, might be a first but decisive step toward overcoming the worst abuses of the overemphasis on winning" (p.37). An overemphasis on winning relegates the other values cited to oblivion. In place of a balanced view we have an unbalanced understanding of the sport experience.

Participation in sport enables contestants to learn about themselves. As they respond to the continuous challenges emerging during the game, self-knowledge is acquired along with improvement in skill execution. As Delattre (1988) suggested, self-discovery and self-creation are attained by all participants, winners and losers. A well-played contest, where the mutual quest for excellence prevails, provides the setting for greater self-discovery because both teams bend their full effort towards winning, but do so in a way that preserves all the positive values attributable to a sport contest. Phrased somewhat differently, there is proper balance present, not only between two evenly matched opponents, but also among the various elements that comprise sport. A fine example of such a case is the 1999 National College Athletic Association (NCAA) final basketball game between the University of Connecticut and Duke University. U Conn emerged victorious by a narrow margin, but every participant benefitted from a superbly played game. After such a fine display it is regrettable that one team had to be called a loser.

Winning does matter. Striving to win, doing one's best in accordance with the rules, is an integral part of the tacit agreement. One way to solve the problem of overemphasis on winning is to abolish competitive sport. Since this will obviously not come about we need to put winning in proper perspective, or in terms of this ethical principle, restore balance to sport. The overemphasis placed on winning is somewhat ironic; at the end of league play and conclusion of tournaments there is only one winner. The vast majority of contestants are then labeled losers.

Winning does matter but it is not necessarily the most important value. Although the following events occurred outside of sport, the activities were of a competitive nature and hence are applicable. One of the authors was engaged in a card game of War with his 4-year-old grandson. As the game progressed it soon became clear that Grandfather's few remaining cards would be lost, thus ending the game. The grandson voluntarily gave Grandfather a bunch of cards–prolonging the game was much more important than winning. A similar situation occurred some three years later. The card game had been replaced by Monopoly. The grandson landed on Park Place and Boardwalk, built hotels on them, and when Grandfather's token landed on the property, the grandson was in a position to collect all the money and win the game. Instead he gave some of his own money to Grandfather so that the game could continue. The old adage "By our own children we shall be taught" applies here. Going one step further in sport, Ross (1987) has argued the radical thesis that for the athlete, *qua* athlete and as a person, there are times when losing is more important than winning.

A Wider Context

Sport is one activity among a host of others in the lives of people. Those individuals who earn their living from sport are also parents, children, and members of a community. They have fears and aspirations outside of sport and enjoy other things life has to offer. Indeed, there are things more important than sport even among some who have been consumed by sport. One such person was Jim Valvano, former coach of the NCAA championship basketball team, University of South Carolina. In many ways he was the epitome of success in sport and certainly was committed, as they say, 110% to winning. At the height of his success, unfortunately, he was diagnosed with cancer (G. Smith, 1993). His picture was on the cover of *Sports Illustrated*, which also featured a quotation from him: "I am fighting to live." Gary Smith details the background and history of this highly successful coach and then describes the painful ordeal of the cancer patient. The relative importance of each emerges clearly. Whether it is called balance or perspective matters little since the message is so clear.

Questions about priorities, which is another way to approach the notion of balance, emerged dramatically near the end of the 1998 National Football League (NFL) season. Atlanta Falcons head coach Dan Reeves had quadruple bypass heart surgery on December 14, 1998. Four days later he was out of the hospital and back at his job, working to prepare his team for the next game. Two days later he was readmitted to the hospital with an accelerated heart rate. In this case the overemphasis placed on winning took precedent over proper recovery from major surgery. In the eyes of some the behavior exhibited by Dan

Reeves in rushing back to his coaching duties, despite the risk to his health, was laudable, but to others it was an example of unbalanced behavior.

A short time later another incident occurred involving an NFL coach. This time it was Jimmy Johnson of the Miami Dolphins. His mother passed away on a Sunday, but instead of flying home to Texas immediately to be with his family, he stayed with his team to prepare them for their forthcoming Monday night game with Denver. He coached his team Monday night, worked on Tuesday, then flew to the funeral on Wednesday morning. He left for Miami immediately after the funeral, spending virtually no time with his family. He didn't stay to comfort his ailing father.

A few months later a lengthy article on Jimmy Johnson was published. Journalist Le Batard probes into Johnson's personality and scrutinizes his behavior during the period of his mother's death:

> Johnson has sold his soul for success.... He hadn't been a good father or good son or good husband, because he was too consumed with being a good coach. Johnson has always been a football-first mercenary who didn't celebrate Christmas or birthdays, didn't care to see his sons grow up and even waived his first wife. That kind of cold made him a champion in football. It didn't help him much at his mother's funeral (Le Batard, 1999, p.D2).

After the football season ended Johnson had sufficient pangs of regret to prompt him to tender his resignation. Owner Wayne Huizinga refused to accept it and supposedly convinced Johnson to resume his head coaching duties. Johnson vowed to make time for family and other pursuits but that resolve quickly dissipated. He has returned to his former lifestyle where football isn't everything, it's the only thing.

Sport is a form of play, one that is highly organized at times but still, nevertheless, play. *Sports Illustrated*, in its May 10, 1999, issue, devotes its opening section to words of praise for mothers from a number of prominent athletes. Danny Manning, Phoenix Suns forward, pays tribute to his mother: "You taught me to love my family, to be kind to those less fortunate and that basketball is only a game" ("Leading Off," 1999, p.8). Hockey is the most compelling element of sport culture in Montreal where the fans agonize over every loss suffered by their team and respond with elation after every victory. On many occasions when tensions ran high, long-time sports columnist Red Fisher, in an attempt to calm matters, would remind his readers that hockey is a game played by adult men wearing short pants. The allusion to short pants serves to reinforce the view that sport, even at the level of the Nation Hockey League, is a form of play.

When emotions run high and tempers begin to fray as a result of some event or incident in sport, that is the time to pause and ask yourself, "Will This Matter a Year from Now?" (Carlson, 1997, p.45). That question may help restore balance.

Participation in sports competitions will bring joy and sadness, pleasure and regret, achievement and disappointment. Sport is an activity that allows its participants, and spectators as well, to experience the full gamut of human emotions. Contestants are honor-bound to strive to win, in accordance with the rules, but winning cannot be the only value. Winning and losing are part of the range of human experiences we undergo in sport. We gain from both, in a wide array of ways. A balanced approach will enhance the benefits derived and help guide us along proper ethical lines.

General Applicability

Each sport is an arbitrary construct, a rule-governed activity created by human beings. Each was originally designed to enable participants to enjoy an intrinsically satisfying, socially sanctioned experience at a comfortable level of risk. Satisfaction for all is only possible when everyone abides by the rules, when all participants adhere to the tacit agreement entered into at the start of the contest.

Most sports are structured along competitive lines, designed to produce a winner and a loser at the conclusion of the contest. However, it is important to "distinguish the conceptual claim that the goal of competition is victory from the psychological claim that the competitors' primary motive for participating is the desire to win" (Simon, 1985, p.45). People participate in sport for many different reasons. There are times when the goal and the motive coincide but those instances are rare when compared to the wide array of other factors that prompt people to play sports. Camaraderie, testing one's mettle, controlling weight, enhancing one's health, and enjoyment of an exciting atmosphere are some of the reasons usually given for sport participation. We can compete in sport for various reasons and still gain all the benefits without subscribing to the "winning is the only thing" view.

Four ethical principles have been elaborated to serve as guides for proper behavior in sport. Notice that the moral reasoning that explains the applicability of each principle to sport is not unique, nor is it limited solely to that activity. Each time any of the principles is abrogated an ordinary moral rule has been broken. If the four ethical principles sound like they apply to all aspects of life, it is because that is truly the case. Keeping promises, having respect for persons, carrying out one's responsibilities and doing one's duty, and maintaining a proper balance are moral guides that apply to all of life, sport included.

References

Arnold, P.J. (1984). Three approaches toward an understanding of sportsmanship. *Journal of Philosophy of Sport*, 10:61-70.

Bok, S. (1978). *Lying: Moral choice in public and private life.* London: Quartet Books Limited.

Buber, M. (1958). *I And Thou* (R.G. Smith, Trans.). New York: Charles Scribner's Sons.

Carlson, R. (1997). *Don't sweat the small stuff ... and it's all small stuff.* New York: Hyperion.

Delattre, E.J. (1988). Some reflections on success and failure in competitive athletics. In W.J. Morgan and K.V. Meier (Eds.), *Philosophic Inquiry in Sport,* pp.271-276. Champaigne: Human Kinetics Publishers.

Dublin, C. (1990). *Report of the Commission of Inquiry into the Use of Drugs and Banned Practices Intended to Increase Athletic Performance.* Ottawa: Canadian Government Publishing Centre.

Feezell, R.M. (1988). Sportsmanship. In W.J. Morgan and K.V. Meier (Eds.). *Philosophic Inquiry in sport,* pp.251-261. Champaigne: Human Kinetics Publishers.

Fraleigh, W.P. (1984). *Right actions in sport: Ethics for contestants.* Champaigne: Human Kinetics Publishers.

Hoberman, J.M. (1992). *Mortal engines: The science of performance and the dehumanization of sport.* New York: The Free Press.

Hyland, D.A. (1988). Competition and friendship. In W.J. Morgan and K.V. Meier (Eds.), *Philosophic inquiry in sport,* pp.231-239. Champaigne: Human Kinetics Publishers.

Hyland, D. (1990). *Philosophy of sport.* New York: Paragon House.

Kant, I. (1968). *Critique of pure reason.* (N.K. Smith, Trans.). London: Macmillan Publishing Company.

Keating, J.W. (1978). *Competition and playful activities.* Washington, D.C.: University Press of America.

_____. (1988). Sportsmanship as a moral category. In W.J. Morgan and K.V. Meier (Eds.), *Philosophic inquiry in sport,* pp.241-250. Champaigne: Human Kinetics Publishers.

Kowal, J., & Ross, S. (1999). Excellence in sport: Philosophic and performance considerations. *Avante,* 5, 3:18-30.

Leading off. (1999). *Sports Illustrated.* May 10, pp.6-11.

Leaman, O. (1988). Cheating and fair play in sport. In W.J. Morgan and K.V. Meier (Eds.), *Philosophic Inquiry in Sport,* pp.277-282. Champaigne: Human Kinetics Publishers.

Le Batard, D. (1999). The mellowing of Jimmy Johnson. *The Ottawa Citizen,* May 11, p.D2.

Lehman, C.K. (1988). Can cheaters play the game? In W.J. Morgan and K.V. Meier (Eds.), *Philosophic inquiry in sport,* pp.283-287. Champaigne: Human Kinetics Publishers.

Lumpkin, A., Stoll, S.K., & Beller, J.M. (1994). *Sports ethics: Applications for fair play.* St. Louis: Mosby.

Malloy, D.C. (1996). A perspective on ethics in sport administration curricula. *Avante,* 2:79-87.

Malloy, D.C., & Taylor, M. (1999). A qualitative inquiry of athletes' perception of the ethical climate in sport: A Canadian context. *International Sports Journal,* 3, 2:112-129.

McIntosh, P. (1979). *Fair play: Ethics in sport and education.* London: Heinemann.

Osterhoudt, R.G. (1973). The Kantian ethic as a principle of moral conduct in sport and athletics. In R.G. Osterhoudt (Ed.), *The philosophy of sport: A collection of original essays,* pp.282-290. Springfield: C.C. Thomas Publisher.

Rosenberg, D. (1993). Sportsmanship reconsidered. *International Journal of Physical Education,* 30, 4:15-23.

Ross, S. (1987). Winning and losing in sport: A radical reassessment. In F.A. Carre (Ed.). *Conference Proceedings. ICHPER/CAHPER World Conference,* pp.269-271. Vancouver: The University of British Columbia.

_____. (1989). Locus of responsibility: Ethical behavior in sport. *International Journal of Physical Education*, 26, 4:19-22.

_____. (1994). Sport sciences and the whole person. *CAHPER Journal Research Supplement*, 1, 1:109-116.

Ross, S., & Malloy, D.C. (1999). *Biomedical ethics: Concepts and cases for health care professionals*. Toronto: Thompson Educational Publishing.

Sartre, J. (1957). *Existentialism and human emotions*. Secaucus, N.J.: Carol Publishing Group.

Shea, E.J. (1996). *Ethical decisions in sport: Interscholastic, intercollegiate, Olympic and professional*. Springfield, Ill.: C.C. Thomas.

Simon, R.L. (1985). *Sport and social values*. Englewood Cliffs, N.J.: Prentice-Hall, Inc.

Smith, C. (1993). As time runs out. *Sports Illustrated*, January 11, pp.10-25.

Thomas, C. (1983). *Sport in a philosophic context*. Philadelphia: Lea & Febiger.

Weiss, P. (1969). *Sport: A philosophic inquiry*. Southern Illinois University Press.

8

Putting Theory into Action:
Case Studies for Model I

The Application of Model I

At this point in the text the focus shifts away from the more theoretical aspects of ethics to the practical side (i.e., praxis–putting theory into practice). The case studies in Chapters 8 and 9 will enable you to apply the knowledge you have acquired up to this point in the text. As you address each incident, you will have ample opportunity to engage in moral discourse. In addition, a number of questions to help guide some discussion are presented at the end of each case. These questions will not only guide the reader's own exploration of the case but they also will promote group discussion. As each case is presented there will be times when the issue or situation is described sufficiently to allow you to proceed directly with the moral discourse. At other times additional background material will be presented to provide an appropriate context or to draw your attention to certain factors or conditions that may not seem obvious or pertinent based solely upon reading the case. Brevity and relevance are the guidelines used to ensure that your attention is directed to the actual ethical issue involved in that particular case study.

In this particular chapter, case studies have been selected with the "five-step model" in mind. To assist you we have provided a sample analysis using the first four steps of the "five-step model." No judgment will be rendered; that will be left to the reader. In this analysis we will (1) provide a reasonably accurate account of the situation, (2) describe the steps to be taken, (3) indicate the need to explore the three ethical bases to determine which one(s) is/are appropriate for the ethical maxim, (4) provide additional information that may be germane to the situation at hand, and (5) lead you to the point where you may well be ready to take the final step and render moral judgment.

Example Case: Fresno State Hires a Head Coach

Early in April 1995, Fresno State College (California) announced the hiring of Jerry Tarkanian, a graduate of the class of 1955, as its new head basketball coach. Tarkanian is a veteran basketball coach, having spent many years as a coach at the University of California-Long Beach State and at the University of Nevada-Las Vegas, as well as a short (but unsuccessful) stint in the National Basketball Association (NBA). Tarkanian's tenure as a Division I coach has been marked by success (including a national championship) and controversy, including lawsuits and counter-suits with the National College Athletic Association (NCAA), the governing body for college sport in the United States.

Even before the contract had been signed, rumors began circulating about Tarkanian's recruitment of players for the team. According to an article in *Sports Illustrated* (Wolff & Stone, April 17, 1995)

> Don Marbury Jr., the brother of Brooklyn High School guard sensation Stephon Marbury, would be hired as a Fresno State assistant coach, and Stephon would renege on his oral commitment to Georgia Tech and follow Don to the San Joachim Valley; and Stephon's buddy Kevin Garnett, the 6'10" schoolboy star from Chicago's Farragut High with abysmal test scores but skills so sublime that some NBA executives predict he'll be a first-round pick in the June draft, would join them. (p.11)

Additional rumors circulated about Tarkanian's interest in three other players, Richie Parker, the Manhattan schoolboy guard who had pleaded guilty to first-degree sexual assault earlier in the year, guard Rafer Alston, who was attending a junior college despite being a chronic truant in high school, and "7-foot Mark Blount, a discipline case who, after drifting through six high schools, [had] committed orally to [the University of] Massachusetts last August" (Ibid.). All of the players named had at least two things in common: apparently excellent basketball skills and problematic histories that seemed to foreshadow future difficulties.

These recruitment practices were not new for Tarkanian. In previous college coaching positions he had sought the best players while disregarding their histories and academic qualifications. Tarkanian justifies his practice by pointing to the need to recruit good players. Talented athletes are needed to ensure a winning team. It appears that college basketball coach Jerry Tarkanian has no qualms about recruiting players who are neither academically qualified nor have the ability to benefit from a college education.

Fresno State had only had two winning seasons in the previous 10 years. To justify the hiring of such a controversial coach, "Fresno State president John D. Welty seemed to embrace the curious goal of providing quality sports entertainment for the community" (Ibid.).

In one sense the account just given would seem to be adequate for Step One, but more information is presented in order to provide a broader context within which to conduct the moral discourse. At least three additional factors merit consideration:

1. Division I college basketball has become increasingly more visible and is a significant addition to the major sport scene in North America. Commensurate with this growth has been an enormous increase in the amount of money available from television sponsorship.

2. There is a need to understand both the procedure used to hire a coach and the hierarchy of responsibility existing in a university. Generally speaking, it is the director of athletics, along with a search/selection committee, who is responsible for the hiring. Within the hierarchy, the director of athletics reports to, and is responsible to, a senior university administrator who is, most often the vice-president, administration, or vice-president, student affairs. It is important to note that the vice-president reports to and is responsible to the president of the university.

3. There is a need to discuss the role of sport in the university, be it high-profile sports, such as basketball and football, or low-profile games, such as badminton, squash, or soccer. What is the function of sports and games in an institution of higher education? Whose needs and interests should be considered when these activities are planned and organized?

Now that this additional context has been provided attention can be directed to three specific issues that merit consideration from a moral perspective. In effect three separate, yet interrelated, subjects emerge, each of which becomes the focus of attention of the three rounds of moral discourse.

1. Was it right or wrong, good or bad, proper or improper, for Fresno State to have hired Jerry Tarkanian, given his well-documented record of success, controversy, and known recruitment practices?

2. Since Jerry Tarkanian did not deny the accusations made, we can assume he attempted to recruit the players mentioned above. Given that he sees his mandate as producing a winning team, was he justified in doing what he did?

3. What, if any, responsibility does Fresno State have to provide quality sports entertainment for the community? Is the president right or wrong to identify this as the role for the team? As an additional challenge it would be worthwhile attempting to define what is meant by "quality sports entertainment."

Moral Discourse

Attention is now turned to the first issue: Was it ethical for Fresno State to have hired Jerry Tarkanian?

Step One: Obtain and Clarify All the Facts

This step has been covered, to some degree, in the information provided. Anyone having additional knowledge should contribute it now.

Step Two: Identify the Ethical Maxim

Recall that there are three major bases from whence an ethical maxim can be derived. Each will be explored in turn.

1. Deontology/non-consequentialism. Are there any rules stated or laws promulgated by a search/selection committee as it proceeds to hire someone for the position of head basketball coach? In contemporary times, in many jurisdictions, equal opportunity laws are in force, which means that race, color, religion, or gender cannot be a factor in hiring. No other rules or laws appear to be applicable.

What usually exists is a tacit agreement to hire the best candidate. Problems arise in individual interpretation of best, particularly where there are no educational-sanctioned or profession-sanctioned tangible qualifications. For example, a team seeking to hire a physiotherapist would require each candidate to hold a university degree in physiotherapy and membership in the national professional association, but no such qualifications exist for coaches.

Can "hiring the best candidate" stand as a rule? If the answer is yes, then it can serve as the ethical maxim, but if the answer is no, another source must be explored.

2. Teleology/consequentialism. For this ethical base the notion of the greatest good for the greatest number serves as the general guide. Would the hiring of Jerry Tarkanian, in preference to all the other applicants, produce the greatest good for the greatest number? Which categories of good are invoked here? Is there conflict or compatibility between the good produced for the members of the team, the good produced for the entire student body at Fresno State, the good produced for the institution itself, the good produced for the greater community, and the good produced for the coach? How can the intangible good produced for each one be quantified? How then can this calculus of good be compared to the tangible good as measured by the coach's salary or the revenue derived by a winning basketball team?

3. Existentialism. Authenticity and genuineness are the major features in this ethical base. That being the case a major question emerges: Can the hiring of Jerry Tarkanian be regarded as an authentic act by an institution of higher education?

Step Three: Time (Motivation and Intention)

What motivated the president of Fresno State to hire Gerry Tarkanian? What were his intentions in seeking out such a high-profile coach who was so well connected?

The second issue can now be addressed: Was Jerry Tarkanian justified in recruiting the new players named at the beginning of this case study?

Step One: Obtain and Clarify All the Facts

Already completed.

Step Two: Identify the Ethical Maxim

1. Deontology/non-consequentialism. There are rules published by the NCAA governing the recruitment of players. These rules include the specification of the time of the year recruiters can approach prospective players, the number of prospective players that can be invited to visit a campus, prohibitions against a wide variety of inducements, and the academic qualifications required to compete. In addition each institution would have a set of rules governing admission. These rules can serve as the ethical maxim. Not every situation, however, can be covered by rules. At such times the notion of the spirit of the law, rather than the letter of the law, is invoked. At times the letter of the law, as specific rules, are amenable to various interpretations; the spirit of the law lends itself to more interpretations.

2. Teleology/consequentialism. Without talented athletes the prospects of a winning season are very low. In order to win, better athletes need to be recruited. Implicit in this line of reasoning is the notion that winning is good and also produces more goodness than losing. Is this a valid view? If winning is good and produces more goodness and losing is bad and produces more "badness," then this notion can be used as a potential ethical maxim.

3. Existentialism. We may speculate that, from the coach's perspective, as he (in this case) interprets his role and responsibility to produce a winning team, his recruitment practices can be regarded as authentic behavior.

Step Three: Time (Motivation and Intention)

What motivated Gerry Tarkanian to recruit the players named at the beginning of this case study? What were his intentions in seeking out these individuals? Another question emerges within this context: Are his views and behavior compatible with our general conception of a university?

The third issue, Fresno State's responsibility to provide quality sport entertainment for the community, is now the matter of consideration.

Step One: Obtain and Clarify All the Facts

Already completed.

Step Two: Identify the Ethical Maxim

1. Deontology/non-consequentialism. There are no known rules that govern the responsibility a university has to provide sports entertainment for the community. This does not appear to be a viable source for an ethical maxim.

2. Teleology/consequentialism. What good will be produced by Fresno State providing quality sports entertainment for the community? Who will benefit from the good produced? Is this an exercise in public relations? If it is, how can the amount of good be calculated? What implicit message is being conveyed when a university undertakes to entertain the community with its basketball team? How much good will that produce compared to the bad produced?

3. Existentialism. Can the provision of quality sport entertainment for the community by Fresno State be deemed an authentic act?

Step Three: Time (Motivation and Intention)

What motivated Fresno State to assume responsibility for the provision of quality sport entertainment for the community? What is the intention of Fresno State in becoming involved in this area of community life?

This completes our quest to find an appropriate ethical maxim to use in each of the three issues identified. It has not been a simple task but the effort itself has produced some immediate benefits. Involvement in the quest has promoted a greater understanding of the ethical bases, along with a keener awareness of the moral dilemmas. Analysis is required to identify matters so that the most pertinent source is explored to find the applicable ethical maxim.

Step Four: Extenuating or Special Circumstances

For the sake of clarity each of the three moral issues will be explored in turn.

1. The search and selection committee. Jerry Tarkanian, a graduate of the university, is an unemployed yet previously highly successful coach. His return to Fresno State could be interpreted as a return home. Since Fresno State has had only two winning seasons in the previous 10 years the need for a good coach is obvious. Are these truly extenuating or special circumstances?

2. Recruitment practices. Due to the date of the hiring–April is very late in the recruiting timetable–almost all of the best high school players have already been recruited. There is an extremely small pool of talent left, yet in order to have a winning team, a requisite to justify his employment, fine athletes are required.

3. Is there any circumstance imaginable that would justify a university offering quality sports entertainment for the community?

Discussion of extenuating or special circumstances assists us in moving to the final step, rendering moral judgment, which you are now better able to do as a result of engaging in this step-by-step moral discourse as outlined in the model provided.

Case Studies

Case 8.1

Rulings, Responsibilities, and Consequences

During the second week of August 1995, the Canadian Little League Baseball championship tournament for 14- and 15-year-old boys was held in Port Coquitlam, B.C. The team winning the tournament would be crowned Canadian champions and, as such, would earn the right to represent Canada at the World championships in Orlando, Florida.

As hosts, the Port Coquitlam team was automatically accorded a spot in the tournament. A neighboring community, Langley, B.C., represented British Columbia and advanced to the finals against a team from Orleans, Ontario. Due to many rain delays, Orleans was scheduled to play three games in two days, one on Wednesday and two on Thursday, with the championship contest scheduled for 6:00 p.m. on that day.

Orleans won the game they played Wednesday, thus enabling them to go on to the two games on Thursday. N.W., the star pitcher for Orleans, pitched in the Wednesday game but did not toss in the first game on Thursday. In that contest Orleans beat the host team, Port Coquitlam, setting up the championship contest versus Langley, B.C.

Little League rules state that no pitcher can throw in consecutive games or on consecutive days during a tournament. Both stipulations apply before a pitcher is eligible to throw again in a game. Because the rain delays had fouled up the pitching rotations so badly, the Orleans coach and manager requested permission from the tournament director for N.W. to pitch, if needed, in the final game. Because more than 24 hours had elapsed between the end of the Wednesday game and the start of the championship game, the tournament director ruled that N.W. was eligible to pitch.

There are two versions of what happened. In one version, reported in the press, the umpires and the Langley team were informed of the ruling by the tournament director. In the second version, it seems that the umpires and the Port Coquitlam team, as tournament hosts, were told of the decision but the Langley team was not informed.

During the final game between Orleans and Langley, N.W. came in to pitch in the fifth inning, getting the final two outs to retire the side. Orleans then came to bat in the top of the sixth inning and one of their players hit a home run to make the score 8-3. At that point Langley protested N.W.'s pitching appearance, halting the game. After a 45-minute discussion, N.W. was not allowed to pitch any more. The game resumed, Orleans held on to win 8-7 and, they assumed Thursday night, the national championship and a trip to Orlando a day or two after that.

Friday morning the members of the Orleans team were informed that the protest lodged by Langley had been upheld by the president of Little League Canada and by the officials in the international Little League headquarters in Williamsport, Pennsylvania. That ruling meant Orleans forfeited the game; Langley was declared the champion and flew to Orlando to participate in the international championship tournament.

The request by the Orleans team to allow N.W. to pitch in the final game Thursday was approved by the tournament director, an adult sanctioned in that position by Little League Canada, and by logical extension, also by the international Little League organization. Although the tournament director admitted afterwards that his interpretation of more than 24 hours elapsing was incorrect–a full calendar day must pass–that did not prevent other adult officials (the president of Little League Canada and officials at the international headquarters) from ruling N.W. ineligible after his brief appearance in the final game. Approval to pitch was granted by a sanctioned official before N.W. entered the game yet the second ruling, declaring him ineligible, came after the game. The second ruling also turned victory on the field by Orleans into a loss after the game was over.

Questions to Consider for Discussion

1. Did the Orleans coach and manager act ethically when they requested permission for N.W. to pitch in the final game?

2. Did the tournament director act ethically in approving the request?

3. Did the Langley team behave ethically in lodging a protest?

4. Did the president of Little League Canada behave ethically in upholding the protest?

5. Did the international Little League office behave ethically in upholding the protest?

6. Is it ethical for youth to suffer consequences due to inappropriate behavior by adults?

Case 8.2

Challenging Authority: Who Has the Final Say?

In common with most regulating sports-governing bodies, the Illinois High School Association (IHSA), the state high school athletic association that supervises scholastic athletics in the state, sets limits regarding participation. In wrestling, schools are allowed to take part in four meets. In early February 1995, the IHSA received a report from a rival school that M.C. High, a school with a strong wrestling program, had competed in five meets, apparently violating the rules. Once the complaint was verified, the IHSA ruled that M.C. High was ineligible to compete in the state team tournament.

Bylaw 5.162 (*Sports Illustrated*, March 6, 1995, p.18-19), which governs participation, does not distinguish between varsity and junior varsity wrestlers. However, other (IHSA) "bylaws pertaining to the *minimum* number of events required to qualify for a state tournament specifically mention that those tournaments must be of varsity status" (*Sports Illustrated*, p.18). In its defense, M.C. High argued that it had sent only junior varsity wrestlers to the fifth tournament. As no varsity athlete had competed, the bylaw had not been violated since only varsity events counted.

This line of argument failed to sway the IHSA despite evidence that other schools had done the very same thing. M.C. High was banned from the state tournament; the original decision stood.

M.C. High went to circuit court, sued, and won a decision directing the IHSA to include it in the state tournament. The decision by the lowest court was taken to the Appeal court where the ruling by the circuit court was upheld. That decision, in turn, was taken to a higher tribunal, the State Supreme court, where, again, the original decision was upheld. Three courts now ordered the IHSA to include M.C. High in the state tournament.

In reaction to the rulings by the three courts, and rather than allow M.C. High to participate, the IHSA suspended, then cancelled, the tournament for that year.

Questions to Consider for Discussion

1. Was the wrestling coach of M.C. High right, and justified, in assuming that he could enter a fifth tournament using junior varsity wrestlers, although there was no specific written exemption for such behavior in wrestling?

2. How are we to categorize the behavior of the rival coach who reported M.C. High to the IHSA?

3. Was the IHSA justified in their ruling M.C. High ineligible for the

state tournament? Can that decision be sustained when we know that other schools committed the very same violations, were reported, yet went unpunished?

4. Was M.C. High justified in resorting to court action?

5. How do you categorize the behavior of the IHSA that cancelled the state tournament?

Case 8.3

Rules Are Rules: Children and Adults

Twenty tykes from Vaquero and Verdugo, communities outside Los Angeles, who were members of their respective Southern California Little League all-star teams, participated in a benefit tournament. The event was held to raise money for the community and to honor the memory of a local child who had died a year earlier (*Sports Illustrated*, July 24, 1995, Canada Edition, p.11).

Their participation violated Regulation IV-a, which stipulates that no more than six players from a Little League tournament team "may participate on another team except authorized elementary and junior high school teams" (*Sports Illustrated*, July 24, 1995, Canada Edition, p.11). As a consequence of this violation, Little League headquarters in Williamsport, Pa., ruled the players ineligible to compete in a forthcoming district tournament. An appeal, based on the fact that the players participated in an event designed to benefit the local community, failed to deter Little League headquarters officials from applying the rule as written.

In reaction to the ruling from Little League headquarters, both teams decided to forfeit their eligibility rather than replace the players who had participated in the charity event.

Questions to Consider for Discussion

From an ethical perspective the behavior of at least three groups merits assessment: (1) team organizers, (2) league officials, and (3) the players.

1. Were the adult organizers and managers of the two teams involved aware of this Little League rule? If not, on what basis could they justify assuming positions of responsibility?

   There is a second event that must be scrutinized: after Little League headquarters ruled the twenty players ineligible for the district tournament, what ethical judgment is to be rendered on the decision of the team organizers to forfeit their eligibility, thereby penalizing those players who did not violate Little League rules?

2. Officials at Little League headquarters applied the letter of the law even though the event was organized to raise money for a worthy cause. Was that proper?

3. Should children, even at the Little League level, where they can be as young as 7 or 8 years, be responsible for knowledge of the rules of the game? Should that responsibility extend to regulations about participation beyond their own league or local tournament? Should these youngsters be expected to know, and therefore obey, all of the Little League eligibility and participation rules?

Based on what occurred in this case another issue emerges that merits ethical consideration. On the assumption that it was the adults involved, and not the children, who made the decision to participate in the charity event, what ethical assessment is to be made of a situation that affects the children, since they are the ones denied the opportunity to play, though they were not involved in the decision that led to the sanction imposed?

Case 8.4

Residency Requirements for Minor League Hockey

For many young Canadian boys, hockey is the most important, and in one sense, the most glamorous sport. A large, complex organization has evolved to manage the many leagues and tournaments involved. At the apex of this organization is the Canadian Hockey Association, the body that establishes national standards and formulates policies that apply to all leagues under its jurisdiction across the country. Each of the 10 provinces and two territories has a provincial association that supervises minor hockey in its own jurisdiction. Another administrative level exists, namely the organizations found locally, in cities, towns, and villages, throughout each province and territory. It is at this level that local leagues are organized, supposedly for the benefit of the children who live in these communities.

Eligibility and residency requirements are two items among the many issues these sport-governing bodies address.

A story appeared at the top of the front page of *The Toronto Star* (March 16, 1995) bearing the headline, "Private eye stalks kids in hockey league battle," and the following subheading, "Parents outraged at eligibility tactic." Oakville is a separate municipality located just west of Toronto, the largest city in Canada. Toronto, as the most populous city, has the largest minor hockey league. From the perspective of some viewers, Toronto is the most attractive place to play, offering a more intense level of competition and a greater potential for exposure to the scouts from the National Hockey League.

An unusual situation evolved that merits an explanation. Motivated by a desire to ensure that all the Oakville youngsters who resided and attended school in the community played in the local league, the organizers hired a private investigator to stalk certain "suspicious" youths in an attempt to quash their eligibility in Metro Toronto: "The Minor Oaks Hockey Association (MOHA) tried to prove that five players, *aged 9 to 13* (emphasis added), were ineligible to play in the Metro Toronto Hockey League (MTHL)" (*The Toronto Star*, March 16, 1995, p.A1). Videotape evidence was presented to buttress the argument that, since the boys actually lived in Oakville, the Ontario Hockey Federation (OHF), the provincial body, should compel them to play for their hometown teams.

A hearing was conducted by the OHF to allow all parties to have their say. It was at this hearing that information about the undercover surveillance was made public. The parents of the five boys involved reacted furiously when they heard what had happened, claiming that their family privacy had been violated. Furthermore, they maintained, no deceit had been used, nor had there been any attempt to hide the identity of the teams the youngsters were on or where they were attending school. All five players involved "liv[ed] in Oakville and attend[ed] school there, but [were] allowed to play hockey [in the MTHL] because their parents [had] obtained court custody orders giving them Metro-area addresses with family members or long-time friends" (p.A1). At the hearing the fathers of all five boys admitted that they had agonized over the decision to seek custody orders, which costs $400, but justified the action on the basis that their sons really wanted to play in Metro.

Both organizations involved, the Minor Oaks Hockey Association and the Metro Toronto Hockey League, expressed sharply differing views before, during, and after the hearing. The president of the MTHL denounced the actions of the MOHA, asserting that a new low had been reached with the hiring of a private investigator to spy on children. For its part, the MOHA accused the MTHL of doing anything to ensure a position of dominance in minor hockey in the province of Ontario.

The problem of residency requirements and custody orders had arisen many times before. The Ontario Hockey Federation had prohibited the use of custody orders to meet residency requirements to comply with a recent Canadian Hockey Association rule, which states that no one can move for the sole purpose of playing hockey. At this point it seems pertinent to recall that this case involves boys aged 9 to 13.

A few days after the weekend hearing, the Ontario Hockey Federation ruled that since the custody orders had been obtained before the September 10, 1994, deadline the boys would be allowed to play in Metro–at least for the remainder of that season.

Questions to Consider for Discussion

This somewhat unusual case–a sport-governing body taking extraordinary steps to compel youngsters to play in its own league–provides us with many opportunities to engage in moral reasoning. The behavior of at least five groups merits ethical assessment: (1) the Canadian Hockey Association, (2) the Ontario Hockey Federation, (3) the Minor Oaks Hockey Association, (4) the Metro Toronto Hockey League and the parents of the five boys.

1. In our society we generally accept the view that parents have full jurisdiction over their children except in cases where the courts rule otherwise. If that is an acceptable practice in society, what is the ethical basis for the CHA to restrict parental rights by legislating residency requirements or forbidding the use of custody orders, obtained legally, that determine residency in the eyes of the law?

2. Two points merit consideration. How ethical is it for the OHF to abide by the CHA's ruling on residency requirements that, in effect, restricts parental rights? It is generally well known that many youngsters registered with teams in the MTHL reside outside that territory. With that as background information, what ethical assessment is to be made of the OHF ruling in this case?

3. Two issues need to be addressed within this context. What is the ethical status of the MOHA's attempt to compel boys in Oakville to play in their own league? What ethical judgment can be rendered on the decision made to employ a private investigator to spy on 9- to 13-year-old boys?

4. Given that there is an overabundance of boys within Metro Toronto who wish to play hockey, is it right for the MTHL to register players from outside Metro even if these boys have established residency through court custody orders?

5. Since the parents of the five boys involved each applied to a judge to obtain court custody orders granting their sons Metro-area residences, it is safe to assume they knew the residency requirement rules. From an ethical perspective, what can be made of the fathers' behavior?

Case 8.5

Post-Game Handshakes

A number of high school sports leagues in Southern California have eliminated the post-game mandatory handshake, reasoning that too often these handshakes touched off fist fights. Another reason expressed in support of the decision is that the lineup, with both teams facing each other, provided many opportunities for trash-talking and uttering insults and threats. Rather than risk additional untoward incidents, with potentially negative consequences, it was decided to remove the temptation by stopping the practice.

Additional arguments have been offered in support of the decision to eliminate post-game handshakes. Shaking hands after a game is not really a gesture of good sportsmanship at all. Compelling youngsters and teenagers to do something they do not really want to do makes a mockery of the notion of sportsmanship. It is a contrived action rather than a genuine display of goodwill and respect. Rather than viewing the handshake as tangible evidence that whatever occurred in the game is now history, forgiven and forgotten, the gesture is seen as masking true feelings and thus is hypocritical.

Those who support the retention of the traditional post-game handshake view it in a much different light, one that focuses on education and the inculcation of positive values. Youth need to be taught the importance of appropriate social graces that, in turn, leads to the modification of attitudes. Shaking hands after a game teaches the participants to respect each other in both victory and defeat and transmits a tacit message that what occurred in the game is now behind all parties involved. Shaking hands is tangible evidence of the acceptance of responsibility for one's own behavior. Shaking hands is also a gesture of cooperation that counterbalances the competitive element found in the sports contest. Life has both competitive and cooperative elements in it.

Deciding to retain or eliminate the post-game handshake has enormous educational and ethical implications. Many southern California school sports leagues have opted to eliminate the post-game handshake. That decision invites ethical assessment.

Questions to Consider for Discussion

1. What responsibility do league organizers have for the moral development of athletes?

2. Are there different responsibilities depending on the age level of the athletes involved?

3. What moral benefits, if any, will be gained by the elimination of post-game handshakes?

4. Were the league organizers right in eliminating the mandatory post-game handshake?

Case 8.6

A Padded Resume

One of the most prestigious appointments in U.S. college sports is the position of coach of the Notre Dame Football Team. Five days after being named to that position, George O'Leary's tenure ended with his resignation. He admitted having lied on his resume where he claimed he had earned three letters as a college football player and had a master's degree in Education from NYU. "In fact he never played a down for New Hampshire and he took only a few courses in NYU" (Author, 2001, p.32).

At the press conference when he announced his resignation, O'Leary defended his action by calling the misrepresentation "a youthful in discretion" (ibid.). In his younger years, he had "padded" his resume to enhance his chance of being hired to coaching positions. He admitted that these misrepresentations had never been stricken from his resume.

When personnel problems or difficulties arise at such senior levels, often the employee is given the option of resigning instead of being fired. From the reports reviewed we do not know if that is what happened in this case.

Questions to Consider for Discussion

1. If Notre Dame had practiced due diligence prior to appointing George O'Leary as head coach, the inaccuracies in his resume would have been detected. Since that, seemingly, was not done, was it right for Notre Dame to accept O'Leary's resignation?

2. From an ethical perspective, is the punishment of (forced?) resignation commensurate with the inappropriate behavior of padding the resume?

3. Since the misrepresentations referred to "non-events" many years ago that had no bearing on his track record as a football coach nor his ability to coach, how ethical was it for Notre Dame to expect and accept O'Leary's resignation?

4. Generally speaking, what harm, if any, can there be in padding one's resume in order to enhance one's chance of obtaining the position sought, particularly when it is assumed that many people resort to this tactic?

Reference

- Author. (2001). Great exaggeration. *Sports Illustrated*, December 24-31.

Case 8.7

The Quest for Records

In 1982 Cheryl Miller established a record for girls high school basketball by scoring 105 points in one game. Early in 1990, breaking that record was the aim of Lisa Leslie, a senior at Morningside High in Inglewood, Calif., and, at 6'5" tall, its star player (*Sports Illustrated*, Feb. 19, 1990, p.30-31). Lisa Leslie was considered by many observers to be the best female high school basketball player in the United States.

On February 7, 1990, in a game against an injured, overmatched squad from South Torrance High, the score at the end of the first quarter was 49-6. All 49 Morningside points had been scored by Lisa Leslie. At the end of the first half the score was 102-24, with Lisa tallying 101 points, just four short of equaling the existing record.

During the halftime intermission Gilbert Ramirez, coach of the South Torrance squad, met with his players. Two girls had already fouled out and another was injured, leaving only four healthy players available to start the second half. A vote was taken by the team in favor of forfeiting the game. Coach Ramirez then informed the referees and the opposing team.

That news upset Lisa Leslie. She approached Coach Ramirez with a request for his team to continue playing until she had scored three more baskets. This would give her sufficient points to become the new record holder. Immediately after establishing the new record, the South Torrance team could forfeit the game. They refused to comply with her request.

The referees allowed Lisa to shoot four technical foul shots, which were awarded for delay of game, at the start of what should have been the third quarter. Although she scored on all four attempts, giving her 105 points and ostensibly tying the record, league officials nullified those points, ruling that the game had ended officially at halftime.

Coach Ramirez was suspended by League officials for one game for forfeiting but that ruling was revoked. He was reinstated before his team's next game.

The behavior of at least four people merits ethical review: (1) the coach of the Morningside High basketball team; (2) Lisa Leslie, the scoring machine; (3) the referees at the game; and, (4) Coach Ramirez.

Questions to Consider for Discussion

1. Since one player scored 101 of the team's 102 points in the first half, it appears that the game plan devised by the coach was to feed the star player, making her the only one allowed to score in order to break the record. Is this ethical behavior on the part of the coach?

2. What is the ethical status of Lisa Leslie's request to Coach Ramirez to continue the game until she had broken the record?

3. What ethical judgment can be rendered on the decision made by referees to allow Lisa Leslie to shoot four technical foul shots?

4. Did Coach Ramirez act properly in allowing his team to vote to forfeit the game?

5. From an ethical perspective, is it ever right to run up the score against a weaker team?

Case 8.8

Is Lying Always Lying?

University of Michigan Booster, E.M., was indicted by the U.S. attorney's office in Detroit, which accused him of laundering $616,000 dollars from illegal gambling operations. He did this by lending money to basketball player Chris Webber and other stars (known as the Fab Five) on the 1992 and 1993 Wolverine Teams that made it to the NCAA final tour. Three investigations by the University, including a 1997 probe that banned E.M. from association with Michigan Athletic Programs, "uncovered little wrongdoing because players denied taking money or wouldn't talk" (Dohrmann, 2002, p.26).

However, when a grand jury investigated, some of the players admitted they took money from E.M., in effect, recanting earlier denials, according to their lawyer, Steve Fishman. "'Lying to the NCAA is one thing,' says Fishman. 'Lying to a grand jury is another. That's perjury'" (ibid.). According to sources Webber often complained during his college days that he didn't have enough money to buy dinner while Michigan made millions off him.

Questions to Consider for Discussion

1. From an ethical perspective, is it fair to offer "student-athletes" athletic scholarships that may be worth $20,000-$40,000 per year maximum, when the institution, as Webber claims, "makes millions off them"?

2. Since it is the college athletes whose performance spectators and the media pay to see, from a fairness perspective, what portion of the income, if any, should be allotted to them?

3. According to lawyer Steve Fishman, lying to the NCAA is one thing, but lying to a grand jury is another. One plausible interpretation of this comment is that it is morally defensible to lie to the NCAA because it is not perjury, but you had better not lie to a grand jury because the potential penalty is far more severe.

   Is it morally acceptable to lie to the NCAA? It is morally acceptable to lie to a grand jury? Can lying ever be justified?

Reference

• Dohrmann, G. (2002). A tangled Webber. *Sports Illustrated*, April 1, p.26.

Case 8.9

Unethical (?) Ethical Advice

A column, "The Ethicist," written by Randy Cohen, appears in the magazine section of the Sunday New York Times. Readers are invited to write to him with ethical issues, which he then addresses. An explanation and rationale are provided for the stand he takes so that readers can comprehend how he arrived at the judgment rendered.

On April 28, 2002, the following question appeared: "Preparing for softball season, I read a book on hitting that said batters can maximize their averages by aiming line drives right between the pitcher's eyeballs. I tried it and hit nine singles in a row but nearly hit the pitcher in the face every time. Is it ethical to aim at the pitcher?" (Cohen, 2002, n.p.)

This question was answered in a way that is open to debate. Here is part of Mr. Cohen's reply: "To hit a line drive deliberately at the pitcher's face is morally acceptable to the extent that it's physically unlikely. And that is a great extent indeed" (p.?) He then avows that hitting a pitched ball is the single most difficult thing to do in sport. "To place your hits precisely is still harder. Thus, by aiming at the pitcher, you have no intent and little likelihood of doing harm; you are simply employing a visualization technique to improve your batting. And nothing in softball forbids hitting one up the middle" (p.?).

Additional elaboration is provided. Players entering a sport contest implicitly accept a degree of risk (supposedly mitigating the deliberate intent to aim at the pitcher's face). Various tactics used in other sports serve as examples of the range of risks. He then notes that in tennis it is legitimate to hit a ball directly at your opponent to win a point. Mr. Cohen draws a moral distinction between being hit by a tennis ball and a softball due to the damage that can be inflicted. "By you becoming [sic] so good at placing your hits that you could knock one into the pitcher's face on command, you would have to forswear this tactic. The moral stricture against doing harm would supersede the rules of the game" (n.p.). In another words, if you are a poor hitter, it is morally acceptable to aim for the pitcher's face, but if you are an excellent batter," if you really can hit with such precision, aim a little higher physically and ethically: place your hits just over the pitcher's head and swing for the fences" (n.p.).

Questions to Consider for Discussion

1. Is it ethical for the author of the book on hitting to advise readers to aim for the pitcher's faces?

2. Is it ethical for any batter to aim for the pitcher's face?

3. If it is ethical to advise a batter to aim for the pitcher's face, and the advice is heeded, how can the intent to harm not be present?

4. How valid is the argument that it is highly unlikely to occur in maintaining it is ethical to aim for the pitcher's face?

5. How valid is the final position taken by the ethical advisor that, if you are a poor hitter, it is ethical to aim at the pitcher's face, but if you are an excellent batter and can hit with precision, it is unethical to do so?

Reference

- Cohen, R. (2002). The ethicist: Swing away. *New York Times,* Magazine section, April 28.

Case 8.10

Health Risk and Sport Participation

A.B., the star linebacker at BTU, who has established records for the most single-season and career tackles for linebackers, is about to enter his senior year. There are questions about his health status; serious concerns have been raised about his continued participation in football due to the potential risk involved.

During spring training following his junior year he lay paralyzed on the turf after a tackle but recovered shortly afterwards. On many prior occasions following tackles he has felt numbness in both arms and hands. That feeling was much different from a stinger, or burner, which creates a tingling sensation in one arm or the other due to extreme pressure on a nerve. To determine the cause of the numbness, A.B. was referred to a neurosurgeon.

Following a thorough examination involving X-ray and magnetic resonance imaging (MRI), which produces an image of bone and soft tissue such as muscles and nerves, the assessment made was that of spinal stenosis, a narrower than normal spinal canal. Based on that assessment the neurosurgeon recommended that A.B. not play football due to the increased risk involved. Aware of the disappointment his recommendation caused, the neurosurgeon suggested obtaining a second opinion. Another neurosurgeon, in a city some distance away, was consulted. This physician confirmed the assessment and concurred with the recommendation to stop playing football. At that point it appeared that A.B.'s football career was finished.

Shortly after that, the head football trainer attended a meeting of the National Athletic Trainers Association. There he heard a presentation by an orthopaedic surgeon, an expert on cervical spinal stenosis, who claimed that men with that condition were not necessarily in any more danger of paralysis than those with normal spinal columns. Some medical research was cited to support his position along with the explanation that paralysis due to football injury was caused by improper tackling technique, head first (now penalized as spearing), and when that happened the diameter of the spinal column was irrelevant. This information was conveyed to A.B., who now had some basis for a possible return to the football team for his senior year.

As the season approached, A.B. started leaning more towards playing. He had maintained game level fitness by training in the gym with his teammates. Head coach J.M., who obviously would welcome him back, exerted no pressure, stating he would accept the decision made by A.B. and his parents. N.P., the director of athletics, became involved as well because the school has certain responsibilities in such cases and the legal liability aspect merited consideration. After discussing the matter with A.B., the director of athletics concurred with the stand taken by the head coach.

Another doctor, one of the BTU's team physicians, considered forbidding A.B. to play but ultimately left the decision to the athlete himself.

A.B., a young man of 23, discussed the matter with his parents who agreed with his decision to play in his senior year. His love of the game was the deciding factor. When the season started A.B. was at his usual linebacker position. In the third-to-last game of the season, he made a tackle, fell to the turf, and lay still, paralyzed. He was transported to the hospital where he spent three days. During this time both sensation and movement returned. A.B. decided to forego the final two games in the schedule.

Questions to Consider for Discussion

Every football player, indeed every athlete, accepts some risk when entering the sports contest. When does that risk become unacceptable? This basic query provokes a series of additional questions.

1. Who should make the decision that the level of risk is unacceptable? In this case, should the decision have been left to the student?

2. From a broader perspective the question can be posed: What rights does a student-athlete have?

3. Who should be authorized to forbid a student to play because of health risks? Should it be the physician? If yes, what happens if there is a divergence of opinions? Should it be the coach? Can a coach make an unbiased decision? Should it be the director of athletics?

4. Can a young man, one who has played football for more than half his life in an environment where football is exalted, make an "unbiased" decision?

Case 8.11

Acts of Commission, Acts of Omission

Thousands of spectators sitting in the aquatic stadium in Seoul, South Korea, and countless millions around the world watching on television gasped collectively as U.S. Olympic diver, Greg Louganis, hit his head on the diving board while attempting a reverse two-and-a-half pike during the 1988 Olympic Games. Louganis, a double gold medal winner at both the 1984 and 1988 Olympic Games, split his head open enough to require stitches. As he plunged into the water his blood dripped into the pool.

After he climbed out of the pool, Louganis said nothing as his bleeding wound was stitched up by a U.S. team physician who was not wearing latex gloves. Neither did he say anything to the organizers of the meet. It was only seven years later, during an interview on a U.S. national television network, that this silence assumed ominous significance. Louganis, who was on television to promote his soon-to-be-released autobiography, admitted that he had AIDS. He also admitted that at the time of his ill-fated dive he knew he was HIV positive.

Louganis recounted how he had been paralyzed with fear after the accident, aware that the blood he shed into the pool contained the virus. His failure to speak up might readily be regarded as an act of omission. His silence potentially put the health of the physician who stitched him up and the health of all other divers in the competition at risk. Further, any other person who might have entered the pool was also put at risk.

Questions to Consider for Discussion

1. From an ethical perspective, in terms of an act of omission—the silence of Greg Louganis—how do we assess his behavior

    a) in actually competing in the Olympics while knowing he was HIV positive, thus posing a risk to others?

    b) in not informing the U.S. team physician about to stitch his bleeding wound without wearing latex gloves?

    c) in not informing the organizers of the competition?

2. After these issues have been addressed, it would be worthwhile to extend the moral discourse one step further to examine the existing situation. Now, in Canada, athletes are asked, but not compelled, to provide medical information to sports officials. Would it be ethical to compel athletes to reveal personal medical information? Should there be one set of rules for the disclosure of non-communicable diseases and another set of rules for the disclosure of communicable diseases? What ethical rationale can be presented to support your stand?

Case 8.12

Medical Care, Medical Business, and the NFL

Medical care in the United States is regarded, in many ways, as just an other business, where services are rendered for a fee and profit is expected. While it is true that most of the American population, but not all, has medical insurance that remunerates physicians and surgeons and pays for hospital care, the realm of medicine operates as much by a business ethos as by appropriate medical treatment. Fee-for-service is the usual arrangement. Physicians and surgeons are paid based on each procedure performed.

Since physicians and surgeons earn their income based on the services they render, it follows that those who render more services will generate greater incomes. Continuing in a business vein, physicians and surgeons "compete" for patients; those who attract the most patients have the busiest practices resulting in the highest incomes. A similar scenario applies to hospitals. Other than referrals from other physicians and surgeons, or recommendations from patients who tell their friends and neighbors about a particular medical practitioner, the number of avenues available to attract new patients is limited.

One way of attracting new patients is through media exposure, in particular through unpaid media appearances. Each professional sport team has at least one physician attending at all games. Whenever there is an injury to an athlete the person most often interviewed is the team physician. It is the physician who explains the nature and extent of the injury, and who predicts a date of return to action by the player. Due to the intense publicity that accompanies the appointment of the team physician "doctors and hospitals are willing to pay handsomely to become a team's `official health-care provider'" (Author, 1995, p.12).

There are reports that both NFL 1995 expansion teams, the Carolina Panthers and the Jacksonville Jaguars, have encouraged a bidding war among medical professionals interested in working for their respective teams. In their solicitation of proposals the teams invited the prospective bidders to state what funds they would make available for the purchase of such things as executive suites, radio and television commercials, advertising signs in the stadium and program ads (Author, 1995, p.12). It appears that the qualifications and experience of the medical practitioners who would attend the injured players are relegated to a secondary position.

It is reported by *Sports Illustrated* (Author, 1995, p.12) that the group that won the Panthers' contract was committed to donating medical supplies and X-ray equipment worth some $400,000 to the team beyond providing medical services at a predetermined (managed-care) rate. Winning the contract must produce lucrative results if the magnitude of another bid is calculated. "In Jacksonville one medical group's bid of $4.8 million over five years–and its commitment to pay the salaries of the three Jaguar trainers and to buy at least $500,000 a year in advertising–wasn't deemed good enough" (ibid.). Imagine how much that medical group expected to garner in fees and hospital charges–from the team and from other patients in the wider community who would be drawn to them due to the publicity–if they were willing to spend more than $2,000,000 per year during the life of the contract.

With the focus almost entirely on the business side, questions must be raised about the attention devoted to the medical side. Football is a violent game, more so at the level of the NFL where all the players are big, strong, and fast. Injuries occur frequently since there is considerable body contact on every play. Where business factors appear to outweigh the qualifications of the medical practitioners and the proximity of the hospital one can safely assert that the priorities are skewed.

Questions to Consider for Discussion

1. Should the same procedure be used, that is, open tendering, to acquire medical services as the process used for the acquisition of all other goods and services (e.g., team uniforms, travel agency service and hotel accommodations in cities where away games are scheduled)?

2. At least three groups merit having their behavior examined from an ethical perspective: (1) NFL teams, (2) medical groups, and (3) the NFL.

   a) Is it proper for NFL teams (or any other teams) to invite bids from medical and hospital groups who want to provide these services to the team? What is the ethical status of the team when it stipulates that the proposal must include a declaration of funds committed to sponsorships?

   b) Should medical groups (physicians and hospitals) become involved in bidding to provide services to NFL teams? Donating medical equipment, paying trainers' salaries, and purchasing advertising adds to the overhead of running a medical practice and operating a hospital. Since most hospitals in the U.S.A. are privately owned, the costs just cited must be recouped by charging all patients higher fees. Is this fair?

   c) Does the NFL have a moral responsibility to regulate these matters?

Reference

• Author. (1995). Scorecard. *Sports Illustrated*, May 8.

Case 8.13

Professional Tennis Age Restrictions

In September 1994, the Women's Tennis Association (WTA), the organizing and ruling body for women's professional tennis, announced new age restrictions, effective January 1, 1995. These new rules prevent girls under 18 years of age from becoming full-time professionals. Fourteen-year-old girls will be prohibited from regular participation in tour events, while players aged 15 to 17 will be phased in on a gradual basis.

These rules were enacted because of many unhappy events in the recent past and the presence of two young players, both only 14 years old, about to turn pro. There are sufficient cases of young girls who turned pro and then suffered serious injuries (Tracy Austin and Andrea Jaeger) or encountered serious psychological problems

(Jennifer Capriati) for the WTA to take action. In effect, the new rules, hopefully, will prevent future problems of this nature.

Not everyone agrees with these new rules. The International Management Group (IMG) signed Martina Hingis to a five-year contract when she was only 12 years old. IMG has already obtained endorsement contracts for her with a sporting goods manufacturer, a designer clothing line, and an automobile maker. A considerable amount of money is involved, not only for Martina Hingis but also, obviously, for IMG Furthermore, if a player is good enough to compete at a higher level, despite being younger, why should she be prevented from doing so? It is only by testing oneself against better players that an athlete will improve. Competing against those who are better helps an athlete really develop her potential.

Questions to Consider for Discussion

1. Is it ethical for the Women's Tennis Association to have age-limiting rules that prevent players from competing in tournaments where they can earn considerable money? If a player has the ability to beat other players on the tour, why should she be prevented from playing, improving her game, and earning money simply because she has not yet reached a certain age?

2. Is it ethical for the IMG to sign a contract with an athlete who is only 12 years old?

Case 8.14

Employees, Unions, Sponsors, and Sport Teams

Employees, whether blue-collar or white-collar workers, professionals, or athletes in major league sports such as baseball, hockey, basketball, and football, form unions. The formation of unions protects individual employees and enhances their bargaining power. Unions, as a group, are better able to deal with management than individual employees regarding many aspects of employment.

Cheer leaders are, in one sense, only an adjunct to the actual sports contest, yet in another sense they are an integral part of the sport event itself. Cheer leaders add color and excitement, promote more spirit, and, in general, help make the game a more enjoyable experience for the spectators. Cheer leaders are often seen at basketball and football games. Very often the cheer-leading squad is sponsored by some business group other than the team.

"The Buffalo Bills, the cheer-leading squad allied with the NFL's Buffalo Bills, voted to unionize in their blue-collar hometown" (Author, 1995, p.16). In response to that decision, the local fast-food company refused to renew its sponsorship of the squad. That did not necessarily mean the end of cheer leaders at Buffalo Bills home games. Very shortly after that, in a second move, the Buffalo Bills announced the signing of a three-year contract with two other companies who will be sponsoring an all-new cheer-leading team. In effect, the members of the cheer-leading team who unionized were fired for their effort.

Questions to Consider for Discussion

1. Was the fast-food company justified in its refusal to renew its sponsorship of the Buffalo Bills simply because they had formed a union?

2. Did the management of the Buffalo Bills behave ethically when they signed a deal with two other companies as sponsors of an all-new cheer leading group?

Reference

- Author. (1995). Shop stewardess. *Sports Illustrated*, August 14.

Case 8.15

To Bet or Not To Bet on Track and Field

Track and field meets are often very exciting spectacles featuring a variety of demanding events requiring, at various times, speed, endurance, strength, skill, and strategy. Many would argue that track and field is the foundational sport since its events encompass the basic skills found in most of the other sports.

From the competitive aspect, according to *Sports Illustrated,* "the U.S. remains the most powerful track and field nation in the world" (Author, 1995, p.13). Despite that distinction attendance at meets has been declining, sometimes so precipitously that some longstanding events have been cancelled. Commensurate with declining attendance at meets has been a decrease in television coverage.

Spurred by these sad developments, the U.S.A. Track & Field (USATF), the sport's national governing body, secured sponsorship from three major corporations for a series of five indoor meets to be held on consecutive weekends during the months of February and March of 1995. Along with the sponsorships was a contract from a major American television network to broadcast the meets. To this point matters are routine and follow a generally accepted pattern, and therefore provoke almost no interest in the ethics involved.

A subsequent step was taken, however, one that certainly invokes the need for ethical assessment. Just before the second event in the series, a meet to be held in Reno, Nevada, where gambling and bookmaking is legal, the USTFA announced "that it had persuaded the Eldorado Race and Sports Book in Reno to take action on the meet" (Editorial, 1995, p.13). A line was set on 8 of the 16 events. Betting on the outcome of various events, be it the sprints, middle- or long-distance races or the jumps, was not only allowed but, in effect, encouraged. The introduction of betting was justified based on the need to make track and field more entertaining, thereby attracting more fans.

As a precautionary measure, to protect the integrity of the meet, "the USATF required all athletes to sign a statement saying they would not place any bets, even on themselves" (Editorial, 1995, p.13).

All major sports leagues, including the NBA, NHL, NFL, and Major League Baseball (MLB), have clear, strong, explicit statements forbidding their athletes from betting on games. None of these leagues would agree to have authorized bookies, such as those found in Nevada, become involved in their games. While it is accurate to say that various Sports Book operations in Nevada set the odds for games played in the NBA, NHL, NFL and MLB, it is done without the consent or cooperation of the leagues.

Questions to Consider for Discussion

1. From an ethical perspective what assessment is to be made of the behavior of the USATF in persuading the Eldorado Race and Sports Book to handicap various events in the Reno meet?

2. What ethical assessment is to be made of the USATF action that has the effect of encouraging betting on events in track and field meets?

Reference

- Editorial. (1995). On track betting. *Sports Illustrated,* February 20.

Case 8.16

Division I-A Football on Campus

In U.S. college athletics Division I-A is regarded by many as the top of the pyramid, the highest level of intercollegiate sport. Universities who participate in Division I intercollegiate sports are allowed a pre-scribed number of athletic scholarships according to National Collegiate Athletic Association (NCAA) rules. Colleges who can offer athletic scholarship are, obviously, in a position to entice more highly skilled high school athletes to enrol at their institutions compared to Division II and Division III schools, where no scholarships are offered. Recruitment of better athletes usually results in more highly skilled teams. Better teams, the logic continues, attract more spectators and generate more publicity for the institution.

Branches of state universities can now be found in various cities in that particular state. There is a campus of the University of Alabama (UAB) in Birmingham. In December 1994, the city council "voted to give the University of Alabama at Birmingham $2.2 million in public funds to start a Division I-A football program" (Editorial, 1994, p.8). Funding for state universities is the responsibility of the state government; municipal governments usually do not provide funds for these institutions of higher education.

Question to Consider for Discussion

1. In Birmingham 25% of the population lives in poverty and 11% has less than a Grade 8 education. Given the extent of poverty present and the low level of education among its population, what is the ethical status of the city council's decision to allocate $2.2. million to UAB to start a Division I-A football program?

Reference

- Editorial. (1994). Scorecard. *Sports Illustrated*, December 12.

Case 8.17

Home Exercise Videos

Home exercise videos are among the hottest selling items wherever videos are sold. Some surveys suggest that 8 out of the 10 best-selling videos are devoted to some general or specific aspect of physical fitness. Very often media celebrities or movie or television stars are featured. When such is the case, that video is usually named after the featured star. Featuring celebrities as fitness instructors or fitness gurus apparently guarantees increased sales.

Many claims are made on the package. Basically they all say the same thing: follow the exercise program in the video and you will attain various health and fitness benefits. All too often the unstated, but intended nevertheless, message being delivered is "just follow this videotape and you, too, will have this svelte, fabulous body and super good looks." What is never stated, nor explained, is the amount of money these celebrities spend on personal trainers, personal chefs, personal managers, and makeup artists. With rare exception, none of these celebrities tells the viewers (or the general audience) what the plastic surgeon has contributed to slimming, nipping, tucking or re-configuring various body parts. One exception is Cher, who has publicly acknowledged countless operations, undergoing plastic surgery on just about every part of her body.

Occasionally supposed fitness experts have been consulted to advise on the formulation of the fitness program presented in the video. Research conducted in the School of Human Kinetics at the University of Ottawa seriously calls into question the fitness claims made and the purported health benefits advertised on the video package. Indeed, there are indications that some video fitness programs may be contributing to the onset of certain medical problems.

Even those home exercise videos that are based on sound exercise principles cannot, by their very nature, address one important feature of all proper fitness programs, namely, increased resistance. What appears on the video is repeated every time the person who owns that video inserts it into the VCR and sets about following the exercises. Repeated sessions produce no advancement or gains since the level of exercise remains the same. On this count alone, fitness claims made on the labels of home exercise videos need to be challenged.

The celebrities who perform in these exercise videos earn large sums of money, as do the producers, distributors and retailers. Production costs are high and the money must be recouped to pay back the investors. Increased sales provide more profits for the companies involved.

Caveat emptor: buyer beware. This warning to purchasers is based on common sense since individuals are expected to exercise good judgment when it comes to spending their own money. In the marketplace many products come with certain warranties or money-back guarantees if the item does not live up to the buyer's expectation. Some products are sanctioned by a national body, such as the Canadian Standards Association, while other products, pharmaceuticals, for example, are subject to rigorous governmental scrutiny such as the FDA in the U.S.A. No guarantee, warranty, government scrutiny, or official sanction is applied to home exercise videos with one minor exception. A professional association, based in California, offers their seal of approval if the exercise program in the video closely follows the organization's safety guidelines and standards. While the seal of approval has been awarded to about a dozen exercise tapes put out by professional trainers, only one celebrity video has earned the association's approval.

Questions to Consider for Discussion

1. What is the ethical status of the celebrities who assume the role of fitness instructors when they have no professional or scientific basis for what they are doing? Is it ethical for these celebrities, aware

as they are of the benefits and discipline they have received from personal trainers, personal chefs, full-time, highly paid managers, and plastic surgeons, to pitch the benefits of exercise when they know, full well, that the goals they are espousing are beyond most of the purchasers?

2. What is the ethical status of the professionals in the field of Human Kinetics (Physical Education, Kinesiology), the professors of exercise physiology, biomechanics, biochemistry of exercise, and fitness training who remain silent (act of omission), considering the false or misleading claims made in these home exercise videos and the potential risks to the health of those who actually follow the programs?

Case 8.18

Winning and Job Tenure

D.S. was born and brought up in Toledo, Ohio, attending elementary and high school there. He then went on to attend the University of Toledo, where he was the starting quarterback in 1963 and 1964. After graduation he stayed in his hometown, married a local girl, and started his career by coaching at two high schools. In 1971 he was hired as an assistant coach by the university and was promoted to the position of head coach in 1982. This is a story of a local boy succeeding. Throughout his tenure as head coach, D.S. was very well liked and respected by his players and assistant coaches. Coach D.S. stressed the importance of academics to his players. Graduation rates for athletes on football scholarship exceeded the graduation rate for the entire student population. All the National College Athletic Association (NCAA) rules were followed scrupulously; there was no hint of any wrongdoing at any time. In many respects D.S. could serve as a model for other young coaches to emulate.

In 1989, with a victory in the final game of the season, Coach D.S. became the "winningest" coach in the history of the school. Then, four days later, he was fired. That action enraged the local community who showed their resentment by wearing large buttons and T-shirts supporting the fired coach. Petitions for his reinstatement were circulated and within five days some 20,000 people had signed on. These petitions were delivered to F.H., the president of the university, but he ignored the plea. The dismissal was final. F.H. had recently been appointed to his present position after spending 1985 to 1988 as the president of a large southwestern university with a strong winning tradition in football. That school was a perennial contender for the "mythical" national collegiate championship.

A.B., the person who made the decision to fire the coach, had been appointed director of athletics in July 1987. He had left his position as an assistant director of athletics at the Ohio State University, the large state university and a major national football power, to assume full control of the athletic program at this smaller, lower-scale, lower-key institution.

Before the start of the season, A.B., in his capacity as director of athletics, gave coach D.S. an ultimate bottom line: a 7-4 season or be fired. Based on the record achieved by the football team over the past few seasons, which had not measured up to the level expected by the director of athletics, and based on the 6-5 record in 1988, one victory short of the 7-4 season demanded, A.B. avowed that firing the coach was fully justified.

Coach D.S. had a 49-38-2 record over a period of eight years. In six of his eight years, he had had a winning season. Even the year just completed, a 6-5 season, put his team on the winning side of the ledger. Before the start of the season, the pundits predicted a sixth place finish for his team, but they actually finished tied for second place. Included in the season was a victory over the eventual conference champion. The reason given for his firing was that he did not win enough games.

A.B., the director of athletics, vigorously defended his decision to fire the coach. Despite D.S. holding the record as the "winningest" coach in the history of the school, his overall record was mediocre. That record was simply not good enough for him to retain the position of head coach. A.B. had higher aspirations: the school's football team should set the benchmark for victories in the conference. A clear target existed: win the championship about half the time, and for the other half, the other schools should need to beat them to win the championship. A record of 6-5 is just not good enough; it is not a mark of distinction nor is it a mark of excellence. Won-lost records no worse than 9-2 were expected, but since that was not in the offing, the director of athletics felt fully justified in terminating the coach's contract.

Questions to Consider for Discussion

1. From an ethical perspective, was the director of athletics justified in firing the coach?

2. Was a 6-5 record, instead of the targeted 7-4 goal, sufficient grounds for dismissal? (Model II can be applied here to account for the wide range of factors that need to be included in the discussion.)

3. In an institution of higher education, how ethical is it to base a personnel decision on the won-lost record?

Reference

• Looney, D.S. (1989/90). The axe falls at Toledo. *Sports Illustrated*, December 25-January 1, Double Edition, pp.32-33.

Case 8.19

Competition, Cooperation, and Revenue

As with all sports leagues, the National Football League (NFL) is an organization that features and promotes competition among its member teams. Although competition appears to be the prime feature, there are many facets of the league where cooperation predominates. For example, the owners cooperate in drawing up schedules that are to their respective benefit, have agreed upon and implemented a system for drafting players into the league and have worked together to negotiate a collective agreement with the players' union.

Another area where cooperation existed was in the creation of a corporate entity called NFL Properties. This corporation has a responsibility to recruit corporate sponsors. Those companies who sign up are entitled to call themselves an "official supplier" of (type of product) to the NFL. In addition, NFL Properties is also responsible for marketing a wide array of products (such as caps, sweaters, jackets, and so on) bearing the NFL logo or the logo/crest of all the teams. Revenue derived from the sale of these properties is shared equally among the teams in the league.

In 1993, Cola company A paid the league $250 million for a five-year deal for the exclusive right to be named the official cola drink of the NFL (Editorial, 1995, p.66). In August of 1995, Jerry Jones, owner of the Dallas Cowboys, announced the signing of a 10-year, $40 million deal with Cola company B for the Texas Stadium. This deal, legal and permissible (Editorial, 1995, p.B1), circumvents the spirit of the league contract with Cola company A for exclusive marketing and promotional rights. This new deal is a contract between a soft drink company and the Dallas Cowboys; it is not a deal with NFL Properties. As a result all the revenue from the contract goes to the Dallas Cowboys; none of the money derived is shared with the other owners.

Dallas Cowboys owner Jerry Jones is a businessperson. His goal, in this regard, is to maximize the income and profits gained from his team. His move, to sign a separate contract with a competing soft drink company, is legal but it obviously conflicts with the contract signed by NFL Properties with the other soft drink company. Furthermore, signing a separate deal runs contrary to the notions of cooperation and partnership, requisite features that allow both the league and NFL Properties to function well.

Question to Consider for Discussion

1. From an ethical perspective, was Jerry Jones justified in signing a separate, exclusive deal for Texas Stadium with Cola company B?

References

- Editorial. (1995). *Sports Illustrated,* Canadian Edition, September 4.
- Editorial. (1995). *The Toronto Star,* August 13.

Case 8.20

College Sport or Business

Head football coach Lou Saban of L.S.U. (Louisiana State University) has a clause in his contract that stipulates he will be paid $1 million "above the highest paid football coach in U.S. college ranks should the Tigers win the National Championship" (Editorial, 2002, p.28).

Since he is not the highest paid coach, the actual amount of money he would receive should his team win the National Championship would be much more than $1 million. How much more pressure does this put on the coach to win at any cost?

Question to Consider for Discussion

1. Given that the notion of the student-athlete relationship implies total human development rather than a narrow focus on winning, what ethical justification is there for such an incentive clause?

Reference

- Editorial. (2002). Go figure. *Sports Illustrated,* February 25.

Case 8.21

NFL Expansion Draft

Both the Jacksonville Jaguars and the Carolina Panthers paid $140 million U.S. in expansion fees to join the National Football League (NFL) and would begin play in the fall of 1995. As part of the deal, both teams would participate in a special expansion draft held on February 15, 1995, to select players made available by the existing 28 teams in the league. Each of the 28 teams was required to contribute six signed players, thus making 168 players available. From this pool the two new teams would choose the 30 to 40 players who would constitute the core of their first season's roster. No other restrictions were placed on the existing 28 teams regarding which signed players they could make available. No directives were issued regarding positions or number of years experience in the league. In effect, each of the existing 28 teams had free rein in deciding which signed players would be made available to the expansion teams. When the list of names was published, an assessment of the talent available was made: "Many of the unprotected are aging players with $2 million-plus salaries" (Editorial, 1995, p.9) and many others are backup players or second stringers whose inflated salaries were much too high compared to their relative worth to their respective existing teams.

Although Jacksonville and Carolina had each paid $140 million in expansion fees they had no say in deciding the criteria established for the special expansion draft player pool. From the perspective of *Sports Illustrated*, "this all looks like another case of the NFL's established franchises gouging the new kids on the block" (Editorial, 1995, p.9). Ideally, for interest in the league to remain at a high level, which in tangible terms translates into high attendance, parity among the teams is a desirable goal. Based on the assessment made of the talent in the expansion draft pool–overpriced, over-the-hill, second stringers–it appeared that many years would have to pass before the expansion teams reached parity with the existing teams.

Since the expansion teams paid such a large entry fee would it not have been fairer to (1) grant them some say in deciding the criteria established for making players available from the existing teams, and (2) have some first string players allocated to them so that the goal of parity could be attained more quickly? It would be worthwhile to assess the behavior of the league itself and the actions of the 28 member teams.

Questions to Consider for Discussion

1. Did the NFL behave ethically in setting the entry fee at $140 million U.S.?

2. What procedure would you recommend be established to ensure a fair entry fee?

3. Was the player distribution procedure established by the NFL really fair?

4. What procedure would you recommend to ensure fairness in the player distribution process?

Reference

• Editorial. (1995). *Sports Illustrated,* Canadian Edition, January 30.

Case 8.22

Female Participation in Sport

Issues about female participation in sport have a long history. Basically, sport has been seen as a male preserve. Furthermore, women are often viewed in a stereotypical manner. This is what is often identified as femininity. As more and more women and women's events have been admitted to international sport competitions, these factors have led to some questionable practices by those organizing sport. The following cases provide some data on how sport leaders have sought to control women's entry into sport in the face of equal opportunity and of questionable medical evidence and practices. It is argued by administrators that their decisions are necessary for the continuation of fairness in sport.

Soon after the former Soviet Union (USSR) was admitted to the international Olympic movement in 1951, Soviet athletes began to win many medals and top the "unofficial" standings. A large part of this success came through the triumphs of Soviet female athletes. The USSR had a highly formalized sport system where scientific methods and early identification of athletes were key elements. With this rationalized program, Soviet women were selected for different sport events based on size, musculature, mental ability, and skill. Towards this end, many of the women did not represent idealized stereotypes of women and of femininity, but they were highly successful in Olympic and world competitions.

The result of strict and rigorous training made many women appear more "masculine." As their achievements grew, especially when nearing men's records, they were labeled and their sex was questioned by many officials, journalists, and athletes. The questions started in Tokyo in 1964.

A chromosome test (Barr test, 1949) had been developed. At the 1968 Mexico Games the International Olympic Committee (IOC) initiated a program of gender verification. This meant that "female" athletes would have to submit themselves to an inspection process to establish their sex and their qualification to compete in women's events. In the early days of the gender verification process this meant presenting themselves naked to a panel of doctors who would do an internal evaluation of their reproductive organs to compliment the external visual inspection. At the 1968 Games and at future Olympic Games this testing would take on a more scientific guise as the women would have cells scraped from the inside of their mouths (buccal smear), which would then be analyzed genetically through the Barr test.

In this process the women would have to have a XX sex gene

configuration to be allowed to compete. Geneticists know that humans do not only carry XX and XY (male) sex genes. There are several inter-sex configurations–XXY, XYY, and XO. Some women were banned from competition because their external genitalia or the sex chromosomes were not as they "should be." In some cases this had a devastating effect on the women that had been raised as females and viewed themselves as nothing less. There were cases of suicide, psychological trauma, and overt discrimination.

In 1986 a geneticist wrote in the *Journal of the American Medical Association* that this form of testing was inaccurate and discriminatory as it excluded women (e.g., those with the XXY chromosome configuration) who should in fact be allowed into the Games. This report did not, however, do away with the testing. A new test was developed in the early 1990s (Dingeon, 1994). This test also uses a buccal smear for analysis. The test is based upon "the principle of gene amplification (PCR polymerase chain reaction), automated in 1987 by Mullis (1993 Nobel Laureate biochemistry), which enables the prime masculinization gene, the SRY gene described in 1991 to be isolated" (p.65). The argument here is that a cheaper, more reliable, more convenient biochemical technique is available as "gender verification tests are still necessary. As organized by the IOC they are very safe in their execution, and achieve their fundamental ethical objective: to be a deterrent" (p.68).

Men undergo no such testing. It is assumed that "men are men" (simply by the genitalia they possess). Here the premise is that all male athletes have the same basic characteristics and that any qualities that could be classed as "female" or "feminine" would not benefit them in competition. This argument, however, has caused considerable debate around sports that have some aesthetic elements (e.g., gymnastics, diving).

Many women, and men, argue that this test is demeaning and should be abandoned. It appears that as women become better trained and continue to set records closer to those of men, men in positions of power initiate guidelines and rules to put these women "in their place."

Questions to Consider for Discussion

1. There are several very large issues in this situation. Using a two-column format, identify the positive and negative bases of the reason the administrators of sport make this an issue. Next to those columns, compare these reasons to the consequences for female athletes. Comment and discuss the various moral bases for each of the items identified.

2. What is the moral position of the sport administrators in the case? Debate their position and discuss the style of leadership actually evidenced.

3. What are the rights of female athletes in this situation? Debate the issue from their position.

4. As many experts argue that these tests are not conclusive, why do the administrators continue to demand such tests?

5. Who are the people behind the new gender testing and what benefits do they potentially garner from their new improved sex test?

6. Why, with so few real examples of fraud, do the IOC and other global sport bodies continue to seek and carry out such tests?

References

- Blue, A. (1988). *Faster, higher, further: Women's triumphs and disasters at the Olympics.* London: Virago.
- Dingeon, B. (1994). Gene biochemistry and gender testing. *Olympic Message*, 40:65-68.

Case 8.23

Becoming A Boy

One part of the socialization into private boys' schools was to complete a set of initiation rituals. In most cases these were demeaning, dangerous, and disgusting. They were established to ensure that the individuals would become honorable members of the group and would learn their place in the group. When the boys left these schools, they would take many of these activities with them to other parts of their lives. As sport was a central element of these schools, it was often in sport that the tradition of initiation and hazing continued. This case deals with this age-old form of socialization and the ethics of its existence and its excess.

Most sports have these activities; they are particular in sports where team loyalty and rank are maintained, and also where toughness and courage are necessary. They seem to be part of the process of being an athlete in that sport. In many cases they are seen as good, clean fun, a part of the tradition of the sport. In other cases they have led to injury and death. In certain cases they have met with public outcry for their abandonment.

In one club a particular group of new, young members completed certain of these rituals on "rookies' night." The members of this young group of athletes were talented and exuberant. In fact, they took the initiation rituals to a higher level and identified themselves as unique in the club. Following this first ritual, they formed their own sub-group and held their own annual ceremonies.

Their status rose in the club, mainly based upon their playing ability, but also because of their uniqueness in the club's culture. They carried out their own ceremony for a number of years without major incident. One year, however, a journalist friend of one member was invited. It turned out that the "performance" that evening included a mock rape of a woman that mimicked a recent real-life situation. The performance was in bad taste but was a private matter, or that was the perception of the club and its members. A second performance had strong racial over-tones. This combination of sexist and racist material was made public by the journalist who witnessed the activities.

When the group's activities "hit the press," there was a huge public outcry. The overall achievements of the club and its illustrious history of sporting achievement were reduced or ignored in the scandal. Several city groups demanded that the club be disbanded, while other groups de-manded public apologies and the prosecution of the offending members. City hall became involved as the club and clubhouse occupied city park property. In the end the club was able to "ride out the storm." Certain members of the offending sub-group were singled out for punishment. The sub-group was disbanded.

A serious rift within the club resulted from the club executive's ac-tions. Many solid, long-term members quit the club over its handling of the affair. Others lost their interest and attachment to the club, be-coming silent and limiting their participation in the wider club activi-ties. It did not make sense to them that these activities, which had been present from the club's origins (in some similar form), were now being attacked. The club lost much of its original prestige, both inside and outside of the club.

Question to Consider for Discussion

1. In this day and age, is hazing really necessary? What could be the benefit of this ritual?

2. Is there a time or place for this activity?

3. When does it *cross the ethical line*? Why?

Case 8.24

Musical Parents

The extent to which parents will go to ensure their children's success often reaches rather dramatic levels in many professions–not the least of which is sport. This case is included here to foster discussion regarding what is reasonable support and what is potentially damag-ing for children and families alike.

Particular clubs, teams, schools, and leagues have histories of suc-cess. This success is based on a number of factors, with the quality of the individuals and organizations involved being key. This success can be seen in the production of elite athletes, coaches, and administrators. These successes attract more strong and talented athletes, coaches, and members. Success breeds success. In a number of the more established sports, geographic boundaries are clearly established and strictly enforced. This occurs at both the club or community level of sport and in school sport.

Athletes, and their parents, seek to work with or compete in the strongest competitive situations so that they may develop as far as possible. In order to be part of these strong clubs, teams, schools, and leagues, they must, most often, reside in the area in which that unit exists. That is, the right to register for particular teams or clubs is based upon the athlete's place of residence. Because these situations exist, athletes and their parents seek different ways to establish a place of residence whereby the athlete will be allowed to play in the local league.

One well-known example of how athletes and their parents circumvent this guideline is that of Wayne Gretzky. The original purpose in having the 14-year-old Gretzky go to Toronto was to play in the Metro Toronto Minor Hockey League, a league seen as a premier competitive situation that had fostered several top professional players. According to information in biographies of Gretzky, the parents of his teammates were also making life unbearable for him. They were constantly abusive and sought to make his life miserable. Toronto would, in fact, provide a refuge as well as a higher level of competition.

As the Gretzky family lived outside of the boundaries for this league, Gretzky's parents had to "legally give their fourteen-year-old son away" (MacGregor, 1995, p.75). A couple by the name of Cornish became the legal guardians of Wayne, which allowed him to play in the Metro league. With the adoption, Wayne Gretzky was able to play in this premier league, and in fact he played at a higher age category (Junior B) because of his talent. As a result of this ruse, a court challenge was launched by the Canadian Amateur Hockey Association (now the Canadian Hockey Association [CHA]) to bar Gretzky from playing outside of his minor hockey association. In the end Wayne Gretzky continued to play in the Metro Toronto league until he was drafted by the Sault St. Marie junior hockey club after he turned 16. The irony of the situation is that the Gretzky family tried to convince the Sault St. Marie team not to draft Wayne so that he might play with a junior team closer to his parents' home. The guideline stated that at 14, Wayne should not be outside of his home association, yet at 16, he could go hundreds of miles away. The hypocrisy of the situation continues as young players are forced to leave home to follow their dream of elite competition and development.

The Gretzky case is not unique. There are likely hundreds of stories such as this. One other case that MacGregor (1995) mentions in his book *The Home Team: Fathers, Sons, and Hockey* is that of Jason Boudrias. The young Boudrias, from Quebec, had at one point sought better competition in Ontario. Jason had crossed over into Ontario when he had a chance to play for the Gloucester Rangers in the lesser junior leagues, and to allow this to happen his father and mother, Hélène, "doctored it" to make his dream possible. The father laughs. "We had him adopted." Working with a lawyer and an agreeable family, they signed the legal papers and Jason Boudrias became someone else's child while he played in Ontario. When Laval (a Quebec major junior team) drafted him in 1992, Andrew (Jason's father) says, "we had the deal reversed." Jason was re-adopted by his blood mother and father. The Boudrias family all moved to Montreal to be closer to their son and his new team (MacGregor, 1995, p.31).

In both cases the biological parents gave up their legal relationship with their son, giving him an opportunity to play hockey in a higher caliber league. These situations involve a great deal more legal and logistical effort than having a daughter or son move in with an aunt or uncle across the city to be within the boundaries of a particular high school. Likewise, it has different parameters than "red-shirting" (holding a youth back a school year to retain a year of eligibility and to be bigger and stronger than others on the team and in the league) a youth.

In these situations the leagues or organizations are most often acting to maintain equality among the clubs or schools. This blocks some schools, especially those with more resources, from raiding players from other towns, communities, or neighborhoods. On the other hand, a series of bureaucratic regulations ("red-tape") result, often removing individual freedom. The above situations must be observed from several positions: that of the athlete, the parent, the coaches, the administrators, the clubs (and club executives), the schools and school boards, and local and national sport-governing bodies. One may ask: What about the athlete and the maximum possible development of that athlete? There are many other such situations in which parents and other individuals operate for reasons other than that of the athletes. All of these elements of the sport system must be included in the discussion of this matter.

Questions to Consider for Discussion

1. Would you have your child adopted in order to play elite sport in another city or town? Why?

2. Is the possibility of fame worth the price of the loss of a *normal* experience of family?

3. What does this behavior say about the world of sport and the sanctity of parental obligation? How can this behavior be justified?

Reference

- MacGregor, R. (1995). *The home team: Fathers, sons, and hockey.* Viking: Toronto.

Case 8.25

Changing Medals

The Salt Lake City 2002 Winter Olympic Games (WOGs) will go down in history as a watershed Games. The bid scandal crisis of late 1999 and early 2002 led to a number of reactions from the IOC as to how it operates (not to mention the post 9/11 issues) and to its attempts to be more transparent and equitable in the competitions. It was with some relief that the 2002 WOGs opened and the athletes began to compete.

Olympic historians have documented the issues that occurred at previous Olympic games. It is a history rife with wrangling and posturing. This Olympics was to be no different. Of the many issues that arose in the 2002 WOGs, the gold medal for pairs figure skating gained worldwide attention.

Canadian pairs figure skaters Jamie Sale and David Pelletier had, according to all accounts, skated a flawless, technically sound program. It was a gold medal skate. It was, however, the Russian pair of Yelana Berezhnaya and Anton Sikharulidze who were awarded the gold. There was considerable shock over the decision. Sale and Pelletier, while disappointed, accepted their fate with humility. They were in fact feted widely and invited onto many television programs.

Shortly after the event more details of the judging became known. A French judge for the pairs competition openly admitted that she had traded points for the Russian pairs skaters in return for additional points being awarded to the French ice dance pair. This was a pre-arranged vote-swapping arrangement.

Later the French judge recanted her admission of vote swapping. She said she had been put under pressure by the president of the French figure skating union to vote in this manner. In the end an investigation was held to try to sort the whole mess out. With the irregularity in voting fully in public view, the IOC decided to award the Canadian pair a gold medal and thereby a share in the win. From media reports and general conversation, this seemed just for all concerned. The furore, however, did not subside. Nor did the questioning of how subjectively judged competitions are held.

Questions to Consider for Discuss

1. Sport is seen to have elements of equality, egalitarianism, and fair play. What does this case indicate about sport in general and sports such as figure skating in particular?

2. Why is sport law a growing discipline in sport? What implications for sport are there when legal issues grow unabated and demand tribunals and specialized legal advice?

3. There are many historical issues with sports that are subjectively judged. Identify some of these issues by researching sport history journals and books. Analyze past judging issues in light of this case. Are there common human behaviors and outcomes for each case? How might international sport-governing bodies and the IOC deal with such issues?

4. Evaluate the actions of the French judge and skating union president in this case.

5. Was the IOC correct in its decision to award the Canadian figure skating pair an equal gold medal? Provide moral and ethical standards for your response.

6. What would your actions have been if you were the Canadian *chef de mission* at these games? What ethical principles would you have espoused?

References

- Casert R. (2002). ISU investigators question two key witnesses in skating scandal. Canadian Press, February 20 (accessed on canada.comNews, 3/1/02).

- Cole. C. (2002,). The Whimper Olympics. *National Post*, February 23 (accessed on canada.comNews, 3/1/02).

- Siddons, L. (2002, February 22). Olympic protests continue; Rogge writes Putin to clear the air. Canadian Press, February 22 (accessed on canada.comNews, 3/1/02).

- Editorial. (2002). Revolution on ice. *Montreal Gazette*, February 22 (accessed on canada.comNews, 3/1/02).

- For a general overview of stories and timeline for this scandal go to <http://www.usatoday.com/olympics/saltlake/figure/index.htm>.

Case 8.26

Never! In Hockey!

After several months of investigation a widely known and successful ice hockey coach and administrator was charged with sexual assault and sentenced to three and a half years in jail. The available details of the situation indicate that he had systematically used his power of influence over the careers of several male ice hockey players to sexual abuse them.

As success in major junior ice hockey is central to a player's prospect of being drafted by a professional club, ice time and achievements at the junior level are imperative to career development. Clearly, the coaches, managers, administrators, boards of directors, and league officials have considerable power over the players and are able to influence their behavior in many ways.

In the case under discussion, the coach of a major junior club had used his position to literally obtain control of young male hockey players from their parents. This control extended to the minds, bodies, and souls of the young men involved. The coach was able to have the players' rights traded to his club. The player who publicly acknowledged the abuse had endured over 300 episodes of sexual abuse, starting with a visit to this coach's home when the player was 14 years old.

The abuse continued until this player was drafted by a National Hockey League team. Although there were attempts to deal with the abuse and attention focused on particular players, much of the issue was suppressed. It was not until the players collectively complained about the increasing odd behavior of the coach (including some odd behaviors during hockey games) that they were able to force the club to deal with their concerns.

The coach resigned from this particular major junior club but went on to another city where he was part owner and managing director of the club. It was during his time with this club that the legal proceedings against him were initiated, after more than ten years of his controlling impressionable young men. As a result of this coach's abuse the identified player went through serious emotional problems that led to alcohol and substance abuse as well as his seeking psychiatric and psychological counseling to deal with his suffering. Clearly the emotional, psychological, and personal suffering of the player cannot be rectified. The player stated that he felt his youth had been robbed by the coach's abuse.

What made this case of coach-athlete sexual abuse so alarming and difficult to believe was its occurrence in the macho world of men's ice hockey. The tough, heterosexual image of ice hockey was disturbed by the circumstances of this case. Disbelief that such a thing could happen in this sport denied the fact that it did occur and likely occurs much more frequently than is believed.

Questions to Consider for Discussion

1. What are the external moderators operating in the public's mind over this case? How can one rectify this in terms of the evidence of this case?

2. Discuss the situational modifiers that were likely a part of the players decision making to seek the dismissal of the coach with the first club.

3. Put yourself in the place of the abused player. Identify and discuss a possible decision-making process he went through to have the coach charged and to disclose the abuse that he had endured.

4. As an administrator with the ice hockey club that employed this coach, work through a decision-making process in terms of dismissing the coach. Remember that this coach had led the team to a Memorial Cup Championship (champions of major junior hockey in North America).

References

- Board, M. (1997). The Graham James Case: Abuse case wake-up call for hockey. *Calgary Herald*, January 7, p.C1.
- Goyette, L. (1997). Hockey players display true guts. *Calgary Herald*, January 7, p.A9.
- Kimberley, T. (1997). Players confronted James in 1994. *Calgary Herald*, January 7, p.A1.
- McCarten, J. (1997). Kennedy hailed for going public. *The Globe and Mail*, January 7, p.A18.
- Stewart, M. (1997). Kennedy revelation could prompt others to seek help, counsellor says. *Calgary Herald*, January 7, p.A2.

Case 8.27

Sweatshop Shoes and Global Icons

Many major companies have moved the manufacture of their products to Third World countries, especially those in Southeast Asia, so that they can avoid the higher labor and benefits costs that unionized workers in North American and Europe obtain. The companies are also able to avoid stringent workers' compensation rules and costs, and are able to find governments that will support their production demands. This is achieved by setting very low minimum wages, not allowing unions, not having labor laws to protect wages or hours of work, by using child labor, and by giving tax breaks and government money to establish the manufacturing enterprise. As a result of this arrangement many major sporting good manufacturers have closed plants in North America and Europe, throwing many people out of work.

Ballanger (1992) provided information about how this process works. Nike has not had a plant in North American since the early 1980s. This well-known company has a shoe manufacturing plant in

Indonesia, one of five in Asia. The plant discussed produces a mid-range shoe that sells for approximately $80 U.S. It is estimated that twelve cents is spent in labor costs to manufacture a pair of these shoes.

A woman working in this Indonesia plant earns $1.03 U.S. per day. She works ten and a half hours a day, six days a week. Her monthly pay totals $37.46 U.S. This includes 63 hours of overtime for which she was is paid only a few extra cents per hour. She is expected to manufacture 13 to 14 pairs of shoes per day. This woman is barely able to make enough to survive in poverty conditions marked by malnourishment, shanty housing, no running water, no power, and poor sanitation.

Nike's revenues are in the billions of dollars each year. This results in profits in the hundreds of millions each year. The company has one sports person, among many other athletes, endorsing their products who receives $20 U.S. million for his efforts. It would take a female worker over 44,000 years to earn the one-year endorsement fee paid to this athlete.

Questions to Consider for Discussion

1. What is social responsibility? Who can afford it?
2. What obligation, if any, does Nike have to its Third World workers? What is the rationale for this obligation or the lack of obligation?
3. Will you continue to wear Nike apparel? Why?

Reference

- Ballinger, J. (1992). The new free-trade heel: Nike's profits jump on the backs of Asian workers. *Harper's Magazine*, August, pp.46-47.

Case 8.28

Cybersport

This case deals with the obvious as well as the subtle. It concerns individual responsibility and systemic (political and economic) encouragement to act unethically. It forces the reader to consider the relativity and universality of rules and the underlying rationale for these rules.

In 1988, during the Seoul Olympic Games, many Canadians were focused on their television during the men's 100m final. The race itself represents the "citius" of the Olympic motto; the fastest or swiftest human on earth in a footrace. Canada was particularly interested as Ben Johnson was in this final. He was currently the world record holder in this event. It was anticipated that he would win and likely set an Olympic record. The media and national interest had been piqued for months before this race. Much was at stake.

Johnson did not disappoint. He destroyed the competition, looking back as he approached the tape. He had won the gold medal and set a world and Olympic record in the race. All of Canada rejoiced. The prime minister is said to have used this moment to call a federal election as nationalistic pride was high and other matters would be shadowed by the ongoing focus on Johnson's feat. In victory, Johnson carried the Canadian flag around the stadium, proclaiming his country.

Subsequent to the medal ceremony, another moment of supreme pride, it was found that Johnson had an illegal (under the regulations of the IOC's drug commission) amount of a banned substance in his urine. The Canadian *chef de mission* had a duty to retrieve the medal and inform Johnson that he had been disqualified. From the height of nationalistic fervor and pride, this represented a moment of national disgrace. Johnson was denounced in the media.

In an attempt to implement a damage control program, the federal government, the national sport federation, and the athletics national sport-governing body began what some perceived to be a "witch-hunt." A federal government commission was established to investigate the nature and degree of the use of banned substances in Canadian sport.

Known as the Dubin Inquiry, after the judge appointed to head the commission, the "dirty laundry" of international sport was aired. This became a standard item in newspapers, daily television news coverage, general public discussion, academic study, and (much like the OJ Simpson trial) a form of real "soap opera."

A lengthy report published by the inquiry contained revelations of rampant illegal practices in sport. These practices were part of sport at all levels, but particularly at the elite international level. The guilty parties were identified, suspended, and demeaned. The adage of "hero to zero" came to be part of the general vocabulary. What seemed lost in this soul searching was the fact that the practices were rampant, well beyond what the Canadian cases revealed.

There is no question that the culture of elite sport fosters the philosophy of "winning at all cost" (cf. Hoberman, 1992; Zakus, 1992). This culture was clearly seen after the fall of the Berlin Wall and German re-unification. When the East German sport system was exposed, the degree of the use of banned substances and practices was startling, but not unexpected. While not condoning the use of drugs, the situation presents a plethora of ethical issues–not the least of which is individual responsibility and that of the sport delivery system that fosters winning at all costs.

Questions to Consider for Discussion

1. Was Ben Johnson responsible for his fate? Why? To what extent?

2. Is the system of corporate-sponsored sport responsible? Why? To what extent?

3. Is there any "fair sport" being played at the elite level?

4. Is the "winning at all cost" philosophy unique to sport?

References

- Hoberman, J. (1992). *Mortal engines: The science of performance and the dehumanization of sport.* New York: Free Press.

- Zakus, D.H. (1992). The International Olympic Committee: Tragedy, farce, and hypocrisy. *Sociology of Sport Journal,* 9:340-353.

Case 8.29

Sportsmanship and Football/Soccer: The Letter of the Law and the Spirit of the Law?

In February 1999 a football match was played between Arsenal and Sheffield United with the first outcome being a 2-1 victory for Arsenal. However, this score was not upheld, for the winning goal was scored in a manner that was contrary to the *informal* rules of the game.

This is what happened. In the game a Sheffield player went down with an injury, and the Sheffield goalkeeper immediately kicked the ball out of bounds–a standard yet informal play. Once the injured player was removed and replaced, the *understood* next play for the Arsenal player would be to throw the ball back to Sheffield and play would commence. However, when the ball was thrown in to Sheffield, it was intercepted by a young Arsenal player (a Nigerian who was not aware of the informal "culture" of English football) who proceeded to kick the ball to another player on his team. This player then instinctively fired it into the Sheffield goal.

Both teams were in shock that this unwritten yet deeply held rule had been violated. The referee chose to uphold the goal despite the arguments from both sides that it should be disallowed. According to the official rules, it was a "legal" goal. Immediately after the match the Arsenal coach declined the victory and stated that he "offered the replay because it wasn't right to win that way–it wasn't Arsenal." The game was replayed, fans were offered tickets at half the normal price and Arsenal won the game 2-1 for the *second* time.

The English referees were outraged because they felt that the game was being taken out of the proper context of the rule book.

David Bowen of the Irish Football Association stated: "I believe this could open a can of worms. The English FA [Football Association] may be hanging its hat on the fact that both teams agreed but we would have said tough, these things happen in football. There is no way we would have interfered with the laws of the game." The famous German player Beckenbauer suggested that the decision was "populist." There was no reason to replay the game.

Questions to Consider for Discussion

1. What ethical approaches are at odds in this case?

2. How would you characterize the comment by Beckenbauer?

3. Should this informal rule be formalized?

4. Discuss the ethics of informal and formal cultures. How are they relevant to each other?

5. What do the terms "the spirit of the law" and "the letter of the law" mean? How does this case relate to these terms?

References

• Vecsey, G. (1999). Don't worry: Sportsmanship won't be catching. *The New York Times*, February 21, p.39.

• Warshaw, A. (1999). Football—"Rematch" protest instigated by Celts. *Arsenalnews*, February 28 (from web version of paper: http://www.pcug.co.uk/~satchmo/arsehome/Arsenews.htm).

Case 8.30

Positions of Trust—Coaches

A 1993 study carried out in Quebec indicated that 96% of athletes "absolutely trusted" their coaches (versus their teachers at 62% and their parents at 55%). The study was reported in the April 24, 1993, edition of *The Globe and Mail* (April 24, 1993) under the heading, "Quebec acts to wipe out sexual abuse in sports." In these positions of trust, coaches are given a tremendous amount of power to control the lives of their athletes. Athletes, parents, administrators, sport organization boards of directors, and the public assume that coaches act morally in their interaction with athletes. The following two cases provide information about two incidents that received considerable mass media attention. It must be remembered that many such situations exist and are not reported (and therefore not sensationalized).

Shortly after the newspaper report of the Quebec study, an investigative piece of television journalism outlined several incidents of systematic sexual misconduct and abuse by coaches. Male coaches of female athletes in the sports of rowing, swimming, and volleyball were exposed as being sexual abusers in their positions of trust. A newspaper article commenting on the television program stated that the "report on harassment said to be `tip of iceberg'" (Jollimore, 1993, p.A19).

The television program reported that male coaches had carried out practices in which the female athletes had to appear naked in front of the coach, be measured while naked, were inappropriately (sexually) touched, and had direct sexual relationships with the coaches. The coaches used their power to maintain the silence of the female athletes. This power is rooted in the coach's decision to play or sit an athlete, to select or drop an athlete, or to control the amount of playing time the athlete receives. The coaches were also able to set the athletes against each other and "divide and conquer."

As the athletes were serious and longed to compete they were easily pressured. It took a great deal of strength to raise the abuse issue. Many suffered for years until they had the strength to expose the abuse. In only one case was the coach charged. In court, however, the judge ruled that, while he believed the girl, there was still reasonable doubt and thus dropped the charge. In two other cases the coaches were allowed to resign and thus avoid overt damage to their lives and careers. Simply stated, the system covered up the abuse and allowed the guilty to escape formal punishment for their misdeeds. It is assumed that their reputations have been damaged and that the informal network will ensure that they are not in such positions of power again.

This line of thinking, however, does not work. Two of the coaches are currently in direct contact with female athletes. A third attempted to coach, but was blocked; he has a non-coaching position with the national sport organization in the same sport in which he abused athletes. While the coaches may have suffered some private punishment, the victims remain aggrieved. Their lives and their enjoyment of sport has been damaged. The system of justice has apparently left them to their own devices.

Many have argued that this is somewhat natural. It is a female/male thing, a natural occurrence when members of the opposite sex spend considerable time together in close relationship. In two cases the coaches were married, so they were adulterers as well. Can the argument be made that this is just something that males do? Is it, as is so often argued, something to do with male hormones and primal behavior? Is it, as is also so often argued, the female's fault in that they somehow cause their own abuse by being young, attractive, and available? Overall, does this mean that this sort of behavior is acceptable in society? If the official legal system does not punish the coaches, what solution is there to this type of behavior?

At the time that this issue became public there were few, if any, ethical codes of conduct for coaches. Many sport organizations began to review their guidelines. The ruling body of sport demanded that sport organizations have such codes and that they be fully implemented. Still the question of punishment remains. How does one deal with abuse of trust wherever it occurs in sport?

Questions to Consider for Discussion

1. Although the coaches were not charged under the laws of the land, many did move to other positions (often in the same sport). Some continue to deny their actions or to show remorse for the suffering they caused their athletes. What morality directed their behavior?

2. How were the athletes in these situations responding to the coaches' unethical behavior?

3. During the interviews in the television program, several sport administrators supported the coaches accused of such aberrant behavior. What is their source of decision making and what reasons were likely given to justify their decision (or lack of action)?

4. Will codes of conduct alleviate these situations? Why or why not? What ideas are behind your decision?

References

- Jollimore, M. (1993). Report on harassment said to be "tip of the iceberg." *The Globe and Mail,* November 6, p.A19.
- Editorial. (1993). Quebec acts to wipe out sexual abuse in sports. *The Globe and Mail,* April 24.

Case 8.31

Conflict of Cultures: Snowboarders and the IOC

With the commercialization of the International Olympic Committee (IOC), its Games, and sport generally, new products are required to enhance revenue generation. As the IOC seeks to expand its control over sport and broader commercial revenues, inclusion of the more trendy, youth-oriented, and media-friendly sports in the Olympic Games is sought.

As a result, freestyle skiing, short course speed skating, and snowboarding are now on the Winter Olympic Games schedule. These sports represent future commercial and media possibilities. Each of these sports, however, has its own sub-culture; that is, values, beliefs, behaviors, and shared understandings. They differ considerably from the traditional winter sports of luge, bobsleigh, biathlon, and skating. They also vary in culture from the mainstream of the

IOC and other members of the Olympic "family."

This clash of cultures became overt when the first gold medal for the new Olympic sport of snowboarding was awarded to Canadian Ross Rebagliati in the giant slalom event. In a press release the IOC Executive Board decided to disqualify with immediate effect athlete Ross Rebagliati (snowboarding) of the Canadian delegation of the XVIII Olympic Winter Games in Nagano for testing positive in a doping control (Carrard, 1998, n.p.). This decision was immediately appealed to the Court of Arbitration for Sport (CAS), set up as an ad-hoc division (of the CAS in Lausanne, Switzerland) in Nagano. Reeb (1998, np) wrote of this arbitration in the *Olympic Review*:

> In its award, the CAS noted that the IOC's decision to penalize the athlete was based on article III-B ... of the Medical Code: "In agreement with the International Sports federations and the responsible authorities, tests may be conducted for cannabinoids (e.g., marijuana, hashish). The results may lead to sanctions." During the hearing, it was clearly established that there was no such agreement between the International Ski Federation and the International Olympic Committee. Moreover, the Drug Formulary Guide published for athletes' information by the Nagano Olympic organizing committee did not include marijuana in the list of banned substances. Consequently, the panel of arbitrators in charge of the case concluded that there was no valid legal basis for imposing sanctions on Ross Rebagliati, and overturned the decision of the IOC Executive Board. The discussions therefore focused on the legal problems, and the CAS did not enter into the ethical issues raided by the case.

As the policy and the agreements between elements of the Olympic family were unclear and unwritten, the IOC formed a working group to deal with the issue of marijuana (Meeting of the IOC, and International Olympic Committee). This group was established to clearly delineate a policy on this particular drug issue and to exhibit some action by the IOC executive for having their legally suspect decision overturned. It was partly to save face and partly to continue the IOC's self-proclaimed war on drugs in sport.

In the press coverage of this issue, it was noted that Regabilati had used marijuana prior to April 1997 but had only encountered "second-hand smoke" since that time. His flat-mates and other associates were regular users (Hughes, 1998a, 1998b). He had, in fact, been exposed to second-hand smoke just prior to his departure for Nagano (Goodbody, 1998, n.p.). The medical community argues that the metabolites can remain in the body for up to four weeks after exposure. The initial decision apparently also floundered as the IOC Executive Board did not consider or verify Regabilati's claim of non-use; that is his claim of innocence. Their decision was in camera and without due process.

When looked at in its entirety, the Rebagliati expulsion points to several issues with the substance and form with which the IOC regulates sport and its business. By attempting to portray itself with a sport with good "potential television ratings and the fan excitement that it creates" (Bryant, 1998) the IOC erred. While the commercial possibilities appeared great, and it appeared that the Olympic movement was moving with the times by making snowboarding part of the Games program, the IOC failed to consider the nature of the sport. That is, the IOC and FIS failed to understand this sport fully and perhaps embraced it without full aforethought. Or, perhaps, the IOC felt that snowboarding athletes would conform in order to be part of the Olympic aura. Or, failing that, the IOC would be able to exert control. All of this adds to the difficulty evident in the arbitration decision.

Perhaps more poignant is the apparent lack of accord between the IOC and its list of banned substances and the wider community, as well as between elements of the Olympic family. Part of the CAS's decision is that, while not condoning the use of marijuana by Regabilati, the IOC has not made explicit its guidelines. As Hughes (1998a, n.p.) wrote, "If sport authorities wish to add their own sanctions to those edicted by public authorities, they must do so in an explicit fashion. That has not been done here." The CAS also found that the Games organizing committee had not listed certain recreational drugs such as marijuana on their list of banned substances. Finally, it seems that the FIS and the IOC do not have complete agreement over the list of banned substances. Clearly the accords between elements of the Olympic family are not explicit or aligned. Overall, there are several gaps in the case that was brought against Regabilati that point to the IOC Executive Board's decision being in error, even if it was morally sound.

Questions to Consider for Discussion

1. Does the IOC have the legal right to control athletes in terms of their private habits? How far does this control go? In terms of the behavior of IOC members, do they have the moral right to dictate athlete behavior?

2. If you were appointed to an IOC commission that was to develop an athlete's code of conduct during the Olympic Games what considerations would you include in the philosophical basis of the code and what sanctions would be included?

3. The FIS and IOC seem to have by organizational fiat made snowboarding part of the sport federations purview and then part of the Winter Olympic Games. Identify, from an ethical perspective, the rationales for this and then comment on the rationality and morality of this process.

4. Can the IOC actual fulfil its role as the vanguard in the war on drugs in sport? In this discussion include the moral and ethical position of the IOC in this role.

References

- Bryant, J. (1998). Surfers accused of taking sport downhill. *The Sunday-Times*, February 12, np (from web version of paper http://www.sunday-times.co.uk).
- Carrard, F. (1998). Ross Rebagliati disqualified. International Olympic Committee. February 11, Press Release #26.
- Goodbody, J. (1998). Rebagliati to appeal against his expulsion. *The Sunday-Times*, February 12, np (from web version of paper http://www.sunday-times.co.uk).
- Hughes, R. (1998a). IOC forced to back down over drugs case. *The Sunday-Times*, February 13, np (from web version of paper http://www.sunday-times.co.uk).
- _____. (1998b). Marijuana offence is soft target for IOC. *The Sunday-Times*, February 12, np (from web version of paper http://www.sunday-times.co.uk).
- International Olympic Committee president appoints working group on the issue of marijuana. (1998). International Olympic Committee, February 14, Press Release #29.
- Meeting of the IOC working group on the issue of marijuana. (1998). International Olympic Committee, February 19, Press Release #44.
- Reeb, M. (1998). The court of arbitration for sport in Nagano. *Olympic Review*, XXVI-20, April-May, np (from web version of journal: http://www.olympic.org/news/review/1998_20/en/j_tas_e.html).

Case 8.32

Corporate Ethics: Is the IOC Different from Other Organizations?

The International Olympic Committee has long held itself as the morally sound leadership group of a movement based on the historic precepts of its foundation. Most of these ideas originate from IOC founder Pierre de Coubertin. The IOC holds itself as the "supreme authority of the Olympic Movement," in that its leadership role emanates from Olympism, the foundational philosophy of the movement.

Looking into the Olympic Charter we find elements of this guiding moral framework. The second, third, sixth and seventh of these fundamental principles provide further elements of the concept of Olympism (these can be found on the IOC's web page—www.olympic.org). We see the overall pattern of the philosophy. The ideas of overall human development, education, and peace are repeated. What we do not see, however, are the high moral principles that are to guide the action of the actual IOC membership.

While most organizations of this size, wealth, and international stature have developed or have been forced to instigate codes of conduct, this organization has seen itself as above such matters and done nothing in this regard. The Olympic Charter has some guidelines that sanction members. In chapter two of the charter, sections 1.3, 1.4, 1.6, all of 2, and all of 3 delineate the obligations and responsibilities of members. Most are, however, open to broad interpretation and are not based on a clear code of conduct.

In late 1998 serious allegations surrounding the Salt Lake City bidding process were exposed. IOC president Juan Samaranch was informed of the allegations in early December 1998. An ad hoc commission was proposed towards meeting in late January 1999 on these allegations. The IOC moved into damage control over the allegations.

In early 1999 the president and his deputy of the Salt Lake Organizing Committee (SLOC) resigned over the "bribery scandal." The Federal Bureau of Investigation (FBI) also began investigations into this scandal. In early February 1999, the Board of Ethics of SLOC presented a "report to the board of trustees." Among the allegations were that IOC members or their family received: consultancies (and fees); education, medical, or direct monies; funds to support athletes and scholarships; extensive trips, gifts, and entertainment; and the opportunity to play with the Utah Symphony. The report runs to 59 pages.

The matter also led to an inquiry in the U.S. Senate, a potential U.S. Justice Department investigation of criminal activity by IOC members, as well as a widespread, severe media critique of IOC operations. In all of this Samaranch claimed his innocence while 25 other IOC members (according to a newspaper chronology of this scandal) were placed under suspicion. Samaranch announced the finding of the first ad hoc commission report in December 1998 and the second meeting report in March 1999. In the extraordinary IOC session in March, and for the first time in its history, the IOC membership voted to expel 6 members, warn another 10, and accept 4 resignations (one member died before being expelled).

From this an IOC Ethics Commission was formed. This commission met in early May 1999. According to IOC press releases, "the IOC Code of Conduct will govern the actions of IOC members and that of officials of candidate cities for the Olympic Games and Organizing Committees of the Games (OCOGs) as they interact with IOC members" (May 3, 1999). The mission of this commission was identified: "The mission of the IOC Ethics Commission is to provide advice and guidance on how the IOC operates in accordance with the best practices of international business and government" (ibid.). All of this will, it is stated:

bear in mind the Olympic Charter as they [the commission] build on the Olympic Movement to promote positive ethics and ensure transparency and accountability. The commission will also establish standards and rules that are understandable and applicable in the forthcoming IOC Code of Conduct, as well as verify that the response to ethical issues is active, comprehensive, and effective (ibid.).

The commission of eight persons (five external to the IOC) began by discussing several of the issues arising from the Salt Lake and then the Sydney bidding processes.

After 105 years the IOC has expelled members, admitted it requires reform, that it has been tarnished, and is responsible to the public. All of this is a result of practices that existed for much of the Olympic movement's post-World War II history (Simson & Jennings, 1992).

Questions to Consider for Discussion

1. What would you suggest that the IOC's Code of Conduct contain? What rationales are basic to this code? What ethical principles are central to this code?

2. Due to the lack of transparency, the nature of the IOC's structure and operations, the IOC's ability to rebuke journalistic critiques of its accepted behaviors (e.g., Simson and Jennings revelations), and a history of condoning the actions of its members as identified in the SLOC report, is it justifiable that some members were expelled while others were merely warned? What ethical elements form the bases of your decision?

3. Can the IOC overcome the long-term behavior of its members through a Code of Conduct? Why or why not?

4. If Samaranch is implicated in the bribery scandal, or at least, has accepted expensive gifts (against the IOC's own guidelines), what and how should he be dealt with generally (following what ethical principles)? Or under a code of conduct?

References

*   International Olympic Committee. (1997). *The Olympic Charter* (from web page: http://www.olympic.org).
*   Simson, V., and Jennings, A. (1992). *The Lords of the Rings: Power, Money and Drugs in the Modern Olympics.* London: Simon and Schuster.
*   Press Release. (1999). International Olympic Committee, May 3.

Case 8.33

Moral Character in Professional Sport

The eve of the 1999 Super Bowl saw the arrest of one of the NFL's supposed icons of moral character. Eugene Robinson, the defensive back for the Atlanta Falcons, was arrested on charges of soliciting oral sex from an undercover police officer. The star player had received the Bart Starr Award for moral character the morning of the incident. After his arrest, the player said that he would return the award. He made the following public statement of apology:

> What I want to do now is apologize first to my lord Jesus Christ, secondly to my wife and kids, and thirdly to my teammates and the entire Atlanta Falcons organization for the distraction that I may have caused them. And I say that sincerely, I really say that sincerely. (Associated Press, 1999)

Interestingly, another player was arrested on a similar charge five days after the Robinson episode.

At a superficial level, these cases are more or less simple to assess–a crime was committed, charges were laid, and the guilty party will suffer the consequences that the laws of the land deem necessary. However, we need to probe what lies beneath these charges and other legal and ethical transgression that well-known sport figures have committed (e.g., the IOC scandal, Mike Tyson). Is it the case that some of these individuals perceive their status as famous and rich professional athletes as the go-ahead for any kind of behavior? Do they suffer from what Ludwig and Longenecker (1993) termed the "Bathsheba Syndrome," in which those that wield power become blind to their responsibilities as professionals and members of the community?

Questions to Consider for Discussion

1. How much credit should be given to Robinson's gesture to in returning the Bart Starr Award?

2. How would you describe the ethical culture of professional sport?

3. To what extent are players to blame for their behavior in this environment?

4. What punishment, in addition to legal sanctions, should be given to these players? Why?

5. To what extent are "elite" athletes obligated to be role models? Why?

References

- Associated Press. (1999). Falcon's Robinson says he'll return Bart Starr Award. *Ottawa Citizen*, February 5.

- Associated Press. (1999). Raiders defensive end Audray Bruce accused of solicitation. *Ottawa Citizen*, February 6.
- Ludwig, D.C., & Longenecker, C.O. (1993). The Bathsheba syndrome: The ethical failure of successful leaders. *Journal of Business Ethics*, 12:265-273.
- Editorial. (1999). Robinson to return award. *Ottawa Citizen*, February 6.
- Editorial. (1999). Falcons FS Eugene Robinson plays shaky game after arrest. *Ticker*, February 1.

Case 8.34

Violence in Hockey: When Is It "Part of the Game"? When Is It a Crime?

In a minor league game in Fresno California, Dean Trboyevich, a defenseman for the Anchorage Aces, cross-checked an opposition player. This action triggered a bench-clearing brawl that resulted in 11 players being ejected and Trboyevich receiving a major penalty for high sticking and an additional penalty for attempting to injure the opposition player, Jacques Mailhot. Mailhot was not injured in the incident and, in fact, went on to score his first goal of the season. The penalties handed out by the referee were not the end of Trboyevich's problems. He was later charged by the Fresno police with using his stick as a deadly weapon and, in addition to being fined and suspended from further league play, he faces a possible four-year jail sentence.

To someone who has never watched the game of hockey, the charge of assault-with-a-deadly-weapon would be expected, for a violent act *is* a violent act whether it occurs on the ice or in the parking lot. However, to the "knowledgeable" hockey fan, such behavior is typically perceived as "part of the game," as is the penchant for hockey players to fight on the ice when tempers flare.

Questions to Consider for Discussion

1. Can violent behavior ever be justified in sport?
2. Why is there a "double standard" in hockey?
3. Who benefits from this double standard?
4. What could be done to eliminate violence from hockey?
5. What effect would this have upon the various stakeholders (e.g., fans–children and adults, players–children and adults, owners, other business stakeholders)?

Reference

- The Associated Press. (1999). Hockey player suspended, fined. *The Ottawa Citizen*, February 6, p.B2.

Case 8.35

Ethical Consistency

In 1999 Czech tennis star Petr Korda tested positive for steroid use at the prestigious Wimbledon Tournament. His punishment from the Czech Tennis Association involved his being banned from playing tennis in his home country for one year–but only in his home country. In addition, the International Tennis Association (ITA) punished him by taking away the ranking points accrued as a result of his playing in the quarter finals and his forfeiture of $94,529 in Wimbledon prize money. The International Tennis Federation (ITF) found the player guilty. However, it took no action to ban him from play as they accepted his explanation that he had no idea how the drug Nandrolene had entered his system.

Other tennis players reacted negatively to what they perceived as the unjust non-punishment of Korda. For example, Jonas Bjorkman of Sweden demanded the suspension of Korda and criticized the ITF. He stated that "we've heard so many things that guys are positive and they just cover it over–they are just so scared of putting it out.... I think it's the worst decision the ITF could have made. It is totally the worst that could happen to tennis, I hope all the players in Australia [the current tournament] will go together and really put pressure on the ITF and the ATP (Association of Tennis Professionals)." Further, Bjorkman suggested that "if you cheat, you should be suspended for two, three, four, five years.... Why be tested 15 times a year when we are still not going to be really hard on the guys who are cheating."

Questions to Consider for Discussion

1. Does the ITF have a vested interest in accepting Korda's rationalization?

2. Does the Czech Tennis Association have a vested interest in charging him?

3. What external factors could be influencing the decision-making processes at the Czech national level and the international level?

4. To what extent is Korda responsible for what he ingests? What is the ethical basis of his defense? What other drug charges in sport do you know of in which the athlete claimed ignorance or blamed their trainer/physician? Is this acceptable? What does this tell you about the moral and social development of elite athletes?

5. What kind of pressure should the other players place on the ITF or the ATP?

References

- CBS SportLine Wire Reports. (1999). Korda wins ruling against ITF. January 29.
- Reuters. (1999). Bjorkman calls for ban on Korda. January 6.
- Reuters. (1999). Czech star to face media crush on Tuesday. Steroid issues cloud defense of Australia Open crown. January 11.
- *The Ottawa Citizen.* (1999). Czech federation bans Korda. February 6, B2.

Case 8.36

IOC Ethics and the Drugs in Sport War

A Foxsportsnet sport journalist program, "GoinDeep" (November 11, 1998) featured a piece on drugs in sport. In that television journalism piece evidence indicated that the IOC has been implicated in covering up positive drug tests. These revelations come from scientists, medical practitioners, and other informed individuals. They support the claims made by Simson and Jennings (1992) and Jennings (1996). Clearly there is a contradiction here.

The eighth purpose of the IOC, as defined in Chapter 1 of the Olympic Charter, is to lead the fight against doping in sport. At the IOC sponsored and led World Conference on Doping in Sport (3-4 February 1999 in Lausanne, Switzerland) the IOC proposed the formation of a global anti-doping agency (Olympic Movement Anti-Doping Agency), setting a uniform set of drug use penalties across all sports, and placing IOC President Samaranch as chair of this agency. In the end the IOC had to back down over its leadership and centralized control of such an agency. The involvement, policy reviewing, and investigation by the European Council and the United States government, and the intransigence of several international sport federations for input and power over this agency, met with incredulousness and fear by the IOC.

A new agency (the International Anti-Doping Agency) will operate with a $25 million U.S. input from the IOC but will be independent from the IOC. The uniform penalties were fought by certain large sport organizations (e.g., cycling, soccer, and tennis) and ultimately were watered down. The legal implications and possible further court actions, focused mainly on the restraint of athletes' right to obtain a livelihood, were seen to be difficult and costly. In the end, the six-point "Lausanne Declaration" (see appendix below, pp.203-204) resulted from this conference that outlined the "global fight against drugs." Samaranch declared this a "great victory for clean sport." The agency will have representatives from the Olympic family, government, and intergovernmental organizations. Rather than centrally locate the IOC in this agency, it has been relegated to a coordinating role, although it will still have a central functional role.

If we return to the televised and written accusations of the IOC, we can observe why this occurred. Jennings (1996) wrote, "When the Games were last in America a dozen years ago [1984], the Olympic committee hid the true number of dopers they caught" (p.7). Further in this book Jennings (1996) notes that there was a general clamoring within sport (i.e., by athletes, coaches, administrators) about the hypocrisy of the doping issue. He wrote, "Samaranch is feeling the heat. In December 1995, speaking in Berlin, he asserted that `In Atlanta, there will be very few cases of doping or none.' That's what the sponsors want to hear but many athletes have had enough; they know doping is rampant and despise the Olympic committee for the cover-up" (Jennings, 1996, p.299).

Foxsports investigative sport journalist Diana Nyan interviewed a number of people in the segment "Blood Feud" that corroborate Jennings accusations. Among those interviewed were Dr. Don Catlin and Dr. Robert Voy. The former is director of the Los Angeles IOC-accredited drug lab. He confirmed that nine positive sample B tests were found during the 1984 Games that the IOC did not announce (that is, no action was taken on them). Catlin reported nine positive tests to the IOC, but the IOC had the codes that identify the athletes with the samples.

Dr. Voy resigned from the USOC's medical commission over the lack of integrity in dealing with drugs in sport. He finds that the IOC does not match their philosophy against drugs with action. New tests based on research were needed, but the funding was limited even though the IOC has a billion-dollar budget. Voy is a highly regarded expert on drugs in sport and has published many works on the subject.

Clearly there is considerable confusion and contradiction in all of this. On the one hand, the lack of transparency of the IOC conflicts with the reality of its practices. Whether the truth will prevail, and whose truth it will be, is questionable. If the IOC does further its current, meager attempts to be more transparent, it may be some time before deep, ongoing issues are resolved.

Questions to Consider for Discussion

1. If we assume that the accusations are correct from the Foxsport investigative report, how would you identify and explain the words and actions of the IOC?

2. Journalists are often accused of being smut mongers and of low moral standing. Considering the corroboration of the information

from a variety of sources (including trained scientists and medical practitioners), how would you make sense of the allegations of an IOC cover-up of positive drug tests?

3. Identify and discuss the moral and resultant ethical action of each side of this debate.

4. Is the war on drugs being won? Who is winning it? What in the end should be done about the issue?

5. Should Ben Johnson's gold medal and record (only equaled in June, 1999) be restored? What are the moral aspects of your decision?

References

- IOC. (Various, web page: http://www.olympic.org).
- Jennings, A. (1996). *The New Lords of the Rings: Olympic Corruption and How to Buy Gold Medals.* London: Pocket Books.
- Simson, V., & Jennings, A. (1992). *The Lords of the Rings: Power, Money and Drugs in the Modern Olympics.* London: Simon & Schuster.

Lausanne Declaration on Doping in Sport

Adopted by the World Conference on Doping in Sport; 4 February 1999, Lausanne, Switzerland

Considering that doping practices contravene sport and medical ethics, and that they constitute violations of the rules established by the Olympic Movement, and concerned by the threat that doping poses to the health of athletes and youth in general;

Recognizing that the fight against doping in sport is the concern of all: the Olympic Movement and other sports organizations, governments, inter-governmental and non-governmental organizations, sportsmen and sportswomen throughout the world, and their entourage;

The World Conference on Doping in Sport, with the participation of representatives of governments, of inter-governmental and non-governmental organizations, of the International Olympic Committee (IOC), the International sports Federations (IFs), the National Olympic Committees (NOCs), and of the athletes, declares:

1. Education, prevention and athletes' rights

The Olympic oath shall be extended to coaches and other officials, and shall include the respect of integrity, ethics and fair play in sport. Educational and preventive campaigns will be intensified, focusing principally on youth, and athletes and their entourage. Complete transparency shall be assured in all activities to fight doping, except for preserving the confidentiality necessary to protect the fundamental rights of athletes. Partnership with the media shall be sought in anti-doping campaigns.

2. Olympic Movement Anti-Doping Code

The Olympic Movement Anti-Doping Code is accepted as the basis for the fight against doping, which is defined as the use of an artifice, whether substance or method, potentially dangerous to athletes' health and/or capable of enhancing their performances, or the presence in the athlete's body of a substance, or the ascertainment of the use of a method on the list annexed to the Olympic Movement Anti-Doping Code.

The Olympic Movement Anti-Doping Code applies to all athletes, coaches, instructors, officials, and to all medical and paramedical staff working with athletes or treating athletes participating in or training for sports competitions organized within the framework of the Olympic Movement.

3. Sanctions

The sanctions which apply to doping violations will be imposed in the framework of controls both during and out of competition.

In accordance with the wishes of the athletes, the NOCs and a large majority of the IFs, the minimum required sanction for major doping substances or prohibited methods shall be a suspension of the athlete from all competition for a period of two years, for a first offence. However, based on specific, exceptional circumstances to be evaluated in the first instance by the competent IF bodies, there may be a provision for a possible modification of the two-year sanction. Additional sanctions or measures may be applied. More severe sanctions shall apply to coaches and officials guilty of violations of the Olympic Movement Anti-Doping Code.

4. International Anti-Doping Agency

An independent International Anti-Doping Agency shall be established so as to be fully operational for the Games of the XXVII

Olympiad in Sydney in 2000. This institution will have as its mandate, notably, to coordinate the various programmes necessary to realize the objectives that shall be defined jointly by all the parties concerned. Among these programmes, consideration should be given in particular to expanding out-of-competition testing, coordinating research, promoting preventive and educational actions and harmonizing scientific and technical standards and procedures for analyses and equipment. A working group representing the Olympic Movement, including the athletes, as well as the governments and inter-governmental organizations concerned, will meet, on the initiative of the IOC, within three months, to define the structure, mission and financing of the Agency. The Olympic Movement commits to allocate a capital of US $25 million to the Agency.

5. Responsibilities of the IOC, the IFs, the NOCs and the CAS

The IOC, the IFs and the NOCs will maintain their respective competence and responsibility to apply doping rules in accordance with their own procedures, and in cooperation with the International Anti-Doping Agency. Consequently, decisions handed down in the first instance will be under the exclusive responsibility of the IFs, the NOCs or, during the Olympic Games, the IOC. With regard to last instance appeals, the IOC, the IFs and the NOCs recognize the authority of the Court of Arbitration for Sport (CAS), after their own procedures have been exhausted.

In order to protect athletes and their rights in the area of disciplinary procedure, the general principles of law, such as the right to a hearing, the right to legal assistance, and the right to present evidence and call witnesses, will be confirmed and incorporated into all applicable procedures.

6. Collaboration between the Olympic Movement and public authorities

The collaboration in the fight against doping between sports organizations and public authorities shall be reinforced according to the responsibilities of each party. Together, they will also take action in the areas of education, scientific research, social and health measures to protect athletes, and coordination of legislation relative to doping.

Done in Lausanne (Switzerland), 4 February 1999.

9

Putting Theory into Action: Case Studies for Model II

Basic Assumptions for Case Study Analysis Using Model II

The following cases have been written with the advanced or Model II analysis in mind. As with the cases in Chapter 8, we wish to encourage the development of the student's ability to assess and resolve dilemmas as well as to encourage creativity and logical thinking. Each case contains a brief preamble and a subsequent offering of questions for discussion. We suggest that the reader endeavor to do two things. First, whenever possible, place the case in your own context. For example, if you are in Australia, bring your intimate understanding of this culture and its perceptions, norms, and values of sport and recreation to the analysis. Similarly, if you are living in Canada, Ireland, or the U.S., identify these unique cultural and systemic conditions and explore them in your writing. Second, when making assumptions about certain aspects of the case, state explicitly that you are in fact making an assumption (i.e., that conditions X or Z are perceived to exist in this province, state, and/or country and therefore the impact of these conditions probably will be A, B, or C). Be creative—be logical!

Model II—Comprehensive Analysis

For the reader who intends to employ the advanced method of case study analysis, this section provides a plan of attack.

Step One: Information Gathering

Once the case has been read (and reread), all relevant information should be gleaned and categorized based upon the layers of moderators presented in Chapter 4. We recommend that the reader not try to incorporate information from all layers in the first few case study analyses. Rather, it may be best to proceed with one layer of moderators at a time for the first two or three cases and then gradually add layers until the case is being analyzed using information based upon all moderators of ethical decision making.

For example, for the first few cases the student should try to describe the extent to which the main characters' psychological, ethical, and demographic profiles contribute to a better understanding of the circumstances that surround the dilemma and its eventual resolution. This section should be written and situated as the opening paragraph of the case study. Once this has been done the student should then proceed to the second step–the decision process.

Step Two: The Decision Process

The student, having described one or more layers of moderators, can proceed to the decision process. In this section each of the seven stages of the decision process are addressed. The information gathered in Step One should be incorporated into the student's analysis of each of the seven stages of the process. If the student fails to do this, the work done in Step One will be wasted.

Step Three: The Conclusion and Maxims

The final step in the case analysis is reserved for concluding remarks from the student. These remarks should not only refer to the dilemma and its resolution but also discuss the manner in which the layers of ethical decision making influenced the decision process.

It is also recommended that students identify any maxims, practical or conceptual, that they may have discovered from their analysis of the case and from their examination of their own orientation or attitudes prior to and following their investigation of the particular ethical issue. That is, what have you learned? How have your opinions or beliefs changed?

Example Case: Gender and Sport

In the fall of 1992 a female high school student, Ruth, of exceptional skill in the sport of soccer, attended a high school training camp for the senior boys' team. She believed that the boys' team would play at a skill level comparable to her own and that the involvement at a "higher" level would develop her soccer abilities physically and mentally. She was successful in gaining a position on the team based upon her athletic skills.

This region was very traditional in its way of thinking. It was an agricultural community, which often held in disdain that which filtered in from the "cosmopolitan" centers in the east. News of Ruth's success quickly found its way to the local and provincial media. As word spread of the "girl playing on the boys' team," the executive director of the

Provincial High School Athletic Association (PHSSA), Ted, was contacted by a number of parents, board members, and interested individuals who expressed mixed feelings regarding the incident.

Ted is the 43-year-old father of two teenage daughters. He has a diploma in Sport and Recreation Management from a local community college and is extremely committed to his work and the association. He has always been a strong advocate of women's sport, particularly for his own daughters. They know Ruth well and support her position as athletes and in their understanding of the notion of equality.

The association itself is rather conventional and male-dominated, as are most of the associations in the Sport Federation. It has yet to develop a gender policy apart from the traditional advocacy and support for segregation. Many individuals believed that they were being "sensitive men of the '90s" by consenting to equal funding for a separate system for women.

The PHSAA has the final say in all high school matters of policy. Though Ted, as the executive director, is to report to the board for a final decision, he knows that the board will look to him for guidance as they have done for the past 13 years of his tenure. Thus Ted feels this decision weigh heavily upon his shoulders. He feels a great deal of mixed pressure from his family, from his friends and peers, as well as from the public that seem not too anxious to embarrass "women's lib" to this extent.

Ted is faced with the following dilemma: Should Ruth be allowed to continue playing with the boys' team or should she be restricted to "girls only" teams?

Case Study Analysis

The case study analysis will be carried out in two phases. The first phase will involve a general description of the moderators of ethical decision making in the context of the case. The second phase will describe each stage of the ethical decision-making process as it pertains to the case and is influenced by the situational moderators.

External Moderators

External moderators include societal, political, economic, and technical influencers. From a societal perspective, competitive sport has traditionally been segregated along gender lines. The public view, as received and interpreted by Ted, is that "boys compete with boys" and "girls compete with girls." The public's argument for segregation includes the beliefs that girls will be injured playing against boys, that the standard of competition will be unfair for girls, and that, because fewer girls would excel in an "open" league, fewer female sport role models would exist. These views are held despite the general trend in North America of breaking down the barriers in terms of gender equity and the potential for skill development in a more highly competitive sport environment.

Politically, the issue of integration in competitive sport has not yet received attention locally or provincially. Ruth's case may be the first of a trend, a "politically correct" trend at that, and therefore may become politically significant should the consciousness of the public be raised. While lobby groups and parent associations have been proactive regarding integration generally and gender equity specifically in educational contexts, there as yet exists no political will, provincially or nationally, to desegregate boys' and girls' competitive high school sport.

The economy may have an effect upon Ted's decision in terms of the ability of the association to withstand the costs of potential litigation should Ruth decide to proceed with a human rights court case. The cost of co-ed facility rental (e.g., dual locker room facilities) may also enter as a potentially unacceptable cost to the association. There may, however, be savings realized from program integration. For example, a parallel sport system, that is, separate boys' and girls' leagues, would be reduced to a single-gender, "neutral" sport system, which may reduce costs by half for the association and for the schools.

Finally, technical factors may involve facility and/or logistic concerns that presently exist and/or those that may come about should gender integration occur. Integration may require the association to make rule, facility, and/or equipment changes to accommodate co-ed teams. In addition, the association would have to rewrite all policy and procedures for each sport in order to organize competitive schedules, official assignments, and facility and equipment rental.

Situational Moderators

Situational moderators include organizational ideology, culture, and climate. The association's mission statement (i.e., its stated ideology) is committed to the pursuit of athletic excellence through equitable yet separate programming for male and female student athletes. The association, at present, does not recognize the notion of integration in terms of competitive sport in the high school setting.

The association's culture is predominantly reflective of the traditional view of gender segregation in sport contexts. The staff and the board of directors, with the exception of the office manager, are male and are committed to the association's implicit belief that equitable and segregated high school sport programming is right and just treatment for male and female student athletes. The association's membership has thus far supported the view of gender segregation. There has been no previous suggestion that integrated sport in the high schools is desired or desirable.

The association's climate, that is, the shared perception of what the organization actually does, has a potential role to play in this dilemma. While the members of the association are aware of the movement towards integration in terms of the administrative aspects of sport (i.e., combining boys' and girls' teams in terms of fundraising activities and sponsorships), the notion that boys and girls will play on the same team is beyond the grasp of most. Conceptually, some are in agreement, but in practice, it is too radical a thought to put into action or to support.

Significant Other Moderators

Three cohorts of significant others are identified in the model. They are extraorganizational, interorganizational, and personal significant others. The extraorganizational influencers in this case have expressed varied opinions regarding Ruth's fate. Generally, the female executive directors from other provincial sport-governing bodies, such as volleyball, basketball, swimming, and field hockey, have supported Ruth's efforts. However, their male counterparts in such sports as football, wrestling, track and field, and hockey, who form the majority of the professional staff in the Provincial Sport Centre, do not. Within the school context the male physical education teachers are somewhat ambivalent towards the notion of integration, whereas the female physical education teachers are supportive of the notion of integration. Other members of the staff accept the notion of integration generally, as it has been a focus of many other programs in the curricula (e.g., students with mental and/or physical disabilities).

Within the organization, those who have influence with Ted are in favor of the status quo (i.e., segregation). The board of directors is supportive of maintaining the policy of segregation as is the general membership as polled by Ted. Ted's friends and immediate family represent both sides of the issue with his teenage daughters in favor of integration.

Issue Specific Moderators

The characteristics of the ethical issue represent the fourth category of moderators of ethical decision making. An ethical issue may be described in terms of the following characteristics: immediacy, proximity, concentration, responsibility, magnitude, social consensus, probability of effect, as well as its strategic and tactical significance. This case requires an immediate response from the association; it affects directly the local and provincial high school community sport system; it is focused upon one girl yet has implications for all female student athletes; it is the responsibility of the executive director and his board to make a ruling; its magnitude is significant as it may change the face of high school athletics as it has been practised (i.e., to sanction integration rather than segregation); any decision (including no decision) will have an effect upon Ruth and the future of integration in sport; it does not have social consensus, though there is a trend towards traditional beliefs in segregated sport. Finally, the decision that Ted must make is a strategic (policy) decision, which implies it will have a more global impact upon the association than a tactical decision (procedural). In summary, this issue is morally intensive and requires a comprehensive ethical analysis in order to seek a favorable resolution.

Individual Moderators

Perhaps the most significant of the moderators are those that describe the individual's demographic, philosophical, and psychological make-up. Ted is a 43-year-old white male with a diploma in sport administration from a community college. He is married with two teenage daughters. His philosophical orientation is eclectic with some strong teleological tendencies (i.e., his focus is predominantly organizational ends). If Ted's philosophical orientation were deontological, his focus would be organizational policy, procedure, and tradition; were it existential, his focus would be upon individual free will and individual responsibility for all behavior. Ted can also be described, in terms of his moral development, as falling into Kohlberg's (1969) conventional level. As a result, Ted is highly influenced by nomothetic values and significant others. If he were pre-conventional in his moral development, his behavior would be characterized by selfish careerism, whereas if his level of development were post-conventional, he would demonstrate strong tendencies of individualism and universal/objective justice.

The Ethical Decision-Making Process

The process of ethical decision making in the model consists of seven stages: recognition of ethical dilemma, generation of alternatives, ethical evaluation of alternatives, ethical decision, intention, overt ethical and/or unethical behavior, and evaluation of behavior. To make ethically complete decisions one must assess each stage in terms of existential, deontological, and teleological criteria.

Figure 9.1: Gender Conflict in High School Soccer

Ethical Decision Making Process	Teleology	Deontology	Existentialism
Recognition of ethical dilemma	Sport vs. litigation	Policy	Free will and responsibility
Generation of alternatives	Ends	Means/policy	Free will and responsibility
Ethical evaluation of alternatives	Best ends	Best means	Best possibility of free will and responsibility
Ideal ethical decision	Decline player	Decline player	Allow player
Intention	Decline player with support	Decline player with support	Allow player without support or decline player with support
Overt decision	Decline player: teleological behavior	Decline player: Deontological behavior	Decline player: Inauthentic behavior
Evaluation of behavior	A good decision	A right decision	Not an authentic decision

The following involves a discussion of each cell of the matrix found in Figure 9.1.

Stage I: Recognition of ethical dilemma. From the teleological perspective, Ted may recognize the dilemma in terms of its impact upon the traditional view of segregation within high school sport and/or upon the association in terms of potential costs of litigation should Ruth proceed with a human rights case. Deontologically, Ted may view the dilemma as a matter of organizational policy. Existentially, Ted may perceive the issue as primarily one of Ruth's need for free will and responsibility for her own action.

Stage II: Generation of alternatives. Alternatives that will be generated by Ted will include those that attempt to achieve the best ends for the sport in general and the association in particular (teleology), those that follow the best means in terms of adhering to the association's policy, procedure, and tradition (deontology), and those that reflect his authentic belief in the need for all individuals to exercise their free will and take personal responsibility for all their actions (existentialism).

Stage III: Ethical evaluation of alternatives. Each alternative generated will be juxtaposed with the three perspectives to determine their ethical viability. The teleological criterion will determine the extent to which an alternative satisfies the best end result for the dilemma (e.g., what is best), ultimately, for the sport of soccer. The deontological criterion will assess each alternative in terms of its adherence to existing organizational policy, procedure, and tradition. The degree to which an alternative provides for the individual's free will and personal responsibility is the existential criterion.

Stage IV: Ethical decision. Based upon the ethical evaluation, one alternative will be selected as meeting the ethical demands of the teleological, deontological, and existential perspectives. It may not, however, be possible for any one alternative to meet all criteria. For example, Ted may deny Ruth's request because it is inconsistent with the wishes of the majority of the association's membership (teleology) and because it is against stated organizational policy (deontology). Existentially, he may accept her request because to refuse it would be to deny her free will.

Stage V: Intention. This phase suggests that though the decision-maker may know what the right decision ought to be he may not necessarily intend to carry it out for a variety of reasons. Ted's teleological intent to deny Ruth's request, based upon the supposed greater good of the high school program, is supported by his membership. He has, therefore, weak teleological rationale to support Ruth's position. Ted's deontological intent to deny is based upon existing organizational policy, which supports segregation. Therefore he receives additional philosophical support for his intent to prevent Ruth from participating. Ted's existential intent contrasts with the former two positions. He feels that Ruth's free will is being denied, yet realizes that he has no support for this position. As Ted looks externally for moral direction (i.e., Kohlberg's conventional level) his existential intent is overridden by his teleological and deontological intentions.

Stage VI: Overt ethical and/or unethical behavior. Ted's overt behavior in denying Ruth's request to participate with the male team is guided by teleological and deontological considerations. It is not existential. Ted's behavior is teleological in nature as it results in what the association and the membership in general support as being ultimately best for high school sport. His behavior is deontologically oriented because he adheres to existing organizational policy, procedure, and tradition (i.e., in favor of segregation). Ted's behavior is not authentic as he submits to external pressure, including the association's membership and organizational policy, despite his belief that Ruth ought to be able to choose and take responsibility for her own actions as a student athlete.

Stage VII: Evaluation of behavior. Ted's behavior can be considered as teleologically "good," deontologically "right," yet existentially unauthentic. As a result, Ted, while receiving support for his decision from external sources (i.e., the association's board and its membership) feels an inner tension as he was not able to support his authentic desire to uphold Ruth's free will and choice. While his behavior did not satisfy all ethical criteria it did receive support from the membership and from the organization. A decision meeting the teleological criterion (i.e., that which results in the best end) and the deontological criterion (i.e., that which follows organizational policy) is generally accepted as optimal in most organizational contexts (e.g., the Janus Head model as proposed by Brady, 1985). The existential criterion, which is lacking in Ted's overt behavior, is overlooked typically in administrative contexts as the "ideal organizational person" is encouraged to refrain from personal or authentic input in organizational affairs and behave in a value-neutral (Weber, 1947) or value-free (Simon, 1976) manner that is consistent with policy and procedure.

Summary

This case study demonstrates the utility of Model II to analyze ethical dilemmas in a comprehensive fashion. The model, while prescribing the process of ethical decision making, does not attempt to prescribe what behavior ought to be actualized. It does, however, provide the reader with three perspectives to assess the ethical comprehensiveness of decision-making behavior. Its practical use is to assist the decision-maker in understanding, in a holistic manner, the moderators and the process of ethical decision-making in organizations.

References

Brudy, N.F. (1985). A Janus-headed model of ethical theory. Looking two ways at business/society issues. *Academy of Management Review*, 10:568-576.

Kohlberg, L. (1969). Stage and sequence: The cognitive-developmental approach to socialization. In D.A. Goslin (Ed.). *Handbook of Socialization Theory and Research*, pp.347-480. Chicago: Rand McNally.

Simon, H. (1976). *Administrative Behavior*. New York: The Free Press.

Weber, M. (1947). *The Theory of Social and Economic Organizations*, A.M. Henderson & T. Parsons, Trans. London: Oxford University Press.

Case Studies

Case 9.1

The Young Coach and the Old Tradition

As students graduate to become professionals in their chosen field, often they may be technically competent to take on their new role yet be unprepared to undertake the somewhat more subtle responsibilities of leadership. As a result a variety of situations may arise that will challenge their personal ethics as well as their personal and task-relevant maturity. This particular case was developed to provide an example of the conflict (internal/external and personal/professional) that an individual might face as he or she becomes a "professional" and is faced with additional responsibility and accountability.

Maggie was a 26-year-old graduate student in Kinesiology at one the country's more prestigious universities. She had also been a top-ranked volleyball player in her years of competition. Her career as a player had been cut short as a result of a back injury sustained at a national championship. Maggie had managed, however, to continue her involvement in the sport as an assistant coach of the women's varsity team for two years.

In the second year of her graduate program the head coach, Rob, went on sabbatical and Maggie was offered the job of interim head coach. Maggie felt that this was indeed a major turning point in her career. As a graduate student she was in love with university life and felt that this opportunity to be a head coach would make her curriculum vitae very strong for any future university positions to which she may apply. She was extremely ambitious. Her competitive drive as an athlete was successfully transferred to her career as an "apprentice" academic.

The season began very well. The players, many of whom had played their first seasons with Maggie, respected her not only for the ability she displayed as a player but also for her academic success, her knowledge of the sport, and for her intense loyalty to the team. All seemed well. The team was preparing for an exhibition "road trip" and its members were getting rather excited about the season's first competition as well as the first overnight trip. The team members had a rather dubious reputation as "party animals." They tended to drink and carry on as hard as they played in competition, which was rather intense. This tradition had existed long before Maggie was the interim head coach and had in fact been promoted to some extent by the head coach, Rob. His road trip motto was: "Nobody gets hurt, nothing gets broken, everyone plays to the best of their ability, go crazy!" Maggie had actually been one of the more popular and crazier players during her career. Now that she was head coach, her attitude towards drinking on the bus trips was somewhat different, particularly after learning that the athletic administrator, Dr. Belt, was a firm believer in athletes not drinking alcohol at all. This was a university policy. There was also some suspicion that Dr. Belt was anxious to catch the team in the "act" in order to punish Rob for the insolence that he had displayed towards the administration for the last 15 years.

The team boarded the bus and thought that the first stop would be to pick up a supply of beer and wine for the bus-party on the way to the tournament. Maggie had dreaded this moment; she had been, after all, one of the worst offenders as an athlete and her current puritan attitude may not be terribly popular, and was, to say the least, somewhat hypocritical (and inauthentic) based on her past. Nonetheless, Maggie stuck to her initiative to change the team's party culture and said that there would be no stops until they had reached the destination four hours away. The team was not amused. Upon arrival, rooms were assigned at the hotel, and the women were instructed to meet for warm-up in 45 minutes.

The tournament began and Maggie's team performed extremely well, as expected. They won all of their games in the first match and lost once in the second match. Following the matches, the team went out for a few beers at the local bar and were reasonably restrained since the next game was at 8:30 the next morning. As things turned out, Maggie's team won the tournament in wonderful form; the season was off to an excellent start. On the way home a few of the players asked Maggie if a few beers on the bus would be okay. Maggie's resolve weakened and she said it was permitted. The trip home was reasonably calm; some were doing homework, some were singing songs, and several were drinking and being a bit loud all the way home. Upon arrival at Sydney Hall (the Kinesiology building) one of the players dropped a bottle of beer as she got off the bus—it broke and her friends became uncontrollable in their laughter. Unfortunately for them, the head coach of the field hockey team, Professor Penny Rudent, witnessed the incident. The following morning Maggie was asked to meet with Dr. Belt—her heart sank. As she felt her bright career slowly slip away, she wondered what on earth she was going to say and do to resolve this dilemma.

Questions to Consider for Discussion

1. What was the nature of Maggie's conflict in this case?

2. What do you think was the dominant moderator influencing Maggie's behavior?

3. How do you think that this situation could have been avoided?

4. How would the existentialist view this situation?

5. Why do we so often believe that players can become coaches? What is the fallacy in this argument?

Case 9.2

The Benevolent Autocrat

In the administration of many sport- and recreation-related associations, volunteers often play a significant role in organizational decision making. Volunteers join organizations for a variety of reasons, many of which are personal rather than organizational in nature. As a result the commitment of these individuals to the organizational goals may be overshadowed by their personal agendas. This case was written with a focus on decision making within committees and the reality of abuse of power. It provides an example of the ethical complexity of committee decisions and the variety of factors that may influence one's ethical decision making and influence the manner in which one reacts to perceived unethical decisions.

Jim was a 30-year veteran of the provincial government and a former professional boxer. He had held just about every high profile volunteer position, as well as being the executive director of the athletic association for 10 years. He was currently the athletic director of the local university. To put it mildly, Jim believed himself to be well connected and experienced in the nuances of the political climate of provincial and national sport. He was also known for his zealous and often fixated concern for efficiency and short-term effectiveness as well as the habit of running meetings exactly on time whether issues were completely explored or not. His decisions were based upon the bottom-line only.

In June the lobbying of many in the community for additions to the Derry Centre, an indoor aquatics complex, was successful as the state government agreed to provide a substantial grant to commence construction in the fall. Jim was asked to be the chair of the committee. He decided that a report to the Minister of Sport, Recreation, and Culture would be completed after eight meetings, no more and no less.

The committee consisted of members of the aquatics community, university coaches, athletes, and parents. A number of issues were on the table, not the least of which was the problem of what to do with the elite synchronized swimmers who would be displaced by the construction. There were several national and international athletes using the facility, and finding them another venue in which to train was a concern. A number of suggestions were made for these athletes and what appeared to be a simple solution fast became an extremely heated political debate. This debate involved a number of sport organizations who felt that their interests were being compromised by the support offered to this group of swimmers. For example, the synchro team (the daughter of the dean of his faculty was a team member) felt threatened because they perceived that their hours were going to be reduced; the community swim program felt equally concerned because of reduced hours as well as the perception that the elite synchro swimmers were being favored over the grassroots speed swimmers once again (the son of the university's president was one of these athletes); and the all-male Old Dogs Triathlon Club, whose members always felt that they were being discriminated against (and were now facing reverse gender discrimination) were ready to go to the local paper with their concerns. It seemed that the members of the committee and the various groups that were going to be influenced by the construction had lost sight of the long-term potential for the new addition to enhance the swimming community at large. Jim, however, did not lose sight of this fact and was "on task" despite the tangents that seemed to be multiplying as weeks passed.

The committee members, after much debate, believed that they had reached decisions regarding the nature of the addition to the aquatics center as well as the displacement of the swimmers. Regarding the latter, the following was the committee's proposal:

1. As the Olympics were fast approaching, priority should be given to the displaced elite synchro swimmers at the city's other aquatics center;

2. The speed swimmers would have to arrange their schedule to share morning and evening pool times;

3. The community swim program would not be affected;

4. The Old Dogs would have to cancel their training in the pool until after the synchro team left for the Olympics.

These recommendations were unanimously supported by the committee at the seventh meeting. Prior to the eighth meeting, Jim sat beside the dean of the faculty at a varsity basketball game and discussed the progress of the committee. The dean made the comment that he sincerely hoped that his daughter's synchro team would not be affected by the new construction.

At the end of the eighth meeting, Jim read to the committee the recommendation that he was going to bring forth to the Minister. It was as follows:

1. The speed swimmers would share morning and evening practices
    with the Old Dogs;

2. The synchro team and the speed swimming club would not be ef-
    fected because we must maintain the integrity of the grassroots de-
    velopmental initiatives as well as our Olympic aspirations;

3. The community swim program would be temporarily cancelled.

The committee members were stunned. They did not respond to the
"edict" out of shock and perhaps out of fear of crossing the imposing,
autocratic, and omnipotent figure of Jim. The recommendations were
delivered to the Minister. Shortly afterward, however, the Minister was
informed that this recommendation in no way represented the will of
the committee. He was apprised of the committee's wishes and was
then faced with a dilemma.

Questions to Consider for Discussion

1. How would you explain the behavior of the committee members?

2. What was the value orientation of Jim?

3. What influenced his decision-making behavior?

4. What role do you think that Utilitarian philosophy played in this
    particular case?

Case 9.3

The Only Coach in Town

The influence and power of the coach in sport is often underestimated. The coach's power to control the behavior on and off the
field is significant and more often than not unquestioned. Within this
athlete-coach dyad there exists the potential for physical and psychological abuse. This case was developed for the reader to explore the
ethical tension between a variety of issues, which include societal values and human sexuality, violence between coach and athlete, and
the conflict between the deontological/societal right and the Utilitarian greatest good for the greatest number.

    The village of Thames was a quiet community about 70 kilome-
ters from Newlondon, a large city with a population of about 2.5 million. There was only one secondary school in the village that served
a considerably large area of the county. The village population had
decreased in the past 10 years as the opportunities for young people
were few and most left as quickly as possible for jobs and university
in Newlondon. The school, Sir W. Church Secondary School, was

able to support a few interscholastic athletic programs. These teams, despite having a relatively small population of students from which to draw, always seemed to be very successful not only in county competition but also in tournaments in Newlondon where they were playing against much larger schools.

One of the school's most successful teams was the women's rugby team. They had been county champions for the past four years thanks to the outstanding and demanding coaching of Mike Murphy—a former national team member. Mike had attended Sir W.C. in the 1980s and, after completing his bachelor's and master's of education degrees and his career as an international competitor, was able to return to Thames to teach in his old secondary school. Mike was a strict teacher. He taught biology, physical education, and health with expectations that exceeded those of most academics in the school. His credo was "Pursue excellence on the pitch, in the classroom, and in your life." This was welcomed and encouraged by the principal, Dr. Jane Smith who felt that the academic performance of the school had slipped in recent years. Needless to say, Mike was very well respected by the students, teachers, parents, and the village-at-large.

All seemed to be going well with Mike until his behavior began to change at the beginning of the fall semester. He became unusually quiet in staff meetings, and his temper was extremely short in class and on the pitch. Rumors started flying and the change in his behavior was the talk of students and staff alike. Dr. Smith had heard these rumors as well as the staff's banter and felt that she needed to speak to Mike to find out the nature of his problem. She decided that she would try to meet with him after rugby practice one evening and take him for coffee. She observed part of the practice and noticed that he was being extremely hard on his athletes, bordering on being verbally abusive to them. Jane was glad that she had chosen to meet with him to prevent this situation from escalating further. After practice the two went for coffee and Mike, with little prodding, gave Jane a story she had not expected.

Mike confided in her that he was gay and that the relationship he had been in for the past seven years had suddenly ended. Most of his family had been unaware of this side of Mike until it was accidentally revealed to them by his sister. There was more—his mother was not well and he was experiencing a number of stress-related symptoms as a result. Mike's life was coming apart.

Jane made a number of suggestions to help, including his taking some time off and seeking out counseling. Mike was unwilling to accept this suggestion since he was not the kind to admit "defeat." Jane left him with the assurance that, if he needed to talk, she was always ready to listen.

The season progressed, the team was winning, but Mike's attitude and behavior were degenerating. The situation came to a crisis during a tournament in Newlondon when Mike, in front of the crowd and the local television cameras, directed a number of profanities at his team, kicked over the announcer's bench after a penalty was missed by the referee, and finally slapped his team captain after a poor play. Mike was ejected from the game. The rugby union disciplinary committee was called immediately in order to determine Mike's fate.

The committee met and was unanimous in their shock regarding Mike's behavior and its decline. Dr. Smith was invited to provide some background on the situation and proceeded to reveal some of the chaotic details of Mike's life. An additional variable was thrown into the mix. If Mike were suspended, there would be no coach and therefore no team. The players had absolutely no one in the community who could intervene; the program would have to be cancelled. The committee was faced with a complex array of variables yet they had to make a decision quickly for the sake of the players, for Mike, for the village, and for the public. The local press was eager to report the details of the story, which had the potential to make national news.

Questions to Consider for Discussion

1. What do you think of the power position between the coach and athlete in general?

2. Is this case of violence an isolated incident or is there an aspect of the culture of sport that would allow Mike to believe that he could strike an athlete?

3. How would you describe the actions of Mike's significant others?

4. Should Mike be asked to coach again in the near future? At all?

Case 9.4

Walden Sportplex—Fighting Change

In many urban centers around the world, population demographics are rapidly and radically changing as we become more and more multicultural and multiracial. With the increasing heterogeneity of cultures, the need to accept alternative paradigms becomes necessary if the evolving community is to survive and prosper. The case of Walden Sportplex was developed to have the reader explore, not only the reality of changing societal demographics and their effect upon organization dynamics, but also upon the nature of cross-cultural relations and ethical behavior.

The Walden Sportplex was build in 1985 in the middle of one of the country's major urban centers. The staff of the Sportplex was made up of individuals recruited locally and internationally from Canada, the United Kingdom, and the U.S. Ten years had passed and the Sportplex clientele had begun to decline in numbers. The executive director, Jake, felt that the "problem" was a function of the downturn in the economy and that if things were going the way they always had all would be well in the next few fiscal quarters. There were those who disagreed. Jake, 61, was the first ED of the Sportsplex. He had retired from the navy and then from his position of intramural director at one of the country's larger universities. His philosophy for the Sportsplex seemed to be quite similar to his former position at the university. His programming, as a result, was extremely popular for the middle- and upper-middle-class professional clientele that accessed the facility before and after work as well as during noon hour. However, during the day and on weekends, the building was gradually becoming more and more dormant.

In the 1970s and 1980s the population demographics of the city steadily began to shift from the dominance of the white, 30-something, middle class of European descent to an increasingly young Asian mix. Nearing the twenty-first century, the city had changed drastically from its profile of 10 years earlier. In particular, the demographics of center town, where the Sportsplex was located, indicated that it was a mecca for a variety of ethnic groups.

Despite the fact that Jake believed the declining numbers to be economically based, he also believed that much of the problem was due to the "ethnic" teenagers hanging around the building after school and during the weekend. The assistant director, Zoe, had another perspective. She believed that rather than being an unwanted nuisance, the youth were in fact a group that the Sportsplex had traditionally neglected and could be very successfully integrated into the center. She believed that not only could these youth be welcomed into current programming, but also new and culturally relevant opportunities could be made available to them. Further, she believed that this segment of the population was the key to the future of the Sportsplex as the population statistics demonstrated. Programming must therefore be developed to include this group as well as their parents in the ethnic community. Zoe was able to convince many of her co-workers as well as the majority of the board of directors.

Jake became quite disturbed with this shift in focus and considered it to be, in fact, a mutiny of his staff. He became so incensed at one staff meeting that he completely lost control and blew up at his staff, in particular at Zoe, whom he blamed for much of the new thinking. He went so far as to suggest that Zoe was doing all of this because she herself was of aboriginal descent and was trying "to get back at the white man." With this, he left in a huff. The incident was reported to the board of directors.

Questions for to Consider for Discussion

1. What demographic changes have you noticed in your community?

2. Have these changes affected you directly? How?

3. How would you go about learning more about the demographic profile of your community?

4. How do the philosophies of existentialism, deontology, and Utilitarianism differ in their approach to this dilemma?

Case 9.5

SPORTPLAY—The Lure and Peril

The trend in many nations, such as Canada, in recent years has been to supplement government funding for sport, recreation, health, education, and cultural programs through a variety of fundraising strategies. One of the more popular and successful methods has been lottery ticket sales. The revenue generated by the lotteries has been the savior of many not-for-profit organizations. However, has there been a subliminal cost connected to this method of survival? This case was developed to allow the reader to explore the ethics of lotteries. The reader will be able to test deontological, existential, and teleological theories in this very contentious realm of not-for-profit fundraising.

The Provincial Arts Board (PAB) had been hit recently by substantial government funding cutbacks. It failed to meet three of five of the fundamental categories for full federal funding based upon the newly developed funding criteria. As a result, the executive director, Chris, had to begin looking for alternative sources to keep the PAB running. As a child he had been a national award winner in piano and was well on his way to a career in music. His ambitions changed after his first degree and recently he had completed a graduate degree in arts marketing at the largest university in the country.

The membership had traditionally been made up of the extremely well-to-do. For years, money had not been an object of concern for the board of directors. Recently, however, there seemed to be many more "middle class" members and, as a result, seeking external funding sources for daily operations became a dominant issue for the membership. The culture of the board was indeed in a state of flux. When the federal funding was cut, Chris knew that something drastic had to occur because the old money that had historically kept the board viable was no longer guaranteed; in the 1990s, art was no longer for the so-called upper crust of society.

Chris, thinking beyond the PAB's traditional views of fundraising, came up with the idea of connecting with sport. He felt that if he could garner the support from the sport community (which was always in a state of need) then in partnership they could use legalized gambling on sporting events to satisfy both their financial woes. All wagers and payouts would be controlled by a centralized not-for-profit organization. He mentioned this idea to his colleagues in the national sport center and it took off. After four months of hard work and a great deal of lobbying, 33 associations, art and sport alike, had jumped on the bandwagon as well as several politicians who saw the potential of such a scheme to replace eventually all government support for the art community as well as elite sport.

After one year of extremely hard work, the government agreed to seed the initiative with money to assist in the marketing and advertising of the gambling "game" called *Sportplay.* In the first few months *Sportplay* created quite a stir throughout the country. Sales were unbelievably successful as people flocked to various locations to purchase *Sportplay* forms. The public was told that only a bit of sport knowledge was required in order to make them instantly wealthy, or so they hoped. The advertisements encouraged people to play often to give them a chance to quit working, to insult their boss, to sit by the beach and relax for the rest of their life, to be with beautiful men or women, to be "free," and so on. Despite the fact that the odds of being hit by lightning were better than winning substantially in *Sportplay,* the advertisements emphatically stated that it was impossible to win without "BT-PG," that is, Buy a Ticket and Play the Game. Further, you were "a miserly unpatriotic sod if you didn't play at least once a month to support the arts and amateur sport."

Sportplay was a financial savior for the PAB as well as sport in general. It allowed for the development of new artists as well as teachers, coaches, officials, and administrators; it provided funding for supplies, equipment, and national and international travel; it allowed associations to further enhance their marketability to attract other sponsors; it was directly linked to the country's National Arts Festival and the best showing at the last Olympic Games.

It was not until several years into this scheme that anyone cared to investigate the effect of *Sportplay* upon variables other than arts and sport. For example, government statistics tracking client's seeking counseling for gambling addiction increased by approximately 43% in the second year of the lottery to 64% in the third year. Stories abounded of families that were being broken, juvenile crime was up, and family fortunes were being lost. Several studies correlated these statistics to the new wave of gambling brought on by *Sportplay*. The somewhat imprudent response of the "stewards" of *Sportplay* was that it was the individual's excessive gambling, not *Sportplay*, that was to blame. An additional finding was that primarily members of the lower socio-economic class were the most frequent players–seeking the ultimate escape from their poverty. It appeared that *Sportplay*, not religion, was the new "opiate of the masses."

Chris had, in the meantime, received overwhelming support for his efforts in developing this new manner to fund national artistic and sport programs; he had saved many associations from closure as a result of his initiative. Chris was no longer convinced that his idea was in fact such a marvelous thing. He was having a difficult time justifying the benefits reaped by the art and sport communities (generally consisting of the upper and middle class) as compared to the burden of the optimistic lower class, who generally did not benefit from the elite system. The rich were indeed getting richer and the poor were providing funding. Was the advertising deceptive? Was the typical buyer making informed decisions? Chris wondered if there wasn't something that he could do to make this situation seem more just for all.

Questions to Consider for Discussion

1. Are lotteries ethical?
2. What do you think about lottery support for not-for-profit organizations?
3. Who are the winners and who are the losers?
4. Are you aware of any social disorders that have been caused by gambling–legal or sanctioned?
5. What is the alternative to lottery revenue?
6. What are the competing principles in this case?
7. What is the greatest good for the greatest number?

Case 9.6

A Little Help from Her Friends

Unscrupulous people and naive people do exist. In many cases, for a variety of reasons (i.e., personal relations), we tend to be unable to perceive the ulterior motives (e.g., personal gain or personal friendships) of individuals that may result in personal or organizational damage. In this case the reader will be able to explore the ethics of organizational nepotism and careerism. The often conflicting concepts of objective justice and subjective relationships may provide a useful backdrop for the analysis of this particular case.

Britt was a relatively new administrator in the Sport Centre, a federation of sport-governing organizations. She was liked by more or less everyone in her work setting and in the professional associations to which she belonged. She had been employed by the Sport Centre for several years and had gradually worked her way up the ranks to the administrative level. She had one flaw: she found it difficult to say "no." As a result she was part of virtually every committee, every fundraiser, and every social function that she was asked to attend.

This "flaw" became rather serious when her department's computer system finally broke down after years of glitches. Replacing the system was going to be expensive. News got out to the computer sales network that a rather lucrative contract could be had at the Sport Centre and, needless to say, the "sharks sensed a feeding frenzy." One of these "sharks" was an old friend of Britt's from university. This former roommate, Beth, felt that she definitely had the inside track to this contract because Britt was, to no surprise, the chair of the computer committee.

Britt's department was relatively new and many of the managerial functions were carried out in a less-than-administratively-pristine manner. Many of the decisions that could have been handled by a general manager were made by committee because only as a collective would the best decisions be made, or so they felt. In reality not one of the administrators had the background to make such a purchase, yet they were afraid to seek outside help for fear that others would perceive that the department was not being run effectively. As a result, they relied upon the safety of numbers–decision by consensus. The work environment was extremely positive, yet not terribly efficient.

Beth was a careerist in the full meaning of the word. She was prepared to use every bit of influence and old history to convince Britt to buy from her company in order to reap the substantial commission. It may be interesting to note that Beth had not contacted Britt since university seven years ago, despite the fact that they had both been living in the same city for the past six years–this was known to Beth and unknown to Britt.

Beth began to lobby Britt in a most dramatic way. Lunches, dinners, squash games, movies–life seemed just like it had been in the good old days at school when they were roomies (the "good old days," unknown to Britt, did include the fact that Beth constantly chased after all of the men that ever showed any interest in Britt). The date for tendering fast approached, and Beth was relentless. Britt was so overwhelmed by the reunion with her friend that she lost sight of her objectivity relative to the tender. She provided Beth with information to which Beth should not have been privy. When the bids came in Beth's lobbying intensified, including an offer to help Britt with some of the technical information she lacked and was directed, obviously, to Beth's product.

Britt and the committee met several times to discuss the merits of each tender. The decision came down to three, one of which was Beth's. Thanks to her many in-depth and informal discussions with Beth, Britt was able to answer many of the questions the committee had about Beth's product–this was not the case with the other two. The result–Beth won the contract.

It was at least six months after the installation of the computer system before the staff became extremely concerned with the quality of the product. It seemed inordinately slow and would often shut down without warning or cause. Britt had been attempting for months now to calm the staff and assure them that it was only the bugs of a new system that had to be worked out. As time passed, the poor service that Beth's company provided became even worse and created a great deal of frustration and anger among the staff.

Rumor began to escalate regarding the original deal. It was suggested that Britt had been "taken," that the tendering process was flawed, that Britt was involved romantically with Beth, that Britt had, in fact, taken a "kickback" from Beth. Britt herself was feeling increasingly uncomfortable with the entire situation. Strangely, Beth had not called her since the sale, and when Britt tried to call Beth at work or home she spoke only to voice mail and an answering machine, respectively. Where had her old roommate gone? What was she to do about the computer system?

Questions to Consider for Discussion

1. What is Beth's value orientation? What is Britt's?

2. At what level of moral development would you place each of the two women?

3. How could this dilemma be avoided in the future?

4. Who is to blame? Why?

Case 9.7

Pulling at Heart Strings?

The phrase "the ends justify the means" can often be associated with the organizational functions of marketing and public relations. Particularly in the setting of not-for-profit organizations, the good outcome that is achieved may, for some, provide significant rationale for condoning questionable methods to achieve that "good" end. In this case, readers are encouraged to explore the lengths individuals will go to in order to accomplish "good" ends. This case is richly utilitarian in its theme and demands full use of other ethical theories for its resolution.

The Special People Association (SPA) is a not-for-profit organization that provides programming for individuals with disabilities leading towards local, regional, national, and international arts and cultural events. It is a very active fundraiser, and must be, because the SPA receives proportionally fewer dollars from government sources than other "mainstream" organizations.

Traditionally the SPA's fundraising strategies have not involved high-profile marketing. Rather they have relied on bingos, dinners, and raffles. Until recently, these avenues have been enough to meet the financial demands of the association. However, it is now apparent that the current level of support from external sources is not enough to allow the association to keep up with its ever-increasing program demands. New ideas for fundraising have to be developed and implemented quickly.

Sargit is the executive director of the SPA. He is 38, a graduate of a small university, with a B.A. in Religious Studies from the University of Madras in India and an M.A. in Human Movement Studies from the University of Southern Cross in Australia. He is married and has three children, aged 3, 5, and 9. The eldest child, James, has Down's Syndrome. Sargit and his wife, Helen, are rather vocal supporters of integration for their child in all aspects of his life.

Sargit had lobbied his rather conservative board of directors for years to allow him to be a bit more aggressive in the ways in which he sought external sources of funding. Now that the economy was pressing, the board was willing to take some chances with his creative ideas.

Sargit believed that the faces of their clients had to be exposed to the public–that these special people should not be hidden away or feared or simply tolerated. He felt that the community should be involved in their successes and be proud of their participation at all levels of art and cultural festivals and competitions–local and international. He decided that he would begin with a city-wide billboard campaign. A salesman for a billboard company was a good friend of Sargit and had offered him three free billboards if he were able to sign a contract to pay for five over the next 18 months. This was a very generous offer. However, it was a gamble because it would empty the advertising budget for the association. Sargit felt that it was worth the gamble and proceeded to work on the content of the message that these posters would display.

He met several times with the staff to discuss the strategy and encountered a wide range of opinions regarding the orientation and intent of the billboard. Two camps formed. The first believed that the billboard should be created to show how the younger individuals with the more serious disabilities struggled to overcome tremendous odds to compete. The donations of the public would allow these disadvantaged kids to overcome one less hurdle. This was the "pull at the public's heart strings" orientation, and market research had shown that this was the most effective means for acquiring emotional and financial support among the public. The second camp was not in favor of going for the sympathy donation. Rather they believed that these people, young and old, could warrant public support without using an approach that appealed to public sympathy and guilt. This position was the one that was generally favored by those actually caring for children with disabilities. The committee was at a stalemate—pragmatism versus idealism. Sargit had to present the decision to the board for approval. His was the deciding vote.

Questions to Consider for Discussion

1. What are the competing ethical principles in this case?

2. Do the ends justify the means?

3. What are other examples of "social marketing"? Are they ethically contentious?

Case 9.8

Winning

A common contemporary indictment against elite sport has been its basic assumption to "win at all cost." As a consequence of this dominant value, the abuse of athletes by coaches is not an uncommon incident. This case is clearly one of power and the abuse of position in the pursuit of victory. The reader may feel compelled to re-examine his or her own local or national sport system to question the tacit or latent philosophy of elite and recreational sport systems.

In 1992 Attila immigrated to this country from eastern Europe. He had been his national team coach and was hired by our national program. He was, without question, an extremely knowledgeable coach, perhaps one of the best technicians in world. His success in his former country was impressive and the potential of his impact upon the national team was tremendous.

The national program had undergone a number of coaching changes in recent years. It seemed as though the athletes were not progressing as quickly as many in the gymnastics community believed that they should be. The community was adamant about producing a medallist for the next Olympic Games and the pressure for high performance was becoming more intense. Additional pressure came from the sport's major corporate sponsor. They had recently joined the gymnastics program under the assumption that exposure of their product in an Olympic context would make their annual investment of $250,000 U.S. worthwhile. If a solid performance was not realized in the next Olympics and World championships, the sponsor threatened withdrawal.

As far as the athletes were concerned, they were extremely motivated to be in the run for medals in all of their international competitions. The atmosphere among them was highly competitive. As a result there were some athletes who had gone over the edge and were suffering from various maladies, ranging from anorexia and bulimia to chronic stress injuries.

Prior to Attila's arrival, the former coach had had a very close relationship with most of his athletes. He was technically very good, yet his real forte was his ability to demonstrate concern and empathy for the athletes; he was very much a father figure to many. However, he was not getting results and therefore lost his position to Attila.

Attila wasted no time in taking control of the program. He fired two of the assistant coaches and completely rearranged practice schedules, competition dates, and instituted a spartan regime of diet, sleep, and controlled socializing for the entire team. This, of course, was in addition to the qualitative and quantitative shift in the manner in which the team trained.

Initially, this new approach was accepted by the athletes, who were aware of Attila's successes in his home country and felt that this shift would result in a positive outcome at the World championships and the Olympics. This optimism was, however, short-lived as the morale of the team steadily declined. Attila abused the athletes both physically and mentally. He constantly ridiculed their ability to perform as well as their appearance, and spent much of his time calling most of the females "fat." One athlete, who was a recovering anorexic, ended up in hospital after collapsing in practice. She had been fasting for days following an abusive comment from Attila.

The board was made aware of the situation and opted to do nothing. The team had returned from a dual meet with China where they had nearly upset this gymnastics powerhouse. Despite the complaining of the team members, results were being achieved. The team continued facing the grueling training regime and the abuse at the hands of Attila.

Following another successful dual meet in Europe, the seven senior members of the team wrote a letter to the Gymnastics Association requesting the termination of Attila's contract. The athletes stated that they could no longer continue with the abuse and the pressure that Attila was putting them through. The board responded by threatening to revoke the athletes' funding if they didn't follow the leadership of Attila, who was obviously taking them to competitive heights they could never have hoped to reach without his kind of coaching. The matter was dropped.

The team was still touring Europe when the most unfortunate incident occurred. One of the younger athletes, who showed a great deal of promise, performed exceedingly well throughout the competition until she fell from the uneven bars, thus losing the overall competition for the team. Attila was furious. He chastised the young woman for a full three minutes in front of everyone in the arena. He then roughly escorted her back to the locker room to continue his tirade. The young woman was overwhelmed with shame, embarrassment, and tears; she was completely distraught. Two hours later she was found in her hotel room, having overdosed on sleeping pills. The young woman survived this suicide attempt and was flown home immediately after her release from the hospital.

At this point the team had had enough. All members signed a petition to have Attila ousted from his position. The petition was delivered to the national office upon the return of the team from the most successful gymnastics competition the country had ever experienced.

Questions to Consider for Discussion

1. What ethical theory seems to be the basis for elite sport?

2. How could existentialism be incorporated into the culture of sport?

3. Is the behavior of Attila unique? Why?

4. What external variables influence the current culture of the sport world? What do you think of this trend?

Case 9.9

Everyone Else Is Doing It

"The way we do things around here" is often used as the layperson's definition of organizational culture. This common understanding of organizational behavior provides the background for all socialization of new members. The problem arises when the culture fosters behavior that is perceived to be counterproductive for the overall survival of the organization. If the norms of the organization encourage budget embellishment or a poor work ethic, then the responsibility lies with the leadership to transform the culture to support more positive organizational behavior and commitment. This case is focused upon careerism and situational ethics. The challenge for the reader concerns not only the general analysis of this particular case but also the notion of socialization within any organizational context to prevent the status quo from being ethically unsound.

Lila is a coach of a intercollegiate field hockey team. She is a graduate and former player on the field hockey team of the university which now employs her. Lila, at the time of these events, was completing a postgraduate diploma in coaching from the country's coaching center housed at a large university in the east. Lila had inherited a team that had not won a game in three years. Pressure was being exerted to cancel this sport as it was not achieving any form of athletic excellence nor was it enhancing the reputation of the university. Lila, being a well-credentialed alumna, was expected by many to be the savior of the team. The enthusiasm generated by the athletic director over Lila's interest in the position seemed to bias a thorough search of her professional conduct since she had, after all, graduated from the university.

Lila, as a rookie coach, was given some room to make errors in terms of the administration of her program. Her excuse was, "After all, I'm a coach, not a paper pusher. Where I used to coach someone always did this for me." This behavior was also overlooked because she was winning, a phenomenon unusual with this team. The athletic director, Karen, was reluctant to get rid of a good coach simply because she wasn't filling out forms on time or at all.

Lila began her second year with a successful first season's record to her credit coupled, however, with a disastrous administrative record. The latter was a significant burden for Karen and her administrative staff, who were constantly required to do Lila's work for her. There also seemed to be some growing suspicion that Lila was taking some extreme liberties with her program budget. She was a relatively free-spending entertainer when she was supposedly on university business. Trips away for the weekend with her partner were "expensed" (i.e., charged to her university account) as recruiting trips. Purchases of the most outlandish nature were often slipped through as team expenses (e.g., costly computer screensavers, framed sport posters, and a telephone headset for her office).

At this time, the university was under pressure to reduce its funding and sport always seemed to be the first target for the accountants. The dean of the faculty, Dr. Smith, had to use every ounce of political moxie to prevent the accounting axe from falling on the programs. He made it quite clear that any cut in funding would result in some teams being eliminated from the university completely. Efficiency and effectiveness in all programs was the driving force in the university in these tight economic times. This pressure filtered down to Karen who had to make the teams accountable to the university and to the public.

Karen was becoming extremely upset with Lila's behavior—its effect upon the budget and its influence upon some of the other coaches in the varsity program. Initially, Karen believed that Lila was just a focused and perhaps an eccentric coach. However she soon became convinced that Lila was very shrewd and was using the "Gee, I didn't know I couldn't do that—nobody told me" routine for her personal benefit. Finally Karen had had enough. She was willing to take action.

Lila was asked to make an appointment with Karen. They met and Karen explained how Lila's behavior was and had been unacceptable for the 19 months of her employment. She itemized why Lila's behavior was unacceptable with special reference to her near-fraudulent expense claims. Lila was informed that if there was any hint of the behavior continuing she would be fired. Lila, in true Lila form, feigned shock and assured Karen that she was not aware of these expectations. She promised to shape up and walked to the door. Before she left, however, she said, "Karen, you may be right, but everyone else is doing it."

A month later Karen was informed that Lila had taken on a part-time job without informing the administration. She was also told that Lila was using her university budget to pay for trips she was taking as part of her outside involvement with the soccer association. Further, it was reported that Lila had been overheard as saying, "I'm not paid what I'm worth. I have a master's degree and should be the highest paid coach in this place (she, in fact, was still taking courses and had been saying she was "almost" finished for 19 months). If they can't pay me, I'll *expense* everything."

Questions to Consider for Discussion

1. What does the behavior and attitude of Karen imply about the organizational climate of the athletic department?

2. As a "professional" is Karen's conduct ethical?

3. What factors bred this attitude?

4. How should the athletic director handle this case? To what values should the director appeal in order to enhance Karen's responsibility and professionalism?

Case 9.10

Groupthink

Organizational psychology theorists have assigned the term *groupthink* to the situation in which individuals in a participatory decision-making context will think in uncharacteristically similar ways and resolve problems with rather narrow views. More often than not, the result of groupthink will be weak decisions that have been based upon the informal leader's perceptions. In this case we encourage the reader to consider the potential weaknesses of group decision making. Here the reader will see in action the potential pitfalls in the notion that the majority may be wrong (utilitarianism) or that the traditional view is correct (deontology).

The Sport Federation (FD), in preparation for the next Olympics, was searching for a marketing plan that would generate revenue to support the nation's Olympic team in its final year of training. The FD relied heavily upon public and corporate philanthropy, yet was in need of more funding to meet the expanded demands of pre-Olympic training. For years the FD had been extremely conservative in its marketing strategies. It depended largely upon federal funding, gifts from the country's major corporations, and some very subtle attempts at public fundraising. Despite these sources, the FD needed more money.

The current president of the FD had been appointed in 1998 after the retirement of Colonel "Johnny" Fitzpatrick, a highly respected figure in the international sport community. Johnny had operated the FD for 17 years, very much as benevolent autocrat. He structured the FD not unlike an extension of the military bureaucracy (in which he had served with distinction in World War II). As a result, the FD had always operated with surprising precision in a culture of quasi-autocracy.

The new president, Winston Michael Moore, was appointed to continue the corporate philosophy established by Fitzpatrick. His was not a mandate for change. The appointment of Moore was not met with overwhelming enthusiasm. A core of sport administrators in the FD, though they highly respected and even loved the Colonel, felt that his philosophy was no longer representative of the FD as they neared the twenty-first century. However, this desire for change was not shared by all.

The senior management committee decided to establish a sub-committee devoted to resolving the FD's financial needs. This committee was made up of 12 individuals, 8 of whom were staunch supporters of the FD's "old guard." The first meeting established the tone for what was to follow in the next six weeks of planning.

Moore, as the chair, explained to the members that the planning stage would be consensually based. Each member should speak his or her mind without thought to its immediate relevance to the problem. He suggested that "free thinking is the basic premise of this phase. I encourage each one of you to throw off the chains of what is possible or impossible. Let us all be as creative as we can!" The immediate reaction of at least four members of the committee was one of shock. Since their interaction with Moore had not been positive and free thinking, this was the last concept they expected would leave his lips.

After this first statement, Winston Michael Moore asked if he could make a few comments as a member of the group, *not* as the chair. He stood up and proceeded to lecture the committee on the evils of corporate sponsorships for the next 30 minutes. He argued that to accept anything from a corporation that was not philanthropic was virtual slavery to the will of the corporate agenda. If sport was to remain free of immorality and be the bastion of character building, it *must* stay clear of the hazards of the business realm. To do otherwise was to contravene the successful culture that the Colonel had taken so long to build. The destruction of this culture would be something that Winston Michael Moore would not tolerate. Winston Michael Moore resumed his position as chair as eight individuals sat nodding their heads in agreement; the remaining members were silent and dumbstruck.

Olivia, a newly appointed sport administrator, was speechless. She had just arrived at the FD and had been hoping to build her career with this organization. Her background was in sport fundraising and marketing and she was thrilled to be chosen as a member of this committee. She had spent many hours developing ideas for some very aggressive campaigns for sponsorships. She was prepared at this first meeting with charts, overheads, slides, and computer graphics for a completely new strategy for the FD. She had shared her ideas with two other members of the committee who were equally excited with the prospect of a much-needed new vision for the FD.

These three individuals were the most junior members of the committee. All of them were relatively recent graduates (still paying student loans) and all were parents of very young children.

The fourth member of the group, Tastuhiko, was not a firm believer in the old guard. He was a veteran of the FD and had been in conflict with the Colonel as well as with Moore on several occasions. He was tolerated by the old guard and by the current regime not only because of his abilities as an administrator but also because of his sheer popularity among the employees of the FD. He was, unfortunately, soon to retire.

At the first coffee break, the four members of the "outgroup" met in the hallway. Tastuhiko implored the other members to present their ideas and not let "old Moore-the-bore" scare them. As they returned to the meeting they were thinking of a variety of scenarios—not the least of which included their children, their loans, and their mortgages.

Questions to Consider for Discussion

1. Is there a relationship between Utilitarianism and the concept of groupthink?

2. How does the notion of "intent" influence the ultimate behavior of the outgroup? What factors will influence their "ideal" resolution? Why?

3. What is the culture of the organization? How could it be changed or transformed?

Case 9.11

Sweatshops and Not-for-Profit Fundraisers

It is not uncommon for companies from industrialized nations to make use of Third World production environments in order to save costs and make a profit. For example, the price of the running shoes you are wearing might be substantially higher if a particular firm were not able to manufacture their product using the extremely cheap labor of Third World people. Your benefit? Their exploitation? A variety of arguments can and ought to be made concerning the potential benefit or exploitation that "industrialized" nations bring to these contexts. In developing this case, we hope that the reader will challenge the assumptions and breadth of the utilitarian stance (that is, the greatest good for whom?), the deontological argument of Kant, and the existential role as demonstrated by Donna, who must overcome the lure of organizational efficiency and cultural relativism.

The city of Rideau is a mid-size metropolitan center with a population of approximately 1.5 million people. An estimated one-quarter of the population is of aboriginal descent and generally falls into the lower socio-economic strata. Rideau has a very well developed municipal culture and recreation council that attempts to provide programming for all clientele within the city's core area.

The council's theme for the twenty-first century was "Healthy Activity-for-All." The intent was to encourage everyone within the community to find some form of healthy activity to which they could commit at least 15 or 20 minutes every day or every second day. In order to promote this theme and raise funds to support it, a variety of marketing strategies were initiated. One was the sale of a T-shirt with a very brightly colored design on both the front and back. The initial sales of the shirt were overwhelming. It seemed as though the council had inadvertently created a new fad among the teenagers of Rideau. The result was that they couldn't keep enough shirts in stock. In fact, there was a demand for sweatshirts, shorts, and even socks that had the same design on them as the original T-shirt. Based upon this new market for clothing, the council felt that they could create a clothing store and expand their sales significantly. Space was available in a vacant municipal office. All they had to do was hire a few employees and spend a minimal amount of money to design and stock the store and they were away!

Coincidentally, Tom, one of the members of the council, was about to go on holiday. His plan was to tour a number of countries in Asia and Southeast Asia. He offered to look around for any deals on clothing while he was there. Tom was very much a machiavellian sort and had always been quite vocal about his missed calling as a businessman—he wanted the store to be his "baby." He was determined to bring back a "sweet deal" on clothing for the council's newly developed clothing venture.

When Tom returned, he indeed had the makings of a very lucrative deal with a company operating in a Southeast Asian country. With all taxes and import fees included, the purchase of clothing from this company was extraordinarily inexpensive, less than half the local price. The store would make a significant profit from its sales (better than would result from a local firm) and as a result actually be able *to enhance its support for its cultural and recreation programming for the underprivileged individuals of the city's inner core.*

The store was prepared, the clothing was imported, and sales were better than expected. This phenomenon turned out to be a rather stable and very successful source of revenue for the council. They soon needed to expand their quota from their Asian supplier.

It was decided that the executive director of the store, Donna, would make a special trip to the supplier to further enhance the existing arrangement. Upon her arrival there, she was immediately taken aback by the outright poverty of the country. She had never traveled to a Third World country and was not prepared mentally or physically for what she was now experiencing.

Donna contacted the supplier and was picked up by the owner, Skip, at her hotel. They quickly made their way to the factory in a village about 30 kilometers from the nation's capital. During the trip, Donna had so many questions about the living conditions of the people in the country that Skip was barely able to keep up with her. They finally arrived at the factory and Donna was astonished. The workers of the company were all children. The conditions were, from her point of view, deplorable. She asked how much they were being paid and was told about 25 cents per day, for 12 hours per day, six and a half days per week. Her next question was about the children's schooling; the response was that it was taken care of on the half day off. Skip then proceeded to discuss the business at hand–expanded imports for her store.

Donna feigned having to call her superior (she had none) to confirm the deal and asked if she could be taken back to her hotel.

Questions to Consider for Discussion

1. What is cultural relativism and how does it apply to this case?

2. What effect will Donna's behavior have on the children in this Third World country?

3. What ethical principles are in conflict?

4. If you knew that your running shoes were made by children in poor working conditions in a land far away, what would you do? What ought you to do? Why?

Case 9.12

Harassment and Chivalry

Our conscience can be a very powerful force in our behavior. Authentic behavior is often pitted against other teleological or deontological standards. The existentialist's challenge has always been to consider the deontological and the teleological and choose the genuine. This case of harassment and chivalry is an interesting one, illustrating the conflict between duty and existential authenticity. The "hero" of the case finds himself in a very pressing and ethically laden position from a variety of angles.

In 1994, Lee Ward attended an international fitness equipment conference in Mexico representing the vice-president of his company, who was unable to attend. Lee, as a manager and as a person, was not well respected by his peers and by members within the organization. He displayed few leadership qualities and was held in disdain by most, but he was tolerated. He also had a very nasty side to his character and was extremely jealous of those who had risen through the ranks of the company faster than he had. He would take every opportunity to criticize those who were successful, those who were innovative, those who demonstrated any sort of enthusiasm. His style of conflict resolution was never to confront face-to-face. Rather, he sent memos. In fact, much of his day was spent sending memos to the president of the company indicating how various individuals were not doing their job. Despite the fact that he was considered to be a bit of a joke, he was described by many as a "dangerous little man."

At the conference he followed the "in" group of sales personnel to the various functions and visited the same sights and took the same tours just to be part of the action. One afternoon, a group decided to venture out to the beach to relax while there was a lull in the three-day event. On this occasion, Janice, an individual that was held in extremely high regard both professionally and socially, joined the group to swim and lie in the sun. She also happened to be a very attractive woman.

During the afternoon Lee was busy trying to be part of the group. He decided to get his camera out to take some picture for the company's newsletter. His ulterior motive was to get as many shots of Janice in her bathing suit as possible and was successful, unbeknownst to Janice.

Several months later Lee met Janice at a show. She was there with her partner, Errol. Lee proceeded to tell Janice how great she looked in the pictures he took of her. Janice was speechless. She told the story of the afternoon on the beach to Errol, who was noticeably upset but agreed not to do or say anything. Janice said that she would handle it in her own way.

The incident bothered Errol considerably. He was a rather old-fashioned sort, and he felt that Janice's honor and reputation had been impugned by Lee. He thought of many ways to resolve the issue, one of which was to fatten Lee's lip, an option he rejected despite relishing it. The matter was dropped.

Later that year, Lee happened to be in Errol's organization on business. As Errol was returning to his office, he spotted Lee leaving the building. Errol reacted quickly, not really caring about the reputation of the "dangerous little man." He turned on his heels and ran after Lee. He caught up with him and introduced himself with extreme formality. Errol began by stating that he was aware that Lee had in his possession (in fact on his wall at work) pictures of a friend taken without her consent. Further, Errol suggested, Lee would be wise to deliver the pictures and the negatives to Janice and then the matter would be dropped. Lee was quick to agree to Errol's request.

Following this confrontation, Errol felt that he had done the right thing. Janice's honor was in someway restored, he felt. He called Janice and told her of his action, knowing that she may not see things the same way he did. He was right. Janice was extremely upset. She was worried about the repercussions of Errol's actions. Janice knew that Lee was rather spineless and would take revenge on her in subtle ways for his own embarrassment at the hands of Errol. She was also upset because Errol had taken action after they had agreed none would be taken. Errol had no excuse other than his somewhat lingering sense of chivalry, which told him that it was the *only thing* he could have done as a "gentleman."

Questions to Consider for Discussion

1. Was Errol being authentic? How?

2. What other ethical view did his behavior reflect?

3. What circumstances exist in the workplace or in society that would allow Lee to believe that his behavior was acceptable? Why is this? How could it change?

4. What do you think of Errol's belief in the concept of "chivalry"?

5. How does Lee view women? Using ethical theory, how would you describe or critique his behavior?

Case 9.13

Faculty of Kinesiology Student Society: Freedom and Responsibility

In any educational setting, regardless of the level, it is up to the educator to foster independent critical thinking and individual responsibility and accountability. Only when students feel this sense of responsibility do they begin to mature socially. However, "letting go" has its pitfalls. What if the student makes a bad decision—to what extent is he or she held accountable? Can the educator stand by while mistakes are made? This case centers around the notions of freedom and responsibility and the paternal tension experienced when it is supported by administrators, coaches, and parents alike.

The Faculty of Kinesiology was established in 1945 at the university, and it has supported a student society for the past 15 years. The society had been operated by the students and a faculty member whose task it was to oversee on- and off-campus activities. The society had been successful in conducting its own business and felt that faculty involvement was becoming a bit too patronizing. In 1990, the students felt that they were capable of "running their own show."

The executive committee of the society met with the assistant dean of the faculty and provided her with the details and rationale for their request for more autonomy. The assistant dean was pleased to see the students taking this initiative and agreed wholeheartedly to this new arms-length relationship–let the students take responsibility and learn from their decisions and mistakes.

All was well for the society for several years. They were active in a variety of aspects of campus life. From the first-year orientation to the graduating dinner-dance, society-run events were overwhelming successes among the students as well as with their parents. Pre-game pubs were well attended and were never allowed to get too rowdy. The relationship with the faculty was excellent.

In the fall of 1995, a request came to the society from a student seeking assistance in a fundraising scheme. The student, Jane, told the society that she was a volunteer member of the International Sport Management Case Study Association (ISMCA) that was meeting in Spain in December of that year. The student, an extremely charismatic individual, wanted the society to pay for her travel in return for a very vague promise to include the society, the faculty, and the university in a promotional campaign supported by the ISMCA. Jane never presented any formal plan or provided any contract. Despite this, the society was still keen to continue negotiations with her.

Jane had asked the dean for special consideration with regard to writing final exams as they would be taking place while she was in Spain. Her letter of request was on the dean's desk but no action would be taken until all details were made available.

In October an unfortunate incident occurred. Jane was implicated in a drug-peddling scheme (steroids) involving both male and female body builders. The charges were laid against her and three friends who were regulars at the local Bodyplus gym. As soon as the news became public, a variety of stories began circulating about Jane and her questionable past. She was charismatic and machiavellian because she had to keep one step ahead of the trouble she had created in her last job, her last school, or her last relationship.

Certain members of the society fast became rather uneasy about the fundraising scheme that Jane had more or less convinced the society to orchestrate. There were however, several members of the executive committee who still believed that Jane merited financial support. It is important to mention that, in general, the committee members in support of Jane were males, and those who suspected her, females.

A growing body of anecdotal evidence was mounting to suggest that Jane was not trustworthy. The dean was pleased that she had delayed her response to Jane regarding the deferment of exams. The society was, interestingly enough, still willing to pursue the fundraiser for Jane's travel. The assistant dean was made aware of the society's dilemma and was prepared to intervene and put a stop to the fundraiser altogether. However, she remembered the agreement she had made with the students—to let them carry out the operations and learn from their decisions and mistakes.

Questions to Consider for Discussion

1. How does this case represent the existentialist values of freedom and responsibility?

2. How can one be an existential leader? Is the assistant dean acting existentially?

3. Why do you think Jane received as much support from the student society as she did?

4. Should the society be allowed to continue in this independent manner? Why?

Case 9.14

A Free Ride

In all walks of life there are those who are committed to their jobs, their profession, or their organization, and there are those who are not. This case focuses upon professional responsibility. A question arises concerning the individual's duty to an organization and profession, and presumably the organization's and the profession's duty to instil a sense of responsibility in its members.

Gary is a graduate of a mid-size university with an undergraduate degree in botany. He has been working in the field for 28 years. He has always worked for the Municipal Horticultural Department, where the basis for moving through the ranks was and continues to be seniority. This philosophy of management was a result of very strong influence from a provincial government that had traditionally been socialist in nature. The notion of meritorious service was an expected (but not necessarily rewarded) characteristic of every unionized public servant—this was lost on many who adopted the "it's a free ride once you're in" attitude. Ralph Gimli, the administrator of Gary's department, had been extremely frustrated by this attitude and was looking for some way to alter the status quo culture of this organization.

In the 1960s the government had hired a number of graduates in an effort to replenish the organization following a wave of retiring senior managers. Gary had given up trying to improve himself academically or technically almost immediately after receiving his permanent position in the municipal government.

He contributed very little to the organization—but always enough to keep himself from being fired. He refused to take on new tasks, to learn new technologies, and to adhere to any concerted attempts to change the "work ethic" and organizational culture. His cynical perception of any of these initiatives was that it was just another theory—it would not work and it would go away. And so it went for years.

The next wave of mandatory retirements from the city was approximately five years away. This caused mixed reactions among the employees. For some this meant that some very capable and experienced administrators, who had been mentors to so many, would be forced to leave while they still had a tremendous amount to offer. For others, in particular Ralph, this meant that a number of individuals would finally, and thankfully, be leaving the organization after a career that was uninspiring at best, a drain on the rest of the employees at worst. Gary was one of the worst offenders from this latter group.

Graduates from recent years were desperate for positions in a field where few jobs existed. Many opted out in favor of jobs in the insurance industry, the military, sales, and other unrelated occupations. Gary continued on, doing almost nothing, learning little, contributing less, collecting his checks, drawing on the system, and taking up space. In addition, Gary had three years remaining before he could collect full pension and was bound and determined to collect it.

With a new retirement package now available, Ralph felt that he had an opportunity to finally rid the system of Gary. The file that Ralph had been keeping for the past five years was full of documentation indicating that Gary was incompetent. Ralph believed that the union would have put up too much of a fuss with the accusations Ralph wanted to make and so he had not pursued the matter. Now that a retirement package was available to Gary, Ralph wondered whether he should present the file to Gary and suggest that he should take the package (which would be significantly less than what he would receive at full retirement).

Questions to Consider for Discussion

1. How would you define professional ethics?

2. What are the responsibilities of the professional in our field?

3. What could Gary's supervisor do to enhance this behavior of Gary's?

4. How would Kohlberg describe Gary's behavior?

5. Is there any responsibility on the part of the organization for Gary's outcome?

Case 6.15

Academic Fraud

In the academic world, particularly today when the Internet provides the student and researcher alike with the opportunity to cut corners and submit work that is less than academically or ethically sound, academic fraud has become a concern. Individuals commit acts of fraud for a variety of reasons. Professors under the gun of "publish or parish" and students attempting to get the marks to pass or go on to graduate school and well-paying jobs are often tempted to forgo the *right* means to succeed at university. In this case duty is split between a number of masters.

Sam is a graduate student in the second year of his master's program. He is very hard working and has been a strong addition to the faculty as an instructor, a developing scholar, and as a personable and honorable young man. Sam is the student of one of the country's leading scholars in his area. His ambition is to continue his education to the doctoral level in the hope of becoming a professor. His advisor, Dr. Milton, is known as a thorough and caring mentor to all of her students.

Sam's thesis was well on its way. Three chapters were completed and he was preparing to begin his data collection when a personal tragedy occurred. In June, Sam's brother James announced to the family that he had been diagnosed as having cancer, and was not expected to survive past Christmas. This news was a terrible shock to the family.

The news was devastating to Sam, who revered his older brother. James had always been a strong supporter of Sam, who had become a solid student more by his hard work and tenacity than by his natural abilities. Sam wanted to finish his degree before James died. He wanted James to be present at his convocation as a way to thank him for all that he had done for Sam in his all-too-brief life. Sam had a problem. Analyzing the data and writing the final chapters was possible. However, he worried that he would not be able to collect his data in time to make all the pieces fit together.

Sam's data collection involved both surveys and interviews of individuals involved in elite sport. The focus was on the individual's perception of himself or herself through the periods of injury. Sam believed that the only way that he was going to make the September deadline for fall convocation was to "cook" his data. He decided to arrange, as planned, 30 interviews from the sample he and Dr. Milton had accessed. However, the accompanying questionnaires would be "fudged" by him prior to conducting the interviews. He believed that Dr. Milton would never find out about this bit of fraud as long as he did a solid job of making up the findings.

By the time the interviews were completed, Sam's survey data had been analyzed and he was half-way through his discussion chapter. Sam let Dr. Milton believe that he was anxious to begin data input and that he was planning to work night and day to get things finished in time for the convocation deadline. Dr. Milton had her doubts about Sam meeting this date. However she said that she would work as hard as Sam needed her to work since she was aware of his brother's condition and wanted to help.

Sam, in his efforts, went so far as to make the occasional phone call to Dr. Milton's office very late at night to ask a statistical question or one regarding qualitative interpretation. He was well aware that her answering machine automatically told her the time of the call. The intent of all of this was to try to convince her that he was in fact working night and day and could conceivably finish on time.

From Sam's perspective all seemed to be going well. He was leaking just enough information to Dr. Milton in order to keep his lie alive. In the first week of September, Dr. Milton received a phone call from a former graduate student with whom she had spoken about Sam's research several months ago. The person was quite interested in Sam's work and was aware of the triangulated methodology that was being used. He had been expecting a questionnaire from Sam but had not received it. Dr. Milton was puzzled by this omission and was about to dial Sam's number at home to ask him about it when a disturbing thought popped into her mind: Had the data been made up? If this was the case, not only would Sam not graduate while his brother was still alive, but he would also be tossed out of graduate school for academic fraud. Sam answered the phone and Dr. Milton said ...

Questions to Consider for Discussion

1. What factors led to Sam's decision to commit academic fraud?

2. What was Sam's intent? What do you think of it?

3. What alternative courses of action could he have taken?

4. How could this have been prevented from Sam's perspective? From Dr. Milton's perspective?

5. Is Sam's behavior authentic or hedonistic?

Case 9.16

Code of Ethics: Is It Enough?

In the last decade the concern for ethical conduct or at least for the appearance of ethical conduct in a variety of organizational sectors has been pervasive. As organizations attempt to demonstrate that they are indeed ethical in order to gain the trust of stakeholders, many have opted to develop codes of ethics or conduct to guide the behavior of employees and volunteers. The adoption of a code of ethics was thought by some to be sufficient to handle all the ethical ills of the organization. As the reader will see in the following case, a code alone will not result in ethical behavior. In this case, the focus is the inculcation of the notion of corporate ethics into a firm where no such culture exists. The concepts of climate and culture may be useful for the reader in resolving this particular case.

Tony B. was the general sales manager of Grendal Inc., a small and innovative company that had been surviving well in the very competitive world of recreation and fitness software technology. Tony felt himself to be an extremely progressive leader. He was constantly reading the current trade journals and the occasional academic journal to keep up with current trends in the technology as well as management styles (e.g., Japanese management methods, TQM, chaos theory, leadership styles of Attila the Hun, and so on). He attended all the management seminar "road shows" that passed through the city. He was, as the old adage goes "always sharpening the saw."

The latest "tool" that he felt was worthy of implementing was a code of ethics. He read that a code of ethics would provide his employees with moral guidance in the workplace, which would result in more trust, honesty, productivity, and meaning for the employees as well as less turnover, absenteeism, and sabotage. Tony, without delay, gathered his business partners together and began to develop the code, which was to be implemented before the next quarter began in two months. The committee of four worked quickly and efficiently. They developed a comprehensive list of ethical do's and don'ts that seemed to cover the relative universe of questionable conduct in the realm of software production and sales. It was printed, distributed, and placed on the wall of the coffee room, locker room, production room, and it was bronzed and hung on the wall in Grendal's boardroom. "There," Tony thought, "it's done, now I've got to get on with that joint venture with Malaysia. We're falling behind and the boys in KL don't like to be kept waiting."

Grendal Inc. had not been known externally as an icon of moral conduct in the software industry, but neither had it experienced internally the flagrant acts of corporate sabotage and spying that some of its larger competitors had faced recently. It was a dynamic business whose basic premise was *sales, sales, sales,* and therefore survival.

Grendal's primary competitor for its new product was a Brazilian company, Beawulf Inc. It was a relatively new player in the market and was trying desperately to obtain a significant market share. Beawulf had had a number of incidents of corporate sabotage in the last three months, none of which had been uncovered. These acts were starting to hurt the company more from a perspective of morale and production than from sales.

Joan A., an employee in her first year with Grendal, was at home one Sunday morning when she received a rather unusual call from Beawulf. They offered her a position, a substantial raise, and a signing bonus if she would join their firm and assist them in competing against Grendal.

Joan was excited and a little frightened. Why was she, of all people, being contacted? What would her co-workers think of her? What would happen to her own career? How would the information she had benefit the competitor? How would it damage Grendal? Joan knew that the owners had recently developed and distributed a code of conduct or ethics or something and that all employees were to read it and supposedly act morally though this was never observed in the behavior of Tony and the other managers. Most of the employees did not give it much thought—another dictum from the golf course, they sarcastically believed. Joan asked herself, "What is it that is truly valued in this company?" She was able to answer this question with little hesitation. The ultimate values of Grendal were market share and profit—all else was "window dressing" (i.e., the concern for the well-being and growth of each individual). Profit was *the* basic assumption that was implicitly and explicitly drilled into the head of every new employee, regardless of their status within the organization.

Questions to Consider for Discussion

1. What is the purpose of a code of ethics?

2. What are the limitations of organizational codes of ethics? Why?

3. How can a code be put into action?

4. From what value orientation is Joan coming?

5. Is Tony committed to the code of ethics? Why? Does he understand the concept fully?

6. What could he have done differently? What is missing in this organizational culture?

Case 9.17

Vices and Fundraising: Compatibility Paradox?

Corporate sponsorship, like lottery sales, can become a very contentious issue for organizations wishing to raise funds for their survival. Sponsorships can create at least two difficulties for the recipient. The first problem may be that when a corporation gives an organization money, it will inevitably expect input in the manner in which the organization conducts its business. This is problematic when the sponsor may wish to move in directions that are antithetical to the mission or vision of the organization. Second, what the sponsor represents (i.e., the product they manufacture) may be problematic for a recipient. This case raises the questions of the ethics of organizational survival, corporate sponsorship, and individual values.

Lea was a newly hired "communications" officer for the National Arts Alliance (NAA). She had recently graduated with her M.B.A. with a focus on marketing. Lea's previous connection with the arts was non-existent, with the exception of her enjoying a good play or listening to the odd opera CD as she studied for exams. She was hired by the NAA because she demonstrated a great deal of knowledge and enthusiasm throughout the interview process. The NAA hoped that Lea could breathe some life into the chronically poor financial health of the Alliance.

Lea immediately began to review the mandate of the NAA, its values, and its philosophy. She found that the organization had been run, more or less, from the kitchen table of the board of directors. Few formal policies existed and a state of administrative chaos was the accepted and perhaps the preferred mode of operation. This situation did not dissuade Lea. In fact, she believed that as a result of this perceived chaos she could explore just about any avenue to raise funds and she would not be hampered by an organizational dictum stating, "Policy does not allow us to do A, B, or C." The environment, she thought, was perfect to develop her own career and allow her to move up to a larger marketing firm, with the NAA as her first major success.

Lea took the lead from the realm of sports. She arranged a meeting with three of the largest beer companies in the province as well as the district managers of two tobacco companies. Her feeling was that if sports fundraisers can access companies that sell products considered to be rather unhealthy, then why in the world could the arts not jump on the alcohol and cigarette bandwagon? Lea's meetings were initially very successful. One tobacco company was interested in sponsoring an upcoming jazz festival; two of the beer companies were very interested in making some headway into the arts world–a realm they had not yet explored because their focus had been traditionally on sports.

Lea reported the results of her meetings to the board and the reaction was, to say the very least, diverse. Nigel M. was outraged that the NAA had to look for sponsorship at all–he questioned the very existence of Lea's position. He believed it was the responsibility of the public (i.e., the government) to support the arts in all their endeavors. Supporting all cultural projects was to him self-evident. Yukio S. was thrilled with the prospect of "big, dirty companies" wanting to give the NAA money. She perceived it to be their moral obligation to support the arts because they had done so much damage to the health of consumers of their products–a fundraising quid pro quo. Julia P. also supported the idea but purely for pragmatic reasons–the bottom line was her primary concern. Whose money was made available was not relevant–the survival of the NAA was the primary objective. James N. thought that alcohol and tobacco and the arts had always gone hand in hand as part of the lifestyle of the community. He had a hard time justifying their partnership with sport, but who among them would be first to cast the stone when everyone in the room was smoking. The meeting continued in this fashion for hours. In the end they decided that more information should be presented at the next meeting and the matter was tabled.

Lea had never considered any of these arguments. She, like Julia, was only concerned with the bottom line for the NAA and for her own career. However, the debate about partnerships with debatable social consequences made Lea seriously consider her own values, her own paradigm of what she was and what she wanted to become. The next meeting of the board was held the following month and the motion to pursue these ventures was passed by a slim majority. Lea resigned after the meeting.

Questions to Consider for Discussion

1. What was Lea's dilemma? What principles were in conflict for her? For the organization? Why?

2. What factor led her to rethink her own standards?

3. What do you think of sponsorship? Where would you draw the line?

4. Can an organization be altruistic? Is there always an agenda or an ulterior motive?

Case 9.18

Put on Your Administrative Hat

This case is about "whistle blowing." The main character, Jim, must decide whether or not he is willing to follow his conscience or the "party line," despite the very difficult outcomes that may result from either course of action.

Jim was a senior manager in a steel company. He was a professional engineer with a M.B.A. and had been in charge of the production end of Southern Aero Inc. (SAI) for 15 years. Jim was married with children. He was a devoted father, member of the school's PTA, and an active member in the church. Jim tended to be rather conventional in his political leanings and this characteristic spilled over into his work-related behavior; he was cautious and conservative. He was never one to jump on the bandwagon when a new idea was mentioned. In fact, he had held a great many younger, more aggressive employees back because their schemes were a bit too reckless for the company as Jim perceived it. Nonetheless, Jim was extremely well respected by most employees and was often the focus of attention when new employees were being told the history and "myths" of SAI.

SAI had been the nation's leading manufacturer of aircraft frames for the past 20 years. However, in the last five years their dominant position in the market had begun to erode as several multinational companies jumped into the competition with lower prices, faster deliveries, and, some believed, a better product. SAI's board of directors was more than a little concerned at the loss of market share and called a meeting early in January to get some answers from the senior management team. The meeting was held and the atmosphere seemed to be panic-stricken. This giant was not accustomed to being threatened and no one really knew how to handle such a crisis. Halfway through the morning of the second day of meetings, one of Jim's senior researchers boldly raised her hand and asked if she could address the meeting. Susan was a brilliant scientist in her own right. She had a Ph.D. in chemical engineering and was sought after by every major company prior to the completion of her doctoral research on aluminum alloy. She had been with SAI for five years and had been working in her lab without a great deal of pressure to produce. She often felt that she was just "window dressing" for Southern because they believed that they really didn't need any new ideas–they had been, after all (until recently), the giant of the industry. Despite the fact that SAI placed little pressure on Susan, she had been extremely busy. She had continued her research where her doctorate left off, attempting to design a better aluminum alloy that could be used not only for aircraft engines but also for the hull of the national team's bobsled in the next Olympics (SAI had been forced to diversify its range of products to keep in the market). Perhaps not surprisingly, the development of a new bobsled material was a very lucrative venture, particularly in Europe where the sport is much more popular.

Susan approached the podium with a prepared presentation, complete with computer graphics that would make any marketer proud. She presented the results of her past five years of research and stunned the board with her proposal. They had been in such a state of panic that any new idea would have been accepted. However, Susan's was an unbelievable departure from anything the industry in general had known.

Susan's proposal called for a complete change in the chemical structure of the steel that SAI was using to build its products. It demanded some reorganizing of the production process but, as it turns out, not a radical departure from the flow of production. Yet the product, as Susan suggested would be similar in structural strength but twice as light as anything currently on the market, foreign competitors included. The advantage of lighter aircraft engines and bobsled frames with similar qualities was obvious to the board who, more or less, dropped everything to endorse Susan's work. Susan was given carte blanche for her research and the board quickly began setting its strategy for retaking the lead in the industry.

Jim was skeptical. Susan's work seemed thorough, the results appeared, thus far, to be plausible, but he was not ready to join in the sudden sense of organizational euphoria. The production line was reorganized and ready to begin the new process in April, four months after the initial meeting. A news conference was held to introduce the new revolutionary product and it was to be Jim's responsibility, as senior engineer, to make the announcement and answer questions from the media. Prior to the meeting Jim received two reports on the new product. Both reports identified the steel as being lighter, and both found the steel to be similar in structural strength. However, one of the reports found that the steel failed at 120% of recommended torque. In other words, under normal flying conditions, the SAI steel frame was superior to that of other manufacturers. However, under unusual conditions, it was less superior. In a dive situation, it would break up faster than the old SAI frame and that of the competitors. While this stress would not be experienced by the bobsled competitors, the implication of aircraft failure would most certainly influence the purchase of the material for a sport context.

The industry standards allowed for this margin of error, that is, 20% over limits, but SAI had never accepted safety at the status quo level. Were they to do so now? Jim knew that he did not have to raise this point at the press conference since the steel was within acceptable legal limits. But to Jim, this was simply not what he believed SAI was about. It seemed to him to be a contradiction in company philosophy. He was well aware that the board was extremely excited about the possibilities of the new steel and the repercussions that he might face if he were publicly to cast some doubt on its quality and safety.

Jim asked SAI's president, Sam Takahashi, if he could meet with him to discuss his concerns about the new product. Mr. Takahashi listened carefully to Jim's concerns, not only about the minimally safe steel but also about the perceived contradiction in the philosophy of SAI. Mr. Takahashi was silent for a few uncomfortable minutes after Jim had finished and then said, "Jim, you are an engineer and a good one, but for this situation, you've got to put your *managerial hat* on and take your *engineering hat* off."

The following day, Jim welcomed the press to the conference, made his official introduction and overview of the new SAI product, then took a deep breath, introduced Susan, and left the podium.

Questions to Consider for Discussion

1. What is meant by switching hats? Is there a third hat that is you? Is this one ever taken off? Should it be?

2. What has happened to this organization? What moderator is at work and changing the climate?

3. How would you describe Susan? Is she at fault? What is her culture? How is it different?

Case 9.19

Playing the Big Leagues

This case deals with interpersonal conflict and ethics in the "hard-nosed" world of corporate finance and sport marketing. Once again, personal integrity is challenged by organizational climate.

Chris James was an "up-and-coming" manager in a very large multinational corporation, Atlas-Rand Inc., which specialized in sport apparel and equipment. It had originally made its name in the world of running shoes in the early 1970s and had since expanded to become a huge multinational company with annual profits exceeding $4 billion. It had several very lucrative contracts with sport superstars in tennis, golf, football (i.e, soccer, American, Australian, and Canadian rules football), basketball, baseball, hockey, and so on. Chris was extremely happy to be involved with such a prestigious company; it was her first "real" job after graduating with her B.A. in

Commerce. Her parents were also very pleased with her career progress though they really didn't know a great deal about the world of business. Her mother had stayed at home with five children and her father was a career naval officer who tended to shun all financial matters. He believed the navy would look after his family from "cradle to grave." Although both her mother and father were role models to Chris, it was her father who had planted the seeds for her drive to succeed in a "man's world," her desire to travel, and her respect for the "chain-of-command."

Chris believed that Atlas-Rand represented and demonstrated important values and notions of community responsibility. Chris was not of the mind that the business world had its own set of values or ethics that were separate and distinct from the rest of the society or other professions. She was under the impression that Atlas-Rand believed in this premise as well. In other words, her ethical conscience was rarely challenged by being a loyal employee of Atlas-Rand.

The senior management of Atlas-Rand had been watching Chris' progress very carefully as she was being groomed for a very important position in the international trade division. Her enthusiasm, work ethic, and managerial skills were excellent as was her potential to grow and be a role model to male and female employees alike (she was also fluent in French and Spanish and semi-fluent in Cantonese).

Upon her return to work following winter holidays with her family, Chris was invited to the office of the CEO of domestic operations and was introduced to the vice-president of personnel of Atlas-Rand's international office. Chris' initial nervousness was soon replaced with extreme joy as she was offered a position at the head office as assistant director of joint ventures. Chris was thrilled: she would be traveling internationally, she would be able to experience many of the places her father had traveled to with the navy, and her salary would be monumentally increased. Her career was well on its way!

After six months, Chris was beginning to feel a bit more comfortable in her new position. She had made four trips to offices in Malaysia, Japan, Australia, and Singapore and was already making progress on a number of ventures that had been left dormant in the early stages of negotiation by her predecessor. Chris received an e-mail from her boss, the director of joint ventures, who was returning to the head office from recent conferences. She wanted to meet with Chris about their strategies for an important negotiation because she said she wanted Chris to be involved in a new dimension of the business. Chris felt that this message was somewhat mysterious, but was excited by the prospect of a new challenge as well as the faith that her boss, Darlene, seemed to place in her.

Darlene arrived and they met for breakfast prior to their meeting with an unnamed group of individuals. Darlene, who had very much taken Chris under her "wing," stated that she wanted Chris simply to observe what transpired at the meeting and they would talk afterwards. The meeting was in a large conference room in a hotel in the outskirts of the city with few of the trappings or formalities that were usually associated with important clientele. As the meeting progressed, Chris became aware that the individuals in the room were three of Atlas-Rand's fiercest competitors, yet the conversations were far from confrontational.

After the meeting, Chris was dumbfounded. She had no idea what to say or do. Chris' conscience was screaming, "I was just involved in price-fixing!" Darlene and Chris met for dinner that evening. Chris was still in a state of shock. Darlene, somewhat anticipating Chris' reaction, was prepared. "Business," she said, "has its own code of ethics. It's not like anything else. We all play the game and we play by our rules, our ethics, our values. All of those guys around the table understand this, it's how we all have to survive, how we all make a profit that, in the end, allows us to do all the good things that Atlas-Rand is known for throughout the world." Chris reacted by stating, "But we say that we don't do this sort of thing, it's in our code of ethics, for crying out loud! The guys in the legal department spend half their lives drawing up policies on this! Damn it, I thought that we were the good guys, with values and corporate responsibility and all the rest of it." Darlene responded, "Chris, it's true, but the guys in legal don't run the business. They are not making the deals, they are not in the trenches, and what they don't know and what the public doesn't know won't hurt them In fact, the more money we all make the better it is for the public anyway. It's like bad cough medicine—it might taste bad now but in the end it's good for you. These are the big leagues, Chris, and all the players know the rules—written and unwritten. If you don't play by our rules, well, you don't survive. Chris, your future is incredibly bright, you know you will go far in this company, farther than I will. I suppose you've got to make the choice: do you play to win for the company, for the shareholders, and for yourself? Or do you quit the game and do whatever the average Jane does out there? Have you ever read *Atlas Shrugged*? You should!"

Questions to Consider for Discussion

1. Is there a difference between business ethics and ethics generally? Should there be?

2. Can you survive in the world of business and keep your own ethical position intact? Why? Or why not? Can you defend your position?

3. What alternatives does Chris have?

4. Can anything be done to change this? Is this unrealistic?

Case 9.20

Marketing High-Schoolers

Obtaining an athletic scholarship to an American college is highly desirable for many high school students due, in part, to the high cost of tuition fees. It is also desirable because being on a varsity college team is the best venue for attracting attention from the major league scouts. In today's market, being drafted into that level means riches for the young athlete with $1 million signing bonuses almost routine in contemporary times.

A new company, College Baseball Advisers Inc., charges $600 "to enhance high school player's college scholarship prospects by analyzing his playing ability and devising a marketing plan for him" (Editorial, 2002, p.32). Since high-school players are scouted by the colleges, what benefit would there be for the player to have his playing ability analyzed by the company? Why would a high-school player need a marketing plan?

Questions to Consider for Discussion

1. How ethical is it for the family of a high-school student to pay a company to analyze the student's playing ability?

2. How ethical is it to pay a company to devise a marketing plan for a high-school student?

3. From an ethical perspective, has this company crossed the line separating education and business?

Reference

• Editorial. (2002). Go figure. *Sports Illustrated,* 14 January.

Case 9.21

Stealing Signals

To receive satellite TV programs, a monthly fee is paid by the viewer. In addition, from time to time pay-per-view programs are offered. In order to receive the signal ,an encoded card is needed so that the viewer (household) can be charged for watching the program.

New York radio host S.R. is being sued by satellite services provider Direct TV for alleged piracy. He had boasted on a nationally syndicated show that he had used an illegally modified access card to steal sports and movie programming. By having his card "zapped," he was able to avoid paying for the programs.

Using a "zapped" card is illegal. However, a person using such a card does so in the privacy of his or her own home. Hence, the likelihood of being caught is very slight, if at all. The use of, or abstaining from using, such a card then becomes an ethical matter.

Question to Consider for Discussion

1. Is it ethical to obtain satellite programming by using a "zapped" card when other people are paying for it?

Reference

• Editorial. (2002). Blotter. *Sports Illustrated*, April 1, p.28.

Case 9.22

Cyberbodies, Cyborgs, or Clean Athletes

With the mapping of the human DNA through the Human Gemone Project, advances in digital, electronically controlled prostheses, and ongoing research by pharmaceutical companies the possibilities for the way sport is performed in the future take on more intrigue. The history of sport is rife with athletes using performance-enhancing substances and practices (see Hoberman, 1992, and Todd, 1987). The issue of use of performance-enhancing substances and practices is likely to be overtaken by issues of cyberbodies and cyborgs.

Michael Featherstone (1991) identifies cyberbodies as a result of research leading to the manufacturing and cloning of humans. It will not be long before in vitro fertilization "designer babies" are born. The genetic factors sought in these babies could potentially be those necessary to produce top sport performers (Cole, 1994). Featherstone (1991, cited in Cole, 1994) noted that

the potential consequences here for, to take an example, sport are tremendous. Not only is there the capacity to enhance performance and repair, or replace body parts to produce cyberbodies. There is also the potential to genetically design optimum types of bodies best suited for particular sports. (p.22)

Here the notion of repaired and replaced body parts is the focus. The "cyberathletes" will be fundamentally human but might have man-made body parts, as distinct from cyborgs.

We are familiar with the notion of cyborgs from, among others, Arnold Schwarzenegger's *Terminator* films. Cole (1994) discussed the concept of cyborgs in terms of man producing humanoids that might supplant humans or cyberathletes in sport competitions.

Both of these future possibilities do not, however, seem as prescient as those of genetic identification and manipulation. While this discussion has been around since the early 1980s, it is only with the completion of the Human Genome Project in June 2000 that genetic engineering became reality. An Australian television program (Willis, 2002) reported that identifying sport scientists had identified two of many possible genes that make for better athletic success, one related to heart function and the other to explosive muscle function. If these and other discovered genes can be "turned on" or a person's gene extracted, modified, and replaced in that person to produce better function, then sport takes on a different identity. In other words, manipulation of a person's natural genetic endowment to possibly create better athletes results, and genetically modified (GM) athletes are created.

A number of ethical issues have been identified by Miah (2001), mainly around protecting the athlete's genotype but also ensuring that genetic modification has not occurred. Here again sport faces a type of cheating that might be difficult to detect. While research continues on genetic modification and humans genes, it might not be that far in the future that sport will face an insurmountable question.

Each of these future possibilities points to a change in the fundamental way in which humans participate and perform in sport. The very nature of sport continues to be challenged by science. Science, both as the rational method to improve sport (better training regimes, diet, etc.), but also as the way to produce non-natural participants and performers, continues to provide challenges for sport, sport management, and sport organizations (especially to ensure a "level playing field").

All of this echoes a criticism that Ross (1994) leveled against the field of sport sciences in general. He suggested that the athlete is perceived to be little more than a machine to do the bidding of the coach, the scientist, the nation, and now the corporation (i.e., *homo mechanicus*). As a result, the "whole" person, that is, an existential individual with freedom and responsibility or the Kantian person as an end in oneself, is not considered or developed. The focus is on outcome, and process is lost.

Questions to Consider for Discuss

1. Aside from issues of "scientific possibilities," what does the production of cyberbodies, cyborgs, and advanced pharmaceuticals hold for the future of sport?

2. Most of the issues around steroid use and other substances and practices to enhance sport performance have challenged the basic premise of what sport is. How do these newer forms of enhancement challenge sport?

3. What does the GM athlete present to sport?

4. To what degree might GM or cyberbody enhancement be condoned?

5. How can we understand what would make an athlete seek the above-mentioned modifications to their body?

6. What does the culture of sport do to foster this?

7. If we feel the need to change this perception, how would we do it?

8. Describe what you think *homo mechanicus* means in your sport?

9. Can there be an existential athlete? Why or why not?

References

- Chester, R. (2002). Future shocks: Science-fiction fantasies, such as robotic maids and talking kitchen utensils maybe only a few years away. *The Courier-Mail*, Brisbane, Australia, February 23, p. 29.

- Cole, C. (1994). Resisting the canon: Feminist cultural studies, sport, and technologies of the body. In C. Cole & S. Birrell (Eds.), *Women, Sport, and Culture*. Champaign-Urbana, Ill.: Human Kinetics.

- Featherstone, M. (1xxx).

- Hoberman, J. (1992). *Mortal engines: The science of performance and the dehumanization of sport*. New York: Free Press.

- Miah, A. (2001). Genetics, privacy, and athletes' rights. *Sports Law Bulletin*, 4, 5. (Accessed online at http://www.sportslawbulletin.com/Current/Analysis/Analysis.htm on 2/22/02).

- Sports threat: Gene transferring. (2001). Associated Press (Accessed online at wysiwyg://46/http://www.wired.com/news/print/0,1294,41428,00.html on 2/22/02).

- Ross, S. (11994). Sport sciences and the whole person. *CAHPER Research Supplement*, 1, 1:109-115.

- Todd, T. (1987). Anabolic steroids: The gremlins of sport. *Journal of Sport History*, 14:87-107.

- Willis, P. (2002). Gene sport. *Catalyst*, ABC-TV, producer L. Heywood, February 21. (accessed online at http://www.abc.net.au/catalyst/stories/s479512.htm on 2/22/02).

Case 9.23

Should Equal Rights Work Both Ways?

In 1993 the Massachusetts State Superior Court ruled that the Equal Rights Amendment applies to athletics. "That meant boys could not be barred from playing on girls' teams" (Reilly, 2001, p.100). In most instances it has been girls who have petitioned the courts to be allowed to play on boys' teams, but in Massachusetts, the effect of the court ruling has been to allow boys to play on girls' field hockey teams. Boys are bigger and faster than girls and hence their participation seems to have altered the girls' games considerably. Since there are no boys' field hockey teams in U.S. high schools, the only venue available to boys who are interested in playing this sport is the girls' team.

Many girls, their coaches, organizers and supporters have protested the presence of boys on the girls' teams.

A court ruling established the legal right of boys to play on girls' high-school field hockey teams but that does not decide the ethical issue involved.

Questions to Consider for Discussion

1. What is the ethical status of the legal arguments provided by girls who petitioned to play on boys' teams?

2. If girls are allowed to play on boys' teams based on the ethical and legal premises of equal rights, what ethical basis can be involved to prohibit boys from playing on girls' field hockey teams?

3. From an ethical perspective, how valid is the argument that the presence of boys on the girls' field hockey team alters the nature of the game?

Reference

- Reilly, R. (2001). Not your average skirt chaser. *Sports Illustrated*, November 26.

Case 9.24

Spilling the Beans on Major League Baseball

A bold and revealing quotation stands out on the cover of the June 3, 2002, issue of Sports Illustrated. Under the heading, "Confession of an MVP," we find, "At first I felt like a cheater. But I looked around, and everyone was doing it," attributed to former MVP Ken Caminiti. This issue contains a special report on steroids in baseball.

"Totally Juiced" is the title of the special report. Far more telling is the subtitle: "With the use of steroids and other performance enhancers rampant, according to a former MVP and other sources, baseball players and their reliance on drugs have grown to alarming proportions" (Verducci, 2002, p.34).

According to some sources, baseball players did not resort to using performance-enhancing substances in the past. There was a time when the use of chewing tobacco was fairly prevalent, which became a focus of attention when the anti-smoking campaign was introduced. However, that is much different from the current concern. "Steroid use, which a decade ago was considered a taboo violated by a few renegade sluggers, is now so rampant in baseball that even pitchers and wispy outfielders are juicing up-and talking openly among themselves about it" (p.36). That assertion is based on interviews with players, trainers, and executives conducted over a three-month period. Along with an increasing reliance on steroids, other performance-enhancing drugs used include human growth hormone (HGH), and legal and illegal stimulants ranging from amphetamines to Ritalin to Ephedrine-laced dietary supplements. It is the use of illegal steroids that is growing the fastest and having the most profound impact on the game.

Not only is its use rampant but the attitude toward its use has changed radically, from clandestine use and emphatic denial to open discussion on what to use and where to obtain the requisite substances. "The surest sign that steroids are gaining acceptance in baseball: the first public admission of steroid use-without remorse-by a former prominent player. Ken Caminiti, whose 15-year big league career ended after a stint with the Atlanta Braves last season, revealed to Sports Illustrated that he won the 1996 National League Most Valuable Player Award while on steroids he purchased from a pharmacy in Tijuana, Mexico" (ibid.). He also confessed that the heavy use of steroids cause his testicles to shrink and retract; tests showed that his body had virtually stopped producing its own testosterone, having fallen to only 20 percent of normal.

He showed no remorse over his use of steroids and, in reply to a question, admitted that he would not discourage any player, veteran or rookie, from using steroids. His rationale: the money is so good it would be foolish not to go that route. He also estimated that at least half of the players are using steroids and that they talk about it openly. Other observers place the use at 85 percent of the players.

There are both legal and ethical issues involved. "Steroids are illegal in the U.S. unless prescribed by a physician for medical condition such as AIDS or Hypogonadism (an inability to produce testosterone)" (ibid.). Major League Baseball has no steroid policy or testing program for its players. To inaugurate a testing program would require the desire and resolve of the owners and, through collective bargaining, the agreement of the Major League Players' Association, which traditionally has resisted any form of drug testing.

Questions to Consider for Discussion

1. Was it ethical for Sports Illustrated to "spill the beans" about the rampant use of steroids in Major League Baseball?

2. Was it right for retired MVP Ken Caminiti to confess that he had used steroids during his playing career?

3. Was it right for Ken Caminiti to report publicly that the use of steroids is rampant among Major League Baseball players?

4. Is it ethical for the Major League Baseball team owners to have no policy regarding drug testing?

5. What is the ethical status of the Major League Players' Association in resisting any form of drug testing?

Reference

*   Verducci, T. (2002). Totally juiced. *Sports Illustrate*d, June 3, pp.34-40, 42, 44, 46, 48.

Case 9.25

Private and Public Responsibility or Private versus Public Responsibility

Generally speaking it is the responsibility of governments-national, state, and municipal-to build certain recreation facilities. There are many national parks, countless state parks, and campgrounds. At the municipal level, there are playgrounds, arenas, parks, and recreation centres. The need for municipally provided recreation facilities, it could be posited, is less in affluent neighborhoods since the residents have the resources to purchase services from the private sector. However, in low- and lower-income areas, discretionary funds for recreational activities are much more limited for many families, if they exist at all. These areas, often in inner cities, all too often have no recreation facilities provided by local government.

Highly successful former sports agent Dennis Gilbert (he set salary records for clients such as Jose Canseco) grew up in South Central Los Angeles with "guys like Bobby Tolan, Reggie Smith and Bob Watson" (Editorial, 2002, p.22). They played sandlot baseball on a dirt field with a wooden backstop and no fences. At one time baseball played by local youth was vibrant. However, this has not been the case in the recent past because there wasn't anywhere decent to play.

In mid-January 2002, Dennis Gilbert Field opened "less than 3 miles from the sandlot where Gilbert, 54, played as a boy" (ibid.). With funds supplied by Gilbert ($1.5 million), who was approached by a representative of Major League Baseball's Reviving Baseball in Inner Cities (RBI) program, the field was built upon what was a garbage-strewn lot. Gilbert classified his philanthropy as a way of giving something back to his childhood neighborhood.

Questions to Consider for Discussion

1. What is the ethical status of Dennis Gilbert's contribution that helped create a recreation facility in an area where he played as a boy?

2. How ethical is it for the local municipality to allow a private group to usurp their responsibility to provide recreation facilities?

3. What is the ethical status of Major League Baseball's Reviving Baseball in Inner Cities (RBI) program?

4. What is the ethical status of Major League Baseball's RBI program if it only approaches wealthy individuals to the exclusion of municipal governments?

5. From a fairness perspective, what happens to those countless neighborhoods who have not produced a wealthy individual who could be approached to donate funds for a recreation facility?

6. What is the ethical status of an individual who, like Dennis Gilbert, came from a poor neighborhood, became wealthy but, when asked for financial assistance, refused to contribute?

Reference

• Editorial. (2002). Good sports. *Sports Illustrated*, January 28.

Glossary of Terms

Aristotle (384-322 BC). Greek philosopher who, in his book entitled Nichomachean Ethics, suggested that one's telos or goal/purpose as a human is to pursue the "good life." The good life was believed to be a life in which the individual strove to reach full potential as a human, that is, habitually practiced virtuous behavior. Virtuous behavior was framed by two laws–deficit and excess. Therefore the virtuous choice was the mean between excess or deficit and was an end in itself rather than a means to a further end.

Authentic. To be true to oneself in thought and behavior.

Axiology. The study of values (often broadly considered to incorporate the study of ethics and aesthetics).

Beliefs. Objects of faith.

Categorical Imperative. The foundational statement of Immanuel Kant's (1724-1804) ethical position. It reads, "Act only on that maxim that you can at the same time will to become a universal law."

Chaos. The absence of rules. The existence of disorder and confusion.

Consequentialism. Another term for teleology.

De Coubertin (1863-1937). Founder of the modern Olympics.

Deontology. A school of ethical thought that believes ethical behavior is based upon one's duty. This duty originates from divine, societal, or intuitive sources. It is also known as formalism, rule ethics, or non-consequentialism.

Ethics. The study of morals.

Existentialism. A general term for the *school* of philosophical thought that supports the notions of freedom, responsibility, and subjective truths.

Formalism. Another term for deontology.

Freedom. The ability to choose for oneself one's own beliefs, values, and behavior.

Good. From a teleological perspective, this term refers to accomplishing the goal or the end of one's efforts.

Hedonism. The school of ethical thought that believes that ethical behavior is pleasure seeking (physical, social, or intellectual).

Hedonistic Calculus. The method employed by the Utilitarians to determine ethical choices. It attempts to measure quantitatively units of happiness in order to determine the best alternative to follow. It is the basis of the modern rational decision-making process.

Idiographic. Individually based.

Intent. One's true purpose or aim.

Janus Head. Janus is the ancient Roman god of the gates who possessed two faces. One face looked inward from the gate to protect the city from internal perils and the other looked outward from the gate to protect the city from invaders.

Liberalism. An open-minded perspective; a political view leaning towards democratic values.

Maxim. A rule of conduct.

Metaethic. The aspect of ethical theory that is concerned with the logical form of ethical beliefs (i.e., the objectivity or subjectivity of ethical discourses).

Morals. Codes of conduct.

Nihilism. The denial of all reality and the rejection of all moral principles.

Nomothetic. Group or societally based.

Norms. Standards of a particular grouping, culture, or society.

Normative Ethics. Ethical theories that are concerned with the content of decisions and/or behavior.

Paradigmatic. A world view or Zeitgeist.

Plato. Greek philosopher, the student of Socrates and the teacher of Aristotle. Believed in the notion of truth as a rational or cognitive form as opposed to a sensory perception. Like his pupil Aristotle, Plato too argued in favor of ethical behavior being based in virtue (i.e., wisdom, temperance, courage, and justice).

Personalistic. Another term for existential philosophy.

Praxis. One's practice or behavior that is based upon one's reflected philosophy or theory.

Qualitative. What is measured or measurable subjectively or by means of interpretation.

Quantitative. What is measured or measurable objectively, numerically.

Reliability. Repeatable.

Social Contract. An actual or a psychological contract developed for and by the group that one "signs" in order to glean the benefits of group membership (e.g., economies of scale and protection from harm).

Socrates. A Greek philosopher who was the teacher of Plato. He is the main character in Plato's many dialogues and provided us with the dictum that "the unexamined life is not worth living."

Solipsism. The belief that I alone exist–everything I see and perceive in reality is only an object of my consciousness.

Situational Ethics. The belief that a particular behavior is acceptable or unacceptable based upon the particular circumstances surrounding it (i.e., teleology).

Teleology. A philosophical school of thought that believes that ethical behavior is based upon the result or the ends of one's actions.

Utilitarianism. Utilitarianism is the ethical school of thought developed by the British philosophers Bentham and Mill. Ethical behavior to the Utilitarian is that which results in the "greatest good for the greatest number." Two versions of Utilitarianism exist: Act and Rule Utilitarianism. Act Utilitarianism suggests that one should act in such a manner as to bring about the greatest happiness; Rule Utilitarianism on the other hand argues that one should follow the rules that will result in the greatest good for the greatest number.

Validity. What is true.

Value. A concept of the desirable with a motivating force.

Index

MARQUIS

Québec, Canada

HANGRY NO MORE!

KET O
TRICKS
FOR WOMEN WHO LOVE TO EAT

42

24

Contents

Chapter 1: The Basics

66

72

80

Chapter 2: Delicious Recipes

Chapter 3: Keeping Track

58

128

Your Keto Journey

From the hows and whys to delicious recipes and handy workbook pages, get started on your path to success.

While many diets come and go, keto has proven to have some staying power. Why? The very-low carb, low-to-no sugar diet has a whole lot of good stuff to offer. To start, it serves up fast results: It's not uncommon to shed 10 pounds or more in your first few weeks before settling into the more typical (and doctor recommended) .5 to 2 pounds a week. And with more than 40% of the population classified as obese, a highly effective program like this is particularly motivating!

But losing pounds isn't the only benefit. Weight gain in general can put us at risk for health conditions like high blood pressure, diabetes, heart disease, increased inflammation and poor cholesterol readings. That's where keto can also have a big impact. Keto focuses on your macronutrient intake, or the amount of carbohydrates, fats and protein you consume. It places an emphasis on healthy fats (like avocado and salmon) over unhealthy carbs (like white bread, pasta and sugary treats), which can lead to inflammation in the body. By using fats instead of carbs as a primary fuel source, your body will enter a state of ketosis, or the metabolic process in which you burn ketones rather than glucose for fuel. Translation—you're burning more body fat, so you're not just shedding excess pounds, you're also losing inches.

And while we can all be guilty of being a little hangry from time to time, another great thing about eating a keto-centric diet is that you are more likely to feel satiated—and energized—as your body transitions into ketosis and you ween yourself off your dependence on sugar. Plus, we've pulled together more than 40 recipes (including desserts!) to keep you satisfied.

While a ketogenic diet might sound complicated, with the right tools and information it's really very straightforward to follow. That's where the workbook beginning on page 132 comes in. While the experts and resources found in this book provide important information, the workbook section serves as that trusted friend that can lead you on your journey and keep you motivated. You'll find space to outline your weekly goals and milestones, plus sections to track elements like macronutrients, hunger, hydration, sleep and exercise, along with your weight and even your mindfulness. It's a place to reflect and evaluate your progress. It's also full of inspiration that can help give you a boost if you need one—because that's what trusted friends do.

As you work through the pages of this book, we trust that the diet's many benefits, from weight loss to better health, will have you feeling that it's time well spent in no time at all. —*Nancy Coulter-Parker*

Inches off plus confidence gained equals success!

THE
Basics

While going keto sounds complicated, the right tools can make it easy. Let the experts and resources in this section help you begin.

Lesson One

That salad actually isn't very keto friendly.

Welcome to Keto

Wondering what all the buzz is about? (There's a lot of buzz!) Consider this your intro to the ketogenic diet.

It may be the diet of the moment, but don't call keto a "fad diet." Unlike other weight-loss eating plans that have fallen in and out of style (cabbage soup diet, we're looking at you), the ketogenic plan is proving to be more of a long-term lifestyle than a slim-down quick fix. And it's attracting people with various wellness goals. Yes, weight loss is one of them, but it's far from the only reason that people are signing up to go keto.

If you're reading this, you're likely interested in the diet—maybe you've even considered giving it a go. So what's keto all about? We break it all down on these pages, from how it works to the best ways to make it an easy part of your life.

A Brief History

Keto was actually first introduced as a treatment for epilepsy in the 1920s, after doctors figured out that patients with low blood sugar seemed to have fewer seizures with this way of eating. The therapy was widely used for two decades, but the introduction of anti-epileptic drugs pushed it out of popularity. However, interest in the diet has grown again, and today it's often used to treat kids with epilepsy who don't respond well to medication.

The Diet Today

While interest in the medical field is growing, the appetite for the ketogenic diet in the general wellness and weight loss world is *booming*. Keto is one of the top diet search terms on Google and shows no signs of slowing down. Everyone from celebrities to bloggers is praising the diet for its ability to help with weight loss—and keep it off.

But it's not just people with extra pounds to lose who are gushing about the diet. Doctors say that putting their patients on a keto diet has helped with everything from reducing high blood pressure to improving inflammation and chronic pain. They're even adopting the eating plan themselves.

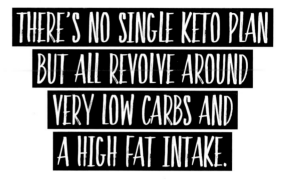

THERE'S NO SINGLE KETO PLAN BUT ALL REVOLVE AROUND VERY LOW CARBS AND A HIGH FAT INTAKE.

Lose It

Weight loss is just one reason people flock to the keto diet.

"I myself was following the standard dietary recommendations, was into endurance sports and thought I was healthy. Then, after having blood work done, I discovered I was prediabetic. I couldn't explain why that was happening," says John Limansky, MD, an internist in Puerto Rico. Limansky switched to the keto diet and his health improved. Now he has his own concierge practice devoted to preventative and longevity health with a focus on a ketogenic or low-carb diet.

Keto Controversy

Not everyone is sold. Celebrity trainer Jillian Michaels has criticized the diet, saying that it was bad for overall health. Moreover, some doctors and dietitians aren't pleased that the diet encourages saturated fat and limits whole grains and some veggies, arguing that this could be harmful for cardiovascular health. Three physicians even penned an article in the journal *JAMA Internal Medicine* saying that the enthusiasm surrounding keto outpaces evidence of the diet's benefits. "Although the temptation is great to recommend a potentially novel approach for otherwise difficult-to-treat diseases, it is important to remain grounded in our appraisal of the risks, benefits and applicability of the diet to avoid unnecessary harm and costs to patients," they wrote.

As with any health change, it's best to talk with your doctor before switching to a ketogenic diet—and it's smart to know what's involved before you jump in. The guidance in this book is a great place to get started. So read on!

Ketosis, Explained

The goal of a ketogenic diet is all about going into ketosis. If you're thinking "ke-what?" here's what you need to know.

BUT FIRST... GLUCOSE

To understand ketosis, it helps to first understand how the body gets its fuel when eating a carb-filled diet. Typically, the body turns two types of carbs into energy: sugar (fruit and dairy, for example) and starches (like bread or pasta). When we eat these foods, the body breaks carbohydrates down into a type of sugar called glucose. Glucose is released into the bloodstream, where it can be used immediately for energy. It can also be stored in the muscles and liver as a reserve source of fuel.

AND NOW... KETOSIS

If you stop eating carbs, the body can't rely on glucose for energy. But it needs to get fuel from somewhere, so it turns to fat stores. Fat is broken down into molecules called ketone bodies, which are released into the bloodstream and used to generate energy. Ketosis occurs when your cells primarily use fat for energy.

THE JOURNEY TO KETOSIS

This shift doesn't happen overnight. It usually takes a few days or even weeks of limiting carbohydrates (20 to 50 grams a day) to produce enough ketones to fuel the body—though some people may need to limit their carbs intake further. And here's a shocker: Many people who follow a keto diet never actually reach ketosis because they're not cutting enough carbs to stop the glucose cycle.

Keto gives some people more energy!

How You'll Really *Feel*

Not at your best during your first few days on the diet? You're definitely not alone. Here's what to expect when you swap carbs for fat.

Any sort of dietary change can make you feel different, and that's most certainly true of keto. The changes can be unexpected—even unsettling—and it's not uncommon for people to ditch the diet in the first week or so because they don't like how they feel. But know this: The symptoms are normal and very manageable. And one of the best things you can do is be prepared for them.

To help you understand how your body reacts to this switch in diet, we got the scoop from expert doctors and dietitians. Learn what changes and symptoms you can expect as you transition to the plan, and get a look at what's happening inside your body as you adjust to eating more high-fat foods.

You'll Switch Fuel Sources

The main goal of the ketogenic diet is to get your body to run on fat as its major source of energy, which happens within a few days to a few weeks after you start following the food plan, says Jeff Volek, PhD, RD, a professor in The Ohio State University Department of Human Sciences, who has studied the keto diet for years. Typically, your body and brain prefer glucose (or sugar, which you'd get from carbohydrates) as the primary fuel source. "But when you're restricting carbohydrates, your body becomes more efficient at breaking down and using fat for fuel," Volek explains.

More specifically, your liver partially breaks down fat into what are known as ketones (hence why it's called the ketogenic diet). The liver then releases these ketones into the bloodstream, and any cell in the body can use them for energy.

Brain fog is normal when you start keto.

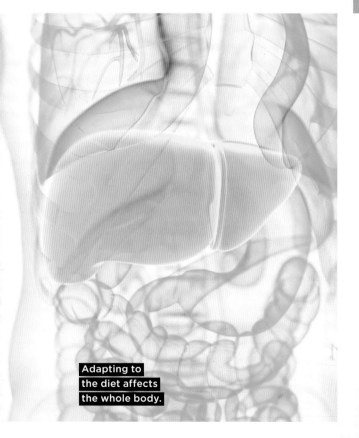

Adapting to the diet affects the whole body.

GIVING UP PASTA AND CARBS CAN TAKE SOME GETTING USED TO.

What Hunger?

After your initial transition to keto, you may find that hunger pangs and cravings—poof!—vanish. Some research has found that keto can have an appetite-suppressing effect. This occurs even when you're cutting back on calorie intake, something that has been shown to typically lead to an increase in appetite in obese people. Many people on a ketogenic diet say that they'll skip meals altogether because they don't feel hungry enough to eat. Listen to your hunger cues and let them be your guide as to whether you're ready to sit down for a meal.

Some people go keto for a few weeks, some for a few months and some for years—or forever! What will you choose to do?

THE BIG SWITCH

BEFORE YOU ADOPT A KETO DIET...
Your body gets energy by breaking down carbohydrates from the diet into a type of sugar called glucose.

Glucose is released into the bloodstream, where it can be accessed immediately for energy. It's also stored in the muscles and liver as a reserve source of fuel.

WHEN YOU STOP EATING CARBS...
Your body needs to find a new fuel source, so it turns to fat stores.

Fat is broken down into molecules called ketone bodies, which are released into the bloodstream and used to generate energy.

Ketosis happens when most of the cells in your body no longer use glucose and instead are relying on fat for energy.

KEEP IN MIND THAT KETONE URINE TESTS, WHILE AFFORDABLE, AREN'T ALWAYS 100% ACCURATE.

Unlike fat, ketones can even pass through the blood-brain barrier, meaning your brain (which usually prefers to run on glucose) can also switch over to running on ketones.

You May Feel Run Down

"As your body transitions from burning sugar to burning fat, it struggles initially," says Chris Palmer, MD, director of the Department of Postgraduate and Continuing Education at McLean Hospital in Belmont, Massachusetts, and assistant professor of psychiatry at Harvard Medical School, who has studied the ketogenic diet's use in psychiatry. "The body is used to burning glucose, so when it's forced to switch over to fat and ketones, it has to go through adaptations in order

HOW TO CHECK KETONE LEVELS

Whether you're going on the keto diet for health reasons or with the primary goal of weight loss, it's a smart strategy to regularly check your ketone levels, says Jeff Volek, PhD, RD. That's because many people think they're following the diet correctly, but unless you check your numbers it's hard to know for sure that your body is creating ketones. Checking your numbers will clue you in to whether you need fewer carbs (ketone levels can easily drop if you eat too

many carbs) or even less protein.

At first, it's a good idea to check your levels daily. This can help determine if you need to make tweaks to your diet. Remember, different people can tolerate different amounts of carbs without getting out of ketosis, and it may take some trial and error to learn what your body can handle. Then, once the weight is coming off and the keto lifestyle comes more naturally to you, you can reduce the frequency of testing—or you may even find that you

can stay in ketosis without needing to test your levels. Read on to learn about three different ways to check your ketone levels at home.

BLOOD TESTS

These are the most accurate—but tend to also be the most expensive. You'll prick your fingertip and put the drop of blood on a strip. A small handheld device called a ketone meter will then report back your levels.

URINE TESTS

These are more affordable,

readily available in drugstores and online, and pretty easy to use. You simply pee on the strip and then look for a change in color. Then match that color to the key that comes with the product to determine your ketone level.

BREATH METER

These meters are more expensive but very easy to use. Simply press start and blow into the device. It measures acetone, a ketone you exhale through your breath, to give you your reading.

Fiber keeps things moving.

AS WITH ANY NEW DIET, BE SURE TO TALK TO YOUR DOC BEFORE YOU BEGIN.

Double-check to see how the diet may affect your meds.

to accomplish that." Those adjustments make the first few weeks of the diet a little difficult to endure, as you might experience low energy, hunger, even dizziness or weakness. "If a car runs on gas and you want to convert to diesel, or a stove runs on propane and you swap it for natural gas, you have to make adjustments to switch that fuel source. Our cells are no different," Palmer says.

You Could Get "Sick"

Those feelings of dizziness, fatigue and light-headedness are referred to as the "keto flu" or according to the experts, keto adaptation. These symptoms are often the result of a loss of sodium, says Volek. That's because during the transition to ketosis, there's a change in how the kidneys function and you will start losing sodium, and with that, water. Luckily, there are ways to avoid this "flu" (see page 23).

Your GI System May Take a Hit

More fat and less fiber can spell trouble for your digestion, explains Robin Foroutan, RDN, an integrative medicine dietitian and a spokesperson for the Academy of Nutrition and Dietetics. Cutting back on fiber-filled carbs (the ones found in both whole grains and in produce) may lead to constipation and bloating. Troubleshoot the situation by adding keto-friendly berries to your diet (they are filled with fiber) and consider taking a fiber supplement. Look for one that contains psyllium husk (such as Metamucil), which can help get things moving again.

You'll Lose Water Weight

While the first few weeks following the keto diet can certainly be a challenge as you ditch foods like cookies and sandwiches, there's one key payoff that motivates people to stick with it: losing water weight. "One of the first changes you see when you restrict to 50 grams a day of carbohydrates is that your body does get rid of a lot of fluid," Volek says. "That's why you have rapid weight loss—because a lot of people are carrying around extra water."

Your Meds Might Need a Dose Adjustment

If you have high blood pressure or diabetes, Palmer says you definitely need to talk to your doctor before starting the keto diet. Because it's been shown to lower blood pressure and blood sugar, anyone who's taking medication to deal with these conditions could have serious side effects. Your doctor can help you avoid that, often by fine-tuning your dosage.

Your Breath Could Start Stinking

You might have heard that some people experience bad breath—a sort of fruity, sharp odor somewhat similar to nail polish remover—when following the keto diet. "One type of ketone breaks down into acetone, which gets exhaled by the breath," Volek explains. But in order for someone to actually catch a whiff of this scent, your ketone levels would have to be quite high—likely to a dangerous level. For example, those with diabetes who get ketoacidosis (a life-threatening condition) often expel this smell.

If your ketone levels aren't in the too-high range and you're still experiencing keto breath, Foroutan suggests drinking more water and eating foods like watercress, fresh mint, basil and other high-antioxidant fresh herbs.

It Will Get Easier!

The first few weeks can absolutely be tough, but most people tend to feel better after a few weeks of the diet, says Palmer. In addition to the quick weight loss, people tout benefits like improved mood and boosted energy. So stick with it and get ready for success!

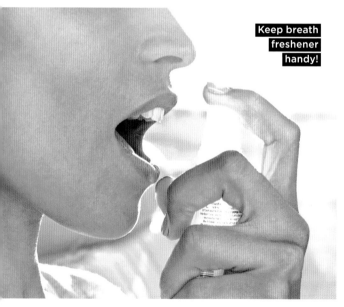

Keep breath freshener handy!

"KETO FLU" SURVIVAL GUIDE

**FEELING ACHY, EXHAUSTED AND SO OVER IT?
USE THESE FOUR STRATEGIES TO BOUNCE BACK FROM THE
KETO FLU—OR, BETTER YET, AVOID IT ALTOGETHER.**

STEP 1
Clear Your Calendar

It's normal to have extremely low energy when you first go keto, as your body transitions from running on glucose to using fat as its energy source. Until it's accustomed to not being able to turn to glucose as fuel, you may experience brain fog and dizziness, too (like you would when you're hungry). That's why it's wise to avoid any activities that will drain you further, whether that's a game of tennis or a long day of gardening or volunteering. But don't worry—this won't last long. You may even find that once you adjust, your thinking is clearer and your energy level is normal again.

STEP 2
Have a Water Bottle Handy

Keep sipping H20 during the first few weeks of your new diet. As you lose sodium, you'll also lose water, which can bring on dehydration symptoms like lethargy, aches and cramps. There's no "right" amount to drink, but be prepared to guzzle more water than you typically do.

STEP 3
Sprinkle on the Salt

Consuming sodium can help keep keto flu symptoms at bay because it helps you retain some water, nixing dehydration side effects. Consider adding high-sodium foods (such as bone broth) or an extra teaspoon of table salt to your meals.

STEP 4
Still Not Feeling Great?

The keto flu should not be accompanied by a temperature. If you're really not feeling well and have a fever, check in with your physician to rule out something more serious.

23

Understanding

The "keto ratio" is about 70-80% fats, 20-25% protein and 5-10% carbs.

There are three types of macronutrients: carbohydrates, proteins and fats. The keto diet supports a moderate intake of proteins, but the real emphasis is on healthy fats. "A normal diet is about 50% carbs, 25% proteins and 25% fats. But on a keto diet, you're looking at your calories coming from about 75% fat, 20% protein and 5% or less of carbs," says Aspen, Colorado-based nutritionist and health coach Lisa Cohen. "All of this is a numbers game."

While healthy fats are key to the diet's fat-burning-for-fuel focus, excess protein is converted into glucose, which can kick you out of ketosis.

You can still include some carbs in your keto diet, but it's important to get the right balance for ketosis to begin. It's recommended that you keep carbs within 20 to 50 grams per day, or 5 to 10% of your total caloric intake. To give you an

idea of what you get with that, consider that half a cup of cooked quinoa has roughly 12 grams of net carbs. (Net carbs are the number of grams of carbohydrates, minus the grams of fiber in a serving.) And whereas 1 medium avocado has 17 grams of carbohydrates, when you subtract the fiber, that number drops closer to 2 net carbs. So it can take a bit of planning to make sure you get your numbers right from the start.

Count Grams, Not Calories

The easiest and most common way to determine macronutrients is by measuring grams. Counting grams is easier and more accurate than counting calories because fat has more calories per gram than protein or carbohydrates. (A gram of fat has 9 calories; a gram of protein or carbohydrate each has 4 calories.) Because fat is more calorically dense, keto meals tend to look a bit smaller portion-wise, even when they have the same amount of calories as (or more than) non-keto meals. Think about it: 2 tablespoons of olive oil has 28 grams of fat and 252 calories, even though it looks like nothing. Visually, compare this to a 3.5-ounce skinless, boneless chicken breast, which has about 165 calories, 3.6 grams of fat and 31 grams of protein.

A typical keto ratio is either 4-to-1 or 3-to-1— that's about 4 grams of fat for 1 gram of protein plus carbohydrate. So for every 5 grams of food you eat, 4 grams will be fat and 1 gram will be protein and/or carbohydrate. The percentages people talk about (75-20-5) are converted to grams.

So here goes: You need to eat 1,800 calories a day using the 75-20-5 ratio. So you'll be getting

Macronutrients

What exactly are your macros—and how do you calculate them to stay in ketosis? Here's what you need to know.

Many keto-compliant foods will keep you satisfied for hours on end, so you'll be less likely to nosh all day.

1,350 calories from fat, 360 calories from protein and 90 calories from carbs every day. Next, calculate the grams you'll be eating of each macronutrient. For fat, that's 1,350 divided by 9 (remember, 1 gram equals 9 calories), or about 150 grams of fat daily. For protein, it's 360 divided by 4, or 90 grams of protein (approximately 30 grams of protein per meal). For carbs, you are allotted roughly 23 grams per day.

For proteins, a common calculation is 0.8 grams of protein per kilogram of body weight. "A lot of people think keto is a high-protein diet, but that's more of the Atkins diet philosophy. If you have too much protein on keto, it gets converted to glucose, so it's best to stick with the 0.8 number," explains sports physician Chris Vincent, DC, co-founder and CEO of Altus Sports Institute, a comprehensive sports medicine and training center. For someone weighing 250 pounds, that's roughly 90 grams of protein daily, or about 30 grams per meal. Then, says Vincent, "It's [about] avoiding all starch, glucose and sugar. Get the limited amount of carbs from high-fiber veggies and maybe a few berries or nuts. The rest is as much as you want to eat in fat, like avocados, olives, and olive and coconut oils."

As far as carbohydrates, the recommendation is often 20 to 30 grams of net carbs per day—or try to keep it under 50 grams. Just remember that net carbs are carb grams minus fiber grams in a food.

But experts say you can get a bit lost in the weeds calculating macros. Often, says registered dietitian and nutritionist Tracey Grant, founder of wholedailylife.com, she'll recommend a higher amount of protein, especially for active people. The key, she says, is that she wants her clients to get enough protein to support satiety. Likewise, she is wary of discouraging her clients from focusing too much on the carbs in high-fiber vegetables. "Don't worry about the carbs in vegetables, even in asparagus and broccoli; you will see carbs that are not fiber, but they're minimal when it comes to blood sugar. I'd rather people eat them and get nutrients, than worry about the carbohydrate number."

How Do You Measure Ketones?

The only real way to determine whether or not you are in ketosis—and reaping the benefits of the keto diet—is to measure your ketones, says Vincent. To track if you are in ketosis, you can measure ketones in your urine, or do a finger-prick blood test. While urine strips work initially, they're not as effective in the long run: "Once you have been in ketosis for a while, the body stops spilling over ketones into the urine," says Grant. A ketone blood meter, where you prick your finger and check your blood for ketones, is more reliable. "There are so many meters that are just a finger prick, and you can track when you are in ketosis. It gets complicated with limiting your carbs," says Vincent. "The easiest way is to follow a sensible ketogenic diet and finger-prick test your ketones; that way you know exactly where you are."

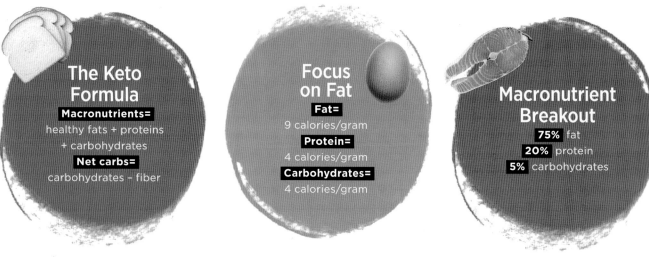

The Keto Formula
Macronutrients=
healthy fats + proteins + carbohydrates
Net carbs=
carbohydrates – fiber

Focus on Fat
Fat=
9 calories/gram
Protein=
4 calories/gram
Carbohydrates=
4 calories/gram

Macronutrient Breakout
75% fat
20% protein
5% carbohydrates

A number of online calculators can help you figure out how many grams to eat based on how active you are.

How Much Protein?

1 kilogram =
2.2 pounds
Protein intake is calculated as 0.8 grams of protein per kilogram of body weight.

Healthy Fats

Eating enough fat is a fundamental part of the keto diet, but it's not always easy to do. Here's how to keep your intake on track.

On a keto diet, fat is your very good friend, helping to improve energy levels and mitigate the energy spikes and dips that too much sugar in your bloodstream can cause. Fats tend to keep you feeling satiated and less likely to snack mindlessly throughout the day. Fats are also key in helping to absorb vitamins like A, D, E and K, regulate inflammation, boost immune function and keep skin and hair cells healthy,

But while fat intake is a cornerstone of the diet, comprising up to 75% of your calories, the high level of healthy fats required to keep you in ketosis can counter weight loss if you don't make the best choices. It may take some time to figure out the right balance of foods for you.

And while you don't need to count every calorie on keto, it is possible to undermine results. "People might go overboard on high-fat foods like nuts and seeds, or eat three whole avocados a day, which is not beneficial if their goal is weight loss," notes Tracey Grant, a Phoenix-based registered dietitian and certified wellness coach.

The Good vs. The Bad

Dietary fats are not all created equal. Some have a number of proven health benefits; others have been shown to be harmful. Here's a guide to the good, the bad and the sometimes in between.

In Moderation

Saturated Fats Thanks to American physiologist Ansel Keys, who hypothesized in the late 1960s that saturated fats caused heart disease, we spent decades avoiding these fats. His thinking was that saturated fats would influence cholesterol and raise "bad" LDL cholesterol levels. Since studies had linked high cholesterol to heart disease, it was assumed that saturated fats *caused* heart disease.

More recent research, however, does not support this theory. Rather, it has shown that saturated fats also increase good cholesterol (HDL) and that the increase in both LDL and HDL does not have a direct correlation to heart disease.

> Lauric acid is the main saturated fatty acid found in coconut and is thought to have antimicrobial properties.

Seeds
(monounsaturated or
polyunsaturated)

Avocado
(monounsaturated)

Excellent Choices

✳ **Avocado** One avocado contains 13 grams of fiber with 3 grams of net carbs, and is rich in monounsaturated fats. It also contains 4 grams of protein.

✳ **Nuts and Seeds** These snacks are full of monounsaturated and polyunsaturated fats and are often a good source of protein, too. Just watch the carb count: One cup of walnuts has 14 grams of net carbs.

✳ **Olives** These snacks are rich in monounsaturated fats—in particular, oleic acid, which may help reduce inflammation. A handful of olives (about seven to 10) contains roughly 1 gram of net carbs.

✳ **Salmon** This flavorful fish is packed with omega-3 fatty acids for brain and heart health, with about 20 grams of protein per each 200-calorie serving.

Salmon
(polyunsaturated)

Olives/Olive Oil
(monounsaturated)

Nuts
(monounsaturated or
polyunsaturated)

Still, given the controversy behind saturated fat, it pays to stay somewhat cautious. "You don't want to eat only saturated fats," says Kendra Whitmire, a nutritionist and dietitian in Laguna Beach, California. Like everything else in nutrition, a healthy balance of minimally processed food sources makes the most sense.

Help Yourself

Monounsaturated and Polyunsaturated Fats There are two main types of unsaturated fats: monounsaturated and polyunsaturated. A key difference in the chemical structure between saturated fats and mono- and polyunsaturated fats is that the latter two remain in liquid form at room temperature. Think olive oil, a monounsaturated fat, versus coconut oil, a saturated fat.

Polyunsaturated fats are primarily known as omega-3 and omega-6 fats. Omega-3s are the healthy omegas; they're found in fish and seafood, and have other animal and plant sources, such as walnuts. Omega-6 consumption is best kept to a minimum, so you'll want to avoid processed foods and seed and vegetable oils, such as corn oil.

On the other hand, monounsaturated fats get the green light, with foods like avocados, olive oil and some nuts. They do the opposite of what trans fats or unhealthy fats do: They help to reduce inflammation and support heart health, and are even thought to help with weight loss.

Avoid At All Costs

Trans Fats Once commonplace in food products, trans fats have been banned in the U.S. "We get it from those already bad vegetable oils and take them through *more* processing to make them solid at room temperature, which enhances shelf stability," explains Grant. "Trans fats are inflammatory for the body and associated with heart disease."

Although in recent years companies have been reformulating products and removing trans fats, Grant says they're not completely gone. "There is a loophole in the law: If a product has less than 0.5 gram per serving of trans fats, it can be listed

Cured Meats (saturated)

A cheese plate can be a smart keto option—just avoid the crackers and other high-carb items.

as 0. If a product says it has monoglycerides or triglycerides in it, those are code words for trans fats. So the product might actually have 0.4 grams of trans fat per serving in it. If you have three servings through the day, you are eating 1.2 grams for that day," she explains.

The exception, says Grant, is grass-fed CLA (conjugated linoleic acid), which is a good trans fat associated with healthy weight management and good health. "If you see trans fat on the label and it is from a grass-fed source and there are no processed animal fats, then it is OK," she adds.

Best Oils

Cheeses (saturated)

AVOCADO OIL

Available both refined and unrefined, avocado oil is full of healthy monounsaturated fat and oleic acid, which has been shown to help lower cholesterol. It has a creamy, rich (yet mild), almost buttery flavor, which makes it an ideal partner for cooking. It has a very high smoke point and is well-suited for roasting, grilling or sauteing veggies. It's also a good choice for salad dressings, pesto or dishes that use a variety of herbs.

COCONUT OIL

Coconut oil is full of healthy saturated fats and lauric acid, both of which are thought to be easily converted to ketones to sustain ketosis. Its health benefits include helping to balance cholesterol and boosting metabolism. Relatively mild in flavor,

it offers just a hint of its coconut roots—not the stronger taste of dried coconut found in baked goods. It's suitable for both cooking and baking. Or add a scoop to a smoothie or even a cup of coffee. Coconut oil can be stored for a lengthy period of time without spoiling.

MACADAMIA NUT OIL

Not your everyday oil, macadamia nut oil's light flavor makes it a good substitute for butter or vegetable oils. High in monounsaturated fats, it's excellent for high-heat cooking, such as sauteing, and it also works well for baking. It can keep on your shelf for up to two years.

OLIVE OIL

With high levels of monounsaturated fat and oleic acid, olive oil is one of the most versatile and trusty oils around. Extra-virgin olive oil is cold-pressed and bottled after the first pressing. It is

unrefined, contains more of the nutrients from the olives and tends to be a bit darker in color and more earthy in flavor. Virgin olive oil is also unrefined, but the production standards are not as stringent and it doesn't tend to be as flavorful. Olive oil is suitable for grilling, roasting and sauteing. Its relatively mild flavor also makes it a reliable choice for salad dressings and drizzles.

SESAME OIL

Often used in Asian-influenced dishes, sesame oil has a slightly nutty flavor. It is extracted from sesame seeds and is available refined or unrefined. It serves up a blend of monounsaturated and polyunsaturated fats and is rich in antioxidants. The unique flavor of unrefined sesame oil is best for salad dressings and drizzles. Refined sesame oil can be used for sauteing and cooking.

Cold-Pressed

This is the term for  oil that has been extracted from nuts, seeds or olives through mechanical crushing or pressing (think expeller-pressed).

31

Drinking water can also help reduce constipation and keep you regular.

Drink Up

A key part of transitioning to keto with minimal side effects is to stay hydrated.

When you first kick off the keto diet, you may notice your pants suddenly feel a whole lot looser. In fact, rapid weight loss is one of the hallmark characteristics of going keto. That's because when you slash carbs from your diet, your body naturally sheds water weight. Carbs are stored in your muscles and liver as glycogen; each gram of glycogen contains about 3 to 4 grams of water. So when your body taps into those glycogen stores for energy, that water weight comes off with it. An estimated 70% of the weight lost in the first week of a keto diet is due to water weight; over time, as you tap into fat stores, that number will slow down and then drop significantly.

Losing this much water can not only cause dehydration; it can also throw your body's electrolytes out of balance, which is in part why you might feel symptoms of the keto flu. "People need sodium, magnesium and potassium when they do a low-carb diet," says Tracey Grant, RDN and nutritionist. Adding these electrolytes—or at the very least, salt— can minimize uncomfortable side effects. "If someone is not feeling well, or is light-headed, dizzy or nauseous, I encourage them to look at electrolytes and hydration," she says. Even mild dehydration can zap your energy, memory and attention, while an electrolyte deficiency can create headaches, weakness and nausea.

Sodium and potassium, in particular, are needed to help maintain adequate fluid levels and blood volume. While you can optimize potassium intake from foods such as avocados and coconuts, if you are having rapid water-weight loss, you may need to add in a supplement or liquid electrolytes.

Because you lose water quickly at the start of the keto diet, make hydrating a daily habit from the start, drinking water or other fluids regularly throughout the day. The best way to remind yourself is to keep a water bottle at your desk or carry one with you. Although coffee and tea have a mild diuretic effect, they still count (just avoid the sugar), as do foods with a higher water content, such as soups and vegetables.

Hydration Rule of Thumb

Divide your weight by two: That's what you should drink in ounces daily. For instance, if you weigh 160 pounds, try to take in roughly 80 ounces, or 10 cups, of water. Be sure to include electrolytes in your hydration plan to avoid side effects like the keto flu.

Keto in Terms of Food

t's time to put the diet into action and take a look at the different food categories—what you can or can't eat from each. As you consider your macronutrient intake, it's important to think about the way in which you implement the diet. "Take two plates, for example: one of bacon, cheese and pork rinds, all keto foods that are high in fat and low in carbs; or one of what I'd recommend—a fatty cut of high-quality animal protein, like good, fatty pork; nonstarchy vegetables like broccoli; and some avocado, nuts and seeds. Focus on whole foods and don't forget fiber, micronutrients, vitamins and minerals," says Tracey Grant, RDN and wellness coach.

Healthy Diet Options

BERRIES

Berries are low-ish in carbs and high in fiber, but you want to use them sparingly. Think of them more like a treat, says New York–based Kristen Mancinelli, MS, RDN, author of *The Ketogenic Diet: A Scientifically Proven Approach to Fast, Healthy Weight Loss.* For example: Try sprinkling a few sliced strawberries on your yogurt. And while blueberries are OK, blackberries, raspberries and strawberries have a higher fiber count, so are lower in carbs.

DAIRY AND EGGS

Believe it or not, cheese is actually high in fat, protein and calcium, but low in carbs. Finally, you can enjoy eating cheese and not worry about it! Cheese even contains conjugated linoleic acid, which has been linked to weight loss. Mancinelli notes that soft cheeses tend to have more grams of carbs, and hard cheeses have fewer. On the dairy front, plain Greek yogurt also fits the bill. Eggs are also OK: They are low (less than 1 gram) on carb content, and one egg serves up just under 6 grams of protein.

> The benefits of losing weight and regulating blood sugar make figuring out what you can eat time well spent.

> You know rice, pasta and potatoes are off the table. But what *can* you eat? A lot more than you may think.

FLOURS AND BAKING INGREDIENTS

While still keeping an eye on your carbohydrate load, there are some flours that are keto friendly. These flours, not surprisingly, are derived from foods that are also keto friendly, such as almonds and coconuts. If you need a binding agent to help these flours act more like wheat flour, xanthan gum will do the trick. And along these lines, salt, pepper and spices can help to enhance the flavor of any meal.

NUTS AND SEEDS

Nuts and seeds will be your friends on this diet, for their healthy fat content and amino acids. They can also be rich in protein, vitamins, minerals, dietary fat and antioxidants. But be sure to focus on low-carb nuts. Cashews and pistachios, for instance, are higher in carbs.

NUT BUTTERS

Nut butters taste good and pack a protein punch. Try some on celery sticks or use them to make fat bombs (see pages 60 and 122). Keep single-serving pouches on hand for when you're on the go. Just make sure they don't have added sugar.

PROTEINS

Recommended proteins include low-carb seafood like salmon; shellfish are also usually low in carbs. Meat and poultry are staples of this diet; they contain no carbs but are rich in nutrients. "The flesh of animals other than shellfish does not contain carbohydrates; it's pretty much protein and fat," says Mancinelli. For the healthiest options, choose grass-fed or organic.

VEGGIES

Even veggies contain carbs. But when you look at the net carb count (subtracting the fiber from the carbs), you usually come up with a low-carb count with vegetables. The exceptions: starchy vegetables, such as potatoes and butternut squash, which should be avoided. Read on for some delicious low-carb veggie options.

8 Low-Carb

LEAFY GREENS

Lettuces, kale, chard and spinach, too. Leafy greens tend to be "all you can eat"-type foods. They're packed with nutrients, including vitamin K, yet they're very low in carbohydrates and have no-to-low impact on blood glucose. You can eat greens raw in a salad; place them in a blender to make a soup or smoothie; or saute, bake or steam them to serve alongside a protein. Romaine lettuce can even be put on the grill.

Cut bell peppers into strips so they're ready to be tossed in a salad, added to a stir-fry or munched by the handful.

Veggies YOU SHOULD KEEP IN YOUR FRIDGE

GARLIC

By the numbers, garlic could be considered a high-carb vegetable—1 clove of garlic contains 1 gram of carbs—but **the amount that we typically eat at one time is so small that it counts as low carb.** And we're thankful for that, because it packs a punch on the flavor front. Plus, numerous studies have shown that it may help to decrease blood pressure, boost the immune system and increase resistance to the common cold.

BELL PEPPERS

Choose from antioxidant-rich red, yellow, orange or green peppers to snack on raw throughout the day, or mix them into a salsa or a salad. Fun fact: A pepper's carb content differs by its color. Green bell peppers have the lowest carb count, at 3 grams per 3.5 ounces; red has 4 grams and yellow has 5 grams per 3.5 ounces. **Of course, the brighter red and orange colors contain more carotenoids, which offer even more protective health benefits.**

Avoid starchy vegetables like potatoes and squash. Go for nutrient dense, low-carb, nonstarchy veggies.

BROCCOLI

Like many of its fruit and veggie counterparts, broccoli (and other cruciferous vegetables, including cauliflower, Brussels sprouts and cabbage) is rich in antioxidants. These crunchy veggies contain active plant compounds called phytochemicals, which research has tied to protective health benefits. Broccoli has around 3 to 5 grams of carbs per 3.5 ounces. Try steaming or sauteing it, or roasting florets at 425 degrees Fahrenheit.

CELERY

Often thought of as the ultimate diet food, celery contains a mere 1 gram of carbs per 3.5 ounces. Despite it seeming like a watery, not-much-to-it veggie, it is in fact an excellent source of fiber and it's loaded with antioxidants, enzymes, vitamins and minerals. So cut it into sticks and keep it in the fridge for when you have a hankering for a crunchy snack, or chop it to add to salads. Store celery in water to keep it fresh and prevent it from wilting.

CUCUMBERS

At just 3 grams of carbs per 3.5 ounces, cucumbers are one of those snacks you could munch on all day. That's a good idea, considering they promote hydration, in addition to being rich in antioxidants. **Pair cucumbers with all of their low-carb buddies—tomatoes, feta cheese, bell peppers, red onions and olives**—for a yummy Mediterranean salad. For the dressing, combine olive oil, minced garlic and lemon juice with some salt and pepper to taste.

ONION

Like garlic, onion is higher in carb content—7 grams per 3.5 ounces—yet it tends to be consumed in smaller amounts, which allows it to qualify as a low-carb veggie. **Onions are rich in fiber and the flavonoid quercetin, which also functions as an antioxidant.** Studies have tied quercetin to many health benefits, including lowering blood pressure. Try chopping up some onions to add to soups, salads and main dishes, or grill slices to eat solo.

GREEN BEANS

Although green beans are legumes, like lentils and chickpeas, they do not carry the same carb load that beans typically have. They have roughly 4 grams of carbs per 3.5 ounces. Green beans are a great source of fiber, and their rich green color is indicative of their chlorophyll content, which research has suggested may help protect against cancer. **Steam beans or saute them in avocado oil, add them to a salad or enjoy them raw as a snack.**

What to Eat (And Avoid)

Fill up your fridge and pantry with these satisfying and delicious keto-friendly staples.

"YES" FOODS
These are all A-OK to eat on a ketogenic diet.

✳ **FATS AND OILS** (butter, olive oil, coconut oil, avocado oil, mayonnaise, ghee and lard)

✳ **AVOCADOS**

✳ **BERRIES** (in moderation; ideally strawberries, blackberries and raspberries)

✳ **BONE BROTH**

✳ **DARK CHOCOLATE AND COCOA POWDER** (check the carb content first)

✳ **EGGS**

✳ **FISH AND SEAFOOD** (think: red snapper, tuna, lobster, crab and scallops; the fattier, the better)

✳ **FULL-FAT DAIRY** (try cheese, sour cream, ricotta, plain Greek yogurt and cottage cheese)

✳ **LEAFY VEGETABLES** (spinach, kale and arugula, for example)

✳ **LOW-CARB VEGETABLES** (asparagus, broccoli, zucchini, mushrooms, cucumber, cauliflower, Brussels sprouts, artichoke and celery)

✳ **MEAT** (steak, chicken, pork, beef, lamb, ham, bacon and turkey; the fattier, the better, and preferably grass-fed and organic)

✳ **NUTS AND SEEDS** (walnuts, almonds, chia seeds, flaxseeds)

✳ **SPICES**

✳ **UNSWEETENED COFFEE AND TEA**

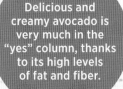

Delicious and creamy avocado is very much in the "yes" column, thanks to its high levels of fat and fiber.

"NO" FOODS

Avoid these for the most part, because they can throw you out of ketosis.

✳ BEANS AND LEGUMES (such as chickpeas, peas and lentils)

✳ MOST FRUIT (exceptions: avocados and certain berries)

✳ FRUIT JUICES AND SUGARY SMOOTHIES

✳ HIGH-CARB VEGETABLES (things like potatoes, turnips, yucca, carrots, parsnips and corn)

✳ LOW-FAT AND FAT-FREE DAIRY PRODUCTS

✳ REFINED AND WHOLE GRAINS (bread, pasta, breakfast cereals, rice, crackers, chips, cookies and baked goods)

✳ SUGAR (including honey, syrups and high-sugar condiments like ketchup and barbecue sauce)

Sad, Angry, Stressed and Noshing

Emotional eating isn't uncommon, but it's not always healthy and it could throw you off your keto diet.

A breakup, tough work deadline or fight with your sister can all send you straight to the fridge—and that's normal. Most everyone comfort eats now and then, says Susan Albers, PsyD, a *New York Times* bestselling author and licensed clinical psychologist at the Cleveland Clinic. "We develop a number of habits to help soothe stressful moments and one of those is stress eating."

Emotional eating typically begins with small bites. You might dig into ice cream as a pick-me-up after learning that you didn't get a job you wanted, for example. "While small doses of stress eating aren't necessarily physically dangerous, they can quickly develop into a habit," says Albers.

But emotional eating doesn't always involve negative emotions. In fact, some people reach for food when they are happy or excited about something like scoring that dream job or even, ironically, hitting a weight-loss goal. "For some, food becomes a reward," says psychologist Ree Langham, PhD.

Regardless of the motive, both men and women can become emotional eaters. However, research has found that females are more likely than males to emotionally eat. And if you're following a keto diet, that could spell trouble for your success. The happy news: There are ways to curb comfort eating before your favorite jeans start feeling a bit too snug. Read on for an easy-to-follow three-step plan.

PSA: Don't use a doughnut as a stress ball.

43

Late-night nosher? You might be eating out of habit.

STEP 1

BE AWARE

Albers says much of emotional eating is unconscious and happens automatically.

One way to become more aware of what you're putting in your mouth? Keep a food journal, like the one beginning on page 138. "Before you jump into changing this behavior, make note of where and when you stress eat," she says. Is it at the office, late at night or when you're around your in-laws? Look for patterns. Then every time you eat, ask yourself how physically hungry you are on a scale from 1 to 10. Albers says pangs of hunger rated six or higher are likely physical hunger, while anything lower is a sign you're emotionally eating.

"Why Did I Choose Keto?"

Ask yourself this question, and ask it often.

Reminding yourself why you decided to go keto could help you stay focused on your wellness goals and may also give you an additional tool for ending emotional eating. If you're tempted to dig into a bowl of chips or bag of cookies, reflect on why you decided to follow keto to begin with. "It's important to identify what attracted you to the keto diet in order to develop—or maintain—a connection with it," says Langham. Did you choose the keto diet because of the health benefits? For an energy boost? To feel more comfortable in your own skin? There's no wrong answer, but keeping your reason top of mind can help you stay motivated and focused.

What was your catalyst for going keto?

STEP 2
REPLACE

Tea time!
A cuppa can
be soothing.

Swap stress eating with non-food activities that give you a quick pick-me-up on a tough day. Three one-minute fixes that you could try:

Sip Black Tea Pinkies up! A study in the *Journal of Psychopharmacology* found that subjects who drank black tea experienced a 47% drop in their cortisol levels, the stress hormone that makes you crave food, compared to 27% among the subjects who drank a placebo.

Treat Yourself to a Foot Rub Instead of a Snack All you have to do is sit down, slip off one shoe and place your foot over a tennis ball. Rub each foot, one at a time, over the top of the ball until you feel relaxed and soothed. According to a study in the *International Journal of Neuroscience*, self-massage slows your heart rate and lowers your level of cortisol, which Albers says can reduce the desire to stress eat.

Just Breathe Mindless eating soothes raw nerves by numbing emotions. "Munching gives you a moment to zone out from daily commotion," says Albers. Instead, clear your mind with a breathing exercise. It can trick your body into thinking you're going to sleep, which in turn relaxes you. Here's how to do it: Slowly breathe in and out, counting each time you inhale and exhale. Continue until you get to 10.

Spending time with good friends can help lower your stress levels too.

STEP 3
PRACTICE!

There are many ways to calm yourself without calories, such as journaling, meditating and connecting with others.

Albers recommends trying these techniques when you aren't craving food so you get them down pat before the urges strike and you really need them.

"You wouldn't want to learn how to swim in rough water," she explains. "Nor do you want to learn the art of soothing yourself without food on a very stressful day." With practice, you can end emotional eating.

No Meat? No Problem!

You can be a vegetarian and have your keto, too! Read on to learn the ins and outs of sticking to a plant-based ketogenic diet.

At first glance, the ketogenic diet doesn't seem to have much in common with a plant-based diet. Some keto devotees even swear off veggies completely because of their carb content. But while more and more health-conscious Americans are catching on to keto, the number of plant-based eaters is exploding as well. Veganism grew a whopping 500% between 2014 and 2017, and the plant-based milk industry is predicted to hit $34 billion by 2024.

If you're wondering whether you should cut back on meat to optimize your health and protect the environment, here's some good news: These two ways of eating don't have to be mutually exclusive. There's a rising trend of plant-based keto, perfect for people who are already vegetarians as well as those who don't want to eat a diet that's high in meat. "Not many people can deny that eating vegetables is good for your health, and with more research showing just how powerful a keto diet can be for your health as well, people are wanting to capitalize on the benefits of both," says Will Cole, IFMCP, DC, a Pittsburgh-based functional medicine practitioner who coined the term for a keto-vegetarian in his book of the same name: *Ketotarian*.

The Best of Both Worlds

By overlapping the principles of keto and plant-based eating, you can reap the benefits of both while avoiding the pitfalls that people following each individual lifestyle can fall into. As a vegetarian, for example, it can be easy to lean heavily on starches in foods like cereal, bread,

A keto diet that's also vegetarian could have added health benefits, such as reduced cholesterol.

baked goods, rice and pasta in order to fill yourself up, which could lead to inflammation and related health problems.

Similarly, those on a ketogenic diet can gravitate toward processed meat and artificial sweeteners while also giving too much credence to labels like "low-carb," "high-fat" or "keto friendly"—all foods that can be low in nutrient quality. "Going plant-based keto focuses on plants, which have been shown to be powerful cancer fighters and next-level detoxifiers," says Cole.

While no studies have looked at plant-based keto diets specifically, medical practitioners like Cole have had patients experience health benefits like weight loss, reduced inflammation, enhanced brain function, increased energy and curbed cravings.

Veg Out

How can you reap the benefits of plant-based keto? First, get your fats from high-quality plant-based products like avocados, olives, nuts and seeds, as well as coconut oil and avocado oil. You should also eat a variety of nonstarchy vegetables like leafy greens, broccoli, Brussels sprouts, peppers

UNSWEETENED PLANT-BASED MILK (LIKE ALMOND, FLAX, SOY AND CASHEW) ARE TYPICALLY KETO FRIENDLY.

and mushrooms. (While some people worry that soluble fiber found in vegetables will take you out of ketosis, studies have shown that soluble fiber can actually lower blood sugar levels, says Cole.) And when you can, choose real, whole foods over prepackaged foods (even when those foods are labeled "keto friendly"!). Finally, before you get started, check in with a medical professional to discuss supplementation, especially with vitamins B12 and D and iron, which vegetarian diets can lack. Then dig in! The best part about going ketotarian is that the meals are fresh and delicious.

The (Fake) Meat of the Matter

Can some of the newest meat alternatives fit into your new diet? These days, most supermarkets are stocked with meatless burgers and hot dogs, and more and more restaurants, from Applebee's to Dunkin' Donuts, offer vegetarian alternatives. Fake meats are a booming business, but are they actually keto friendly? The simple answer: It depends.

"A lot of meat alternatives contain additives and fillers instead of whole foods," says functional medicine practitioner Will Cole. Additionally, they can be higher in carbs than their animal-based counterparts: A ground beef hamburger patty contains zero grams of carbs, while Gardenburger's Black Bean Chipotle Veggie Burger has 16 grams of carbs, for example. But you can also find varieties that are more keto-compatible. One to try: Beyond Meat's plant-based patties, which contain three grams of carbs (along with 20 grams of protein and 18 grams of fat).

THE BOTTOM LINE
Read labels and, when possible, make your own "meat" using keto ingredients like nuts, seeds and coconut oil, says Jillian Kubala, RD, a dietitian in Westhampton, New York. "It's an excellent way to know exactly what's in your food."

SMART SWAPS

READY TO DITCH THE MEAT? USE THESE VEG-FRIENDLY ALTERNATIVES TO KEEP TO YOUR KETO DIET IN CHECK:

↓

Instead of
A bunless cheeseburger
Try
A portobello cap covered in cheese

✳

Instead of
Steak
Try
Cauliflower steak

✳

Instead of
Chicken kabobs
Try
Eggplant, zucchini and squash kabobs

✳

Instead of
Bacon
Try
Tempeh bacon

✳

Instead of
Beef chili
Try
Walnut chili

Cycling allows ketoers to enjoy their favorites, like pasta, then follow the plan again.

What Is Keto Cycling?

This diet hack just may save your sanity.

If you're on the keto diet and are starting to feel like you're about to quit, there's a secret tool you may not know about that can help you stay on track. It's called keto cycling, a period where you eat a normal level of carbs (225 to 325 grams on a 2,000-calorie diet). Incorporating it into a keto lifestyle can help you stick with the plan longer by easing up on the stricter eating guidelines and helping you feel less deprived. Here's how to cycle successfully so you don't find yourself gorging on an entire pizza in one day.

Pick a One- or Two-Day Cycle Length

The first step to keto cycling is figuring out how many days you'll do it for. "There's no set length," says Julie Upton, MS, RD, CSSD, co-founder of the

San Francisco–based nutrition communications firm Appetite for Health. "You can either follow a keto diet for five days a week and cycle for two days in a row, or follow the diet for six days and cycle for one." Figure out what you need; if you find yourself feeling hangry and deprived from a lack of eating carbs, you may need to start with two days and then transition to one as you continue on keto and your body adjusts to your new nutrition intake.

Indulge—But Be Mindful

The point of keto cycling isn't to undo all the work you've done with the keto diet. It's to help satisfy a craving so you don't feel hopeless and quit altogether. And while cycling is a chance to enjoy carbs, like that pasta you've been jonesing for, you're better off eating smart carbs—like sweet potatoes, quinoa, whole grains, or higher-carb fruits, like an apple, some pineapple or a banana. Don't think of this as a "cheat day" but rather a chance to indulge in more carbs if you feel you need a break.

Adjust your protein and fat intake on these cycling days. Aim to get 20% to 35% of your daily calories from fat (44 to 78 grams for a 2,000-calorie diet), and roughly 15% to 20% of your daily calories from protein (75 to 100 grams). Or take your weight and multiply by 0.36 to get the proper protein amount for you, which is the recommended dietary allowance.

Cycling May Not Be for Everyone

Unfortunately, if you're following the keto diet for specific health reasons and are being monitored by a physician, cycling may not be an option for you. But if you're on the keto diet for general wellness and weight loss, Upton says, cycling is something you should practice for longevity. "The downside of a keto diet is that most people just can't stick to it," she says. "It's too restrictive. Keto cycling gives you some flexibility and allows you to eat your favorite foods occasionally, helping you to stick to keto for longer than you likely would be able to."

What to Expect After Cycling

Keto cycling will kick your body out of ketosis—but only for a few days. Since you won't be in ketosis, your body will hold on to more water and your weight will fluctuate. Once you go back to restricting carbs and increasing fat macros, your body will shed the water weight again. Keep in mind that while the scale will creep up a little, you may actually lose more by being able to stick with the diet longer over time.

On cycling days, stick with high-fiber carbs ike quinoa and chickpeas.

Strategic Snacking

No commercial products needed! Homemade keto snacks are easy—and tasty.

Many people say they don't feel the need for between-meal noshes when they're on keto, because a high-fat diet tends to be so satiating. But there are always those moments—maybe the ones in which you used to reach for crackers or pretzels—when you need a little something. Luckily, there are plenty of good candidates to choose from.

Take, for instance, guacamole—a naturally keto-compliant recipe. Avocado plus a little tomato, onion, spices—what's not to like? Of course, you're accustomed to scooping it up with tortilla chips, but there are many other (keto-friendly) options. Or bump up your antioxidant intake with some of the vegetables shown at right.

Try our Ultimate Guacamole recipe on page 101.

NUTS
Best bets: macadamia, pecans and Brazil nuts. Some nuts, like cashews, peanuts, pistachios and almonds, have a bit more carbs, so go easier on those.

BOILED SHRIMP
Buy frozen cooked shrimp, defrost and dip in a cocktail sauce of no-sugar ketchup, with a little lemon juice, horseradish, Worcestershire and hot sauce.

Bell Pepper Strips

Celery Sticks

Jicama Sticks

Cucumber Slices
or Rounds

Dip It!

Replace chips with these healthy scoopers.

Lightly Steamed
Green Beans

DARK CHOCOLATE
Dark chocolate (at least 70% cacao) is packed with antioxidants, and satisfies a sweet tooth with few carbs. Just avoid milk-chocolate blends.

CHEESE
Eat cheese in cubes or slices, or put it on a keto cracker; any way, cheese is an excellent fat- and protein-packed pick-me-up for an afternoon snack.

Get Your Buzz On

Bulletproof-style coffee was popularized by Dave Asprey, author of *The Bulletproof Diet*. **The beverage consists of coffee, grass-fed butter and medium-chain triglyceride (MCT) coconut oil,** which, among other things, reportedly helps to stabilize mood and improve gut health.

Adding high-fat dairy to your coffee will help you hit your fat macros—and keep you feeling more satisfied.

What About the Fun Stuff?

Don't let the word "diet" or even "no sugar" scare you off! There are plenty of yummy treats you can still eat while on keto.

O f course, the term "diet" can elicit a lot of responses. Add in "no sugar or carbs" (yup: bye-bye, potato chips) and it feels like everything fun just flew out the window. But that's not exactly the case with the keto diet, says Rachel Kearney, who says she had tried every diet under the sun and thought she would never be able to lose weight. Kearney started her keto journey at 255 pounds and is now down to 165. "For the first time, it was a diet that I liked, because you could have cheese and lots of things that make you feel like you are not dieting at all. It's crazy—I would have melted cheese with pepperoni and sauce and couldn't believe it was allowed," she says. Kearney also still enjoys her desserts. "I dove into keto baking. I would make treats, like keto cheesecake fluff—that could keep me satisfied in the sweets department."

Kearney's go-to treats include quick-and-easy things like whipped cream, stevia and strawberries. To indulge a little more, she'll go with keto cheesecake or one of her peanut butter and sugar-free jam fat bombs.

More Things to Enjoy on the Keto Diet

✱ **Coffee** is a go-to for many who've gone keto. Lots of people use it as a way to delay eating. "I definitely have a lot of coffee, especially when I am in ketosis. It will keep me full until the afternoon," Kearney notes, adding, "Many people will do coffee as a meal replacement, and Bulletproof-style coffee is a popular choice. It's two tablespoons of butter or ghee, and MCT [medium-chain triglyceride] oil added to coffee and a bit of heavy cream. You blend it up and it gets frothy. It helps you meet your fat for the day and keeps you full for a long time."

✱ **Wine and Liquor** You can still treat yourself to a drink on keto. Just remember that while many hard alcohols like vodka or tequila don't contain carbohydrates, what you mix them with usually does. "You can have a little bit of wine," says Chris Vincent, DC, co-founder and CEO of the Santa Monica, California–based Altus Sports Institute. Wine (5 ounces) or light beer (12 ounces) each contain about 3 to 4 grams of carbs. The best way to tell if any of these options are a fit with your diet is by testing your ketones. "Have a glass of wine with your meal and test," Vincent says. He also recommends a wine lower in sugar, like those from Dry Farm Wines.

✳ Chocolate Dark chocolate, with a minimum of 70% cocoa, is also keto friendly. One ounce of dark chocolate in this range contains 10 grams of carbs or fewer. And eating a little bit of chocolate can help stave off other cravings.

Cacao and cocoa are both derived from cacao beans. Raw or minimally processed cacao nibs are simply cacao beans that have been chopped up into edible bites. Raw cacao is rich in antioxidants and magnesium, and it's also a natural mood elevator. "Cacao is really good for you and very good for your brain. But the trouble is, companies tend to add sugar to cacao. Alone, it tastes horrible," notes Vincent. But there's some good news! "As you eat fewer carbs, your taste buds change, so when you have [regular] sweets they taste really sugary." As this happens, darker chocolate doesn't taste as bad. "You can do 90% chocolate and not throw yourself out of ketosis," Vincent adds.

Cacao in chocolate or powder form is raw and not as processed as cocoa or chocolate. Cacao powder is made by cold-pressing unroasted cacao beans. This process removes the cacao fat or butter, but keeps the enzymes intact. The bean, without the fat, is then ground into fine dark powder, or cacao powder. This can be used in any kind of baked good or treat.

✳ Sweeteners While granulated sugar is not permissible on the keto diet, there are several options out there than can help you satisfy your sweet tooth.

Erythritol This is a sugar alcohol that has a glycemic index of zero, so it won't spike your blood sugar. It's also easy for the body to digest. Use it in place of granulated or powdered sugar in recipes at a ratio of 1-to-1, but it's recommended to add up to ⅓ cup more erythritol than sugar in a recipe.

Stevia This natural sweetener is plant-based and contains few to no calories or carbs.

Fat Bomb

This is typically a no-bake snack made with high-fat ingredients such as coconut butter or oil, butter, nuts and seeds. Popularized by the ketogenic diet, fat bombs are satiating and they can be a great way to enjoy a sweet treat while still staying within the parameters of keto eating.

Available as a liquid or a powder, just 1 teaspoon of stevia is the equivalent of 1 cup of sugar. Stevia is a little bit like cilantro, though—people either really like it or they really don't. And those who don't like it can usually sniff out the slightest hint of it!

Monk Fruit Like stevia, monk fruit sweetener is plant-based. It contains no calories or carbs and is up to 2.5 times stronger than regular sugar. When substituting for sugar, try using half the amount called for. Be sure to read the label carefully, as some brands add in other ingredients that are not keto friendly.

Xylitol You will often find xylitol in sugar-free candies and chewing gum. Like erythritol, it is a sugar alcohol that can be used instead of sugar at a ratio of 1-to-1, but most people find that you can actually use as little as ½ cup of xylitol to replace 1 cup of sugar. Be mindful that xylitol has a tendency to absorb a lot of moisture, so you may need to adjust some recipes to counter this. Also, sometimes xylitol can cause an upset stomach when used in large quantities.

Dark chocolate is OK in moderation. Just try to stick to one that's 70% cacao or higher.

85% to 99%

Chocolates in this range are extra dark and bitter-tasting. This type is almost all cacao, which offers an intense flavor not buffered by dairy or other sweeteners. **It also falls in the better-for-you category, as it's less processed and closer to raw chocolate than its lower-percentage counterparts.**

Dining Out Guide

Let's face it: You're not always in the mood to cook. Whether you're going out for a nice sit-down meal or want to grab a bite to eat on the go, use the advice on these pages to ensure that your order keeps you on plan.

We've said it once and we'll say it again: The easiest way to stay on plan when following a ketogenic diet is to cook at home. But some days, slaving over the stove is the last thing you want to do (understood!). Or perhaps you're planning to go out for dinner to your favorite restaurant to celebrate a birthday, anniversary or other special occasion. Whatever the case, eating out while on keto is possible—as long as you're strategic about what you order. Read on for everything you need to know about sticking to keto outside of your own kitchen.

Keto-Friendly Cuisine

EATING OUT? ORDERING IN? IT ALL WORKS ON KETO!

Chinese

What to Order Lettuce wraps or stir-fry with meat and veggies. Just be sure to ask for the sauce on the side.

What to Avoid Rice, noodles, egg rolls, anything that is fried and most of the sauces and marinades (they can be high in sugar and carb-y cornstarch).

Tweak your order to make it keto.

63

Keto tip: Ask for extra fat on the side.

Shellfish is always a good keto choice.

Restaurant Rules

Headed out for a sit-down meal? Use these tips to stay on track.

PREVIEW THE MENU
Researching what a restaurant serves can help you figure out how doable it will be to keep to keto. Most restaurants have their menus online, making it easy to do some detective work in advance.

CLEAR THE TABLE
Sometimes removing temptations is the best strategy! If the bread basket or complimentary side of fries is difficult to resist, ask your waiter if they would clear it off the table.

BRING YOUR OWN FAT Adding fat to your meal can often be the trickiest part of eating out. So pack your own! For example, take along a small container of avocado oil to add to your salad.

ASK AND YE SHALL (SOMETIMES) RECEIVE If the menu doesn't have anything that fits your diet, ask if it's possible to put together a keto-friendly plate (for example, a burger patty with cheese served with a side of broccoli with butter). Not all restaurants will be game, but it can't hurt to ask!

Italian

What to Order Most Italian restaurants will have fish and shellfish on the menu. Antipasto bites like meat and cheese are also a great bet, as are chicken dishes—and you're in the right place to ask for extra-virgin olive oil!

What to Avoid Pasta, breaded meats (chicken Parmesan, for example) and pretty much everything on the dessert menu (sorry!).

Mexican

What to Order Meat-heavy meals like fajitas and carne asada are a great bet (just leave the tortillas on the side). Load them up with high-fat toppings like guacamole, sour cream and cheese.

What to Avoid The chips, tortillas, taco shells, and rice and beans...and sugary margaritas!

Sushi

What to Order Sashimi and rice-less rolls that are rolled up in nori (seaweed)—you can ask for the rolls to be stuffed with fish, avocado, cream cheese and more. Consider bringing your own MCT oil to add extra fat to the dish.

What to Avoid Anything with rice, tempura—and even some of the sauces, such as eel sauce, which can be high in carbs.

Thai

What to Order Curries made with coconut milk (ask if there's sugar added to the coconut milk) or a meat-based stir-fry—hold the sauce.

What to Avoid Noodles and rice-based dishes are the obvious ones, but many of the sauces can be high in sugar or flour, including seemingly keto-friendly fish and peanut sauces.

9
MENU RED FLAGS

STEER CLEAR OF DISHES THAT
CONTAIN THESE DESCRIPTIVE WORDS.
THEY WILL LIKELY BE FRIED OR
HIGH IN SUGAR—WHICH COULD QUICKLY
KICK YOU OUT OF KETOSIS.

Crispy	Glazed	Sticky
Breaded	Crunchy	Golden
Battered	Honey-Dipped	Teriyaki

Grab, Go and Enjoy!

EVEN FAST FOOD CAN FIT INTO KETO, LIKE THESE ON-THE-GO PICKS.

Chipotle
Keto Pick Burrito Bowl with carnitas, romaine lettuce, cheese, sour cream and guacamole
Calories: 665; Fat: 51 g; Protein: 33 g; Carbs: 12 g

Dunkin' Donuts
Keto Pick Sausage, egg and cheese (no bread)
Calories: 370; Fat: 32 g; Protein: 16 g; Carbs: 3 g

McDonald's
Keto Pick Big Mac (without the bun)
Calories: 330; Fat: 25 g; Protein: 18 g; Carbs: 7 g

Panera
Keto Pick Greek Salad
Calories: 400; Fat: 36 g; Protein: 5 g; Carbs: 11 g

Starbucks
Keto Pick Tall Caffe Misto With Coconut Milk
Calories: 60; Fat: 3.5 g; Protein: 1 g; Carbs: 6 g

Kicking Off
Keto

Ready, set...go!
Here's everything
you need to get ready
for your first few weeks
on a ketogenic diet.

I f you've decided to give the keto diet a go, you may be thinking...*now what?* While you can absolutely dive right in and figure things out as you go along, it's best to head into the diet knowing what to expect. Not only will this help you prepare, but nixing surprises that could throw you off course may help you stick with it.

To help you find the best game plan, we talked to experts who've been there, done that—and have stellar tips and tricks to pass on to help boost your success. Read on for their words of wisdom, but remember: Everyone's journey is different, and what works for them may not be best for you, so feel free to tweak their advice!

YOUR PRE-KETO ACTION PLAN

A Few Weeks Out

Take a Look at Your Schedule A grueling week of work, or a weekend where you have a 5K race planned? Not the best time to start. "The transition period can be brutal, so prepare to start the diet when you have a few light days or a long weekend," says Kristen Mancinelli, MS, RDN. You may even decide to take a vacation day to eliminate the to-dos in your life as you kick off the new eating plan.

A Couple of Weeks Out

Find an Online Community If you don't have questions yet, you likely will soon! Finding an online group now gives you the chance to read up on other people's experiences and tips. Consider jotting down the inspiration and advice that resonates with you so you can reference it later.

A Week Out

Start Bookmarking Recipes Now's the time to begin thinking about what will be on your menu. Luckily, these days the internet is overflowing with great ideas. Want more mealtime inspo? We've got you covered. Check out recipes for mouthwatering breakfast, lunch, dinner, apps, snacks and dessert foods starting on page 78.

A Couple of Days Out

Stock Your Fridge Many people find that it's easier to stick with their ketogenic diet when they cook meals for themselves. Take a trip to the grocery store and load up on keto basics.

The Day Before

Try a 24-Hour Fast You're about to kiss bagels, biscuits and soda goodbye, so why not binge on them the day before starting keto—right? Not so fast, says Mancinelli. She recommends a 24-hour fast before starting the diet to transition the body. But if a fast sounds unappealing, John Limansky, MD, an internist who follows a ketogenic diet, suggests skipping an ease-in period and jumping right into the diet.

The Morning of

Fill Up a Water Bottle Keep sipping throughout the day to counteract the unpleasant dehydration symptoms that can come with cutting carbs.

Want a little something extra to keep you going the first few weeks? Consider picking up these products on your next trip to the grocery store.

COCONUT CREAM OR MILK Rich and decadent, it's perfect to use in smoothies or chia puddings.

TAHINI SAUCE The sesame seed–based sauce is high in good fats. Try drizzling it over vegetables.

CANNED FISH Before you turn up your nose at it, give it a chance! It's an easy, no-cook way to get fat and protein into your diet.

BONE BROTH Filling and comforting, bone broth makes for an easy, satisfying snack.

A FANCY COOKING OIL You're going to be relying on these oils often to add delicious flavor and a shot of fat to your dishes. Now's the time to splurge on a nice olive or avocado oil.

ALTERNATIVE "CRACKERS" Got a craving for something crunchy? There are several low-carb cracker options. Look for ones made from flaxseed, almond flour, cauliflower or even straight-up cheese crisps.

Your Get-Started Grocery List

Sticking to these slimmed-down keto-friendly selections may help make your choices less overwhelming as you transition to the diet while still giving you plenty of options. But of course, feel free to adjust to your taste!

PRODUCE SECTION

☐ Asparagus   ☐ Lemons
☐ Avocados   ☐ Raspberries
☐ Broccoli   ☐ Blueberries
☐ Herbs   ☐ Spinach
☐ Kale   ☐ Zucchini

MEAT AND SEAFOOD

☐ Bacon   ☐ Shrimp
☐ Chicken Thighs   ☐ Tuna
☐ Ground Beef

DAIRY

☐ Butter   ☐ Greek Yogurt
☐ Cheddar Cheese   (full fat, plain)
   (full fat)   ☐ Heavy Cream
☐ Eggs   ☐ Mozzarella
      Cheese (full fat)

OTHER

☐ Almonds   ☐ Frozen
☐ Almond Butter or   Cauliflower Rice
   Peanut Butter   ☐ Macadamia Nuts
   (no sugar added)   ☐ Mayonnaise
☐ Coconut Oil   ☐ Olive Oil

Meal-prep makes life so much easier.

SUCCESS—FROM THE START!

FOLLOW THESE FIVE TIPS TO BOOST THE ODDS OF A REWARDING INTRO TO KETO.

1 Put Fat First "One of the biggest mistakes I see is that people eat too much meat and veggies and not enough fat," says Mancinelli. "I often tell them to cut the meat portions in half and add a fat-rich sauce to the plate." You could, for example, smother chicken in a heavy cream and lemon sauce, or add a pesto made from mostly olive oil to a fish dish.

2 Empty Your Cabinets Getting rid of all of the carb-rich foods in your house—especially those that you know you'll have trouble resisting—will make your transition to keto that much easier.

3 Plan Your Meals At first, you'll likely find that it's easier to stick with the diet if you make your own food. If cooking every day isn't realistic, carve out time over the weekend to prep meals for the week.

4 Ask Yourself "Am I Hungry?" For many people who go keto, breakfast becomes a thing of the past, since they find that they are no longer hungry. (Some even skip lunch as well!) You'll likely find that your appetite changes as well. Pay attention to your new hunger cues and avoid eating simply out of habit. If you're used to grabbing a 3 p.m. snack to break up your workday, for example, consider skipping the snack if you're not hungry—and instead, go for a walk.

5 Talk with Friends and Family It's easier to succeed if friends and family are cheering you on, but people can get a lot of pressure to quit keto from loved ones who think the diet is unhealthy. Talk to your crew in advance and explain that this is important to you and that it would mean a lot if you could have their support.

Hit a Plateau?

The scale is going down, down, down and then—it stops. What gives? Here are a few reasons for the weight-loss lull and how to overcome it:

YOU LOST WATER WEIGHT "When you switch over to a keto diet, you reduce glycogen stores, and glycogen holds on to water," explains John Limansky, MD. "Most people lose 7 to 10 pounds quickly, but it's mostly water and glycogen stores."

What to do: Keep at it. Your body will eventually start losing fat—we promise!

YOU'RE GAINING MUSCLE MASS Reminder: Muscle is more dense than fat. So if you're losing fat but gaining muscle, the number on the scale may not change.

What to do: Keep working out. The scale doesn't tell your whole story. Not only is the exercise good for you, but your metabolism is partly based on your muscle mass, says Limansky. While the weight loss may be slower, in the long run the added muscle can boost your ability to burn calories.

YOU'RE OVERDOING IT ON THE CALORIES A painful truth: "One reason why people stall is because they confuse being in ketosis with losing weight," says Limansky. "But if you're not in a calorie deficit, you won't lose weight."

What to do: Keep an eye on calories. Here's a reality check: A "keto-friendly" Bulletproof coffee is 400 calories. If the scale isn't budging, examine your diet or talk with a nutritionist to see if there are places where you can cut calories.

If five days seems like too much to plan at once, even three or four days will be helpful.

Meal Plan Know-How

Here's the way to map out your breakfast, lunch, dinner and snacks for the week. Hint: Being organized helps.

L et's face it, meal planning is not sexy—at all. Still, it's an underrated and underutilized healthy-living tool, says Aspen, Colorado–based nutritionist and health coach Lisa Cohen. "In my work, I help people create habits they can rely on. Unlike motivation, which comes and goes, these are habits like brushing your teeth. They're something you can fall back on if all else fails." And meal planning is a great habit to have while on keto.

In fact, keto devotees insist that meal prep is one of the most important things they do to stay on track. By meal prepping, you're always prepared with food at the ready, so you're less likely to wing dinner or indulge cravings with foods not on your allowed list.

Cohen offers up these tips to help make your meal-planning a success.

1 Plan for the Workweek

To start, take some time to decide what you'll want to eat for breakfast, lunch and dinner for five days. Pick your recipes and make your grocery list. Then plan to do one big shop for staples on the weekend or when you have time off from work. Plan to shop at least one other day in the week to buy fresh items. "I do one big shop," Cohen says, "and then I still go to the grocery store every day, because I like fresh stuff and we do a lot of smoothies at my house."

2 Load up on Containers

Cohen recommends glass storage containers and mason jars. It's not only important to have these to keep everything organized; they also make everything look beautiful in your fridge. "It looks yummy and you can easily see what you have," Cohen explains. Glass containers, unlike plastic, also make it easy to reheat food in the microwave or oven.

3 Have the Correct Equipment

While Cohen says she doesn't use an Instant Pot, which helps to speed up cooking times, she acknowledges it can be a great tool. She does use a slow cooker and food processor to help prep her food.

4 Designate a Time to Prep

Cohen recommends setting aside a day or an afternoon every week to prep food. "Most people like to do this on Sunday afternoons," she says.

Kitchen Essentials

"It's easier to get into the meal-prepping habit when you have a system," says nutritionist and health coach Lisa Cohen, who recommends these tools for success.

★ **Instant Pot** This appliance is multiple gadgets in one: It's a speedier version of a slow cooker, and also acts as a pressure cooker, steams food— and even makes yogurt. Try using it to make bone broth or keto-friendly stews.

★ **Slow Cooker** With this popular appliance, throw your ingredients in the pot in the morning, turn it on and come back to a yummy, healthy cooked meal at the end of the day.

The dinner hour can be made positively peaceful with meal prep and a slow cooker.

★ **Blender** Invest in the best quality you can afford—you won't regret it! Blenders are ideal for making smoothies, which are a great way to start your day or get a midday boost. For a real treat, try our Blueberry Basil or Green Avocado Smoothies (pages 88-89). You can also use a blender to make pesto or blend soup.

★ **Food Processor** This is handy for so many aspects of meal prep. You can put down the knife and leave the chopping and shredding (for salads, dressings and even cauliflower rice) up to your processor. It's also great for making nut butters or protein balls.

★ **Cast-Iron Skillet** These are inexpensive and easy to work with. They're free of chemical coatings (like Teflon), and when you cook with them, they actually add iron to your food, says Cohen. They are simple to maintain, and like a wok, they get better with age and use.

★ **Muffin Tin or Silicone Muffin Liners** Either one of these will work for you to crank out batches of egg muffins to store in the fridge or the freezer. But once you use silicone liners, it will be hard to turn back —they are effortless to clean!

Having the right equipment on hand can make meal prep easier. Start by stocking up on glass containers.

Combining similar ingredients in different ways keeps each meal unique and interesting.

This is when you can pre-chop vegetables, cook your protein and make any dressings, sauces or pesto. She adds that if you don't end up using everything you make, you can usually freeze the extra food.

5 Diversify

Every week, pick out one or two new recipes to try so you are not always eating the same foods. Lucky for you, Instagram and Pinterest are full of inspiring ideas and recipes for meals. Cohen also features many keto-friendly recipes at lisacohenfitness.com.

6 Take It Easy

Consider how much time you have during the week to make your meals. While you may want something elaborate from time to time, you'll probably want to choose recipes that are manageable and even leave you with some leftovers. Our Broccoli and Cheddar Mini Frittatas (recipe, page 86), for example, are so easy to whip up, Cohen notes. "You can make them to have the exact number of macronutrients that you need based on what you add to them. Then you can either freeze them or keep in the fridge."

7 Double Up

It's OK to eat the same meal twice in a week. If you like salmon, make a double batch and eat it on Monday and Wednesday. And make enough salad dressing to last a week. For roasted vegetables, make extra to keep on hand as a snack. Every meal doesn't have to be unique.

YOUR FIVE-DAY MEAL PLAN

Use this sheet as your starting point. Fill in the blanks, gather the recipes, then make your grocery list. The goal is to create a plan and then to do your prepping over the weekend so you're set for the week ahead. If you've already prepped and you have the ingredients on hand, it's easy to swap meals during the week. We're giving you a head start with Day 1, using recipes you'll find on pages 80 to 125 of this book. Enjoy!

DAY	BREAKFAST	LUNCH	DINNER	SNACKS
1	2 Broccoli and Cheddar Mini Frittatas (p. 86); black coffee with cream	Grilled Salmon and Romaine Caesar Salad (p. 93)	Bacon Cheeseburger Bowls (p. 110); 3-Ingredient Chocolate Lava Cake (p. 120)	Cashews and almonds; homemade guacamole with celery stalks
2				
3				
4				
5				

Delicious

RECIPES

Breakfasts to jump out of bed for, lunches and dinners to keep you sated and smiling—and yes, you can have dessert. These dishes will make you forget you're even on a diet!

Breakfast

Healthy
options
to start
your day.

Chocolate Coconut Smoothie Bowl

This tasty dish is a nutritious way to satisfy your sweet cravings.

QUICK AND EASY
START TO FINISH 5 minutes (all active)
SERVINGS 2

- 2 cups coconut milk
- 1 (10-ounce) bag frozen riced cauliflower
- 1 cup ice
- ¼ cup unsweetened cocoa powder
- ¼ cup sweetener (stevia)
- 1 teaspoon vanilla
- **GARNISHES** chia seeds, hemp seeds, unsweetened coconut flakes, chocolate curls, cocoa powder, chopped walnuts

1 Add all ingredients to a blender. Blend until smooth.
2 Pour into bowls and garnish with desired toppings.

NUTRITION INFORMATION PER SERVING
Calories: 484; Protein: 5 g; Fat: 5 g; Carbs: 7.5 g; Fiber: 5.5 g; Net Carbs: 2 g

Avocado Eggs Benedict

Decadent, rich hollandaise in minutes?
Yes—if you use the microwave.

QUICK AND EASY

START TO FINISH 15 minutes (10 minutes active)

SERVINGS 1

4	egg yolks
1	tablespoon mayonnaise
1	teaspoon lemon juice
¼	teaspoon ground black pepper
½	teaspoon salt
½	cup melted butter
2	slices bacon, cooked
1	avocado, sliced
1	tomato, sliced
2	eggs, poached

GARNISHES cracked black pepper,
snipped chives

1 In a medium glass bowl, whisk together egg yolks, mayonnaise, lemon juice, pepper and salt until smooth.

2 Slowly pour in butter, whisking constantly until mixture is free of lumps.

3 Heat mixture in microwave for 15 seconds; stir. Heat another 10 seconds; stir. Heat 15 seconds more and stir until smooth (mixture will thicken as it sits).

4 Arrange bacon, avocado and tomato slices on plate. Top with poached eggs and sauce. Garnish with cracked pepper and chives.

NUTRITION INFORMATION PER SERVING Calories: 604; Protein: 17 g; Fat: 39 g; Carbs: 15 g; Fiber: 8 g; Net Carbs: 7 g

Sausage and Egg English Breakfast

This colorful dish is perfect for cold mornings.

FAMILY FRIENDLY

START TO FINISH 45 minutes (15 minutes active)

SERVINGS 4

8	pork sausage patties
4	tablespoons butter, divided
4	whole eggs
½	teaspoon salt
½	teaspoon ground black pepper
2	cups baby spinach
2	avocados, sliced
2	tomatoes, sliced

1 In a large skillet over medium-high heat, cook patties for 5 minutes per side. Remove from heat and set aside.

2 Add 2 tablespoons butter to skillet; fry eggs to desired degree of doneness. Sprinkle with salt and pepper. Set aside.

3 Add 2 tablespoons butter to skillet; saute spinach for 2 minutes.

4 On each plate, place 2 sausage patties, 1 egg, spinach, avocado slices and tomato slices.

NUTRITION INFORMATION PER SERVING Calories: 771; Protein: 75 g; Fat: 70 g; Carbs: 16 g; Fiber: 7.5 g; Net Carbs: 8.5 g

French Toast Rounds With Berries and Syrup

This tasty treat is made with keto-friendly bread batter—and it's baked in a coffee mug!

QUICK AND EASY

START TO FINISH 20 minutes (5 minutes active)

SERVINGS 2

- ⅔ cup almond flour
- 2 tablespoons whey protein powder
- ¾ teaspoon baking powder
- ⅛ teaspoon salt
- 2 eggs, divided
- 2 teaspoons granulated sweetener (Swerve or stevia)
- 2 tablespoons melted butter
- ¼ cup heavy cream, divided
- 1 teaspoon vanilla
- 1 tablespoon granulated sweetener
- ½ teaspoon cinnamon or nutmeg
- ¼ cup butter

  GARNISHES sugar-free syrup, mint sprigs, strawberries, blueberries

1 In a medium bowl, add almond flour, whey protein powder, baking powder and salt. Stir until combined; set aside.

2 In a large mixing bowl, beat 1 egg and sweetener together on high for 1 minute, until fluffy and light in color. Beat in melted butter.

3 Add flour mixture alternately with 2 tablespoons cream. Mix for 1 minute or until batter thickens.

4 Pour into 2 greased coffee mugs.

5 Microwave on high for 1½ minutes. Remove and let stand for 5 minutes. Remove from mugs and slice crosswise into thirds.

6 In a medium bowl, whisk 1 egg, vanilla and 2 tablespoons cream. Add sliced loaf rounds to bowl. Set aside.

7 In a small bowl, mix sweetener and cinnamon.

8 In a large skillet, melt butter and cook rounds for 2 minutes per side. Sprinkle with cinnamon mixture.

9 Serve with syrup, mint sprigs and berries.

NUTRITION INFORMATION PER SERVING Calories: 725; Protein: 45 g; Fat: 48 g; Carbs: 24 g; Fiber: 9 g; Net Carbs: 15 g

Broccoli and Cheddar Mini Frittatas

These are delicious either served warm or at room temperature—bring them to the office for a light lunch!

FAMILY FRIENDLY | GRAB AND GO

START TO FINISH 35 minutes (10 minutes active)

SERVINGS 6 (2 frittatas)

- 4 bacon slices, cooked and crumbled
- 2 cups cooked broccoli florets
- ⅓ cup shredded sharp cheddar
- 10 eggs, beaten
- ½ cup heavy cream
- ½ teaspoon salt
- ½ teaspoon ground black pepper

GARNISH chopped parsley

1 Preheat oven to 350 F.

2 Coat a 12-cup muffin tin with cooking spray; divide crumbled bacon, broccoli and cheese among cups.

3 In a medium bowl, whisk together eggs, cream, salt and pepper. Divide mixture among the cups.

4 Bake for 16-18 minutes or until set. Cool on a wire rack for 5 minutes; sprinkle with parsley and serve.

NUTRITION INFORMATION PER SERVING Calories: 186; Protein: 14 g; Fat: 12 g; Carbs: 4 g; Fiber: 1 g; Net Carbs: 3 g

Smoked Sausage Breakfast Bowl

Add other leafy greens and keto veggies to this hearty dish.

FAMILY FRIENDLY | **QUICK AND EASY**
START TO FINISH 15 minutes (10 minutes active)
SERVINGS 1

¼	cup smoked sausage, sliced
2	tablespoons butter
2	eggs
1	cup baby heirloom cherry tomatoes, halved
½	avocado, sliced
½	teaspoon cracked pepper
	GARNISH chopped parsley

1 In a large skillet over medium-high heat, brown sausage, about 2 minutes per side; set aside. Add butter to same skillet; fry eggs until desired degree of doneness.

2 In a shallow serving bowl, place sausage, tomatoes and avocado; top with eggs. Sprinkle with pepper and parsley.

NUTRITION INFORMATION PER SERVING Calories: 663; Protein: 23 g; Fat: 59 g; Carbs: 14 g; Fiber: 8 g; Net Carbs: 6 g

Blueberry Basil Smoothie

Berries pair well with so many fresh herbs. Try some lemon basil or mint for a delicious variation.

QUICK AND EASY | VEGETARIAN

START TO FINISH 5 minutes (all active)

SERVINGS 2

½ cup almond or coconut milk

⅔ cup frozen blueberries

2 teaspoons vanilla

2 teaspoons coconut oil

½ cup protein powder

2 tablespoons chopped fresh basil

GARNISHES blueberries, coconut flakes, basil leaves

1 Place all ingredients in a blender and process until smooth.

2 Serve and garnish with more blueberries, coconut flakes and basil leaves, if desired.

NUTRITION INFORMATION PER SERVING Calories: 109;
Protein: 3 g; Fat: 5 g; Carbs: 13 g; Fiber: 2 g; Net Carbs: 11 g

Green Avocado Smoothie

Coconut milk makes this smoothie, which is loaded with healthy greens, creamy and rich.

QUICK AND EASY | VEGETARIAN
START TO FINISH 5 minutes (all active)
SERVINGS 2

2   ripe avocados, halved and pitted
1   cup spinach
2   cups unsweetened coconut milk
2   cups ice
2   tablespoons granulated sweetener
1   tablespoon lime juice
    GARNISH orchid blossoms

1 Place all ingredients in a blender and pulse until smooth.
2 Pour into glasses and serve. Garnish with orchid blossoms, if desired.

NUTRITION INFORMATION PER SERVING

Calories: 353; Protein: 8 g; Fat: 30 g; Carbs: 27.5 g; Fiber: 18 g; Net Carbs: 9.5 g

Lunch

Healthy midday dishes that will keep you satiated until dinner.

Chicken Cabbage Cups

This colorful Asian-inspired dish will even appeal to your non-keto friends. Not a cabbage fan? Substitute any firm-textured lettuce.

FAMILY FRIENDLY | QUICK AND EASY
START TO FINISH 25 minutes (10 minutes active)
SERVINGS 4

1	tablespoon sesame oil
1	tablespoon olive or avocado oil
1	cup sliced green onion
1	cup shredded carrots
½	cup diced red bell pepper
1	tablespoon ginger
1	tablespoon garlic
1	pound ground chicken
¼	cup tamari
1	tablespoon rice wine vinegar
½	teaspoon red pepper flakes
4	cup-shaped purple cabbage leaves

GARNISHES green onion, red pepper flakes, sesame seeds, hot sauce

1 In a large skillet over medium heat, add oils, green onion, carrots, red bell pepper, ginger and garlic. Saute for a minute or two to soften. Add ground chicken and cook for 8 minutes or until no longer pink, stirring frequently.

2 In a small bowl, combine tamari, vinegar and red pepper flakes. Add to skillet and cook 1 minute.

3 Spoon mixture into cabbage cups. Top as desired with garnishes.

NUTRITION INFORMATION PER SERVING Calories: 390; Protein: 14 g; Fat: 23 g; Carbs: 38 g; Fiber: 10.5 g; Net Carbs: 27.5 g

Muffuletta Wrap

The famed New Orleans sandwich can be easily adapted to a keto diet.

GRAB AND GO | QUICK AND EASY
START TO FINISH 10 minutes (all active)
SERVINGS 1

  2   slices salami
  2   slices capicola ham
  1   slice provolone cheese
  1   large iceberg lettuce leaf
  1   tablespoon olive salad
       (or chopped olives)
  2   strips roasted red peppers
       Drizzle of extra-virgin olive oil

1 Layer meats and cheese in center of lettuce leaf. Top with olive salad and peppers.
2 Drizzle with olive oil and roll up. Secure with picks and serve.

NUTRITION INFORMATION PER SERVING Calories: 478; Protein: 30 g; Fat: 41 g; Carbs: 5 g; Fiber: 2 g; Net Carbs: 3 g

Grilled Salmon and Romaine Caesar Salad

Grilling the romaine adds another layer of flavor to this hearty dish.

CLASSIC | QUICK AND EASY
START TO FINISH 25 minutes (15 minutes active)
SERVINGS 2

- 1 (8-ounce) salmon fillet
- ¼ teaspoon salt
- ¼ teaspoon ground black pepper
- 2 romaine hearts, halved
- 2 eggs
- 2 tablespoons Dijon mustard
- 1 clove garlic
- 3 anchovies
- 2 cups olive oil
- ⅓ cup grated Parmesan cheese
- 1 tablespoon lemon juice
  Salt and ground black pepper to taste
- 6 slices bacon, cooked and crumbled
- 1 cup baby heirloom cherry tomatoes, halved
- ½ cup chopped pecans, toasted

1 Preheat a grill skillet over medium-high heat.
2 Sprinkle salmon fillet with salt and pepper. Grill for 4 to 5 minutes on each side. Use a fork to flake. Set aside.
3 Grill romaine halves for 2 minutes; chop.
4 To make dressing: In a food processor, blend eggs, mustard, garlic and anchovies on high for 2 minutes. Slowly add oil in a thin stream. Add cheese and lemon juice. Adjust salt and pepper to taste.
5 In a large bowl, add chopped romaine; top with flaked salmon, bacon, tomatoes and pecans. Drizzle with dressing to serve.

NUTRITION INFORMATION PER SERVING Calories: 600; Protein: 42 g; Fat: 45 g; Carbs: 7.5 g; Fiber: 2.5 g; Net Carbs: 5 g

Shrimp Salad Stuffed Avocados

Pair this simple but elegant dish with some mixed salad greens and cherry tomatoes tossed with vinaigrette.

FANCY | QUICK AND EASY
START TO FINISH 15 minutes (10 minutes active)
SERVINGS 2

¼ cup mayonnaise
3 tablespoons chopped celery
3 tablespoons sliced green onions
2 teaspoons chopped parsley
1 teaspoon chopped dill
1 tablespoon lemon juice
1 tablespoon Old Bay seasoning
½ pound cooked shrimp, roughly chopped
2 ripe avocados, halved and pitted
 GARNISHES dill sprigs,
 chopped parsley

1 In a medium bowl, combine mayonnaise and next 7 ingredients. Stir well to mix.
2 Fill avocado halves with shrimp salad mixture; top with dill sprigs and chopped parsley.

NUTRITION INFORMATION PER SERVING Calories: 408; Protein: 30.5 g; Fat: 25 g; Carbs: 21.5 g; Fiber: 12.5 g; Net Carbs: 9 g

Chicken Caprese Salad With Arugula

For a low-carb dressing, mix olive oil, balsamic vinegar, dried basil and minced garlic; shake well.

QUICK AND EASY
START TO FINISH 20 minutes (15 minutes active)
SERVINGS 4

1	pound chicken breasts
½	teaspoon salt
½	teaspoon ground black pepper
8	ounces asparagus, trimmed
1	(5-ounce) package arugula
1	cup basil leaves
1	pint grape tomatoes
8	ounces fresh mozzarella pearls
2	avocados, sliced
4	strips of bacon, cooked and crumbled
	Low-carb balsamic dressing

1 Preheat a grill pan over medium-high heat. Sprinkle chicken breasts with salt and pepper. Grill chicken 6 minutes per side or until internal temperature is 165 F. Let chicken rest for 10 minutes, then slice.

2 Grill the asparagus for 2 to 3 minutes. Cool and coarsely chop.

3 On a platter, add arugula, basil, tomatoes and mozzarella. Top with sliced chicken, avocado, bacon and chopped asparagus. Drizzle with balsamic dressing.

NUTRITION INFORMATION PER SERVING
Calories: 338; Protein: 19 g; Fat: 24 g; Carbs: 11.5 g; Fiber: 6.5 g; Net Carbs: 5 g

Turkey Taco Lettuce Wraps

All those yummy Tex-Mex ingredients—
without the shell!

FAMILY FRIENDLY | QUICK AND EASY
START TO FINISH 20 minutes (12 minutes active)
SERVINGS 4

2	tablespoons olive oil
½	cup chopped onion
1	pound ground turkey
1	teaspoon minced garlic
½	teaspoon salt
½	teaspoon ground black pepper
1	tablespoon chili powder
1	teaspoon cumin
¼	cup tomato sauce
¼	cup chicken stock
8	romaine lettuce leaves

GARNISHES shredded cheddar, quartered cherry tomatoes, diced avocado, sliced red onion, sour cream, cilantro sprigs

1 In a large skillet over medium-high heat, heat olive oil. Add onion; saute for 2 minutes. Add turkey and garlic; cook 5 to 6 minutes or until no longer pink. Season with salt and pepper.

2 Add chili powder, cumin, tomato sauce and stock. Reduce heat; simmer 5 minutes or until thickened.

3 Serve mixture over lettuce leaves and garnish with desired toppings.

NUTRITION INFORMATION PER SERVING Calories: 117; Protein: 8 g; Fat: 8 g; Carbs: 9 g; Fiber: 5 g; Net Carbs: 4 g

Bacon and Cauliflower Soup

This flavorful soup is so smooth, creamy and decadently delicious, you'll want to invite company over to enjoy a bowl.

FAMILY FRIENDLY | MAKE AHEAD
COMPANY-WORTHY
START TO FINISH 40 minutes
SERVINGS 6

1	tablespoon butter
1	teaspoon minced garlic
1½	pounds cauliflower florets
2	cups chicken stock
1½	cups heavy cream
1	teaspoon salt
1	teaspoon ground black pepper
4	strips bacon, cooked and crumbled
⅔	cup grated Parmesan cheese

GARNISHES Parmesan cheese, chopped chives, sour cream, crumbled bacon

1 In a Dutch oven over high heat, saute butter and garlic for 3 minutes.
2 Add the cauliflower and stir to coat. Cook for 2 minutes.
3 Stir in chicken stock, heavy cream, salt and pepper. Bring to a boil, then reduce heat to a simmer.
4 Cook for 15 minutes, or until cauliflower is tender.
5 Using an immersion blender, blend soup into a smooth puree.
6 Stir in bacon and Parmesan cheese.
7 Serve soup and garnish, as desired.

NUTRITION INFORMATION PER SERVING Calories: 345; Fat: 34 g; Protein: 15 g; Carbs: 8 g; Fiber: 3 g; Net Carbs: 5 g

Clam Chowder

This five-ingredient soup is ready in less than half an hour, but it tastes like you cooked all day!

CLASSIC | QUICK AND EASY
START TO FINISH 20 minutes
SERVINGS 6

- 2 (6.5-ounce) cans clams, undrained
- 4 cups cauliflower florets
- 1½ cups almond milk
- 1½ cups chicken broth
- 1 teaspoon sea salt
- ½ teaspoon ground black pepper
- 1 cup coconut cream
   GARNISHES cracked black pepper, parsley leaves

1 In a Dutch oven, combine all ingredients except for coconut cream.
2 Bring to a boil. Reduce heat and simmer for 10 to 15 minutes or until cauliflower is tender.
3 Stir in coconut cream. Serve soup and garnish, as desired.

NUTRITION INFORMATION PER SERVING Calories: 228; Fat: 16 g; Protein: 12 g; Carbs: 11 g; Fiber: 4 g; Net Carbs: 7 g

Minestrone

This classic Mediterranean soup is loaded with healthy vegetables. The shredded carrots replace the pasta!

CLASSIC | QUICK AND EASY

START TO FINISH 30 minutes

SERVINGS 6

- 1 tablespoon extra-virgin olive oil
- 1 cup chopped onion
- 1 cup shredded carrots
- 1 tablespoon minced garlic
- 1 (20-ounce) package mild Italian sausage, cooked and drained
- 1 (8-ounce) package sliced white mushrooms
- 3 stalks celery, sliced
- 1 green bell pepper, chopped
- 1 teaspoon dried oregano
- 2 bay leaves
- 8 cups turkey or chicken broth
- 1 (14.5-ounce) can diced tomatoes, undrained
- ½ teaspoon crushed red pepper flakes
- 2 tablespoons chopped basil
- ½ teaspoon sea salt
- ½ teaspoon ground black pepper

GARNISHES basil leaves, pesto

1 In a large Dutch oven over medium-high heat, heat oil.

2 Stir in onion, carrots and garlic and cook 2 minutes. Stir in sausage, breaking up with a wooden spoon as needed. Cook 5 minutes.

3 Add the mushrooms, celery and bell pepper. Cook 5 minutes.

4 Stir in oregano, bay leaves, turkey or chicken broth, tomatoes, red pepper flakes, basil, sea salt and pepper. Cook for 10 minutes.

5 Serve and garnish, as desired.

NUTRITION INFORMATION PER SERVING Calories: 408; Fat: 32 g; Protein: 20 g; Carbs: 10 g; Fiber: 3 g; Net Carbs: 7 g

Snacks AND Apps

Clever ideas
for keto-friendly
noshes.

Loaded Deviled Eggs

Old Bay seasoning adds a ton of carb-free flavor to this dish. Make these for a party or an afternoon snack.

CLASSIC | QUICK AND EASY
START TO FINISH 15 minutes (10 minutes active)
SERVINGS 6

6	hard-boiled eggs, halved, yolks removed
½	cup mayonnaise
1	tablespoon Dijon mustard
1	teaspoon Old Bay seasoning
½	teaspoon salt
½	teaspoon ground black pepper

GARNISHES bacon pieces, green onions, Old Bay seasoning

1 In a medium bowl, add cooked egg yolks and mayonnaise. Combine until smooth. Stir in mustard, Old Bay, salt and pepper. Fill each egg white half with yolk mixture. Refrigerate until ready to garnish.
2 Arrange on a platter; garnish as desired before serving.

NUTRITION INFORMATION PER SERVING Calories: 162; Protein: 8 g; Fat: 12 g; Carbs: 5 g; Fiber: 0 g; Net Carbs: 5 g

Ultimate Guacamole

Dip some veggie chips in this guac, or top a burger with a scoop.

QUICK AND EASY | VEGETARIAN
START TO FINISH 10 minutes (all active)
SERVINGS 2

2	ripe avocados
2	cloves garlic, minced
2	tablespoons fresh lime juice
1	cup chopped white onion
2	tablespoons chopped cilantro
1	jalapeño, chopped
1	Fresno pepper, chopped
2	scallions, chopped
1	teaspoon salt
½	teaspoon ground black pepper

GARNISHES diced red onion, jalapeño or Fresno pepper slices, quartered red and yellow cherry tomatoes

1 In a medium bowl, mash avocados with a fork. Stir in garlic and the next 8 ingredients.
2 Place in serving bowl; garnish as desired. Serve with sliced veggies.

NUTRITION INFORMATION PER SERVING Calories: 371; Protein: 2 g; Fat: 30 g; Carbs: 27 g; Fiber: 15.5 g; Net Carbs: 11.5 g

Bacon-Wrapped Asparagus

For extra-crispy bacon, place a wire rack on top of your baking sheet, then place wrapped asparagus on it and bake.

CLASSIC | FAMILY FRIENDLY

START TO FINISH 25 minutes (10 minutes active)

SERVINGS 6

- 1 tablespoon olive oil
- 6 strips bacon
- 1 ounce cream cheese, softened
- 18 asparagus spears, trimmed
- 1 teaspoon ground black pepper

1 Preheat oven to 450 F. Drizzle a baking sheet with olive oil.

2 Place bacon strips on work surface; spread each with cream cheese.

3 Place 3 asparagus spears across each bacon strip; wrap bacon around spears.

4 Place each bundle seam-side down on prepared baking sheet.

5 Bake for 15 minutes or until crispy, shaking pan once halfway through.

6 Sprinkle with pepper; serve hot or at room temperature.

NUTRITION INFORMATION PER SERVING Calories: 185; Fat: 15 g; Protein: 5 g; Carbs: 3 g; Fiber: 1 g; Net Carbs: 2 g

Creamy Blue Cheese Dip With Chicken Wings

This flavorful dip is also excellent with keto-friendly veggie sticks.

FAMILY FRIENDLY
START TO FINISH 5 minutes (all active)
SERVINGS 10

1	cup sour cream
½	cup mayonnaise
½	cup blue cheese crumbles
2	teaspoons white vinegar
1	teaspoon lemon juice
1	teaspoon minced garlic
1	teaspoon Worcestershire sauce
1	teaspoon salt
½	teaspoon ground black pepper
	GARNISHES crumbled blue cheese, chopped parsley, chopped chives
3	dozen chicken wings, cooked

1 In a large bowl, stir together all ingredients.

2 Garnish as desired and serve with chicken wings.

NUTRITION INFORMATION PER SERVING (dip only)
Calories: 425; Fat: 35 g; Protein: 10 g; Carbs: 4 g; Fiber: 0 g; Net Carbs: 4 g

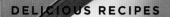
Coconut Shrimp

Swap the deep-fried version for this oven-baked one. It's just as good and the cleanup is a lot easier.

CLASSIC | FAMILY FRIENDLY | QUICK AND EASY

START TO FINISH 20 minutes (10 minutes active)

SERVINGS 4

¼	cup coconut flour
½	teaspoon garlic powder
½	teaspoon salt
⅛	teaspoon cayenne pepper
3	eggs
2	cups unsweetened flaked coconut, finely chopped
1	pound large shrimp, peeled, deveined and butterflied
	GARNISHES mint sprigs, Sriracha mayonnaise (purchase or make with Sriracha, mayo and garlic)

1 Preheat oven to 400 F. Place nonstick bar rack onto a lined baking sheet. Coat rack with vegetable cooking spray.

2 In a small bowl, mix coconut flour, garlic powder, salt and cayenne. In another, beat eggs; in a third, place coconut flakes.

3 Dredge each shrimp in coconut flour mixture, then dip in the egg, shaking off excess; and press in coconut flakes.

4 Place shrimp on prepared wire rack.

5 Bake shrimp for 4 minutes. Flip and cook for 4 more minutes until firm and crispy.

6 Place shrimp under broiler for 1 to 2 minutes or until lightly golden, if desired.

7 Serve with mint sprigs and Sriracha mayonnaise, if desired.

NUTRITION INFORMATION PER SERVING Calories: 443; Fat: 30 g; Protein: 31 g; Carbs: 12 g; Fiber: 7 g; Net Carbs: 5 g

Spinach Dip With Parmesan Crisps

To make Parmesan crisps, drop tablespoons of grated Parmesan cheese on a baking sheet and press down. Bake for 4 minutes at 400 F.

CLASSIC | QUICK AND EASY

START TO FINISH 15 minutes (all active)

SERVINGS 6

- 1 cup frozen spinach, defrosted, drained and squeezed dry
- 1 cup mayonnaise
- ½ cup sour cream
- 2 tablespoons chopped parsley
- 2 teaspoons lemon juice
- 1 tablespoon dried dill
- 1 teaspoon onion powder
- ½ teaspoon salt
- ½ teaspoon ground black pepper
- **GARNISH** parsley leaves, Parmesan crisps

1 In a large serving bowl, combine all ingredients. Garnish as desired.

2 Serve immediately, or refrigerate until ready to serve with Parmesan crisps on the side.

NUTRITION INFORMATION PER SERVING (dip only) Calories: 245; Fat: 20 g; Protein: 8 g; Carbs: 5 g; Fiber: 2 g; Net Carbs: 3 g

Dinner

These mouthwatering dishes
offer tons of flavor
and variety while keeping
you satisfied.

Oven Barbecue Shrimp

Enjoy this savory, spicy treat!

FAMILY FRIENDLY
START TO FINISH 45 minutes (15 minutes active)
SERVINGS 4

½	cup butter
¼	cup Worcestershire sauce
1	tablespoon chopped garlic
1	teaspoon hot sauce (Frank's RedHot)
1	teaspoon Old Bay seasoning
2	pounds peeled raw jumbo shrimp, tails on
	GARNISH parsley, lemon slices

1 In a medium saucepan over low heat, melt butter. Add next 4 ingredients. Stir until combined, remove from heat and let cool.
2 Place shrimp in a 13 x 9-inch baking dish. Pour cooled sauce over shrimp; cover with plastic wrap and refrigerate. Marinate for 30 minutes.
3 Spread shrimp on sheet pan. Broil shrimp for 5 minutes; turn over and broil for 1 more minute. Garnish with parsley and serve with lemon slices.

NUTRITION INFORMATION PER SERVING
Calories: 265; Protein: 46 g; Fat: 6.5 g; Carbs: 5 g; Fiber: 0 g; Net Carbs: 5 g

Kung Pao Pork Tenderloin With Cauliflower Rice

Marinating the pork makes it even more tender in this quick meal.

QUICK AND EASY

START TO FINISH 30 minutes (10 minutes active)

SERVINGS 4

- ¼   cup tamari
- 2   tablespoons cornstarch
- 3   tablespoons chicken broth
- 1   tablespoon rice wine vinegar
- 1   teaspoon salt
- 1   teaspoon garlic paste
- 1   teaspoon ginger paste
- 2   pounds pork tenderloin, cubed
- 2   tablespoons sesame oil, divided
- ⅓   cup cashews
- 1   cup sliced celery
- 1   yellow bell pepper, cubed
- 1   tablespoon olive oil
- 1   (10-ounce) bag frozen cauliflower rice, cooked according to package directions

GARNISHES cilantro leaves, red pepper flakes, sliced Fresno peppers

1 In a medium bowl, combine tamari and next 6 ingredients; divide mixture in half.

2 In a large zip-close bag, add pork cubes and half of the tamari mixture. Marinate for 20 minutes.

3 In a large wok or skillet over medium-high heat, heat 1 tablespoon sesame oil. Add cashews; toast for 1 minute. Add celery and peppers; cook 1 minute. Remove all ingredients from wok or skillet; set aside.

4 Add remaining sesame oil and olive oil to wok or skillet. Add half of pork and cook for 5 minutes; remove and repeat with remaining pork.

5 Add vegetable mixture and cook 1 additional minute or until heated through.

6 Serve over cooked cauliflower rice and garnish with cilantro, red pepper flakes and sliced Fresno peppers.

NUTRITION INFORMATION PER SERVING Calories: 666; Protein: 53 g; Fat: 36 g; Carbs: 29 g; Fiber: 6 g; Net Carbs: 23 g

Beef and Pork Meatballs Over Butternut Noodles

These juicy meatballs taste amazing on top of butternut "noodles."

FAMILY FRIENDLY

START TO FINISH 40 minutes (15 minutes active)

SERVINGS 4

- 1 pound ground beef
- 1 pound ground pork
- ¾ cup grated Parmesan cheese
- ½ cup almond flour
- 2 tablespoons minced parsley
- 1 teaspoon salt
- 1 teaspoon ground black pepper
- 2 cups sugar-free marinara sauce
- 1 (10-ounce) container butternut squash "noodles"
- **GARNISHES** grated Parmesan cheese, chopped parsley

1 Preheat oven to 350 F.

2 In a medium bowl, combine beef, pork, cheese, almond flour, parsley, salt and pepper. Form into 16 meatballs. Place on greased baking sheet.

3 Bake for 20 minutes or until cooked through.

4 In a large skillet, heat up marinara sauce and butternut "noodles." Divide evenly between individual plates. Top with meatballs and serve.

5 Garnish with cheese and parsley as desired.

NUTRITION INFORMATION PER SERVING Calories: 750; Protein: 55 g; Fat: 45 g; Carbs: 22 g; Fiber: 6 g; Net Carbs: 16 g

Bacon Cheeseburger Bowls

Filled with all the delicious toppings and flavors of a burger—but it's a lot neater to eat without the bun!

FAMILY FRIENDLY | QUICK AND EASY

START TO FINISH 30 minutes (15 minutes active)

SERVINGS 4

- 1 pound ground beef
- 1 teaspoon salt
- ½ teaspoon ground black pepper
- ½ teaspoon minced garlic
- 2 tablespoons avocado or olive oil
- 1 large head romaine lettuce, chopped
- 2 cups sliced grape tomatoes
- 1 cup sliced red onion
- ¼ cup dill pickle slices
- 8 slices cooked bacon, torn into large pieces
- 1 cup shredded cheddar cheese
  GARNISHES yellow mustard, ranch dressing

1 In a medium bowl, combine beef, salt, pepper and garlic.

2 Heat oil in large cast-iron skillet; add beef and cook until crumbled and no longer pink. Set aside.

3 For each bowl, add chopped romaine and ¼ of the beef mixture. Top with tomatoes, red onion, pickles, bacon and cheddar. Serve with mustard and ranch dressing.

NUTRITION INFORMATION PER SERVING Calories: 474; Protein: 34 g; Fat: 26.5 g; Carbs: 4.5 g; Fiber: 0.5 g; Net Carbs: 4 g

Strip Steaks With Asparagus and Creminis

This dish looks so elegant—but it's done in one skillet in less than 30 minutes!

FANCY | QUICK AND EASY

START TO FINISH 25 minutes (10 minutes active)

SERVINGS 2

- 2 tablespoons olive oil
- 2 (12-ounce) New York strip steaks (1 inch thick)
- 1 teaspoon salt
- 1 teaspoon ground black pepper
- 1 pound asparagus, trimmed
- 1 (8-ounce) package sliced cremini mushrooms
- 2 tablespoons butter
- 2 cloves garlic, minced
- 2 sprigs thyme
- **GARNISH** thyme sprigs

1 In a cast-iron skillet over medium-high heat, heat oil.

2 Sprinkle both sides of steaks with salt and pepper. Carefully place steaks in skillet and allow to sear for 3 minutes. Flip steaks and cook an additional 2 minutes. Add asparagus and mushrooms to skillet and cook 2 minutes more.

3 Add butter, garlic and thyme and cook 1 more minute. Remove from heat and serve; garnished with thyme as desired.

NUTRITION INFORMATION PER SERVING Calories: 695; Protein: 48.5 g; Fat: 51 g; Carbs: 25.5 g; Fiber: 34 g; Net Carbs: 0 g

Southwestern Skillet Chicken With Seared Avocados

Seared avocado? Yes! They're delicious—and packed with healthy fats.

FAMILY FRIENDLY | **QUICK AND EASY**

START TO FINISH 25 minutes (15 minutes active)

SERVINGS 4

2	tablespoons olive oil, divided
4	(8-ounce) skinless, boneless chicken breast halves
1	teaspoon salt
½	teaspoon ground black pepper
½	teaspoon cumin
½	teaspoon chili powder
2	avocados, halved and pitted
1	red onion, sliced into rings
2	green onions or scallions, sliced
1	jalapeño pepper, sliced
¼	cup fresh lime juice

GARNISHES lime wedges, cilantro sprigs, sliced Fresno peppers

1 Preheat oven to 450 F.

2 Heat a large cast-iron skillet over medium-high heat. Add 1 tablespoon of oil to skillet; swirl to coat.

3 Sprinkle chicken evenly with salt, pepper, cumin and chili powder.

4 Add chicken to skillet and cook for 4 minutes. Turn chicken over and cook for 2 minutes. Remove chicken from skillet.

5 Add remaining oil to pan; swirl to coat. Add avocado halves, cut side down; cook for 2 minutes or until charred. Remove from pan.

6 Add red onion; cook for 3 minutes or until charred. Turn onion; add green onion and jalapeño. Stir in lime juice.

7 Return chicken and avocado to skillet. Bake 7 minutes or until chicken is done.

8 Garnish with lime wedges, cilantro sprigs and sliced Fresno peppers, if desired; serve in skillet.

NUTRITION INFORMATION PER SERVING Calories: 504; Protein: 53.5 g; Fat: 14.5 g; Carbs: 11 g; Fiber: 7 g; Net Carbs: 4 g

Spinach "Pasta" Alfredo

This creamy dish will be a family favorite. Add chicken if you'd like.

CLASSIC | QUICK AND EASY | VEGETARIAN

START TO FINISH 15 minutes
(5 minutes active)

SERVINGS 4

½	cup butter
2	cloves garlic, minced
2	cups heavy cream
4	ounces cream cheese, softened
1½	cups grated Parmesan cheese
¼	teaspoon nutmeg
¼	teaspoon salt
¼	teaspoon ground black pepper
2	(7-ounce) bags spinach shirataki pasta (Miracle Noodle), drained and rinsed

GARNISHES cracked black pepper, chopped parsley, grated Parmesan

1 In a Dutch oven over medium-high heat, melt butter. Add garlic and cook 2 minutes. Stir in cream and cream cheese until smooth.

2 Slowly stir in Parmesan cheese until well incorporated and sauce thickens, about 5 minutes. Stir in nutmeg, salt, pepper and noodles.

3 Serve immediately with cracked pepper, parsley and grated Parmesan on the side so everyone can add the amount they'd like.

NUTRITION INFORMATION PER SERVING Calories: 655;
Protein: 20 g; Fat: 58 g; Carbs: 12 g; Fiber: 3 g; Net Carbs: 9 g

"Mac" and Cheese

This dish is so creamy and satisfying, you'll find yourself preparing it as a light meal or a hearty side.

CLASSIC | FAMILY FRIENDLY

START TO FINISH 25 minutes (5 minutes active)

SERVINGS 4

	Vegetable oil cooking spray
4	cups cauliflower florets
¼	cup melted butter
½	teaspoon salt
½	teaspoon ground black pepper
1	cup shredded cheddar cheese
⅓	cup heavy cream
¼	cup milk

GARNISHES shredded cheddar cheese, cracked black pepper

1 Preheat oven to 450 F.

2 Spray a baking sheet with vegetable oil cooking spray.

3 In a large bowl, toss cauliflower florets, butter, salt and pepper.

4 Place cauliflower on baking sheet; roast for 15 minutes or until tender.

5 In a glass bowl, combine cheddar cheese, cream and milk. Microwave mixture until melted, about 1 minute.

6 Toss cauliflower with cheese mixture, place into casserole dish and bake at 350 F for 5 minutes.

7 Serve and garnish, as desired.

NUTRITION INFORMATION PER SERVING Calories: 283; Fat: 25 g; Protein: 10 g; Carbs: 7 g; Fiber: 3 g; Net Carbs: 4 g

Roasted Turkey Breast With Vegetables

This simple preparation will make your dinner stress-free. If you'd like to serve gravy with it, there are a number of keto-compliant gravy packets on the market.

CLASSIC | FAMILY FRIENDLY

START TO FINISH 2 hours, 30 minutes (2 hours inactive)

SERVINGS 8

- 2 (3 pounds each) bone-in turkey breast halves
- 2 tablespoons extra-virgin olive oil
- 1 cup baby carrots
- 1 cup radishes
- 1 cup baby portobello mushrooms
- 1 red onion, quartered
- ½ teaspoon sea salt
- ½ teaspoon ground black pepper
- GARNISH parsley leaves

1 Preheat oven to 425 F.

2 Place turkey breasts in a roasting pan and brush with olive oil.

3 Arrange vegetables around turkey breasts and sprinkle with salt and pepper.

4 Place turkey in oven and reduce temperature to 375 F. Roast for 1½ hours or until meat thermometer registers an internal temperature of 165 F.

5 Remove from oven, cover with foil and let turkey stand 20 minutes before slicing.

6 Transfer to serving platter and garnish, as desired.

NUTRITION INFORMATION PER SERVING Calories: 310; Fat: 9 g; Protein: 25 g; Carbs: 6 g; Fiber: 2 g; Net Carbs: 4 g

Desserts

End your meal on a sweet note with these tasty treats!

Vanilla Pudding With Cream and Mixed Berries

For a change, try making this with almond extract instead of vanilla—it's so good, especially with berries!

CLASSIC | QUICK AND EASY
START TO FINISH 15 minutes (5 minutes active)
SERVINGS 6

1	cup heavy cream
½	cup unsweetened almond milk
⅓	cup granulated sweetener (Swerve or stevia)
1	tablespoon cornstarch
2	whole eggs
3	egg yolks
1	tablespoon water
1	teaspoon gelatin powder
1	teaspoon vanilla extract
¼	teaspoon liquid stevia
2	tablespoons butter
	GARNISHES whipped cream, mixed berries

1 In a small saucepan over medium-high heat, bring cream and almond milk to a simmer.
2 In a medium heat-proof bowl, combine granulated sweetener and cornstarch. Whisk in eggs and yolks.
3 Put water in a small bowl; sprinkle gelatin over.
4 Pour hot cream over egg mixture, stirring constantly. Whisk in gelatin until smooth.
5 Return mixture to saucepan. Cook over low heat until thickened. Stir in vanilla, liquid stevia and butter until smooth. Pour into 6 serving bowls.
6 Top with whipped cream and berries, if desired.

NUTRITION INFORMATION PER SERVING Calories: 204; Protein: 4.5 g; Fat: 18 g; Carbs: 5.5 g; Fiber: 0 g; Net Carbs: 5.5 g

Mini Brownie Bites

Super yummy and loaded with chocolate, these bites would be a welcome addition to any lunch box.

CLASSIC | QUICK AND EASY

START TO FINISH 20 minutes (5 minutes active)
SERVINGS 20 (1 brownie)

¼ cup butter, melted
¾ cup granulated sweetener (stevia)
½ cup unsweetened dark cocoa powder
2 eggs
½ teaspoon vanilla extract
¾ cup almond flour
¼ cup chopped walnuts
     GARNISH powdered sweetener

1 Preheat oven to 350 F. Grease a mini muffin tin with vegetable cooking spray. (Note that only 20 of the tin's cups will be used in this recipe.)

2 In a medium bowl, whisk butter, sweetener, cocoa, eggs and vanilla. Stir in almond flour and walnuts until just combined.

3 Pour batter evenly into 20 cups of the muffin tin. Bake 15 minutes.

4 Cool in pan for 5 minutes. Remove from pan and cool on wire rack for 10 minutes. Dust with powdered sweetener, if desired.

NUTRITION INFORMATION PER SERVING

Calories: 85; Protein: 1.5 g; Fat: 4 g; Carbs: 12.5 g;
Fiber: 0.5 g; Net Carbs: 12 g

Easy Chocolate Truffles

Store truffles in an airtight container in the refrigerator.

CLASSIC | QUICK AND EASY
START TO FINISH 10 minutes (all active)
SERVINGS 20 (1 truffle)

- 2 tablespoons almond flour
- 2 teaspoons granulated sweetener
- 2 teaspoons unsweetened cocoa powder
- 1 teaspoon sugar-free chocolate chips (Lily's)
- ¼ teaspoon vanilla extract
- ⅛ teaspoon salt
- 1 tablespoon coconut oil
- 1 teaspoon water
  GARNISH unsweetened cocoa powder

1 Combine all ingredients in a bowl and stir until smooth.
2 Scoop out dough with a small cookie scoop and roll into 20 balls. Roll in cocoa, if desired.

NUTRITION INFORMATION PER SERVING Calories: 105;
Protein: 0 g; Fat: 1.5 g; Carbs: 1 g; Fiber: 0 g; Net Carbs: 1 g

Chocolate Lava Cake

If you have 2 minutes and a microwave, you have time to make this dessert.

CLASSIC | QUICK AND EASY
START TO FINISH 5 minutes (2 minutes active)
SERVINGS 2

- 2 tablespoons coconut or almond flour
- ½ teaspoon baking powder
- 2 tablespoons unsweetened cocoa powder
- 2 tablespoons granulated sweetener
- 1 egg
- ¼ cup heavy cream
- 2 teaspoons vanilla extract
- 2 tablespoons sugar-free chocolate chips (Lily's)
- 1 tablespoon butter, melted
   GARNISHES whipped cream, berries

1 In a bowl, add flour and next 3 ingredients. Stir in egg, cream and vanilla. Mix until smooth. Stir in chocolate chips.
2 Brush 2 standard coffee mugs with melted butter; pour batter in evenly.
3 Microwave for 1½ minutes on high. Let rest 1 minute and turn cakes out onto plate.
4 Garnish with whipped cream and berries, if desired.

NUTRITION INFORMATION PER SERVING Calories: 574; Protein: 6.5 g; Fat: 23.5 g; Carbs: 22 g; Fiber: 4 g; Net Carbs: 18 g

Pumpkin Pie Pudding

Try this using other spices you like instead of pumpkin pie spice.

CLASSIC | FAMILY FRIENDLY

START TO FINISH 1 hour 30 minutes (15 minutes active)

SERVINGS 6

1	tablespoon stevia
⅛	teaspoon xanthan gum
1	teaspoon pumpkin pie spice
1	teaspoon vanilla
1	cup heavy cream
½	cup coconut milk
3	egg whites
	GARNISHES whipped cream, pumpkin pie spice

1 In a mixing bowl, combine stevia, xanthan gum and pumpkin pie spice.

2 Add vanilla, cream, coconut milk and egg whites.

3 Beat with a hand mixer on high for 3 minutes.

4 Pour mixture into a saucepan and heat over medium-high heat. Stir constantly for 3 minutes.

5 Transfer pudding mixture to individual dessert serving bowls; let cool to room temperature for about 15 minutes.

6 Refrigerate pudding for 1 hour. Garnish, as desired.

NUTRITION INFORMATION PER SERVING Calories: 325; Fat: 25 g; Protein: 4.5 g; Carbs: 4 g; Fiber: 1 g; Net Carbs: 3 g

Macadamia Nut Truffles

These delicious fat bombs make a yummy dessert or a filling snack.

FANCY | MAKE AHEAD
START TO FINISH 40 minutes (10 minutes active)
SERVINGS 20 (1 truffle)

- 1 (3-ounce) bar Lily's Creamy Milk no-sugar-added milk chocolate-style candy, chopped
- 1 tablespoon coconut oil
- 1 cup macadamia nuts, chopped
- 20 whole macadamia nuts
- **GARNISHES** raspberries, mint sprigs

1 Line a baking sheet with parchment paper.
2 In a small glass bowl, add chopped chocolate and coconut oil.
3 Microwave in 20-second intervals, stirring in between, until chocolate is melted.
4 Stir in chopped macadamia nuts.
5 With a small cookie scoop, form small clusters and place on prepared baking sheet.
6 Lightly press a whole macadamia nut into the top of each cluster.
7 Refrigerate for 30 minutes before serving; garnish, as desired.

NUTRITION INFORMATION PER SERVING Calories: 177; Fat: 18 g; Protein: 3 g; Carbs: 5 g; Fiber: 2 g; Net Carbs: 3 g

Coconut Custard With Toasted Coconut

If your motto is "There's no such thing as too much coconut"—then this is definitely the dessert for you! It's baked right in ceramic serving ramekins, too.

MAKE AHEAD

START TO FINISH 1 hour 30 minutes
(20 minutes active)

SERVINGS 6

1	(13.5-ounce) can coconut milk
2	teaspoons vanilla extract
⅓	cup granulated sweetener
5	egg yolks
	GARNISH toasted coconut

1 Preheat oven to 375 F.

2 In a medium saucepan over medium-high heat, cook coconut milk just until simmering (do not boil). Remove from heat and stir in vanilla and sweetener. Set aside and cool 15 minutes.

3 In a mixing bowl, beat the yolks with mixer for 2 to 3 minutes or until pale and double in size.

4 Slowly pour cooled coconut mixture over egg yolk mixture, stirring constantly.

5 Pour the custard evenly into 6 ramekins. Place in a casserole dish and fill the dish with boiling water halfway up sides of ramekins.

6 Bake for 35 to 40 minutes or until set. Remove from oven and cool for 20 minutes; cover and refrigerate.

7 Serve with toasted coconut.

NUTRITION INFORMATION PER SERVING Calories: 412;
Protein: 16 g; Fat: 32 g; Carbs: 9 g; Fiber: 0 g; Net Carbs: 9 g

Spiced Vanilla Cake

This spiced cake makes for a simple but elegant finish to any meal.

CLASSIC
START TO FINISH 45 minutes (15 minutes active)
SERVINGS 10

4	ounces cream cheese, softened
½	cup butter, softened
½	cup granulated stevia
¼	teaspoon allspice
⅛	teaspoon salt
½	teaspoon baking powder
5	eggs, beaten
1	teaspoon vanilla
2	cups almond flour
½	cup powdered stevia
2	tablespoons heavy cream
	GARNISHES dried cranberries, mint leaves

1 Preheat oven to 350 F. Grease a small tube pan.
2 In a large mixing bowl, use a hand mixer to beat cream cheese and butter until smooth.
3 Add granulated stevia, allspice, salt, baking powder, eggs, vanilla and almond flour; beat well.
4 Pour batter into prepared pan. Bake for 20 to 30 minutes, or until knife inserted in center comes out clean and edges begin to brown.
5 In a small bowl, whisk together the powdered stevia and heavy cream until smooth.
6 Release cake from pan and drizzle glaze over cake. Garnish, as desired.

NUTRITION INFORMATION PER SERVING Calories: 224; Fat: 21 g; Protein: 5 g; Carbs: 18 g; Fiber: 1 g; Net Carbs: 17 g

Cranberry Mousse

If you make this dessert before you start dinner, it'll be chilled and ready by the time you're done with the main course.

MAKE AHEAD | QUICK AND EASY
START TO FINISH 25 minutes (5 minutes active)
SERVINGS 4

- 1½ cups heavy whipping cream
- ⅓ cup sugar-free cranberry sauce
- 4 ounces cream cheese, softened
  GARNISHES mint leaves, dried cranberries, shaved dark unsweetened chocolate

1 In a bowl, use a hand mixer to beat heavy cream for 2 minutes or until stiff peaks form.
2 In another bowl, beat cranberry sauce and cream cheese together until smooth.
3 Fold cranberry mixture into whipped cream until just combined.
4 Spoon mousse into individual serving glasses; refrigerate for at least 20 minutes.
5 Garnish as desired to serve.

NUTRITION INFORMATION PER SERVING Calories: 215; Fat: 20 g; Protein: 4 g; Carbs: 6 g; Fiber: 2 g; Net Carbs: 4 g

Keeping TRACK

Use this journal to list your goals and weekly milestones. Be sure to take lots of photos—you'll want that "before" picture to remind you of how far you've come!

GETTING
Started

Use this keto toolbox to set your goals and
track your progress at your own pace.

This section is set up to kick things off and help keep you motivated on your ketogenic diet journey. Use it to write out your goals, track your progress and to celebrate every step of the way! If you feel like you're hitting a plateau, look back at your starter photo and reread your goals to remind yourself why you are doing this diet and what you hope to get out of it. One keto enthusiast said when she thought she wasn't making progress, she would look back at her photos and realize how far she had actually come. Remember, this is your journey...and just like life, there may be some zigs and zags along the way—and that's OK. If one day or week doesn't go quite as planned, don't worry: There's always a fresh start you can make the next day to get back on your path. We all know life happens, so do the best you can—and let this journal help you track each and every success as you go.

This journal is set up for seven weeks. While experts say the benefits of the keto diet can be felt in week one, with ketosis starting as soon as you begin cutting out carbs, for some it takes a bit longer than a week for the energizing benefits of the diet to kick in. By the seventh week, you should know if this diet is working for you or not. If it is, that will be a good time to evaluate whether you want to make any adjustments to your habits or your macronutrient intake to help keep the diet working for you in the weeks and months ahead. If you've already been following the keto diet, then use this journal to help you find new inspiration and set new goals.

Lastly, we invite you to revisit this journal often and to continue to add to it as you progress with the diet. And remember: There are no right or wrong answers here. This is your chance to be honest with yourself, which will ultimately help you get what you need out of your journey.

Drink Up!

Hydrate, hydrate, hydrate. **Drink at least 60 to 100 ounces of fluids a day, especially when you are starting out.** Drink an electrolyte beverage or take a supplement to help stave off the keto flu.

As with carbs, it's also important to manage your protein—too much can throw you out of ketosis.

The recipes (starting on page 80) and foods listed in "What to Eat (and Avoid)" (page 40) can help you be prepared.

QUICK TIPS FOR KETO

Math Time

To calculate your macronutrient baseline, let an online calculator or app like Carb Manager or MyFitnessPal help you. **These tools will tell you how many grams of each to eat, depending on your age, weight, height, gender and body fat percentage.**

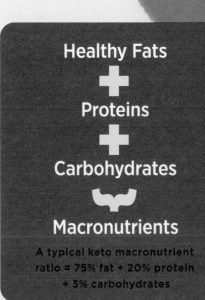

Healthy Fats

+

Proteins

+

Carbohydrates

Macronutrients

A typical keto macronutrient ratio = 75% fat + 20% protein + 5% carbohydrates

9:41
Daily Calories
Today
kcal
896
of
1600
31%
26%
43%
Proteins
Fats
Carbs

Fact Check

Looking for the nutrition data for an avocado? **The USDA food nutrition database (fdc.nal.usda .gov) is the best out there, experts say.**

If you haven't hit ketosis by five to six weeks, there's a good chance you're not following the diet correctly, says nutritionist Kristen Mancinelli.

Hello, Fats

Dietary fats support cell growth and give the body energy. Make sure you're getting enough healthy fats each day by eating avocados, drizzling olive oil over veggies or adding coconut oil to a smoothie. See "Healthy Fats" (page 28) for the best options.

Step Right Up!

Some studies have shown that people who weigh themselves regularly see better weight-loss results than those who don't. The best time to break out the scale? First thing in the morning, experts advise.

It's best to calculate your food intake in grams rather than calories. Fat has more calories per gram than protein or carbohydrates.

Fat = 9 calories/gram
Protein = 4 calories/gram
Carbohydrates = 4 calories/gram

You Can Do It!

Choose a daily mantra that will motivate you. And if your day doesn't go exactly as planned, don't give up—there's always tomorrow! Positive reinforcement has been shown to increase the likelihood that a behavior will be repeated.

YOUR KETO
Workbook

Start Here!

This is your chance to put it all out there! Have fun and be honest with yourself.

What made you decide to give the keto diet a try?

_____
_____
_____
_____
_____
_____
_____

What are you hoping to get out of doing the keto diet? What is the goal that you would like to reach?

_____
_____
_____
_____
_____

Why is this goal so important to you?

_____
_____
_____
_____
_____

Is your current lifestyle in line with your goals?

_____
_____
_____
_____
_____
_____
_____

What lifestyle changes would you like to make to help you reach your goals?

_____
_____
_____
_____
_____
_____

What would make you feel like you've succeeded with the keto diet?

_____
_____
_____
_____
_____
_____

What does reaching your goal look like?

Fill the spaces here with words, a collage or sketches of what your goal looks like in your mind.

How will you celebrate when you reach your goal?

Fill the spaces here with words, a collage or sketches of how you will celebrate reaching your goals.

List three progress goals
you would like to put
in place to help you make
these lifestyle changes.

1 _____

2 _____

3 _____

Is your lifestyle in line with
your diet goals? What,
if anything, do you need to
change to support your
diet goals?

_____

_____

_____

_____

_____

_____

_____

_____

List three people you know
you can lean on if you need a
pep talk to keep you on track.

1 _____

2 _____

3 _____

What makes you happy?

_____

_____

_____

_____

_____

_____

Describe what feeling
good is to you.

_____

_____

_____

_____

_____

_____

What makes you excited
about trying the keto diet?

_____

_____

_____

_____

_____

What worries do you have
about trying the keto diet?

_____

_____

_____

_____

List five tools you have, or
would like to have, in your
personal toolbox to help keep
worries, guilt, stress and
bad feelings about dieting
or yourself at bay.

1 _____

2 _____

3 _____

4 _____

5 _____

If you listed something
you don't currently have in
your life-skills toolbox (like
meditation), can you think
of some ways to incorporate
this skill into your life?

_____

_____

_____

_____

What has kept you from losing weight before?

Write out anything that has held you back before and leave it on these pages.

Reach Your Goals

A key part of achieving success on the keto diet and reaching your goals is believing in yourself and the fact that you can do it. Use these pages to list the books, people, songs or movies that inspire you. Also write down your favorite affirmations, mantras or lyrics that can help keep you motivated! Feel free to draw or paste images here, too.

← *Before*

Before Photo
(paste here)

After Photo
(paste here)

After →

Track Your Progress

Place a current picture of yourself at the top of the page.
As you follow the diet and/or have a great keto day, take a photo of yourself
and add it to this page as a reminder that you are making progress!

YOUR
WEEK-BY-WEEK
GUIDE

*Week 1

FOOD TRACKER		MONDAY	TUESDAY	WEDNESDAY
	Breakfast	MACROS Fat .... Protein .... Carbs .... Calories	MACROS Fat .... Protein .... Carbs .... Calories	MACROS Fat .... Protein .... Carbs .... Calories ....
	Lunch	MACROS Fat .... Protein .... Carbs .... Calories	MACROS Fat .... Protein .... Carbs .... Calories	MACROS Fat .... Protein .... Carbs .... Calories ....
	Dinner	MACROS Fat .... Protein .... Carbs .... Calories	MACROS Fat .... Protein .... Carbs .... Calories	MACROS Fat .... Protein .... Carbs .... Calories ....
	Snacks	MACROS Fat .... Protein .... Carbs .... Calories	MACROS Fat .... Protein .... Carbs .... Calories	MACROS Fat .... Protein .... Carbs .... Calories ....
	Total Daily Macros	TOTAL MACROS Fat .... Protein .... Carbs .... Calories	TOTAL MACROS Fat .... Protein .... Carbs .... Calories	TOTAL MACROS Fat .... Protein .... Carbs .... Calories ....
	Water			
	Hunger	None · Some · Intense	None · Some · Intense	None · Some · Intense

"YOU HAVE A TREASURE WITHIN YOU THAT IS INFINITELY GREATER THAN ANYTHING THE WORLD CAN OFFER."

—ECKHART TOLLE, SPIRITUAL TEACHER

THURSDAY	FRIDAY	SATURDAY	SUNDAY
MACROS Fat .... Protein .... Carbs .... Calories	MACROS Fat .... Protein .... Carbs .... Calories	MACROS Fat .... Protein .... Carbs .... Calories	MACROS Fat .... Protein .... Carbs .... Calories ....
MACROS Fat .... Protein .... Carbs .... Calories	MACROS Fat .... Protein .... Carbs .... Calories	MACROS Fat .... Protein .... Carbs .... Calories	MACROS Fat .... Protein .... Carbs .... Calories ....
MACROS Fat .... Protein .... Carbs .... Calories	MACROS Fat .... Protein .... Carbs .... Calories	MACROS Fat .... Protein .... Carbs .... Calories	MACROS Fat .... Protein .... Carbs .... Calories ....
MACROS Fat .... Protein .... Carbs .... Calories	MACROS Fat .... Protein .... Carbs .... Calories	MACROS Fat .... Protein .... Carbs .... Calories	MACROS Fat .... Protein .... Carbs .... Calories ....
TOTAL MACROS Fat .... Protein .... Carbs .... Calories	TOTAL MACROS Fat .... Protein .... Carbs .... Calories	TOTAL MACROS Fat .... Protein .... Carbs .... Calories	TOTAL MACROS Fat .... Protein .... Carbs .... Calories ....

MINDFULNESS MOMENT

Learning to Love Your Body...

Describe your current relationship with your body—
what do you love and what don't you love?

_____
_____
_____

What would you change in your life if you focused on
what your body can do, versus what it looks like?

_____
_____
_____

The next time you have a negative thought about your body, what thought
can you replace it with that will be more positive?

_____
_____
_____

"TAKE CARE OF YOUR BODY. IT'S THE ONLY PLACE YOU HAVE TO LIVE." —JIM ROHN, ENTREPRENEUR

What was the best thing that happened this week?

_____
_____
_____

What obstacle or challenge did you overcome?

_____
_____
_____

List three milestones you achieved this week.

_____
_____
_____

WEIGHT TRACKER

MONDAY	TUESDAY	WEDNESDAY	THURSDAY
.LBS	.LBS	.LBS	.LBS

SLEEP TRACKER

	Sleep Time	Total Hours	Sleep Quality
M			👍 👎
TU			👍 👎
W			👍 👎
TH			👍 👎
F			👍 👎
SA			👍 👎
SU			👍 👎

EXERCISE TRACKER

	Type	Time	Intensity
M			
TU			
W			
TH			
F			
SA			
SU			

ENERGY TRACKER

How Are You Feeling Today?

Monday

Tuesday

Wednesday

Thursday

Friday

Saturday

Sunday

FRIDAY	SATURDAY	SUNDAY	WEEKLY CHANGE
.LBS	.LBS	.LBS	

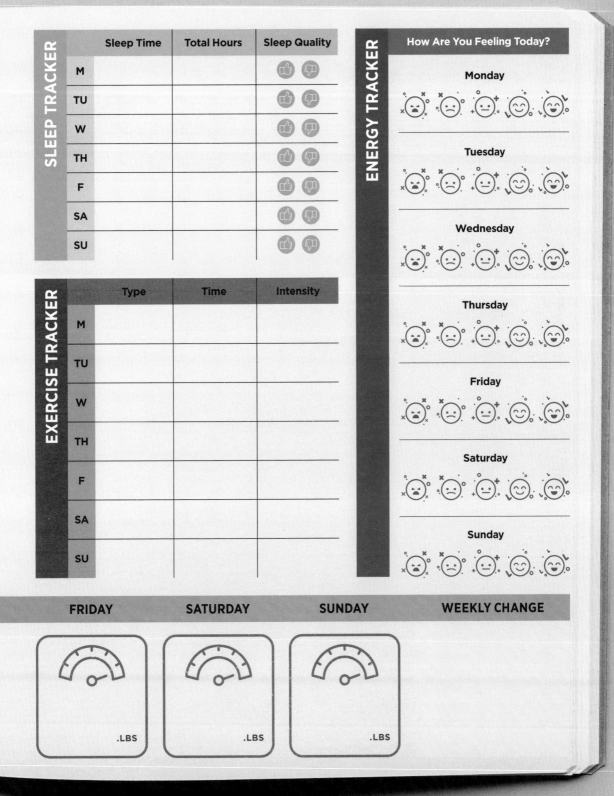

*Week 2

FOOD TRACKER

	MONDAY	TUESDAY	WEDNESDAY
Breakfast	**MACROS** Fat .... Protein .... Carbs .... Calories	**MACROS** Fat .... Protein .... Carbs .... Calories	**MACROS** Fat .... Protein .... Carbs .... Calories ....
Lunch	**MACROS** Fat .... Protein .... Carbs .... Calories	**MACROS** Fat .... Protein .... Carbs .... Calories	**MACROS** Fat .... Protein .... Carbs .... Calories ....
Dinner	**MACROS** Fat .... Protein .... Carbs .... Calories	**MACROS** Fat .... Protein .... Carbs .... Calories	**MACROS** Fat .... Protein .... Carbs .... Calories ....
Snacks	**MACROS** Fat .... Protein .... Carbs .... Calories	**MACROS** Fat .... Protein .... Carbs .... Calories	**MACROS** Fat .... Protein .... Carbs .... Calories ....
Total Daily Macros	**TOTAL MACROS** Fat .... Protein .... Carbs .... Calories	**TOTAL MACROS** Fat .... Protein .... Carbs .... Calories	**TOTAL MACROS** Fat .... Protein .... Carbs .... Calories ....
Water			
Hunger	None — Some — Intense	None — Some — Intense	None — Some — Intense

"THE GREATEST WEALTH IS HEALTH."

—VIRGIL, ANCIENT ROMAN POET

	THURSDAY	FRIDAY	SATURDAY	SUNDAY
MACROS	Fat _____ Protein _____ Carbs _____ Calories _____	Fat _____ Protein _____ Carbs _____ Calories _____	Fat _____ Protein _____ Carbs _____ Calories _____	Fat _____ Protein _____ Carbs _____ Calories _____
MACROS	Fat _____ Protein _____ Carbs _____ Calories _____	Fat _____ Protein _____ Carbs _____ Calories _____	Fat _____ Protein _____ Carbs _____ Calories _____	Fat _____ Protein _____ Carbs _____ Calories _____
MACROS	Fat _____ Protein _____ Carbs _____ Calories _____	Fat _____ Protein _____ Carbs _____ Calories _____	Fat _____ Protein _____ Carbs _____ Calories _____	Fat _____ Protein _____ Carbs _____ Calories _____
MACROS	Fat _____ Protein _____ Carbs _____ Calories _____	Fat _____ Protein _____ Carbs _____ Calories _____	Fat _____ Protein _____ Carbs _____ Calories _____	Fat _____ Protein _____ Carbs _____ Calories _____
TOTAL MACROS	Fat _____ Protein _____ Carbs _____ Calories _____	Fat _____ Protein _____ Carbs _____ Calories _____	Fat _____ Protein _____ Carbs _____ Calories _____	Fat _____ Protein _____ Carbs _____ Calories _____

None — Some — Intense

MINDFULNESS MOMENT

Learning to Love Your Body...

What are your top three health goals?

_____
_____
_____

How would achieving these goals improve your life and how you feel?

_____
_____
_____
_____
_____

What is one thing you can do starting tomorrow to work toward one of these goals?

_____
_____
_____
_____

"TO KEEP THE BODY IN GOOD HEALTH IS A DUTY, OTHERWISE WE SHALL NOT BE ABLE TO KEEP OUR MIND STRONG AND CLEAR."

—BUDDHA, SPIRITUAL TEACHER

What was the best thing that happened this week?

_____
_____
_____
_____

What obstacle or challenge did you overcome?

_____
_____
_____
_____

List three milestones you achieved this week.

_____
_____
_____
_____

WEIGHT TRACKER

MONDAY	TUESDAY	WEDNESDAY	THURSDAY
.LBS	.LBS	.LBS	.LBS

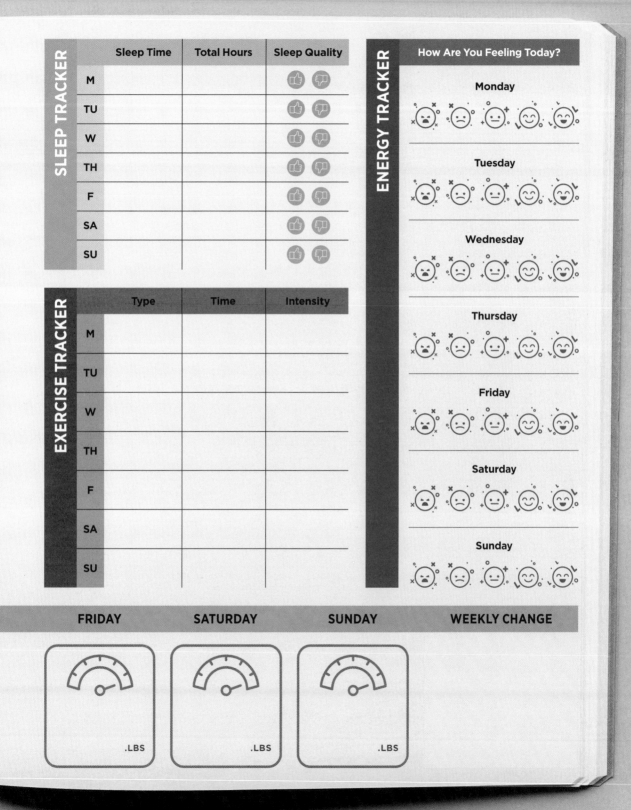

SLEEP TRACKER

	Sleep Time	Total Hours	Sleep Quality
M			👍 👎
TU			👍 👎
W			👍 👎
TH			👍 👎
F			👍 👎
SA			👍 👎
SU			👍 👎

EXERCISE TRACKER

	Type	Time	Intensity
M			
TU			
W			
TH			
F			
SA			
SU			

ENERGY TRACKER

How Are You Feeling Today?

Monday

Tuesday

Wednesday

Thursday

Friday

Saturday

Sunday

FRIDAY	SATURDAY	SUNDAY	WEEKLY CHANGE
.LBS	.LBS	.LBS	

*Week 3

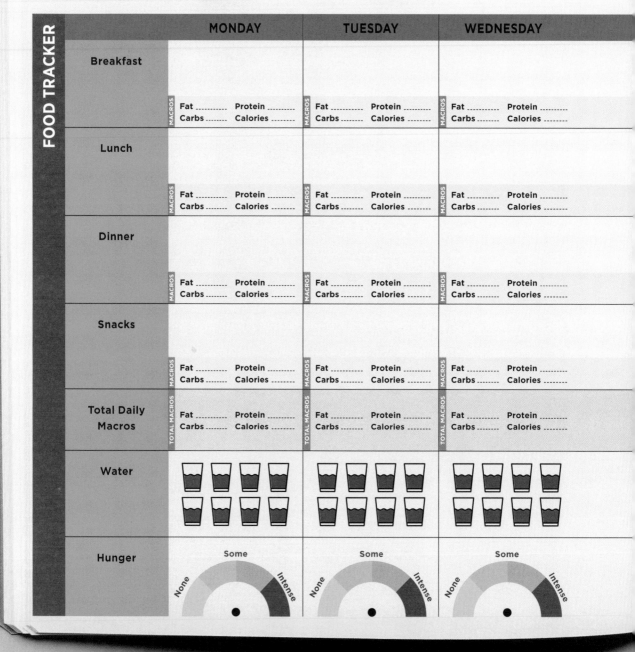

FOOD TRACKER		MONDAY	TUESDAY	WEDNESDAY
Breakfast	MACROS	Fat .... Protein .... Carbs .... Calories	Fat .... Protein .... Carbs .... Calories	Fat .... Protein .... Carbs .... Calories ....
Lunch	MACROS	Fat .... Protein .... Carbs .... Calories	Fat .... Protein .... Carbs .... Calories	Fat .... Protein .... Carbs .... Calories ....
Dinner	MACROS	Fat .... Protein .... Carbs .... Calories	Fat .... Protein .... Carbs .... Calories	Fat .... Protein .... Carbs .... Calories ....
Snacks	MACROS	Fat .... Protein .... Carbs .... Calories	Fat .... Protein .... Carbs .... Calories	Fat .... Protein .... Carbs .... Calories ....
Total Daily Macros	TOTAL MACROS	Fat .... Protein .... Carbs .... Calories	Fat .... Protein .... Carbs .... Calories	Fat .... Protein .... Carbs .... Calories ....
Water				
Hunger		None Some Intense	None Some Intense	None Some Intense

> "EACH NEW DAY IS A BLANK PAGE IN THE DIARY OF YOUR LIFE. THE SECRET OF SUCCESS IS IN TURNING THAT DIARY INTO THE BEST STORY YOU POSSIBLY CAN." —DOUGLAS PAGELS, AUTHOR

THURSDAY	FRIDAY	SATURDAY	SUNDAY
MACROS Fat _____ Protein _____ Carbs _____ Calories _____	**MACROS** Fat _____ Protein _____ Carbs _____ Calories _____	**MACROS** Fat _____ Protein _____ Carbs _____ Calories _____	**MACROS** Fat _____ Protein _____ Carbs _____ Calories _____
MACROS Fat _____ Protein _____ Carbs _____ Calories _____	**MACROS** Fat _____ Protein _____ Carbs _____ Calories _____	**MACROS** Fat _____ Protein _____ Carbs _____ Calories _____	**MACROS** Fat _____ Protein _____ Carbs _____ Calories _____
MACROS Fat _____ Protein _____ Carbs _____ Calories _____	**MACROS** Fat _____ Protein _____ Carbs _____ Calories _____	**MACROS** Fat _____ Protein _____ Carbs _____ Calories _____	**MACROS** Fat _____ Protein _____ Carbs _____ Calories _____
MACROS Fat _____ Protein _____ Carbs _____ Calories _____	**MACROS** Fat _____ Protein _____ Carbs _____ Calories _____	**MACROS** Fat _____ Protein _____ Carbs _____ Calories _____	**MACROS** Fat _____ Protein _____ Carbs _____ Calories _____
TOTAL MACROS Fat _____ Protein _____ Carbs _____ Calories _____	**TOTAL MACROS** Fat _____ Protein _____ Carbs _____ Calories _____	**TOTAL MACROS** Fat _____ Protein _____ Carbs _____ Calories _____	**TOTAL MACROS** Fat _____ Protein _____ Carbs _____ Calories _____

None — Some — Intense

MINDFULNESS MOMENT

Learning to Love Your Body...

What are the biggest time bandits in your life?

_____
_____
_____
_____

What would you rather spend more time on?

_____
_____
_____
_____

What changes could you make to carve out more time for what's important to you?

_____
_____
_____
_____

"THE ONLY WAY TO LIVE IS BY ACCEPTING EACH MINUTE AS AN UNREPEATABLE MIRACLE." —TARA BRACH, PSYCHOLOGIST

What was the best thing that happened this week?	**What obstacle or challenge did you overcome?**	**List three milestones you achieved this week.**
_____	_____	_____
_____	_____	_____
_____	_____	_____
_____	_____	_____

WEIGHT TRACKER

MONDAY	TUESDAY	WEDNESDAY	THURSDAY
.LBS	.LBS	.LBS	.LBS

SLEEP TRACKER

	Sleep Time	Total Hours	Sleep Quality
M			👍 👎
TU			👍 👎
W			👍 👎
TH			👍 👎
F			👍 👎
SA			👍 👎
SU			👍 👎

EXERCISE TRACKER

	Type	Time	Intensity
M			
TU			
W			
TH			
F			
SA			
SU			

ENERGY TRACKER

How Are You Feeling Today?

Monday

Tuesday

Wednesday

Thursday

Friday

Saturday

Sunday

FRIDAY	SATURDAY	SUNDAY	WEEKLY CHANGE
.LBS	.LBS	.LBS	

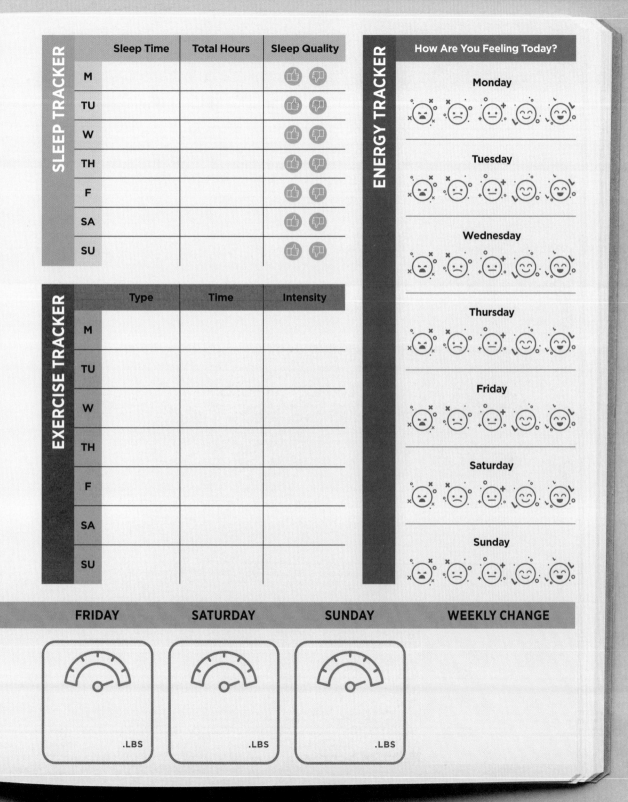

*Week 4

FOOD TRACKER

		MONDAY	TUESDAY	WEDNESDAY
Breakfast	MACROS	Fat _____ Protein _____ Carbs _____ Calories _____	Fat _____ Protein _____ Carbs _____ Calories _____	Fat _____ Protein _____ Carbs _____ Calories _____
Lunch	MACROS	Fat _____ Protein _____ Carbs _____ Calories _____	Fat _____ Protein _____ Carbs _____ Calories _____	Fat _____ Protein _____ Carbs _____ Calories _____
Dinner	MACROS	Fat _____ Protein _____ Carbs _____ Calories _____	Fat _____ Protein _____ Carbs _____ Calories _____	Fat _____ Protein _____ Carbs _____ Calories _____
Snacks	MACROS	Fat _____ Protein _____ Carbs _____ Calories _____	Fat _____ Protein _____ Carbs _____ Calories _____	Fat _____ Protein _____ Carbs _____ Calories _____
Total Daily Macros	TOTAL MACROS	Fat _____ Protein _____ Carbs _____ Calories _____	Fat _____ Protein _____ Carbs _____ Calories _____	Fat _____ Protein _____ Carbs _____ Calories _____
Water				
Hunger		None Some Intense	None Some Intense	None Some Intense

"ENJOY THE LITTLE THINGS, FOR ONE DAY YOU MAY LOOK BACK AND REALIZE THEY WERE THE BIG THINGS."

—ROBERT BRAULT, AUTHOR

THURSDAY	FRIDAY	SATURDAY	SUNDAY
MACROS Fat .... Protein .... Carbs .... Calories	MACROS Fat .... Protein .... Carbs .... Calories	MACROS Fat .... Protein .... Carbs .... Calories	MACROS Fat .... Protein .... Carbs .... Calories ....
MACROS Fat .... Protein .... Carbs .... Calories	MACROS Fat .... Protein .... Carbs .... Calories	MACROS Fat .... Protein .... Carbs .... Calories	MACROS Fat .... Protein .... Carbs .... Calories ....
MACROS Fat .... Protein .... Carbs .... Calories	MACROS Fat .... Protein .... Carbs .... Calories	MACROS Fat .... Protein .... Carbs .... Calories	MACROS Fat .... Protein .... Carbs .... Calories ....
MACROS Fat .... Protein .... Carbs .... Calories	MACROS Fat .... Protein .... Carbs .... Calories	MACROS Fat .... Protein .... Carbs .... Calories	MACROS Fat .... Protein .... Carbs .... Calories ....
TOTAL MACROS Fat .... Protein .... Carbs .... Calories	TOTAL MACROS Fat .... Protein .... Carbs .... Calories	TOTAL MACROS Fat .... Protein .... Carbs .... Calories	TOTAL MACROS Fat .... Protein .... Carbs .... Calories ....

MINDFULNESS MOMENT

Learning to Love Your Body...

Without pausing, make a list of all the things, big and small, that you are grateful for.

_____
_____
_____
_____

What's something you are most looking forward to?

_____
_____
_____
_____

What's something that you're grateful to have today that you didn't have five years ago?

_____
_____
_____

"WEAR GRATITUDE LIKE A CLOAK, AND IT WILL FEED EVERY CORNER OF YOUR LIFE." —RUMI, 13TH-CENTURY POET

What was the best thing that happened this week?

_____
_____
_____
_____

What obstacle or challenge did you overcome?

_____
_____
_____
_____

List three milestones you achieved this week.

_____
_____
_____
_____

WEIGHT TRACKER

MONDAY	TUESDAY	WEDNESDAY	THURSDAY
.LBS	.LBS	.LBS	.LBS

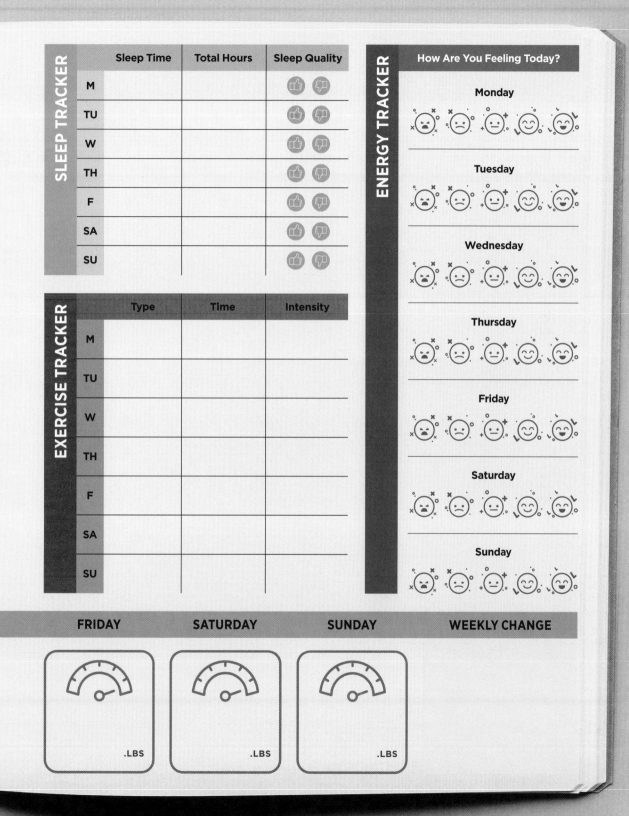

SLEEP TRACKER

	Sleep Time	Total Hours	Sleep Quality
M			👍 👎
TU			👍 👎
W			👍 👎
TH			👍 👎
F			👍 👎
SA			👍 👎
SU			👍 👎

EXERCISE TRACKER

	Type	Time	Intensity
M			
TU			
W			
TH			
F			
SA			
SU			

ENERGY TRACKER

How Are You Feeling Today?

Monday

Tuesday

Wednesday

Thursday

Friday

Saturday

Sunday

FRIDAY	SATURDAY	SUNDAY	WEEKLY CHANGE
.LBS	.LBS	.LBS	

*Week 5

FOOD TRACKER		MONDAY	TUESDAY	WEDNESDAY
	Breakfast	MACROS Fat .... Protein .... Carbs .... Calories	MACROS Fat .... Protein .... Carbs .... Calories	MACROS Fat .... Protein .... Carbs .... Calories ....
	Lunch	MACROS Fat .... Protein .... Carbs .... Calories	MACROS Fat .... Protein .... Carbs .... Calories	MACROS Fat .... Protein .... Carbs .... Calories ....
	Dinner	MACROS Fat .... Protein .... Carbs .... Calories	MACROS Fat .... Protein .... Carbs .... Calories	MACROS Fat .... Protein .... Carbs .... Calories ....
	Snacks	MACROS Fat .... Protein .... Carbs .... Calories	MACROS Fat .... Protein .... Carbs .... Calories	MACROS Fat .... Protein .... Carbs .... Calories ....
	Total Daily Macros	TOTAL MACROS Fat .... Protein .... Carbs .... Calories	TOTAL MACROS Fat .... Protein .... Carbs .... Calories	TOTAL MACROS Fat .... Protein .... Carbs .... Calories ....
	Water			
	Hunger	None — Some — Intense	None — Some — Intense	None — Some — Intense

"A JOURNEY OF A THOUSAND MILES BEGINS WITH A SINGLE STEP."

—LAO TZU, ANCIENT CHINESE PHILOSOPHER

	THURSDAY	FRIDAY	SATURDAY	SUNDAY
MACROS	Fat .... Protein .... Carbs .... Calories	Fat .... Protein .... Carbs .... Calories	Fat .... Protein .... Carbs .... Calories	Fat .... Protein .... Carbs .... Calories ....
MACROS	Fat .... Protein .... Carbs .... Calories	Fat .... Protein .... Carbs .... Calories	Fat .... Protein .... Carbs .... Calories	Fat .... Protein .... Carbs .... Calories ....
MACROS	Fat .... Protein .... Carbs .... Calories	Fat .... Protein .... Carbs .... Calories	Fat .... Protein .... Carbs .... Calories	Fat .... Protein .... Carbs .... Calories ....
MACROS	Fat .... Protein .... Carbs .... Calories	Fat .... Protein .... Carbs .... Calories	Fat .... Protein .... Carbs .... Calories	Fat .... Protein .... Carbs .... Calories ....
TOTAL MACROS	Fat .... Protein .... Carbs .... Calories	Fat .... Protein .... Carbs .... Calories	Fat .... Protein .... Carbs .... Calories	Fat .... Protein .... Carbs .... Calories ....

Learning to Love Your Body...

What emotion would you like to be most present in your life today?

_____
_____
_____
_____

What can you do to achieve that?

_____
_____
_____

What do you need to avoid doing?

_____
_____
_____
_____

"YOU HAVE BRAINS IN YOUR HEAD. YOU HAVE FEET IN YOUR SHOES. YOU CAN STEER YOURSELF ANY DIRECTION YOU CHOOSE."

—DR. SEUSS, AUTHOR

What was the best thing that happened this week?

_____
_____
_____
_____

What obstacle or challenge did you overcome?

_____
_____
_____
_____

List three milestones you achieved this week.

_____
_____
_____
_____

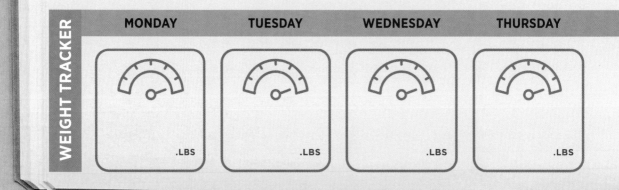

WEIGHT TRACKER

MONDAY	TUESDAY	WEDNESDAY	THURSDAY
.LBS	.LBS	.LBS	.LBS

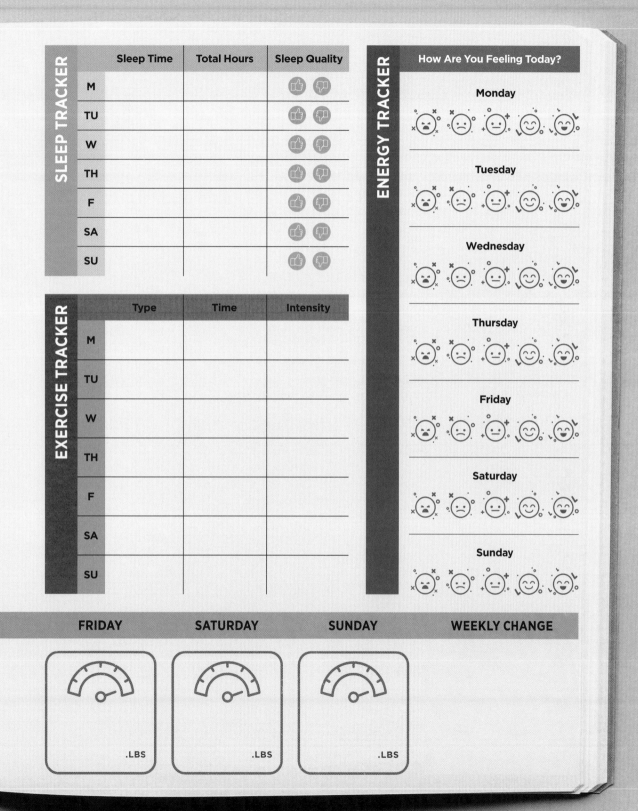

SLEEP TRACKER

	Sleep Time	Total Hours	Sleep Quality
M			👍 👎
TU			👍 👎
W			👍 👎
TH			👍 👎
F			👍 👎
SA			👍 👎
SU			👍 👎

EXERCISE TRACKER

	Type	Time	Intensity
M			
TU			
W			
TH			
F			
SA			
SU			

ENERGY TRACKER

How Are You Feeling Today?

Monday

Tuesday

Wednesday

Thursday

Friday

Saturday

Sunday

FRIDAY	SATURDAY	SUNDAY	WEEKLY CHANGE
.LBS	.LBS	.LBS	

157

*Week 6

FOOD TRACKER

	MONDAY	TUESDAY	WEDNESDAY
Breakfast	**MACROS** Fat .... Protein .... Carbs .... Calories	**MACROS** Fat .... Protein .... Carbs .... Calories	**MACROS** Fat .... Protein .... Carbs .... Calories ....
Lunch	**MACROS** Fat .... Protein .... Carbs .... Calories	**MACROS** Fat .... Protein .... Carbs .... Calories	**MACROS** Fat .... Protein .... Carbs .... Calories ....
Dinner	**MACROS** Fat .... Protein .... Carbs .... Calories	**MACROS** Fat .... Protein .... Carbs .... Calories	**MACROS** Fat .... Protein .... Carbs .... Calories ....
Snacks	**MACROS** Fat .... Protein .... Carbs .... Calories	**MACROS** Fat .... Protein .... Carbs .... Calories	**MACROS** Fat .... Protein .... Carbs .... Calories ....
Total Daily Macros	**TOTAL MACROS** Fat .... Protein .... Carbs .... Calories	**TOTAL MACROS** Fat .... Protein .... Carbs .... Calories	**TOTAL MACROS** Fat .... Protein .... Carbs .... Calories ....
Water			
Hunger	None — Some — Intense	None — Some — Intense	None — Some — Intense

"ONE PART AT A TIME, ONE DAY AT A TIME, WE CAN ACCOMPLISH ANY GOAL WE SET FOR OURSELVES."

—KAREN CASEY, AUTHOR

THURSDAY	FRIDAY	SATURDAY	SUNDAY

MACROS
Fat .... Protein ....
Carbs .... Calories ....

MACROS
Fat .... Protein ....
Carbs .... Calories ....

MACROS
Fat .... Protein ....
Carbs .... Calories ....

MACROS
Fat .... Protein ....
Carbs .... Calories ....

MACROS
Fat .... Protein ....
Carbs .... Calories ....

MACROS
Fat .... Protein ....
Carbs .... Calories ....

MACROS
Fat .... Protein ....
Carbs .... Calories ....

MACROS
Fat .... Protein ....
Carbs .... Calories ....

MACROS
Fat .... Protein ....
Carbs .... Calories ....

MACROS
Fat .... Protein ....
Carbs .... Calories ....

MACROS
Fat .... Protein ....
Carbs .... Calories ....

MACROS
Fat .... Protein ....
Carbs .... Calories ....

MACROS
Fat .... Protein ....
Carbs .... Calories ....

MACROS
Fat .... Protein ....
Carbs .... Calories ....

MACROS
Fat .... Protein ....
Carbs .... Calories ....

MACROS
Fat .... Protein ....
Carbs .... Calories ....

TOTAL MACROS
Fat .... Protein ....
Carbs .... Calories ....

TOTAL MACROS
Fat .... Protein ....
Carbs .... Calories ....

TOTAL MACROS
Fat .... Protein ....
Carbs .... Calories ....

TOTAL MACROS
Fat .... Protein ....
Carbs .... Calories ....

Some — None — Intense

Learning to Love Your Body...

What have you always wanted to do but haven't gotten to yet?

_____
_____
_____
_____

What is stopping you?

_____
_____
_____
_____

What step(s) can you take today to work toward that goal?

_____
_____
_____
_____

"REMEMBER TO CELEBRATE MILESTONES AS YOU PREPARE FOR THE ROAD AHEAD." —NELSON MANDELA, FORMER PRESIDENT OF SOUTH AFRICA

What was the best thing that happened this week?	What obstacle or challenge did you overcome?	List three milestones you achieved this week.
_____	_____	_____
_____	_____	_____
_____	_____	_____
_____	_____	_____

MONDAY	TUESDAY	WEDNESDAY	THURSDAY
.LBS	.LBS	.LBS	.LBS

SLEEP TRACKER

	Sleep Time	Total Hours	Sleep Quality
M			👍 👎
TU			👍 👎
W			👍 👎
TH			👍 👎
F			👍 👎
SA			👍 👎
SU			👍 👎

EXERCISE TRACKER

	Type	Time	Intensity
M			
TU			
W			
TH			
F			
SA			
SU			

ENERGY TRACKER

How Are You Feeling Today?

Monday

Tuesday

Wednesday

Thursday

Friday

Saturday

Sunday

FRIDAY	SATURDAY	SUNDAY	WEEKLY CHANGE
.LBS	.LBS	.LBS	

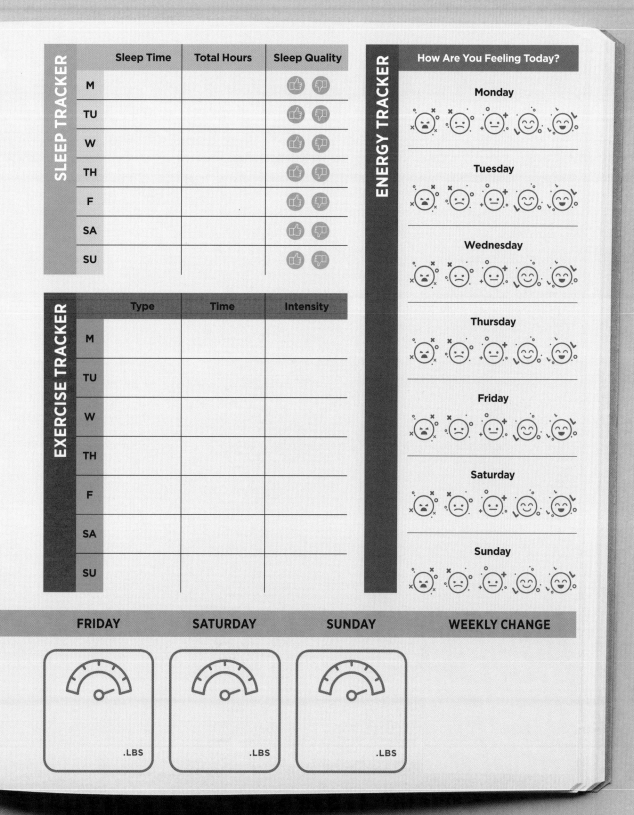

*Week 1

FOOD TRACKER		MONDAY	TUESDAY	WEDNESDAY
	Breakfast	MACROS Fat .... Protein .... Carbs .... Calories	MACROS Fat .... Protein .... Carbs .... Calories	MACROS Fat .... Protein .... Carbs .... Calories ....
	Lunch	MACROS Fat .... Protein .... Carbs .... Calories	MACROS Fat .... Protein .... Carbs .... Calories	MACROS Fat .... Protein .... Carbs .... Calories ....
	Dinner	MACROS Fat .... Protein .... Carbs .... Calories	MACROS Fat .... Protein .... Carbs .... Calories	MACROS Fat .... Protein .... Carbs .... Calories ....
	Snacks	MACROS Fat .... Protein .... Carbs .... Calories	MACROS Fat .... Protein .... Carbs .... Calories	MACROS Fat .... Protein .... Carbs .... Calories ....
	Total Daily Macros	TOTAL MACROS Fat .... Protein .... Carbs .... Calories	TOTAL MACROS Fat .... Protein .... Carbs .... Calories	TOTAL MACROS Fat .... Protein .... Carbs .... Calories ....
	Water			
	Hunger	None / Some / Intense	None / Some / Intense	None / Some / Intense

"THE BEST TIME TO PLANT A TREE IS 20 YEARS AGO. THE SECOND-BEST TIME IS NOW."

—CHINESE PROVERB

	THURSDAY	FRIDAY	SATURDAY	SUNDAY
MACROS	Fat .... Protein .... Carbs .... Calories	Fat .... Protein .... Carbs .... Calories	Fat .... Protein .... Carbs .... Calories	Fat .... Protein .... Carbs .... Calories ....
MACROS	Fat .... Protein .... Carbs .... Calories	Fat .... Protein .... Carbs .... Calories	Fat .... Protein .... Carbs .... Calories	Fat .... Protein .... Carbs .... Calories ....
MACROS	Fat .... Protein .... Carbs .... Calories	Fat .... Protein .... Carbs .... Calories	Fat .... Protein .... Carbs .... Calories	Fat .... Protein .... Carbs .... Calories ....
MACROS	Fat .... Protein .... Carbs .... Calories	Fat .... Protein .... Carbs .... Calories	Fat .... Protein .... Carbs .... Calories	Fat .... Protein .... Carbs .... Calories ....
TOTAL MACROS	Fat .... Protein .... Carbs .... Calories	Fat .... Protein .... Carbs .... Calories	Fat .... Protein .... Carbs .... Calories	Fat .... Protein .... Carbs .... Calories ....

MINDFULNESS MOMENT

Learning to Love Your Body...

What is something you've always wanted to do?

_____
_____
_____
_____

Why have you been putting it off?

_____
_____
_____
_____

Is there a realistic way for you to get started right now? What would that look like?

_____
_____
_____
_____

"IF YOU WANT TO CONQUER THE ANXIETY OF LIFE, LIVE IN THE MOMENT, LIVE IN THE BREATH." —AMIT RAY, SPIRITUAL TEACHER

What was the best thing that happened this week?

_____
_____
_____

What obstacle or challenge did you overcome?

_____
_____
_____

List three milestones you achieved this week.

_____
_____
_____

WEIGHT TRACKER

MONDAY	TUESDAY	WEDNESDAY	THURSDAY
.LBS	.LBS	.LBS	.LBS

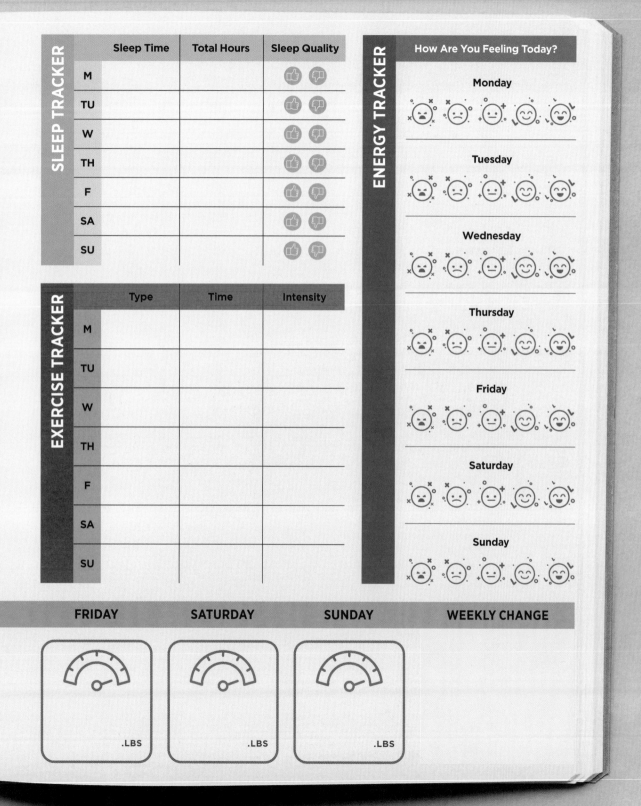

SLEEP TRACKER

	Sleep Time	Total Hours	Sleep Quality
M			👍 👎
TU			👍 👎
W			👍 👎
TH			👍 👎
F			👍 👎
SA			👍 👎
SU			👍 👎

EXERCISE TRACKER

	Type	Time	Intensity
M			
TU			
W			
TH			
F			
SA			
SU			

ENERGY TRACKER

How Are You Feeling Today?

Monday

Tuesday

Wednesday

Thursday

Friday

Saturday

Sunday

FRIDAY	SATURDAY	SUNDAY	WEEKLY CHANGE
.LBS	.LBS	.LBS	

YOU DID IT!

We Knew You

What's next? Where would you like to be this time next year?

Hint: You can use this workbook to help set new goals to keep moving forward on your keto journey.

_____
_____
_____
_____
_____
_____
_____
_____
_____
_____
_____
_____
_____

What new habits would you like to hold on to over the course of the next year?

_____
_____
_____
_____
_____
_____
_____
_____
_____
_____
_____
_____
_____
_____
_____
_____

What's your favorite mantra? Now, keep using it—often!

_____
_____
_____
_____
_____
_____
_____
_____
_____
_____
_____
_____
_____
_____
_____
_____

Could

Goals!

By setting goals and writing them down, you helped set yourself up for success. **A Harvard study found that the 14% of its participants who set goals were 10 times more successful than those who didn't. The 3% who set and wrote down goals** were even more successful than the 14% who set them, but didn't write them down.

By the Numbers

20%

The percentage of the body's energy that the brain consumes in a resting state. The brain uses glucose for energy: While it can't use fat as a fuel source, it can use ketones.

10

Pounds or More

The common amount of weight lost during the first month on keto. That's because you lose a lot of water weight when you first start the diet.

137%–314%

The percentage increase of blood ketone levels in a small study of women who exercised before a meal, versus when they exercised after a meal. Working out while you are fasting—for instance, in the morning, before eating breakfast—has been shown to increase ketone levels.

0.5–2 lbs.

After an initial period of what can be dramatic weight loss due to the shedding of water weight, experts say there will be a leveling-off period. **From this point on, you should expect to lose 0.5 to 2 pounds a week.** This amount is considered to be appropriate for healthy weight loss—the kind you are more likely to keep off.

184 lbs.

The average weight of an American adult, according to federal survey data of approximately 48,000 adults ranging in age from 40 to 64.

75
Million

The number of Americans with high blood pressure. The keto diet can help with this, as it has proven to be helpful for people who have a hard time losing weight. (Being overweight is one of the top causes of high blood pressure.)

100

The approximate number of calories you burn running 1 mile.

SPECIAL THANKS TO CONTRIBUTING WRITERS

Mallory Crevling, Dana Hudepohl, Margaret Monroe, Rachel Morris, Colleen Travers

CREDITS

DISCLAIMER